# TECHNOLOGY LAW

## AUSTRALIAN AND INTERNATIONAL PERSPECTIVES

The regulation of technology is an important and topical area of law, relevant to almost all aspects of society. *Technology Law: Australian and International Perspectives* presents a thorough exploration of the new legal challenges created by evolving technologies, from the use of facial recognition technology in criminal investigations to the rise and regulation of cryptocurrencies.

A well-written and fascinating introduction to technology law in Australia and internationally, *Technology Law* provides thorough coverage of the theoretical perspectives, legislation, cases and developing issues where technology and the law interact. The text covers data protection and privacy, healthcare technology, criminal justice technology, commercial transactions, cybercrime, social media and intellectual property, and canvasses the future of technology and technology law.

Written by leading experts in the field, *Technology Law* is an excellent resource for law students and legal professionals with an interest in the area.

**Marcus Smith** is Senior Lecturer in Law and Course Director at the Centre for Law and Justice, Charles Sturt University, and Adjunct Professor of Law at the University of Canberra.

**Gregor Urbas** is Adjunct Associate Professor at the ANU College of Law, a former Associate Professor of Law at the University of Canberra, and a Canberra barrister.

Cambridge University Press acknowledges the Australian Aboriginal and Torres Strait Islander peoples of this nation. We acknowledge the traditional custodians of the lands on which our company is located and where we conduct our business. We pay our respects to ancestors and Elders, past and present. Cambridge University Press is committed to honouring Australian Aboriginal and Torres Strait Islander peoples' unique cultural and spiritual relationships to the land, waters and seas and their rich contribution to society.

# TECHNOLOGY LAW

## AUSTRALIAN AND INTERNATIONAL PERSPECTIVES

Marcus Smith

Gregor Urbas

CAMBRIDGE
UNIVERSITY PRESS

Shaftesbury Road, Cambridge CB2 8EA, United Kingdom

One Liberty Plaza, 20th Floor, New York, NY 10006, USA

477 Williamstown Road, Port Melbourne, VIC 3207, Australia

314–321, 3rd Floor, Plot 3, Splendor Forum, Jasola District Centre, New Delhi – 110025, India

103 Penang Road, #05–06/07, Visioncrest Commercial, Singapore 238467

Cambridge University Press is part of Cambridge University Press & Assessment, a department of the University of Cambridge.

We share the University's mission to contribute to society through the pursuit of education, learning and research at the highest international levels of excellence.

www.cambridge.org
Information on this title: www.cambridge.org/9781108816014

First published 2021

Cover designed by Tanya De Silva-McKay

*A catalogue record for this book is available from the National Library of Australia*

ISBN    978-1-108-81601-4    Paperback

Additional resources for this publication at www.cambridge.org/highereducation/isbn/9781108816014/resources

# CONTENTS

# PREFACE

Technology law is a diverse, interesting and highly relevant field, touching on some of the most significant legal and social issues of the day. This text explores technology law in its socio-legal context in Australia and around the world. It critically examines law and regulation relating to technology developments, incorporating relevant theoretical perspectives.

Available texts to date in Australia have focused on cybercrime law. Some texts, published further afield in the United Kingdom, have broadened this to information technology law, branching out beyond cybercrime to include allied areas such as privacy, e-commerce and intellectual property. This text takes a broader approach in defining the field of technology law. In addition to encompassing cybercrime, privacy, commercial transactions and intellectual property, it extends technology law to also include healthcare and criminal justice, providing a more complete discussion, and expanding the horizon of the field to incorporate a holistic view of the regulation of technology in our society.

We have taken this approach with a view to better conceptualising the relationships between these related areas of law, in what continues to be a flourishing area of national and international academic study and law reform. It offers a new way forward for this burgeoning area of legal scholarship, and will be of interest to practitioners, policymakers, academics and students.

**Marcus Smith and Gregor Urbas**
*September 2020*

# TABLE OF CASES

# TABLE OF STATUTES

# ACKNOWLEDGEMENTS

The authors would like to acknowledge Cambridge University Press, and in particular Lucy Russell, Senior Academic Commissioning Editor, and Rose Albiston, Academic Development Editor, for their support and input. We are also grateful to the independent peer reviewers for their time and the important feedback they provided. Finally, we would like to thank our families and colleagues for their support and patience throughout the writing of this text.

The authors and Cambridge University Press would like to thank the following for permission to reproduce material in this book.

**Figure 2.1**: Reproduced with permission of Oxford University Press, from *Responsive Regulation: Transcending the Deregulation Debate*. Permission conveyed through Copyright Clearance Center, Inc; **Figure 2.2**: Reproduced with permission of Lawrence Lessig; **Figure 2.3**: Originally published by Routledge, reproduced under STM signatory guidelines; **Tables 3.1** and **3.2**: © Office of the Australian Information Commissioner. Reproduced under CC BY 3.0 AU licence (https://creativecommons.org/licenses/by/3.0/au/legalcode); Extracts from the Office of the Australian Information Commissioner: © Office of the Australian Information Commissioner. Reproduced under CC BY 3.0 AU licence (https:// creativecommons.org/licenses/by/3.0/au/legalcode); Extracts from Commonwealth legislation: Sourced from the Federal Register of Legislation. Reproduced under Creative Commons Attribution 4.0 International (CC BY 4.0). For the latest information on Australian Government law please go to https://www.legislation.gov.au; Extracts from *General Data Protection Regulation*: © European Union, 1995–2020; Extracts from *D'Arcy v Myriad Genetics Inc* [2015] HCA 35; *Honeysett v The Queen* [2014] HCA 29: Reproduced with permission from the High Court of Australia; Extract from National Health and Medical Research Council, *Ethical Guidelines on the Use of Assisted Reproductive Technology in Clinical Practice and Research* (NHMRC, 2017), 21: © Commonwealth of Australia 2019. Reproduced under CC BY 3.0 AU licence (https://creativecommons.org/licenses/by/3.0/ au/legalcode); Extract from Ronald Leenes et al, 'Regulatory challenges of robotics: some guidelines for addressing legal and ethical issues' (2017) 9(1) *Law, Innovation and Technology* 1: Originally published by Taylor and Francis, reproduced under STM signatory guidelines; Extracts from Council of Europe, Convention on Cybercrime, Treaty no. 185 opened for signature in Budapest on 23 November 2001; The Council of Europe's Convention on Cybercrime: Reproduced with the permission of the Council of Europe; Extract from John Richardson, 'Stuxnet as Cyberwarfare: Applying the Law of War to the Virtual Battlefield' (2011) 29(1) *Journal of Computer and Information Law* 1: © Oxford University Press. Reproduced under STM guidelines; Extract from Victorian legislation: © State of Victoria, Australia. Copyright in all legislation of the Parliament of the State of Victoria, Australia, is owned by the Crown in right of the State of Victoria, Australia. This

# 1

# INTRODUCTION TO TECHNOLOGY LAW

# Conceptualising technology law

In recent decades, the regulation of technology and associated information has become an important and topical area of law, relevant to almost all aspects of society. Issues in technology law typically extend beyond specific jurisdictions and have state, national and international implications. Developments in one jurisdiction rapidly have international ramifications, due to the connectedness facilitated by the internet and modern communications technology. The areas of the law that are evolving due to technological developments are diverse: a preliminary list would include finance law, criminal law, medical law, media law and privacy law. New technology creates challenges, because when it becomes available, new regulatory gaps arise. For example, the emergence of cryptocurrencies such as Bitcoin has required public agencies to issue guidelines as to whether they constitute forms of currency, and whether dealings using them are subject to taxation laws.[1] Another example is the legislation enacted in the early 2000s to regulate the use of DNA evidence in criminal investigations. When these laws were enacted, the use of commercial ancestry databases and other modern techniques in genetic analysis to identify suspects in some high-profile contemporary cases was not envisaged.[2]

A primary consideration must be the concept and definition of technology law. As a relatively new area of the law, there has been debate over the definition and coherence of technology law as a field of legal expertise and scholarship. As a somewhat nebulous field, it is similar in this respect to other more recent and diverse fields of the law, such as health or environmental law. Technology law combines several traditional areas of the law and appears to borrow from other fields, such as criminal law, human rights law, privacy law, and political and regulatory theory.[3] One issue for technology law is that there is such a wide range of different technologies, each being applied in various contexts. These all have risks and benefits that must be managed to prevent harms from occurring. Further, adequate regulation in the form of legislation, judicial oversight, policies, standards and procedures spread across different areas of the legal system, fields of business, government agencies, and state, national and international jurisdictions equates to a major challenge for regulators attempting to adopt effective and coherent approaches.[4]

There have been numerous attempts to define the field of technology law. Until the mid-2000s, it was disjointed, lacking a cohesive theory. As more prominent legal issues arose that did not fit well within the existing paradigms, it became recognised that a new field of law was needed to determine 'how to protect interests in particular cases as well as how a decision will affect other interests once it is integrated within the whole law'.[5] From

---

1   Parliament of Australia, Senate Economics References Committee, *Digital Currency – Game Changer or Bit Player* (August 2015). Available: <www.aph.gov.au/parliamentary_business/committees/senate/economics/digital_currency/~/media/Committees/economics_ctte/Digital_currency/report.pdf>. See, also, Australian Taxation Office, *Tax Treatment of Crypto-Currencies in Australia – Specifically Bitcoin.* Available: <www.ato.gov.au/general/gen/tax-treatment-of-crypto-currencies-in-australia---specifically-bitcoin> (last updated 18 June 2019).
2   Chris Phillips, 'The Golden State Killer Investigation and the Nascent Field of Forensic Genealogy' (2018) 36 *Forensic Science International: Genetics* 186.
3   Theodore Ruger, 'Health Law's Coherence Anxiety' (2008) 96 *Georgetown Law Journal* 625, 627; Todd Aagaard, 'Environmental Law as a Legal Field: An Inquiry in Legal Taxonomy' (2010) 95 *Cornell Law Review* 221, 229.
4   Michael Guihot, Anne Matthew and Nicolas Suzor, 'Nudging Robots: Innovative Solutions to Regulate Artificial Intelligence' (2017) 20 *Vanderbilt Journal of Entertainment & Technology Law* 385, 452.
5   Arthur Cockfield and Jason Pridmore, 'A Synthetic Theory of Law and Technology' (2007) 8 *Minnesota Journal of Law, Science & Technology* 475.

a jurisprudential and regulatory perspective, it was argued in the literature at that time that a theory of law and technology could provide 'a structure through which lessons learned from technologies of the past can help make decisions about how to regulate and adapt to future technologies'.[6] Technology law is an interesting and dynamic field. As it continues to grow (as it no doubt will), 'coherence in technology law will become clearer and stronger as we continue to study and identify congruencies among the seemingly disparate topics and the complexity of interactions within the field'.[7] Technology law is now an important and much-needed field of study.

> New technologies create novel issues that press at the extremes of the established laws. As has been argued, the established fields of law, weighed down by the requirements of field coherence, are often slow to respond in time or with adequate answers ... The speed of change, the rate of change, the novelty of the challenges, the rapidity with which they swamp, not only local markets, but the whole world, and the depth of those changes to our society, our environment, and what it means to be human, makes it necessary to have a set of regulatory responses to new technologies that can, well, respond, in time and at a global level ... Technology law must operate where these other laws do not, or cannot adequately. It develops among the interactions between technologies, risks, and their regulation. It works alongside, sometimes with, and sometimes outside of other established areas of law and must be defined accordingly.[8]

It must be noted that in developing a definition of technology law, *technology* is itself a very broad term. What once was considered novel may now be obsolete – and yet it remains a form of technology. Technology is continually evolving across several sub-disciplines such as biotechnology, information technology, artificial intelligence and robotics. There are a number of texts available on information technology, dealing with the law as it relates to computing and the internet. While many areas of technology are closely related to information, either producing it or analysing it, many are not, and this term is too narrow for the burgeoning field that this text seeks to encompass. Defining technology law on the basis of specific areas, such as biotechnology or information technology, would become dated as each developed and morphed into other areas over time. Given the rate of advancement, it is appropriate to approach the subject broadly. For this reason, Donald Schön's definition, outlined in his work *Technology and Change* (1967) has withstood the test of time. This definition of technology encompasses 'any tool or technique, any product or process, any physical equipment or method of doing or making, by which human capability is extended'.[9] In this context, the focus of technology law becomes 'adjusting law and regulation for sociotechnical change'.[10] The complexity of technology is amplified by the pace at which new technologies arise and by the breadth of their impact. Roger Brownsword et al (2017) propose that the unifying question technology law addresses is threefold: first, the

---

6   Lyria Bennett Moses, 'Why Have a Theory of Law and Technological Change' (2007) 8 *Minnesota Journal of Law, Science & Technology* 589, 605.
7   Michael Guihot, 'Coherence in Technology Law' (2019) 11(2) *Law, Innovation and Technology* (DOI:10. 1080/17579961.2019.1665792), 9.
8   Ibid.
9   Donald Schön, *Technology and Change* (Pergamon Press, 1967), 1.
10  Lyria Bennett Moses, 'Regulating in the Face of Sociotechnical Change'. In Roger Brownsword, Eloise Scotford and Karen Yeung (eds), *The Oxford Handbook of Law, Regulation and Technology* (Oxford University Press, 2017), 576.

challenge that new forms of technology pose to 'established legal frameworks, doctrines, and institutions'; second, the 'adequacy of existing regulatory regimes'; and finally, the 'ideas and justifications offered in support of regulatory intervention'.[11]

# Recent developments in technology law

Reflecting on political, social and legal developments over the past decade, there have been many relevant issues subject to public debate that engage with technology and law. Briefly highlighting a number of these provides an introduction to the field and is a useful way of foreshadowing the more detailed discussions of these and many other examples that will take place in the following chapters of this text. These examples indicate the balancing act at the heart of many issues in this area of the law – a trade-off between individual and collective rights – specifically, how technology should be used and regulated. The examples are indicative of the need to regulate the harmful aspects of new technology and the associated challenges inherent in doing so, while facilitating the development and adoption of beneficial technological advancements.

While technology has positive and negative applications and implications, recent technological developments can be contrasted with those in the 20th century. Developments such as air travel, the revolution in computing and the discovery of antibiotics all benefited society greatly and, while of course requiring regulation, were associated with relatively few negative implications for most individuals, particularly when considered in the context of the advantages they provided. An exception to this would, of course, be the impact of the Industrial Revolution on the environment and its implications for society; however, further technology has also provided the capacity to mitigate harmful effects of earlier technologies, such as solar and other renewable forms of energy production. In the contemporary examples from the last decade that will be discussed shortly, vast advances in information and communications technology have been associated with compromised privacy and autonomy, principally due to the development of the internet, smartphones, social media, genomics, biometrics and artificial intelligence. Other areas of development where the complex implications of new technology can be observed include healthcare and cybercrime.

## Communications

In 2013, a whistleblower from the US intelligence community leaked an enormous amount of information to journalists about the extensive surveillance and analysis of communications, social media and internet usage by the United States and allied countries, including Australia, Canada, New Zealand and the United Kingdom. Edward Snowden, a subcontractor and systems analyst for the National Security Agency (NSA), released classified documents detailing global surveillance programs run by the NSA and the Five Eyes intelligence network, which includes the NSA's partner agencies such as the Australian Signals Directorate (ASD) and the Government Communications Headquarters (GCHQ) in the United Kingdom. It has been estimated that Snowden disclosed approximately 1.7 million intelligence files, including 15 000 Australian files. The disclosures included the names and details of various

---

11  Roger Brownsword, Eloise Scotford and Karen Yeung (eds), *The Oxford Handbook of Law, Regulation and Technology* (Oxford University Press, 2017), 7–15.

programs run by these agencies. Among them were the *PRISM, XKeyscore* and *Tempora* programs, which enabled 'almost anything done on the internet' to be intercepted, searched and stored by surreptitious tapping of undersea fibre-optic cables and through confidential agreements with technology companies.[12] The documents also revealed that the United States had spied on the communications of world leaders, including several of its allies.[13] A major report commissioned by the US government following these revelations sets out the arguments and counterarguments that might be used to justify these national security activities.

> One of the government's most fundamental responsibilities is to protect this form of security ... Appropriately conducted and properly disciplined, surveillance can help to eliminate important national security risks. It has helped to save lives in the past. It will help to do so in the future.[14]

The report also recognises the ethical, as well as potential commercial, implications for the United States of these actions. The discrepancy between what is acknowledged in the report, and the practices that led to it being commissioned, is vast.

> In a free society, public officials should never engage in surveillance in order to punish their political enemies; to restrict freedom of speech or religion; to suppress legitimate criticism and dissent; to help their preferred companies or industries; to provide domestic companies with an unfair competitive advantage; or to benefit or burden members of groups defined in terms of religion, ethnicity, race, and gender.[15]
>
> ...
>
> If we are too aggressive in our surveillance policies ... we might trigger serious economic repercussions for American businesses, which might lose their share of the world's communications market because of a growing distrust of their capacity to guarantee the privacy of their international users. Recent disclosures have generated considerable concern along these lines.[16]

The countries implicated by Snowden sought to introduce legislation and create a legal framework that supported some of the activities reported, such as metadata retention. Two years later, the Australian government introduced the *Telecommunications (Interception and Access) Amendment (Data Retention) Act 2015* (Cth). The Act amended the *Telecommunications (Interception and Access) Act 1979* (Cth), to require telecommunications companies and internet service providers to retain phone, internet and email metadata of all their users for a two-year period. According to the legislation, the content of communications is not stored; however, staff in certain government agencies are able to access the information

---

12  Glenn Greenwald, 'Edward Snowden: The Whistleblower Behind the NSA Surveillance Revelations', *The Guardian*, 11 June 2013. Lina Dencik and Jonathan Cable, 'The Advent of Surveillance Realism: Public Opinion and Activist Responses to the Snowden Leaks' (2017) 11 *International Journal of Communication* 763, 765.

13  Ibid.

14  Richard Clarke et al, *The NSA Report: Liberty and Security in a Changing World* (Princeton University Press, 2014), 1.

15  Ibid, xvii.

16  Ibid, 104.

without a warrant. The legislation states that the content or substance of a communication is not required to be kept,[17] but that all the following information must be recorded:

- the subscribers' accounts, services and telecommunications devices
- the source and destination of a communication
- the date, time and duration of a communication
- the type of communication or service used
- the location of equipment or a line used in a communication.[18]

There is no doubt that telecommunications and internet data can be very important in criminal investigations in understanding the activities of perpetrators and victims, and thus contribute to preventing, investigating and prosecuting serious crime.[19] There are many examples of cases where data retention has enabled the collection of pertinent information that could not otherwise have been accessed; and in the case of the serious and expanding problem of cybercrime, it is the only way offenders can be identified in the real world.[20] The alternate perspective argues that data retention is disproportionate, indiscriminately retaining 'data relating to entire populations, irrespective of the nature of the data or whether or not there is a reasonable suspicion of a serious threat posed by those to whom the data relates'.[21] A further argument that is sometimes overlooked is that the distinction between 'content' and 'metadata' fails to acknowledge how much 'metadata' can reveal about an individual's life, particularly when aggregated and integrated with data analytic programs.[22]

## Healthcare

Internet and communications data is not the only area of technology of significance from a legal and regulatory perspective that has advanced rapidly in recent years. The mapping of the genome in 2003, as well as more recent gene editing technologies such as CRISPR/Cas9, have led to a revolution in medical diagnosis and treatment, as well as in reproductive medicine.[23] There are many implications of these new abilities to manipulate DNA. Myriad Genetics is a company providing diagnostic tests that enable doctors to understand the genetic basis of

17 *Telecommunications (Interception and Access) Act 1979* (Cth), s 187A(4).
18 Ibid, s 187AA.
19 Australian Federal Police, *Submission to the Telecommunications (Interception and Access) Amendment (Data Retention) Bill 2014 Inquiry by the Parliamentary Joint Committee on Intelligence and Security.* Available: <https://www.aph.gov.au/parliamentary_business/committees/joint/intelligence_and_security/data_retention>.
20 Attorney-General's Department, *Submission to the Telecommunications (Interception and Access) Amendment (Data Retention) Bill 2014 Inquiry by the Parliamentary Joint Committee on Intelligence and Security.* Available: <https://www.aph.gov.au/parliamentary_business/committees/joint/intelligence_and_security/data_retention>.
21 Australian Privacy Foundation, *Submission to the Telecommunications (Interception and Access) Amendment (Data Retention) Bill 2014 Inquiry by the Parliamentary Joint Committee on Intelligence and Security.* Available: <https://www.aph.gov.au/parliamentary_business/committees/joint/intelligence_and_security/data_retention>.
22 Even encrypted messages can be accessed. As will be discussed in Chapter 3, the *Telecommunications and Other Legislation Amendment (Assistance and Access) Act 2018* (Cth) compels technology companies to provide police and security agencies with access to encrypted messages.
23 Rodolphe Barrangou and Jennifer Doudna, 'Applications of CRISPR Technologies in Research and Beyond' (2016) 34 *Nature Biotechnology* 933.

diseases, including the risk of development, onset and progression, and optimal treatment strategies.[24] This rapidly growing field of personalised medicine will become increasingly important with the further advances in genomics, enabling therapies that give the individual the best chance of recovery, and gene therapies for major diseases such as cancer. In 1994, Myriad Genetics researchers were involved in research that successfully identified and cloned what is now known as the *breast cancer type 1 susceptibility protein gene* (BRCA1), one of the most significant achievements of modern medical science. Myriad subsequently sought to patent the BRCA1 gene, the part of the human genome that they had been involved in identifying and isolating, an action that was immediately controversial. In the United States, the case *Association for Molecular Pathology v Myriad Genetics Inc* went to the Supreme Court, which ultimately found that it was not able to be patented because '[a] naturally occurring DNA segment is a product of nature and not patent eligible merely because it has been isolated'.[25] Myriad Genetics also sought to patent BRCA1 in Australia, which also resulted in extensive litigation. It was eventually heard by the High Court in the case *D'Arcy v Myriad Genetics Inc*,[26] which reached a similar conclusion and held that the invention was not 'a manner of manufacture' within the meaning of the *Patents Act 1990* (Cth).[27]

## Artificial intelligence

The efficiency enabled by new technology is clear, but this can bring its own new problems. An example of this is the way governments and the private sector are now taking full advantage of the efficiencies facilitated by the internet and data analytics in their service provision and business activities. While there are significant efficiency gains to be made, data security remains an ongoing concern, along with other lessons that have been learnt in the first major forays into this area by the Australian government. Automated systems have the potential for efficiency gains in both the private and public sectors that can provide a basis for economic growth. But an understanding of how these systems impact on individual privacy and autonomy must also be taken into account, and is crucial to mitigating the social costs and enhancing the benefits.

One example of the use of new technology in government systems that had a less than ideal outcome was the 2016 Australian Census, subsequently known as #CensusFail.[28] In a process that sought to increase efficiency, the 2016 Census was the first in Australia's history to offer completion of the forms online. However, on census night, 9 August 2016, the Australian Bureau of Statistics' (ABS) system crashed, due to distributed denial-of-service attacks, and was unavailable for citizens to complete their details, making it the most unsuccessful census ever administered by the ABS. It subsequently became known that the ABS shut down the site after it was subject to 'attacks emanating from overseas', which raised questions not only about service provision but data security on the new online platform

---

24  Myriad Genetics. Available: <www.myriad.com>.
25  133 S Ct 2107 (2013), 2111.
26  (2015) 258 CLR 334.
27  Matthew Rimmer, 'An Exorbitant Monopoly: The High Court of Australia, Myriad Genetics, and Gene Patents'. In Duncan Matthews and Herbert Zech (eds), *Research Handbook on Intellectual Property and the Life Sciences* (Edward Elgar, 2017).
28  Doug Dingwall, 'Bureau of Statistics Looks to Avoid the Mistakes of "Censusfail"', *Sydney Morning Herald*, 16 January 2019.

in comparison with the previous paper-based methods. The Senate inquiry that followed made 16 recommendations for future surveys, including greater scrutiny of the technology that would be deployed for the 2021 Census and prompt reporting of data breaches when identified.[29]

In the social security context, Online Compliance Intervention, otherwise known as 'Robodebt', has caused great controversy in Australia. It relates to the use of data matching systems to compare data from the Australian Taxation Office with welfare payments and income declared to the Centrelink agency, and highlights the unintended consequences that can occur when these systems are introduced to increase efficiency. While efficiency was the primary goal in this case, the automated system actually led to unjust outcomes, negative publicity, a loss of trust in government processes, and increased costs associated with reviews, appeals and interventions.[30]

# Social media

While providing important and popular services in internet searching and social networking, it is now well understood that technology companies such as Google and Facebook have become highly profitable and powerful due to the vast amount of data that is provided to them by billions of users around the world and which the companies utilise for advertising purposes. There have been several controversies associated with use of this trove of data; however, the use of Facebook data by the British political consultancy firm Cambridge Analytica in relation to the 2016 presidential election in the United States has received the most coverage. Big data analytics was used in association with information gathered from up to 70 million Facebook users in the United States to develop psychological profiles of voters, which then informed online advertising strategies for the Republican Party. In association with poll results and other intelligence, this strategy was based on the principle that by identifying and understanding individuals in key electorates, different voters could be convinced to have the same opinion on an issue or candidate by using advertisements specifically targeting their personality and social views. The firm was later dissolved after questions arose about the legality of involving a foreign firm in a US presidential election campaign and whether the scale of the activity had compromised the integrity of the election itself. In 2019, Facebook was fined US$5 billion over its management of user data following inquiries into the arrangement.[31]

# Cybercrime

Cybercrime is a very significant emerging threat, recently estimated to cost the Australian economy up to A$1 billion annually.[32] It affects government, businesses and individuals, and there are numerous recent examples. In 2019, it was revealed that the Australian National

29 Senate Economics References Committee, *2016 Census: Issues of Trust* (Parliament of Australia, 2017).

30 Senate Community Affairs References Committee, *Design, Scope, Cost-Benefit Analysis, Contracts Awarded and Implementation Associated with the Better Management of the Social Welfare System Initiative* (Parliament of Australia, 2017). Available: <www.aph.gov.au/parliamentary_business/committees/senate/community_affairs/socialwelfaresystem>.

31 Julia Carrie Wong, 'The Cambridge Analytica Scandal Changed the World – But it Didn't Change Facebook', *The Guardian*, 18 March 2019.

32 Australian Criminal Intelligence Commission, *Cybercrime* (2019). Available: <https://www.acic.gov.au/about-crime/crime-types/cybercrime>.

University (ANU) suffered a large and sophisticated cyber attack, losing a large amount of data over a period of several months. The attack targeted a database holding student and staff records relating to a 19-year period. Investigators determined that the details taken included names, addresses, dates of birth, contact details, tax file numbers, payroll information, bank account details and academic records. Information of this type could be of value for identity theft purposes; however, it was speculated that its level of sophistication indicated it was more likely to have been undertaken by a state actor. It has been speculated that China was likely the actor involved and was interested in the ANU's data because of the large number of students who go on to work in government, the foreign service, and Australia's military and security partnerships with the United States, as well as the large number of Chinese students enrolled at the institution.[33] It was the latest in a large number of cybersecurity incidents affecting political organisations, financial institutions and private citizens around the world.

## Biometrics

The Identity-Matching Services Bill 2019 (Cth), though not yet enacted, seeks approval for a facial recognition database that integrates images from all passport and driver's licence databases. In addition to a facial image verification service that can be used to prevent identity fraud, a law enforcement database was also introduced. This second database can potentially, and at some point in the future almost certainly will, be integrated with other technologies such as CCTV to allow real-time surveillance in public spaces – an approach that is already widely used in China as part of that country's 'social credit system'.[34] This capability has significant potential for mass surveillance applications and would need to be closely regulated, with developments in China indicating how it could also be used in liberal democracies if safeguards are not implemented. Such developments may already be underway, with Victoria Police confirming that it 'utilises facial recognition technology for investigative and intelligence-gathering purposes across the City of Melbourne council's network of 138 surveillance cameras'.[35]

These are just a sample of some of the areas of technology law that have been discussed in the media over the past decade. They will be explored in greater depth later in the text, following a discussion of regulatory and political theory in Chapter 2. There have, of course, been many more instances, not as widely known, but in their own way just as significant, particularly when trends are considered in aggregate. Technology impacts on so many areas of our lives, it is surprising that it has not yet been given the treatment it deserves in teaching and scholarship.

Whether it is the use of a drone received as a gift, a movie downloaded online, images posted on social media, goods purchased from an online merchant, or research into one's genetic ancestry, the legal implications of new technologies are becoming central to everyday living. Technology will continue to influence not just macro events, such as elections, the implementation of national data systems or advances in biotechnology, but

---

33  Australian National University, *ANU Releases Detailed Account of Data Breach*, 2 October 2019. Available: <https://www.anu.edu.au/news/all-news/anu-releases-detailed-account-of-data-breach>.

34  Fan Liang et al, 'Constructing a Data-Driven Society: China's Social Credit System as a State Surveillance Infrastructure' (2018) 10 *Policy and Internet* 415.

35  Elias Visontay, 'Councils Tracking Our Faces on the Sly', *The Australian*, 29 August 2019.

everyday transactions that are integral to our lives. To some extent, everyone has an interest in technology law: not just students of law, computer science or criminology; and not just professionals such as lawyers, police, doctors and business owners. Technology is now so integral to everyday life that whatever an individual's background, interests, activities and future intentions, they should have at least a basic understanding of the relevant law.

# Overview of the text

The coverage of technology law in this text provides the reader with an accessible and integrated resource for learning and understanding the regulation of some of the most interesting and important issues in contemporary law. It will provide a basic understanding of the technology itself, and act as a guide through the context, relevant policy issues, legislation, case law, international perspectives and gaps in the regulatory framework. The text can be divided roughly into three parts. Chapters 1, 2 and 3 provide background material on technology law, as well as associated theory, regulatory principles and privacy considerations that inform the discussion of all areas of technology law throughout the text. Chapter 2, 'Technology: Regulation and Theory' focuses on epistemic, ethical and regulatory perspectives. It moves from a focused discussion of regulatory theory and the regulation of technology through to the central ethical and political theories, such as social contract, consequentialism and deontology; then to an epistemic discussion of the nature of scientific knowledge; and, finally, to case studies and historical examples of how governments and the legal system have responded to new technology in the past and are likely to respond in the future. Chapter 3, 'Privacy and Data Protection', begins the focus on substantive legislation, common law and human rights instruments. It examines the principles of the law of privacy in Australia, including the *Privacy Act 1988* (Cth) and the Australian Privacy Principles, and provides a comparative discussion of equivalent provisions in the United States, the United Kingdom and Europe. How these provisions interact (or are likely to) with respect to new forms of technology, and the ongoing need to manage the benefits and challenges of technology, particularly with respect to personal information, communications technologies and the internet, are also considered.

Chapters 4–9 consider discrete areas of technology law, with a focus on Australian law, but also drawing on international perspectives. Chapter 4, 'Law, Technology and Healthcare', discusses the regulation of technology used in the healthcare sector. It begins with a contemporary discussion of patient rights and regulatory frameworks, before moving on to consider consent, confidentiality and electronic health records, genetic databases, assisted reproductive technologies, human cloning, gene editing and stem cell technology. Chapter 5, 'Law, Technology and Commercial Transactions', examines the regulation of new technologies that facilitate payments, other financial transactions and contracts. These include online payment systems, cryptocurrencies, blockchain, and the significant and growing problem of online fraud and financial crime, along with approaches to mitigate these concerns. Chapter 6, 'Law, Technology and the Criminal Justice System', considers the use of technology in the criminal justice system. It discusses identification technologies, including fingerprint, DNA and facial recognition systems, which are increasingly important to criminal investigations and related areas such as national security. The use of other technologies such as metadata and automated number plate recognition systems to identify suspects in investigations is also examined. A key theme throughout this chapter will be balancing individual rights with the imperative to use available technologies to protect the community from harm.

Chapter 7, 'Cybercrime', examines this rapidly expanding area of criminality and the complexities it presents for law enforcement, with a focus on unauthorised access to and disruption of computer systems. It includes a discussion of phenomena such as hacking and distributed denial-of-service attacks. Chapter 8, 'Social Media and Communications', looks at the regulation of applications such as Facebook, Twitter and Instagram, the regulation of posts on social media sites and the internet generally, the use of personal data for advertising purposes, as well as image-based exploitation, cyberbullying, defamation and harassment. It examines the advent of the internet as a facilitator of instantaneous global communications and the challenges this poses from legal and regulatory perspectives. Chapter 9, 'Intellectual Property', examines how modern technology and developments in data storage and transfer have influenced ownership rights in the entertainment industry, and online piracy through file-sharing systems more broadly, as well as other contemporary forms of copyright and digital trade mark infringement.

Chapters 10 and 11 draw together many of the technology law issues discussed throughout the text and look at their regulation and investigation, before highlighting some common themes and reflecting on how issues in technology law can potentially be anticipated and mitigated. Chapter 10, 'International Investigation and Enforcement', considers the challenges of responding to technology developments by governments and law enforcement. This topic encompasses the international context of many of the areas of technology law that have been discussed, jurisdictional issues in regulating new technologies, as well as investigating and enforcing the law in relation to technology-based offences, including related issues such as interoperability, encryption and data security. Finally, Chapter 11, 'Future Directions in Technology Law', draws together the issues discussed throughout, in light of the theoretical foundation of the initial chapters of the text, and reflects on likely future developments and directions, and on how the law may need to be adapted in the future. The prospect of designing appropriate laws that foresee and can accommodate continual technological advances is a central theme.

The regulation of new technology is complex and subject to ongoing development, and legislation is often contentious and reactive. Legal and regulatory responses to technological advancement, and the risks and opportunities associated with it, must balance competing objectives and be cognisant of ongoing development. The task requires a sufficient understanding of the scientific basis of the technology to appreciate its current and potential applications. Government and courts are tasked with formulating responses to technologies that are continually developing: by the time consultation has been conducted, research and comparative analysis undertaken, advice taken, and laws drafted, passed by the parliament and implemented by the executive – a process that can take years – there is a high probability that the technology itself will have progressed, adapted and been implemented in such a manner as to render that law obsolete and ineffective. This is a fact that should always be borne in mind when engaging with the areas of technology discussed in this text and their associated law and regulation. It means that an understanding of the foundational issues and background – in terms of theoretical perspectives and regulatory approaches, privacy law, and international frameworks and ongoing dialogue in relation to the regulation of technology or investigation of offences – is important when considering specific areas of technology law, whether they relate to healthcare, criminal justice, commercial transactions, cybercrime, social media or intellectual property.

At the forefront of technology law is the area of artificial intelligence (AI), providing ever more efficient means to analyse and solve problems, reduce data processing and storage costs, and provide new financial opportunities for the private sector. AI is an area that offers great potential for human advancement; yet, it also has the potential to encroach upon fundamental human rights, such as privacy and autonomy, as well as potentially compromise data security and the integrity of political systems, and, over time, bring about changes in the labour market and the economy.[36] Developments in data analytics and machine learning in the next decade will have implications for medical diagnosis, human identification and service provision, and will become increasingly based on automation and robotics, with human intervention limited to oversight roles. The challenge for governments and the legal system is to harness the benefits of this technology for society and limit the costs in a globalised world, where there are financial incentives for these technologies to be implemented quickly.

As the examples have highlighted, innovative technologies have a history of being implemented before effective regulation is in place; indeed, historically, technology companies have thrived on a certain level of disregard for government and the established economic and political order. Perhaps as a result of some of these recent occurrences, this attitude has begun to shift and companies are becoming more socially responsible as consumers become more aware of how their data can potentially be used. At least in their public statements, technology companies now acknowledge this fact.

> It's not enough to just connect people, we have to make sure those connections are positive. It's not enough to just give people a voice, we have to make sure people aren't using it to hurt people or spread misinformation. It's not enough to give people control of their information, we have to make sure developers they've given it to are protecting it too. Across the board, we have a responsibility to not just build tools, but to make sure those tools are used for good.[37]

In setting the right level of regulation, the law has an important role to play in balancing the complex and multifaceted impact of AI and other technologies on individuals and society. It must take account of its potential to impact on basic rights and interests, as well as the environment and democratic institutions; and of its potential to change the way humans interact, how we work and access services, and how we obtain information and make decisions. The Australian Human Rights Commission describes the challenges of regulating artificial intelligence as follows:

> Adopting the right governance framework is difficult, because AI technologies are complex, are applied across all sectors of the Australian community, and have enormous capacity for social good, social harm – and often both simultaneously. However, Australian stakeholders need to consider and experiment with innovative models for ensuring that the economic gains, social influence and security impact of AI is [sic] positive for all … Protecting Australians, while powering our future economy, requires

---

36  Australian Human Rights Commission and World Economic Forum, *Artificial Intelligence: Governance and Leadership White Paper* (2019), 5.

37  United States Senate Committee on the Judiciary and the United States Senate Committee on Commerce, Science and Transportation, *Testimony of Mark Zuckerberg* (10 April 2019), 1.

innovation that reinforces Australia's liberal democratic values, especially human rights, fairness and inclusion. Making this vision real is a complex task. It will involve, for example, carefully crafted laws supported by an effective regulatory framework, strong incentives that apply to the public and private sectors, and policies that enable Australians to navigate an emerging AI-powered world.[38]

In ensuring an in-depth understanding of law and regulation as it relates to technology, and of the contemporary and emerging issues in the field, this text provides a foundation for readers to form their own views and make their own contributions to the regulation of technology – a complex, interesting and rich field that will continue to progress and change.

---

38  Australian Human Rights Commission and World Economic Forum, *Artificial Intelligence: Governance and Leadership White Paper* (2019), 6.

# 2

# TECHNOLOGY, REGULATION AND THEORY

# Introduction

This chapter examines science and technology from a regulatory and theoretical perspective, providing an important background to the substantive issues discussed throughout the text. The first part of the chapter looks at regulatory theory as it relates to technology, beginning with the general approach of John Braithwaite, and then at more recent approaches to information technology and the internet, specifically the 'law is code' approach of Lawrence Lessig and its further development by Andrew Murray. Next, the chapter examines political theory, considering the relationship between individuals and societies – how the behaviour of citizens is best managed according to competing interests, and how governments should legislate to manage these interests. The third part of the chapter examines the basic theories of ethical reasoning, deontology and consequentialism. Lastly, the chapter discusses the nature of scientific knowledge that underlies technology, and how scientific knowledge becomes established.

# Regulation

## Regulating technology

The regulation of new technology by law seeks to maximise benefits and limit costs. It is important that technology does not harm or cause other unacceptable outcomes for individuals and the community. A fundamental consideration when examining regulatory approaches for new forms of technology is responsibility for oversight. This includes the role of developing and reviewing policies and responding to complaints. Effective oversight of technology requires technical knowledge (or well-informed advice), resources, and the capacity to balance individual rights, such as privacy, against the benefits to individuals and the community, such as protection from the threat of crime and terrorism. It is important in this area to consider international developments for comparison, and ensure they are integrated into the development of best practice. Regulation often requires consideration of the competing demands between individual privacy and collective security objectives. A number of academics have sought to understand the regulatory process that occurs in relation to technology and have proposed theories that explain and effectively address these types of challenges.

John Braithwaite proposes 'pyramids of supports and of sanctions' that incorporate regulatory and oversight strategies that can be applied by government on a progressive basis.[1] At the bottom level of the regulatory pyramid, support is provided for self-regulation – that is, persuasion. At secondary and higher levels, civil and criminal sanctions are enforced by independent regulators – for example, in regulating police access to and use of personal information such as biometrics and other data in their investigations. In law enforcement contexts, it has been argued that self-regulation (ie the first levels in Figure 2.1) alone is unworkable, as there are insufficient incentives for police to self-regulate their access to and use of personal information in criminal investigations.[2] There is a tendency for the

---

1   Ian Ayres and John Braithwaite, *Responsive Regulation: Transcending the Deregulation Debate* (Oxford University Press, 1992); John Braithwaite, 'Fasken Lecture: The Essence of Responsive Regulation' (2011) 44 *University of British Columbia Law Review* 475.
2   Sabrina Lochner, 'Saving Face: Regulating Law Enforcement's Use of Mobile Facial Recognition Technology and Iris Scans' (2013) 55 *Arizona Law Review* 201, 229–30.

capabilities offered by new technology to overshadow individual rights considerations and the need for greater regulation and oversight.[3] In the absence of a strong and independent regulator, there is likely an insufficient protection of individual rights. Therefore, regulation should occur at multiple levels, ultimately reinforced by independent oversight at the top levels of the responsive regulatory pyramid.[4]

**Figure 2.1** Pyramid of Responsive Regulation[5]

# The internet

In relation to new technology in areas such as health or criminal justice, regulation has built up over time so that when new technology is introduced, there is often an existing regime of legislation and policy that it becomes integrated within, albeit more slowly than is necessary for it to be effective. In contrast with these areas, however, the dawn of the internet in the late 1990s presented a particularly novel and complex regulatory challenge. The rapid access to information of all types that can be facilitated by the internet paradoxically offers opportunities for both personal freedom and government surveillance.

> On the one hand, the internet and associated digital media technologies are presented as revolutionary, emancipatory and even as tools for democratization and the rebranding of liberal internationalism. On the other hand, the internet represents

3   See, eg, Paul De Hert and Serge Gutwirth, 'Interoperability of Police Databases within the EU: An Accountable Political Choice?' (2006) 20 *International Review of Law, Computers & Technology* 21.
4   Ibid.
5   Ian Ayres and John Braithwaite, *Responsive Regulation: Transcending the Deregulation Debate* (Oxford University Press, 1992).

information overload, the 'deluge' of big data, mass privacy and copyright violation and the resurgence of surveillance culture and control.[6]

During the advent of the internet in the late 1990s, a particular form of libertarianism was articulated by John Perry Barlow in his *Declaration of Independence for Cyberspace* that captured the zeitgeist and the views of many pioneers in the field. It was a challenge to regulators, law enforcement and government, along the following lines:

> You have no sovereignty where we gather … You have no moral right to rule us, nor do you possess any methods of enforcement we have true reason to fear.[7]

Barlow argued that when a citizen of a country enters cyberspace, they are no longer subject to the jurisdiction of the country in which they reside – or of any country – and that laws cannot be enforced against individual actors on the internet. The alternative position is that an individual using the internet is not in fact transported into 'cyberspace' at all, but remains within the country they are physically in, and further, if they do commit a crime, it is reasonable to expect that they remain subject to the laws of that country, and indeed, the laws of other countries that might be affected by online conduct where it is committed across borders. Over the 25 years that have elapsed since Barlow published this declaration, the cogency of his position has considerably diminished.

The internet has become ubiquitous – to the extent that it now affects almost every aspect of our lives. Today, almost all transactions can be undertaken in that environment – indeed, many people conduct all their banking transactions on a smartphone. If this libertarian approach were generally accepted in the contemporary world, it would result in anarchy. Although there are certainly limitations in law enforcement's capacity to respond to cybercrime, capabilities have advanced over the past two decades, and there are many examples of success, such as in prosecution for possession of child exploitation material, and more recently, 'image-based exploitation' (otherwise known as revenge porn).[8] A more nuanced version of this argument has been advanced by Johnson and Post,[9] who argue that traditional forms of regulation cannot function effectively in cyberspace and that effective law and regulation in this domain needs to be determined by a free market in which users choose the regulations they believe are likely to be most effective. On this approach, the majority would then be governed by consent and through a 'decentralised, emergent law'.[10] A pragmatic issue with this reasoning that has been identified by a number of authors is the fact that there is a lack of homogeneity among internet users, leading to fragmentation of views, and making it difficult for decentralised collective action to take place, along with the emergence of common standards.[11]

6  Daniel Joyce, 'Internet Freedom and Human Rights' (2015) 26 *European Journal of International Law* 493, 496.

7  John Perry Barlow, *A Declaration of the Independence of Cyberspace* (1996). Available: <https://www.eff.org/cyberspace-independence>.

8  See, eg, *Enhancing Online Safety (Non-Consensual Sharing of Intimate Images) Act 2018* (Cth); *Crimes Amendment (Intimate Images) Act 2017* (NSW); *Criminal Law Amendment (Intimate Images) Act 2018* (WA).

9  David Johnson and David Post, 'Law and Borders: The Rise of Law in Cyberspace' (1996) 48 *Stanford Law Review* 1367.

10  Ibid, 1402.

11  See, eg, Cass Sunstein, *Republic 2.0* (Princeton University Press, 2007); and Andrew Murray, *Information Technology Law* (Oxford University Press, 2019), 59.

# Economic change

Over the intervening period since these views were proffered, the massive expansion of digital information available on the internet, social media, e-commerce and so on, has continued to disrupt legal and economic systems. There has been a marked shift in developed economies from the production of goods, to the production of knowledge. For the time being, Australia is continuing its reliance on the export of natural resources, but it is also undergoing a shift (e.g. in providing a substantial number of its university places to international students), while the United Kingdom (insurance, financial and legal services) and the United States (the global leader in the information technology sector) have already shifted. Companies such as Google, Apple and Facebook are leading examples of the economic shift towards control of information and knowledge being key to wealth, with advertising the main application of this knowledge in the private sector. Andrew Murray describes the change:

> It represents a shift from ownership or control of things to ownership of, or control over, information. It represents the maturity of information technology and most importantly signals a change in economic value from owning things ... to owning information.[12]

The wine bottle analogy has been applied to academic discussion of the disruption caused by the internet. The product has been separated from the package that carried it. For instance, music has shifted from being sold on compact discs, to the digital MP3 format. Barlow summarises that 'with the advent of digitisation, it is now possible to replace all previous information storage forms with complex and highly liquid patterns of ones and zeros'.[13] In the context of cybercrime, the phrase 'old wine in new bottles' has been used in discussions seeking to understand whether cybercrime represents a new type of crime; or simply adopts digital methods in the commission of the same criminal offence, such as fraud, theft and property damage. Peter Grabosky is an adherent of the latter interpretation, stating that cybercrime is 'basically the same as the terrestrial crime with which we are familiar'.[14] A proponent of the former view is David Wall, who views cybercrime as 'new wine, no bottles'.[15]

As the size of computers has reduced in line with technological advancement, greater aggregation of technology has become possible – a smartphone now serves as a phone, laptop, navigation device, camera, notepad and portable music player (among other things), and many traditional devices have become obsolete in the process. Ithiel de Sola Pool first observed that the convergence of technologies occurs along with their advancement: 'electronic technology is bringing all modes of communications into one grand system'.[16] This phenomenon is also relevant to the way companies such as Google, Apple or Facebook are active across an expanding number of platforms, often encompassing news, entertainment, advertising, payment services, physical devices and more. Moreover, a consequence of both the aggregation of technology in smartphones, as well as social media and internet companies, is the fact that it is now much easier and cheaper to record video and images,

---

12  Andrew Murray, *Information Technology Law* (Oxford University Press, 2019), 5.
13  John Perry Barlow, 'The Economy of Ideas: Selling Wine without Bottles on the Global Net', *Wired 2.03* (1994).
14  Peter Grabosky, 'Virtual Criminality: Old Wine in New Bottles?' (2001) 10 *Social and Legal Studies* 243.
15  David Wall, 'Cybercrimes: New Wine, No Bottles?'. In Pamela Davies, Peter Francis and Victor Jupp, *Invisible Crimes* (Macmillan, 1999).
16  Ithiel de Sola Pool, *The Technologies of Freedom* (Belknap, 1983), 28.

package it, and publish 'news'. This has led to an increase in the volume of news, but also to its reduced accuracy (along with reduced personal privacy). Pool's observations, made in 1983, are strikingly prescient today.

> Technology-driven convergence of modes is reinforced by the economic process of cross-ownership. The growth of conglomerates which participate in many businesses at once means that newspapers, magazine publishers, and book publishers increasingly own or are owned by companies that also operate in other fields. Both convergence and cross-ownership blur the boundaries which once existed between companies publishing in the print domain ... and companies involved in businesses that are regulated by government. Today, the same company may find itself operating in both fields. The dikes that in the past held government back from exerting control on the print media are thus broken down.[17]

## Technological capabilities

A further development that requires attention from a regulatory standpoint is the internationalisation of the internet, and how rapidly it is now possible to transfer data across borders. Influential theorists on this phenomenon are Post and Johnson, who argue that traditional state-based sovereignty has been disrupted by cyberspace. In the context of regulating the internet, physical borders have become inconsequential, as individuals and information can move between them instantaneously.

> Clear boundaries make law possible, encouraging rapid differentiation between rule sets and defining the subjects of legal discussion. New abilities to travel or exchange information rapidly across old borders may change the legal frame of reference and require fundamental changes in legal institutions. Fundamental activities of lawmaking – accommodating conflicting claims, defining property rights, establishing rules to guide conduct, enforcing those rules, and resolving disputes – remain very much alive within the newly defined, intangible territory of cyberspace. At the same time, the newly emerging law challenges the core idea of a current law-making authority – the territorial nation state, with substantial but legally restrained powers.[18]

In contrast with the libertarianism of Barlow are the more nuanced approaches of Joel Reidenberg and Lawrence Lessig. Reidenberg seeks to understand the regulatory borders of the rule-making process for cyberspace, involving states, citizens, the private sector and the technology itself. Reidenberg's concept of *Lex Informatica* refers to the 'laws' imposed by technological capabilities and system designs. He considers it possible for the internet to be regulated by government using the internet's architecture itself, rather than by proscribing particular activities an individual can undertake.

> [L]aw and government regulation are not the only source of rule-making. Technological capabilities and system design choices impose rules on participants. The creation and implementation of information policy are embedded in network designs and standards as well as in system configurations ... the set of rules for information flows imposed

---

17  Ibid, 23–4.
18  David Johnson and David Post, 'Law and Borders: The Rise of Law in Cyberspace' (1996) 48 *Stanford Law Review* 1367, 1402.

by technology and communication networks form a 'Lex Informatica' that policymakers must understand, consciously recognize, and encourage.[19]

This approach to regulation was taken further by Lawrence Lessig in his influential work *A Code and Other Laws of Cyberspace*.[20] This work on the regulation of the internet argues, contra the libertarians, that it is possible to regulate cyberspace. Lessig describes four 'modalities of regulation', these being: the law, social norms, market forces, and architecture.[21] Regulators select combinations of these modalities and apply them in a direct or indirect way to control the activities of individuals, in both the real and digital contexts. For instance, the law controls individual activities through the threat of legal sanctions such as fines or imprisonment, social norms through the threat of social sanctions such as stigma, the market through pricing, and architecture (code) through physical constraints such as a lock or, more relevantly, a firewall or a requirement that internet service providers block illegal websites.[22] Lessig describes the individual as a 'pathetic dot' controlled by these modalities (Figure 2.2). On this view, while it may be difficult for traditional law to regulate the internet, when the law is combined in a regulatory framework it becomes possible. Lessig outlines, and then responds to, the libertarian position that control by government in cyberspace is impossible.

> This belief about cyberspace is wrong, but wrong in an interesting way. It assumes either that the nature of cyberspace is fixed – that its architecture, and the control it enables, cannot be changed – or that government cannot take steps to change this architecture. Neither assumption is correct. Cyberspace has no nature; it has no particular architecture that cannot be changed.[23]

The advantage of using architecture (or code) for regulation is that it has a high level of compliance, particularly as the majority of the community lacks the technical skills to

**Figure 2.2** Four Modalities of Regulation[24]

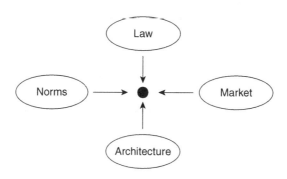

19  Joel Reidenberg, 'Lex Informatica: The Formulation of Information Policy Rules through Technology' (1998) 76 *Texas Law Review* 553.
20  Lawrence Lessig, *Code and Other Laws of Cyberspace* (Basic Books, 1999).
21  Ibid, 43–60.
22  Readers of criminology may be familiar with situational action theory, which addresses a similar point.
23  Lawrence Lessig, 'The Law of the Horse: What Cyberlaw Might Teach' (1991) 113 *Harvard Law Review* 501, 512.
24  Lawrence Lessig, *Code and Other Laws of Cyberspace* (Basic Books, 1999).

circumvent it. This approach physically prevents non-compliance, and is a low-cost option for the government to administer because the costs are often borne by the private sector in building systems that comply with regulatory requirements. Further, in contrast with enacting laws, it can often be done without even informing the public that it has been implemented. This aspect raises questions of democratic accountability: ' ... it muddies the responsibility for that constraint and so undermines political accountability.'[25] Addressing this point, Roger Brownsword suggests that this type of regulation of the internet is problematic in that it takes a sledgehammer to the problem: ' ... techno regulators know how to stop us from being bad only by, at the same time, stopping us from being good.'[26]

In *The Regulation of Cyberspace*, Murray develops Lessig's model into a wider theory in which the dot is a node in a network that forms an 'active dot matrix' (Figure 2.3).[27] Murray argues that the dot is actually an active part of the regulatory process. The dots 'share ideas, beliefs, ideals and opinions ... and are accountable to the community, meaning the regulatory process is in nature a dialogue not an externally imposed set of constraints'.[28] This is described as a form of symbiotic regulation where the regulator takes the views of the community into account and formulates an approach they are likely to accept, as this is mutually beneficial for the regulator and the community. Murray terms this approach 'network communitarianism', contrasting it with Lessig's 'cyberpaternalism'.

> Cyberpaternalism proposes coercion, whereas network communitarianism suggests incentivisation and persuasion. In cyberpaternalism the dot (or dots) acts in a certain way because of 'constraint', whilst in network communitarianism it does so because of 'encouragement'.[29]

**Figure 2.3** Active Dot Matrix[30]

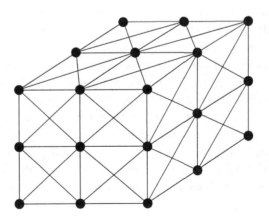

25  Ibid, 96.
26  Roger Brownsword, 'Code, Control, and Choice: Why East is East and West is West' (2005) 21 *Legal Studies* 1.
27  Andrew Murray, *The Regulation of Cyberspace: Control in the Online Environment* (Routledge, 2007).
28  Andrew Murray, *Information Technology Law* (Oxford University Press, 2019), 37, 66.
29  Chris Reed and Andrew Murray, *Rethinking the Jurisprudence of Cyberspace* (Edward Elgar, 2018), 158.
30  Andrew Murray, *The Regulation of Cyberspace: Control in the Online Environment* (Routledge, 2007).

The final aspect of digital regulation that will be considered here is algorithmic regulation. Artificial intelligence systems of this nature are becoming increasingly common. In this case, the code component of regulation is not in the form of fixed architecture, but an algorithm capable of adapting through machine learning to identify new forms of content requiring regulation. An example of this would be an algorithm for identifying unacceptable or illegal content on the web. This is applied by social media sites such as YouTube and Facebook to filter content or, in a slightly different way, Google Maps to identify the quickest route to a destination.[31] While it offers greater efficiency, a problematic aspect of it, and of big data and artificial intelligence more generally, is the lack of transparency in the decision-making process (sometimes referred to as the black box) used by the non-human algorithm, if it were necessary to justify or scrutinise the process. These issues are discussed further in Chapter 3.

## Technology in the courtroom

The use of scientific information or new technology in the legal system involves the interaction of two distinct systems of knowledge to resolve a dispute. It is necessary to consider the nature of each system.[32] Scientific evidence is viewed as reliable due to its ability to appeal to objective instruments and reduce reliance on subjective sensory perception. However, all scientific techniques require some degree of human involvement, such as data collection and recording. The susceptibility of scientific evidence to human error may be easily overlooked due to its well-established theoretical backing. Instances of fraud sometimes occur in scientific research. For example, early in the development of stem cell technology, a prominent South Korean scientist altered the results of his embryonic research to claim an important advancement that was later discovered to be fraudulent and had not been uncovered in the normal peer review process.[33]

Forensic science is one area which has been especially controversial. The use of techniques and technology to compare pairs of marks such as fingerprints, tyre tracks and bite marks in the 1980s and 1990s has been particularly contentious, and it has become apparent that the scientific basis for much of this analysis is not as clear as was previously thought. Wrongful convictions have been caused by unsound forensic science (among other factors). Research examining the factors that resulted in wrongful convictions found the most common reason was incorrect eyewitness testimony, but that this is closely followed by inaccurate forensic science. A contributing factor may be the pressure on law enforcement and prosecution agencies (and the individuals within them) to obtain convictions, which has had a detrimental effect on objectivity.[34] Genetics has provided a sounder basis for forensic science, and DNA evidence has overcome many of the problems of traditional forensic science by providing quantifiable, probability-based assessments of matching DNA

---

31  See, eg, Karen Yeung, 'Algorithmic Regulation: A Critical Interrogation' (2018) 12 *Regulation and Governance* 505, 507.

32  David Faigman, *Legal Alchemy: The Use and Misuse of Science in the Law* (WH Freeman and Co, 1999), Chapter I.

33  Herbert Gottweis and Robert Triendl, 'South Korean Policy Failure and the Hwang Debate' (2006) 24 *Nature Biotechnology* 141.

34  C Michael Bowers, 'Problem-Based Analysis of Bitemark Misidentifications: The Role of DNA' (2006) 159 *Forensic Science International* 104.

profiles. It took a period of time for this form of evidence to become established and for legal requirements to be set in terms of the level of training that was required for technical staff, how match probabilities would be calculated, and how the evidence could be presented in court. While this form of evidence is now generally accepted in the scientific and legal communities, there is still the prospect for mistakes to occur through human error, contamination, or a misunderstanding of the significance of the evidence at trial.

The 1993 case *Daubert v Merrell Dow Pharmaceuticals Inc*[35] transformed the way courts in the United States interpret expert scientific evidence and has also influenced the Australian legal system. It determined that a court must play a 'gatekeeper' role in relation to scientific evidence. According to the court, judges were required to take account of whether the science had been tested, how methodologically sound the testing was and the results that it had produced. In the United States, legal academics have criticised the use of scientific evidence in court, highlighting a number of problems that remain.

> Unfortunately, the adversarial approach to the submission of evidence in court is not well suited to the task of finding 'scientific truth.' The judicial system is encumbered by, among other things, judges, lawyers, and jurors who generally lack the scientific expertise necessary to comprehend and evaluate forensic evidence in an informed manner; defense attorneys who often do not have the resources to challenge prosecutors' forensic experts; trial judges (sitting alone) who must decide evidentiary issues without the benefit of judicial colleagues and often with little time for extensive research and reflection; and very limited appellate review of trial court rulings admitting disputed forensic evidence. Furthermore, the judicial system embodies a case-by-case adjudicatory approach that is not well suited to address the systematic problems in many of the various forensic science disciplines.[36]

These problems have been reiterated by a number of academics who remain critical of the way that scientific evidence is used in courts. Often the scientists or medical experts giving evidence are being paid by one of the parties, potentially providing a conflict over how the scientific results are interpreted; those making decisions on the basis of the evidence, judges or juries, usually do not have scientific training themselves; and there have been high-profile instances of new techniques being used that do not have the backing of the broader scientific community, a fact that may not come to light in a trial. Gary Edmond has written extensively about the importance of improving regulatory standards for scientific evidence.

> On the whole the reports find that many forensic science and medicine techniques are not based on independent scientific research. Many techniques and assumptions have never been evaluated and many practitioners have never had their abilities credibly assessed. Surprisingly few forensic analysts know about, or are trained to deal with, issues and factors that may dramatically influence their performances and the reliability of results. They have been especially inattentive to threats to interpretation and the expression of results. Many practices and techniques are not standardised, and/or described in sufficient detail, to produce consistent results between analysts. Standards

---

35   113 S Ct 2786 (1993).
36   Harry Edwards, 'Solving the Problems that Plague the Forensic Science Community' (2009) 50 *Jurimetrics Journal* 5, 19.

are often imprecise and not based on research. This has meant that – where they exist – accreditation, certification and regulation are generally weaker than they ought to be.[37]

Progress has been made in recent years to improve the quality of expert evidence. Legislative codes of conduct have now been established for expert witnesses that emphasise their roles and duties, independence from the parties, primary duty to assist the court, and obligation to transparently justify their assumptions and reasoning process in reports to the court.[38]

# Political theory

The ethics of a society are reflected in the laws that it creates. In regulating new forms of technology, ethical and political theories can provide a link between the science and technology on one side and law and government regulation on the other, balancing and integrating competing interests within society. The theories that will be considered in this discussion address the concepts of the social contract, liberty, community and justice. Each can be used in different circumstances to evaluate whether the implementation of a new form of technology is warranted.

## Contractualism

Contractualism is a central theory of political philosophy, and is derived from social contract theory. It is used to justify the creation of the state, and the political obligation of citizens. The theory asserts that morality consists of a set of rules that must be agreed upon to ensure that society can function effectively. On this view, ethics, politics and individual moral obligations are related to obligations within society. The political philosophers Thomas Hobbes (1588–1679), John Locke (1632–1704), and Jean-Jacques Rousseau (1712–78) have all made significant contributions to the theory of contractualism. Central to their ideas are the concepts of the state of nature and the social contract. 'The state of nature' describes the situation of humans prior to systems of government being established. It highlights the advantages of political organisation, and that some degree of governmental authority must be accepted if humans are to advance beyond this state. The social contract is a hypothetical device used to describe how a group of individuals without government, division of labour or exchange relations form a society and accept obligations to one another and the state. The social contract is the basis of law and morality within the state, and justifies the social obligation of individual citizens.

In his work *Leviathan*, Thomas Hobbes provided a description of man's situation in the state of nature, which has been widely cited. Hobbes describes this state as *a war of all against all*.

> There is no place for industry ... no culture of the earth; no navigation ... no commodious building ... no knowledge of the face of the earth; no account of time; no arts; no letters; no society; and which is worst of all, continual fear and danger of violent death; and the life of man, solitary, poor, nasty, brutish, and short.[39]

37  Gary Edmond, 'What Lawyers Should Know About the Forensic Sciences' (2015) 36 *Adelaide Law Review* 33, 99.
38  See, eg, *Expert Evidence Practice Note* (Federal Court of Australia, 25 October 2016). Available: <https://www.fedcourt.gov.au/law-and-practice/practice-documents/practice-notes/gpn-expt>.
39  Thomas Hobbes, *Leviathan* (1660; Penguin, 1968), 186.

According to Hobbes, humans are naturally egoistic, and wish to move out of this state, because they cannot otherwise pursue their conflicting goals without frustrating each other. It is argued that, for this reason, rational individuals should surrender their natural rights and become subjects of the sovereign. The sovereign acquires de jure authority and becomes 'that great Leviathan ... to which we owe under the immortal God, our peace and defence'.[40] It is argued that to achieve a long-term existence, individuals must construct a stable society, and that this requires them to surrender their right of nature. However, this does not extend to surrendering the right to respond to immediate threats. In giving their right to the sovereign, the individual has an obligation to obey. The sovereign also has obligations, and in Hobbes' view, determining what is moral or immoral depends upon what action would promote lasting peace.

According to John Locke, while a contract is formed between individuals, rights are not given up to a sovereign, but to the community, ruled by a body politic. Locke's formulation of the ideal society is therefore more democratic.

> Every man, by consenting with others to make one Body Politick under one Government, puts himself under an obligation to every one of that Society, to submit to the determination of the majority, and to be concluded by it; or else this original Compact, whereby he with others incorporates into one Society, would signifie nothing, and be no Compact, if he be left free, and under no other ties, than he was before in the State of Nature.[41]

In moving from the state of nature, individuals 'set up a judge ... with authority to determine all the controversies and redress the injuries that may happen to any member of the commonwealth'.[42] However, the power of the government is not absolute, and is answerable to the majority. Its role is limited to upholding the life, liberty, and property of the individual.

Jean-Jacques Rousseau's version of sovereignty states that the entire population legislates over itself through the general will, which is applied equally to all. The general will promotes liberty and equality, and arises from and promotes fraternity. In Rousseau's view:

> Each of us puts his person and all his power in common under the supreme direction of the general will, and, in our corporate capacity, we receive each member as an indivisible part of the whole.[43]

Under the laws of the state, citizens share sovereign authority. Citizens give their natural liberty to the state, and gain civil and moral liberty. Rousseau stated:

> In order then that the social compact may not be an empty formula, it tacitly includes the undertaking, which alone can give force to the rest, that whoever refuses to obey the general will shall be compelled to do so by the whole body. This means nothing less than he will be forced to be free; for this is the condition which, by giving each citizen to his country, secures him against all personal dependence. In this lies the key

---

40  Ibid, 227.
41  John Locke, *Second Treatise of Government* (1690; Cambridge University Press, 1967), section 97.
42  Ibid, section 89.
43  Jean-Jacques Rousseau, *The Social Contract* (Becket and Hondt, 1762), Book I, Chapter Six.

to the working of the political machine; this alone legitimizes civil undertakings, which, without it, would be absurd, tyrannical and liable to the most frightful abuses.[44]

Laws are viewed by Rousseau as an act of general will made by the people, uniting 'universality of will with universality of object'.[45] Further, because individual judgement can be unenlightened, it is problematic for the public body to implement legislation without submitting their decisions to the vote of the public body.

Like many instances in contemporary society where citizens concede some of their rights to the state in return for the benefits the state has the capacity to provide, it may be argued that in regard to new technologies such as smartphones that provide benefits at the individual and community level, the requirement that governments may record and access data created by these devices where authorised by legislation and warrants for purposes such as the investigation of crime is a form of a social contract between the government and its citizens. While some may assert that the retention of metadata, such as GPS locations and websites visited, is an unwarranted infringement of personal liberty, others may respond that the use of this data by law enforcement and other government agencies is necessary to ensure that the police can effectively prevent crime, and that citizens can enjoy security and freedom.

Traditionally, there have been many instances in which the state intrudes into the personal liberties of citizens. These include when the state requires that cars be registered if they are to be driven on the road, and that photographs and profiles of licensed drivers are retained. The public healthcare system retains personal medical details when subsidising medical costs, and the taxation office maintains details of personal income from which it deducts a significant proportion for use by the state. These actions are all invasive to varying degrees, but are tolerated due to the benefits that the state provides in return. Of course, the arguments will be different according to the specific context; however, some may argue that the requirement that the government retain metadata or other forms of technology-facilitated information for the purpose of upholding the law and investigating crime, or for other legitimate purposes, is arguably no more invasive than many current measures, and would be a reasonable concession in light of the benefits that can be obtained by ensuring the police force can make the best use of available technology in carrying out its function. Depending on the specific context and circumstances, measures such as this reduce the degree to which life is 'solitary, poor, nasty, brutish, and short', and improve living standards throughout the community. These issues are particularly relevant to Chapter 3.

## Liberty and community

*Classical liberalism* favours individual liberty over central government. *Libertarianism* is a stronger form of liberalism that argues the government should have little influence over the individual and that the emphasis should fall on personal responsibility. Liberty is described by John Stuart Mill (1806–73) as 'the nature and limits of the power which can be legitimately exercised by society over the individual'.[46] According to Isaiah Berlin, 'liberty'

---

44  Ibid, Book I, Chapter Seven.
45  Ibid, Book II, Chapter Six.
46  John Stuart Mill, *On Liberty* (Tichnor and Fields, 1859), Chapter I.

has two meanings. According to the first, or negative liberty, a person is free 'to the degree to which no man or body of men interferes' with their activity.[47] According to the second, or positive liberty, a person is free to the extent that they are their own master, 'a thinking, willing, active being, bearing responsibility for their own choices, and able to explain them by reference to their own ideas and purposes'.[48] Gerard MacCallum argues: 'Freedom is always of something (an agent or agents), from something, to do or not do, become or not become something. Any statement about freedom must take the form *x is (is not) free from y to do (not do) z.*'[49]

Historically, the development of political freedom was achieved through the recognition of political rights, and the development of constitutional safeguards. However, the will of the people can involve a tyranny of the majority over the minority through the enactment of laws and the force of public opinion. According to Mill's philosophy:

> The sole end for which mankind are warranted, individually or collectively, in interfering with the liberty of action of any of their number, is self-protection. That the only purpose for which power can be rightfully exercised over any member of a civilized community, against his will, is to prevent harm to others ... Over himself, over his own body and mind, the individual is sovereign.[50]

According to Mill, 'liberty of action' describes freedom of thought, feelings, and preferences, as well as freedom to express opinions, and freedom of association. However, this freedom has limitations to ensure that others are protected from harm.

> No one pretends that actions should be as free as opinions. On the contrary, even opinions lose their immunity when the circumstances in which they are expressed are such as to constitute [in] their expression a positive instigation to some mischievous act ... Acts, of whatever kind, which without justifiable cause, do harm to others, may be, and in the more important cases absolutely require to be, controlled by the unfavourable sentiments, and, when needful, by the active interference of mankind.[51]

Mill argued that in exchange for accepting the protection provided by society, there are two conditions that must be accepted by its members. First, they must refrain from harming the rights of others; and second, they must share in the burden of exercising the protection.

> Acts injurious to others require a totally different treatment. Encroachment on their rights; infliction on them of any loss or damage not justified by his own rights; falsehood or duplicity in dealing with them; unfair or ungenerous use of advantage over them; even selfish abstinence from defending them against injury – these are fit objects of moral reprobation, and, in grave cases, of moral retribution and punishment.[52]

---

47  Isaiah Berlin, 'Two Concepts of Liberty'. In *Four Essays on Liberty* (Oxford University Press, 1969), 118, 122.
48  Ibid, 31.
49  Gerard MacCallum, 'Negative and Positive Freedom'. In David Miller (ed), *Liberty* (Oxford University Press, 1991), 100, 102.
50  John Stuart Mill, *On Liberty* (Tichnor and Fields, 1859), Chapter I.
51  Ibid, Chapter III.
52  Ibid, Chapter IV.

In *On Liberty*, Mill emphasised the importance of non-interference; however, he stated that individual autonomy may be limited if it is likely that harmful consequences to other individuals may result.

> [T]he only purpose for which power can be rightfully exercised over any member of a civilised community, against his will, is to prevent harm to others. His own good, either physical or moral, is not a sufficient warrant. He cannot rightfully be compelled to do or forebear because it will be better for him to do so, because it will make him happier, because, in the opinions of others to do so would be wise, or even right. These are good reasons for remonstrating with him, or reasoning with him, or persuading him, or entreating him, but not for compelling him, or visiting him with an evil in case he do otherwise. To justify that, the conduct from which it is desired to deter him, must be calculated to produce evil to someone else. The only part of the conduct of any one, for which he is amenable to society, is that which concerns others. In the part which merely concerns himself, his independence is, of right, absolute. Over himself, over his own body and mind, the individual is sovereign.[53]

Libertarian objections are likely to be a major basis of opposition to the regulation of new forms of technology. One reply to these objections is based on Mill's comment that the 'only purpose for which power can be rightfully exercised over any member of a civilised community, against his will, is to prevent harm to others'.[54] In light of this quote, it might be argued that biometric databases, for example, fit within Mill's guidelines, as they would contribute to better policing of crime, better conviction rates, decreased recidivism, and therefore, the prevention of harm to others. This will be discussed in detail in Chapter 6.

On the other hand, communitarianism asserts that the value of community is not sufficiently acknowledged by libertarians. On this argument, political philosophy must place a greater emphasis on shared understandings – for instance, the view that community is more than simply a society of equal citizens. An aspect of libertarianism that many communitarians find unattractive is the focus on individualism. Theories that focus on individual rights tend, on this view, to overlook the fact that individual freedom can only occur within a community. Further, communitarians argue that libertarianism fails to understand that the requirement to maintain the common good is as important as individual rights. Liberal societies place restrictions on individual freedom by requiring that citizens comply with principles of freedom and equality, and to some extent, libertarians appeal to the common good when reallocating resources through the taxation system. An important aspect of communitarian philosophy is the focus on guarantees of certain things – for example, access to housing, education or healthcare.

Communitarians are generally more supportive of government intervention in the form of social security. Modern communitarianism developed partly in response to the libertarian political philosophy of the 20th century. For instance, while (according to Rawls) justice is 'the first virtue of social institutions',[55] communitarians argue that justice is remedial in nature, correcting a defect in social life.[56] It is only required where there is a lack of

---

53  Ibid, Chapter I.
54  Ibid.
55  John Rawls, *A Theory of Justice* (Oxford University Press, 1971), Chapter I, section 1.
56  Michael Sandel, *Liberalism and the Limits of Justice* (Cambridge University Press, 1982).

benevolence. Further, Ronald Dworkin (1931–2013) argued that justice provides a means of examining one's beliefs, and ensuring they are not prejudiced: political theory can make no contribution to how we govern ourselves except by struggling, against all impulses that drag us back into our own culture, towards generality and some reflective basis for deciding which of our traditional distinctions and discriminations are genuine and which spurious.[57]

Communitarians would criticise attempts to find a universal theory of justice. They assert that perspectives external to the community are invalid. In their view, the only way to determine what is just, is to understand how a community values its social goods. A just law accords with the shared understanding of its members. Rather than seeking the equal distribution of all goods, a communitarian would try to ensure that inequality in one area, such as wealth, does not influence other areas, such as access to housing, education or healthcare.

A libertarian would argue that society should not take a position on the merit of different lifestyles, rewarding those with lifestyles it values. On this view, the state should be neutral, all individuals are respected equally, and there is no sole measure of what is 'good'. Libertarians would argue that individuals should be free to determine their lifestyle. Conversely, for communitarians, the conception of the common good which defines a community's way of life is taken as the common good for the community. The value placed upon an individual is dependent upon the degree to which they conform or contribute to the common good. This position lacks the neutrality of the libertarian approach, and persuades individuals to adopt the dominant conception of the common good.

There are attractive aspects of both libertarian and communitarian political theory, and it is likely that the best policy position in most cases falls between the two. The community-wide approach of Commonwealth legislation can often be helpful in addressing an area of new technology that was previously unregulated. However, one relevant point to note in this respect is that new technologies, particularly those based on the internet, are global in reach and pose significant regulatory challenges for individual countries. This issue will be discussed in detail in Chapter 7.

## Justice

John Rawls sought to reconcile liberty, equality and justice in his work *A Theory of Justice*, which he promoted as 'justice as fairness'.[58] Rawls attempted to determine the proper political balance of rival claims and interests; the type of justice that 'free and rational persons concerned to further their own interests would accept in an initial position of equality as defining the fundamental terms of their association'.[59] The method proposed by Rawls is a reflective equilibrium.[60] In a reflective equilibrium, one seeks to justify general principles on the basis that they are in accordance with intuitive judgements. In advancing the principles that accord with intuition and reconsidering conflicting intuitions, advancement is made

---

57  Ronald Dworkin, *A Matter of Principle* (Harvard University Pres, 1985), 219.
58  John Rawls, *A Theory of Justice* (Oxford University Press, 1971), Chapter I, section 2.
59  Ibid, 11.
60  Ibid, 20–2.

towards a state of reflective equilibrium where considered principles are harmonious with considered judgements. However, it is debatable whether this is a sound basis for justifying the emergent principles.[61] Rawls' theory is a form of liberal egalitarianism, seeking to nullify discrimination and all forms of social and economic inequality. In legislating for society, one should adopt a hypothetical original position of equality. In this position, one's natural ability, social position, economic status, religion, sex and ethnicity are unknown.[62] An individual in this hypothetical state is acting under a veil of ignorance. This enables the theoretical legislator to be motivated by concern for the circumstance of all persons in society, irrespective of the position in society they are likely to attain. The laws enacted are therefore likely to be general and universal in their application.[63]

Rawls' conception of justice has two principles. First, each individual has a right to the greatest equal liberty that is compatible with liberty for all. Second, social and economic inequalities are to be attached to offices and positions open to all under conditions of equality of opportunity; and further, inequalities are only justified if they are of benefit to the worst off. In applying the principles, the first must be considered prior to the second, and both are used in the formulation of the structures that determine chances in life. The second principle is often referred to as the *maximin* theory of social justice. It refers to maximising the size of the minimum holding of social resources.[64]

Rawls defined hypothetical people under the veil of ignorance, to remove any prejudice that may be inherent in their personal characteristics, such as their race or gender, prior to formulating an appropriate conception of justice. Rawls' 'original position' directly applies in a law and public policy context from the perspective of the legislator. This is particularly useful in the context of evaluating current and future law in a discrete area of public policy. Rawls' theory can also be applied to arguments in relation to technology regulation. From the perspective of a legislator in a theoretical original position, regulatory strategies should apply equally to all citizens; from those holding the highest political and commercial offices in the state, to those performing unskilled labour. They should avoid adversely affecting particular social or ethnic groups. These issues will be discussed further in Chapter 4.

# Ethical theory

Ethical issues in relation to technology can move from judgements about the morality of certain activities, such as the use of assisted reproductive technology, to arguments about how it should be regulated and whether it should be legal. There is a distinction here that should be noted. Someone could hold the view that this technology is morally wrong, but that it should not be illegal; ethical theories can be used to evaluate individual decisions, and laws more broadly. Understanding these concepts is important in clarifying the issues that will be discussed later in this text in relation to technology law. The two most influential ethical theories that will be considered in some detail are deontology and consequentialism.

---

61  Ibid, Chapter I, section 9.
62  Ibid, Chapter I, section 4.
63  Ibid, Chapter III, section 24.
64  Ibid, Chapter II, section 11.

# Deontology

Deontological ethical theories specify that certain acts must or must not be done out of duty, irrespective of their consequences. Therefore, certain acts are right or wrong in themselves. For example, it would be wrong to break a promise, regardless of the negative effects that may result from the act. The most influential modern deontological approach originated in the 18th-century writings of Immanuel Kant, predominantly in his *Fundamental Principles of the Metaphysics of Morals*.[65] Kant proposed universal ethical principles designed to respect the dignity and equality of all human beings. In his view, humans lack the basis for consequential ethical reasoning towards a knowable good.

Kant proposed that moral requirements must be principles of action adopted by all relevant parties, irrespective of their social roles or interrelationships. This form of moral reasoning rejects principles that cannot be universally applied and is described by Kant as the 'supreme principle of morality'.[66] The principle can be formulated in two ways. The first formulation states that one should 'act only on that maxim that you can at the same time will that it become a universal law'.[67] The second formulation focuses on impartial respect for others and states that one should 'treat humanity never simply as a means, but always at the same time as an end'.[68] These formulations are related to one another. For example, if treating others as a means involves restricting their ability to act, it follows that this does not allow them to act on the same principles as ourselves.

To state that we must allow others to act on the same basis as we do is equivalent to stating that we must all act on universalisable principles. The recognition of the rationality and autonomy of individual citizens led Kant to his 'kingdom of ends', which is the union of individual rational beings under common laws.[69] This may be contrasted with consequentialism-based ethics, which would permit the use of people as means if it would allow a better overall outcome. Kant stated that the categorical imperative can be used to justify human duties. For example, if all persons adopted the principle of promising falsely, there would be a breakdown of trust, as people found that their false promises were not accepted. This contradicts the universal adoption of the principle of false promising, and it would therefore be rejected as non-universalisable. A similar line of reasoning can demonstrate that, for example, principles such as acting violently or stealing are not universalisable and should be rejected. Duties such as these that can be observed by humans towards all others are known as complete duties. Duties that cannot be observed toward all others, such as helping all those that live in poverty, are incomplete duties.

Contemporary Kantian theories justify principles of justice by demonstrating that all relevant individuals would agree to them in a hypothetical situation. For example, John Rawls argued that principles of justice are those that would be agreed upon by all rational persons if they were placed in a hypothetical situation ensuring impartiality.

Deontological theory is associated with the notion that the rules (or, more broadly, laws) that ought to be complied with are those that are the most widely applicable. This accords

---

65  Immanuel Kant, *Fundamental Principles of the Metaphysics of Morals* (1785; Dover, 2012).
66  Ibid, Preface, 4:392.
67  Ibid, Second Section, 4:421.
68  Ibid, 4:429.
69  Ibid, 4:433.

with the commonsense notions of fairness and equality. A basic principle in regulating new forms of technology would be ensuring that it is introduced in a manner that is equitable for all members of society, in a manner which accords with expectations of fairness and equality. The universal application of laws is represented in maxims such as that people are equal before the law in liberal democracies.

Let us take the example of gene editing technology: from a deontological perspective, in basic terms, one could argue that a maxim to the effect that gene technology can be used to enhance human wellbeing is universalisable, and does not produce conceptual inconsistencies, such as a maxim to make false promises would. However, on the second formulation of the categorical imperative, it would not be permissible to create a group of humans that have genetic superiority in a way that would limit the freedom of others, or to create humans with more limited abilities in order to make them suitable to serve others. It could also be argued, on this perspective, that using the genetic material of an embryo in either a research or therapeutic context would be wrong, as it is using that embryo as a means to an end.[70] This becomes more complex when more recent technologies such as induced pluripotent stem cells are involved, as will be discussed further in Chapter 4.

## Consequentialism

Consequentialism is another approach used in ethical reasoning. Consequentialist theories view all actions as right or wrong based upon the value of their consequences. The most influential version of consequentialism is utilitarianism. According to utilitarianism, all human actions, inactions and policies result in consequences for the individual and other persons. A utilitarian would argue that society is best structured when it is arranged in a manner that will achieve the greatest overall balance of satisfaction when all of the members of society are considered. Utilitarianism enables commonsense morality to be replaced with a more systematic and uniform approach. Utilitarianism originated in Britain in the late 17th century. It is chiefly associated with the legal theorist Jeremy Bentham, and the philosopher John Stuart Mill. Bentham rejected contemporary religious and social conventions, and focused instead on human wellbeing. Bentham described utility as that property in any object, whereby it tends to produce benefit, advantage, pleasure, good or happiness (all this in the present case comes to the same thing), or (what comes again to the same thing) to prevent the happening of mischief, pain, evil or unhappiness.[71]

In Bentham's view, the best way to construct the laws governing a society is to ensure they provide the most pleasure and the least pain for citizens. This shapes the governance of society, and individual decision-making. The principle of utility approves or disapproves of an action according to the tendency it appears to have to augment or diminish the happiness of the party whose interest is in question: ' ... I say of every action whatsoever; and therefore not only of every action of a private individual, but of every measure of government'.[72] Bentham proposed a utilitarian calculus to measure pleasure and pain, and to compare

---

70  See, eg, Martin Gunderson, 'Seeking Perfection: A Kantian Look at Human Genetic Engineering' (2007) 28 *Theoretical Medicine and Bioethics* 87, 91–3.

71  Jeremy Bentham, *An Introduction to the Principles of Morals and Legislation* (W Pickering, 1798), Chapter I, section 3.

72  Ibid, section 2.

the consequences of different actions. The aim of the calculus was to provide individuals and legislators with a decision-making method. Mill built on the foundation provided by Bentham and outlined the greatest happiness principle: actions are right in proportion as they tend to promote happiness, wrong as they tend to produce the reverse of happiness. By 'happiness' is intended pleasure, and the absence of pain; by 'unhappiness', pain, and the privation of pleasure.[73] Mill used the utilitarian calculus, taking into account overall pleasure and pain, as the moral basis for treating people equally. He argued that actions should be judged as right or wrong depending on their promotion of happiness. According to Mill, individual autonomy and freedom of will should only be limited in the case that there are likely to be harmful consequences to others.

However, opponents of utilitarianism argue that the strict application of this principle could lead to unacceptable outcomes. For example, a utilitarian approach may conclude that it is permissible to sacrifice the life of an individual who contributes little to the community, for the sake of another individual who contributes a great deal. In order to respond to instances such as this, a distinction is often made between act and rule utilitarianism. The former holds that all actions must accord with the greatest happiness; however, according to the latter, one should act in accordance with the rules of conduct that are most beneficial to the greatest happiness. This distinction enables the position to be taken that although there are instances where an action viewed as unacceptable may contribute more to the general happiness, its unacceptability occurs because it contravenes a rule that is beneficial to the greatest happiness. On this formulation, as it is not possible to fully comprehend the consequences of every action one takes when decisions are made, general rules of justice which lead to the greatest happiness are required.[74]

Utilitarianism has been discussed in the context of criminal justice in debates over the appropriate punishment to be imposed by the state. According to Bentham: 'All punishment is a mischief … If it ought to be admitted, it ought to be admitted in so far as it promises to exclude some greater evil.'[75] On this argument, punishment should only be severe enough that it negates the advantage of committing the offence. To deter crime, the harm of punishment should be greater than the expected profit of each offence, divided by the perceived probability of punishment.[76] Utilitarianism provides a valuable cost-benefit analysis that has many applications in law and policy evaluation. In the context of arguments in relation to the implementation or regulation of new technology, its framework can be used to evaluate whether potential costs, such as the possible infringement to personal privacy, are outweighed by the benefits to public safety, law enforcement or other public goods that would be obtained.

# Philosophy of science

Technology is informed by science. It is therefore also important that science is understood at a theoretical level. Science provides humans with a limited degree of understanding and control of the world through a continually developing body of knowledge about natural

---

73  John Stuart Mill, *Utilitarianism* (Parker, Son and Bourn, 1863), 257.
74  Henry West, *An Introduction to Mill's Utilitarianism* (Cambridge University Press, 2004), 74.
75  Jeremy Bentham, *An Introduction to the Principles of Morals and Legislation* (W Pickering, 1798), Chapter XIII, section 1.
76  Frederick Schauer and Walter Sinnott-Armstrong, *The Philosophy of Law* (Harcourt Brace, 1996), 670.

phenomena. The word 'science' is derived from the Latin word *scire*, which means 'to know'.[77] Over time, the development of science has reduced the influence of superstition and supernatural knowledge over public policy, and society in general, historically, through the battles of figures such as Nicolaus Copernicus (1473–1543), Galileo Galilei (1564–1642) and Charles Darwin (1809–82). According to the 20th-century philosopher Bertrand Russell, 'It is not what the man of science believes that distinguishes him, but how and why he believes it.'[78]

Though comprising a wide variety of distinct disciplines such as biochemistry, genetics and physics, science provides a unified understanding of the natural world. Scientists share a common methodology and seek to minimise the influence of human perception and societal and political factors. Scientists share a single view of the universe that is independent of any individual observer, and a representational view of language is adopted by all scientists within a field, allowing a concept such as 'gene' to be associated with a physical object without controversy. Science is concerned with making discoveries and as a way for humans to control their environment. It can potentially cure medical conditions and provide technologies that improve human communication, transport and more efficient use of natural resources. Even well-established scientific knowledge remains a form of inductive reasoning – it is not irrefutable and remains open to being disproved at some future point by a new, more accurate explanation. This is particularly the case with new and rapidly developing fields of science. It is always possible that the current understanding of a particular form of technology will change in the coming decades.

Reasoning involves constructing a valid argument. Deductive reasoning begins at the top with general principles and works down to a more specific conclusion. Inductive reasoning begins at the bottom with specific principles and works up to a general conclusion. Put another way, deductive reasoning moves from an idea to an observation, while inductive reasoning moves from an observation to an idea. If the premises are true in a deductive argument, then the conclusion is necessarily true. However, if the premises are true in an inductive argument, the conclusion is only true to some degree of probability, based on the strength of the supporting evidence. The scientific method provides a means for testing theories and reaching adequately justified beliefs using inductive reasoning.[79]

It can be noted that inductive reasoning generalises from a large collection of particular instances to a general conclusion. For example: where it can be observed that many instances of a phenomenon have a certain characteristic, it is inferred that it always has that property.

In determining when it is appropriate to infer that a universal generalisation about the natural world is justified, it is clear that the number of observations must be large, that they must be repeated in a range of conditions and that there should be no conflicting observations. Scientific knowledge is supposed to be solely derived from observed facts; however, judgements must be made on the basis of prior scientific knowledge. Also, the inductive approach limits knowledge to what can be observed or recorded with contemporary instrumentation.[80]

---

77  Robert Hays, *The Science of Learning: A Systems Theory Perspective* (Brown Walker Press, 2006), 24.
78  Bertrand Russell, *A History of Western Philosophy* (Allen & Unwin, 1945), 527.
79  Alan Chalmers, *What Is This Thing Called Science?* (University of Queensland Press, 2013), 20–2.
80  Ibid.

Karl Popper (1902–94) advocated a solution to the problem of induction, known as *falsificationism*. The problem with induction as an approach to scientific knowledge is that, irrespective of how many instances of a generalisation are observed, it remains possible that it could be proved wrong at some point in the future. Popper believed that science is concerned with falsifying, rather than confirming, theories. This is the key criterion he used to distinguish between scientific and non-scientific theories. For instance, following the development of a hypothesis,[81] predictions are deduced from it and experimental testing is carried out. A hypothesis is abandoned if it is falsified. However, if the hypothesis is not falsified, it is subjected to increasingly stringent attempts at falsification. Popper states: '... this is the way in which we learn from our mistakes; and that in finding that our conjecture was false, we shall have learnt much about the truth, and shall have got nearer to the truth.'[82]

In Popper's view, science proceeds through learning from past mistakes. Rather than providing positive support, successful theories repeatedly survive attempts at falsification. Those that survive are retained. It remains possible that all scientific theories will yet be falsified, and, on this argument, they remain conjectures that have not been refuted, as opposed to confirmed theories. In determining the extent to which a theory is scientific, three factors can be evaluated: its degree of falsifiability, clarity and precision. The more falsifiable a theory, the better it is. A good theory will make the most general and wide-ranging claims about the world and will thus be highly falsifiable yet resistant when subjected to testing. Second, a theory must be clearly stated to ensure that it is falsifiable. If a theory is vague, it may be possible to interpret test results favourably when, in fact, they are not. Finally, precision is necessary for a theory to be good. The more precise a theory, the more susceptible to falsification it becomes. Using this classification, creationism would be classified as pseudoscience because it fails the falsifiability test, whereas the theory of evolution would be considered scientific.[83]

Deduction, induction and falsification have all been used to provide justification for specific scientific theories. The work of Thomas Kuhn (1922–96) analyses scientific knowledge in a different manner. His work focuses on the theoretical framework that is used by scientific knowledge in order to advance. According to Kuhn, science progresses through revolutions or paradigm shifts. The stages of this process are pre-science, normal science, crisis, revolution and a return to normal science.[84] When a single paradigm is adopted by the relevant scientific community, the prior activity becomes structured and focused. A paradigm is a set of theoretical assumptions and their methods of implementation. Kuhn states that the scientists working within a paradigm are practising normal science. Scientists develop the paradigm in an attempt to account for the behaviour of relevant aspects of the natural world through experimentation and falsification. If the theoretical assumptions are challenged to a significant extent, a crisis develops. The crisis is resolved when a new paradigm is developed and attracts a sufficient degree of support among scientists for the original paradigm to be abandoned. According to Kuhn, this process of change is a scientific revolution. The new paradigm guides new, normal scientific activity until such time as a new

81  A hypothesis is an initial proposed explanation made when only limited evidence is available, that can then be tested by further investigation.
82  Karl Popper, *Conjectures and Refutations* (Routledge, 1963), 231.
83  Ibid, Part 2.4.
84  Thomas Kuhn, *The Structure of Scientific Revolutions* (University of Chicago Press, 1962).

crisis and revolution develop.[85] Central to Kuhn's theory is the consensus judgement of a scientific community. The validity of a scientific theory is not determined by applying a set of predetermined standards but by the accumulation of individual judgements in the form of a consensus judgement for the whole scientific community. Individuals who do not accept the consensus judgement become marginalised.[86]

# Conclusion

This discussion has considered the background of theory and policy required to understand the wide range of issues that this text discusses across technology law – spanning privacy and data management, health, criminal justice, social media, digital currencies, cybercrime and intellectual property. The theoretical perspective of political philosophy contributes an important supporting rationale for the positions that will be evaluated, and situates these positions against other areas and historical examples of law and policy. Contractualism provides contextual support for the assertion that individuals must concede some of their rights to the state, in exchange for the protection of property and other rights. In many cases, a utilitarian approach to policy, advocating the greatest overall good, will be most appropriate. However, there are instances where this will lead to unacceptable outcomes – for example, due to the extent to which it may undervalue the rights of the minority. In this case, a Kantian approach, focusing on universal principles, may be more appropriate.

In allowing technology to be used in the legal system, courts have been required to evaluate the scientific validity of techniques, the nature and role of technology in society, and the wider implications of ongoing advancements. Investigating the differences and similarities of the disciplines of science and law has enabled an appreciation of the nature of scientific knowledge. Philosophy of science provides a theoretical foundation for questions related to the reliability, certainty, accuracy and methodology of technologically based evidence. The inductive nature of the reasoning inherent in all scientific knowledge is a key theoretical point. Rather than being certain or logically provable, as with knowledge obtained through deductive argument, it is instead highly probable and based on past observations.

Contemporary knowledge in science and technology must be viewed in the context of the development of the discipline over time, and with the understanding that new technology will likely undermine existing regulatory strategies. Previous legal approaches to evaluating scientific evidence in court, and policy approaches adopted by government, should be considered prior to engaging with the contemporary and developing issues posed by new technology. Finding appropriate regulatory responses to the internet, social media and the regulation of information involves significant challenges for governments and society broadly. Theorists such as Braithwaite, Lessig and Murray have made an important contribution to understanding these developments to date, and further work will be needed as technology continues to advance.

---

85  Ibid, Chapter 7.
86  Gary Gutting, 'Scientific Methodology'. In WH Newton-Smith, *A Companion to the Philosophy of Science* (Wiley-Blackwell, 2001), 429.

# 3

# PRIVACY AND DATA PROTECTION

# Introduction

The rapid growth of information and communications technology over the past two decades, including email, the internet, smartphones, social media, messaging applications and global positioning systems, has enhanced our ability to obtain and share information about the world. However, in the rush to secure the latest mass-produced technology device, many people give relatively less consideration to the implications for the security of the data that they produce and the consequential impact on individual privacy. That data is of great value in the corporate sector, to inform marketing strategies; and to governments to understand the behaviour of their citizens. As was noted in Chapter 1, developments in the past decade, such as the Snowden revelations, and the activities of the former political strategy firm Cambridge Analytica, have increased awareness of the implications of inadequate privacy protections. However, the convenience of new technologies may take precedence for many. As with the other areas of technology that are discussed throughout this text, the rate of development makes it difficult for regulators to ensure that the law remains up to date, although the use of encryption to encode information or messages in such a way that only those who send and receive the information are able to access it has provided some degree of technical protection in the absence of effective law and regulation.

The chapter begins with a consideration of the conceptual background to privacy and data protection law, reflecting briefly on the historical, current and developing contextual issues. The following part progresses to a discussion of privacy law frameworks in Australia, including the *Privacy Act 1988* (Cth) and the Australian Privacy Principles. This includes a consideration of how effective Australian privacy law has been in light of recent technological advancements and their application by government; as well as a detailed discussion of the Australian metadata retention and data access laws, enacted over the past five years, that are among the most expansive in the world. Following this discussion, the chapter considers developments in Europe and the United States, where different legal frameworks are in place and there are a number of interesting cases, such as disputes between Google and privacy regulators in Europe, and the Snowden revelations in the United States. Case studies throughout the chapter investigate the intersection of new technologies and privacy regulation around the world, highlighting the fact that the issues associated with privacy and data protection lie at the heart of technology law.

# Privacy: Concepts and context

The concept of privacy is multifaceted, but can be explained in terms of four key aspects, all of which will be considered at some point in this chapter:

- *Information privacy* (or data protection), which involves the establishment of rules governing the collection and handling of personal data such as credit information, and medical and government records.
- *Bodily privacy*, which concerns the protection of people's physical selves against invasive procedures such as genetic tests, drug testing and cavity searches.
- *Privacy of communications*, which covers the security and privacy of mail, telephones, email and other forms of communication.

- *Territorial privacy*, which concerns the setting of limits on intrusion into the domestic and other environments such as the workplace or public space. This includes searches, video surveillance and ID checks.[1]

Despite the breadth of technology law, privacy is an important consideration in relation to many of its sub-topics. In order to provide some context, this discussion of privacy law will begin with a brief historical background. Academic discussion of privacy law can be traced back to legal scholars in the United States in 1890, although, as indicated in Chapter 2, John Stuart Mill discusses the concept of privacy in his 1859 essay, *On Liberty*.[2] It then began to be discussed in earnest in the latter half of the 20th century in association with the computing revolution.[3] This analysis from legal scholars writing on technology and privacy some 40 years ago remains relevant today, and will continue to be for the foreseeable future. Ruth Gavison, writing in the *Yale Law Journal* as far back as 1980, observed:

> Advances in the technology of surveillance and the recording, storage, and retrieval of information have made it either impossible or extremely costly for individuals to protect the same level of privacy that was once enjoyed … The identification of technological developments as a major source of new concern may be supported by the fact that modern claims concerning the secrecy and anonymity aspects of privacy have not been accompanied by new claims concerning physical access: technological advances have affected the acquisition, storage, and dissemination of information, but gaining physical access is a process that has not changed much.[4]

Thirty years later, Australian privacy advocate Roger Clarke identified four dimensions of privacy that help to explain its importance to individuals and societies:

- *psychologically*, people need private space, in public as well as in their own homes
- *sociologically*, people require the freedom to behave, and to associate with other people, subject to the law and social norms, without the continual threat of being observed
- *economically*, people need the freedom to innovate
- *politically*, people need the freedom to think, debate and act. Surveillance has a chilling effect on behaviour and is a threat to democracy.[5]

Privacy can be understood as a collection of personal interests that an individual has that is free from interference by others. On this understanding, privacy can be viewed as a *right* in a legal sense, but it can also be described as an *interest* because 'a right is always an interest, even if not all interests are accorded the status of legal rights'.[6] This highlights the

---

1   Australian Law Reform Commission, *For Your Information: Australian Privacy Law and Practice: Report No 108* (ALRC, 2008), 142.
2   Samuel Warren and Louis Brandeis, 'The Right to Privacy' (1890) 4 *Harvard Law Review* 193. Briefly stated, the traditional legal and philosophical concept of privacy is the assertion that some aspects of an individual's life are personal and should be free from intrusion. See, also, John Stuart Mill, *On Liberty* (Tichnor and Fields, 1859).
3   Charles Fried, 'Privacy' (1967) 77 *Yale Law Journal* 475.
4   Ruth Gavison, 'Privacy and the Limits of Law' (1980) 89 *Yale Law Journal* 421, 465–6.
5   See, eg, Roger Clarke, 'Privacy and Social Media: An Analytical Framework' (2014) 23 *Journal of Law, Information and Science* 169.
6   Australian Law Reform Commission, *For Your Information: Australian Privacy Law and Practice: Report No 108* (ALRC, 2008), 148.

fact that privacy interests coexist and compete with other interests. Privacy is an important individual right, but (arguably) it does not exist independent of all others: individuals have other rights, such as personal safety, and the exercise of one person's rights can have negative consequences for another. In making laws, courts and governments are required to mediate between competing rights and obligations when enacting law and implementing policy.[7] This is relative; therefore, the need for increased access to personal information to reduce the cost or convenience of providing that information would not provide a strong argument for reducing privacy protections. On the other hand, doing so to increase living standards, to provide essential services such as healthcare, or to achieve other recognised human rights will provide much stronger support for such a change.[8] In practice, the arguments in this area are rarely straightforward, the technology is complex, and the evidence underlying the arguments is often hard to quantify, such as the threat of terrorism. Technologically facilitated social change, such as the advent of smartphones and social media services (and their increasing ubiquity), is likely to have influenced the public's willingness to share personal information and acceptance of a reduction of privacy that may flow on to other forms of digital information.[9]

As will be explained in more detail shortly, an interesting further element to a conceptual understanding of privacy is cultural variation as reflected in different approaches to privacy regulation internationally. The understanding of privacy in the United States has been related to the value placed on liberty and freedom, particularly within the home; while the European approach is considered to be more focused on dignity and the right to control one's public image and how a person is viewed publicly.[10] The difference is even more pronounced in comparison with Asia, where the concept of privacy and its regulation is far less developed, which, combined with an advanced technology sector, has made China a world leader in public surveillance.[11] Using data integration, China has established a 'social credit system' that has the capacity to create a detailed picture of an individual's life and to impose sanctions on citizens, such as restricting access to transport systems, if they repeatedly do not comply with behavioural norms. Governments have the capacity to link databases of biometric templates, CCTV footage, phone and email metadata, and financial, medical and tax records. The establishment of comprehensive, integrated databases of the personal information of citizens by governments has the potential to create a power imbalance between government and citizens, particularly in the absence of a strong regulatory framework.[12]

The Chinese government is also believed to be an aggressive collector of data internationally. Instances of large-scale data breaches involving Australian institutions, governments and businesses are becoming more common. One of the most significant and well-publicised examples of these is the Australian National University (ANU) data breach, made public in 2019, which involved a loss of data relating to 200 000 people extending

---

7   Ibid.
8   United Nations, *Universal Declaration of Human Rights*, GA Res 217A (III), UN Doc A/Res/810 (1948), art 25.
9   See, eg, Patrick O'Callaghan, *Refining Privacy in Tort Law* (Springer, 2012), 7.
10  James Whitman, 'The Two Western Cultures of Privacy: Dignity v Liberty' (2004) 113 *Yale Law Journal* 1151, 1161.
11  See, eg, Cao Jingchun, 'Protecting the Right to Privacy in China' (2005) 36 *Victoria University of Wellington Law Review* 645.
12  Xaio Qiang, 'The Road to Digital Unfreedom: President Xi's Surveillance State' (2019) 30 *Journal of Democracy* 1.

over a 19-year period, believed to have been perpetrated by a 'sophisticated state actor'.[13] All countries engage in some form of covert acquisition of foreign information and offensive cyber activities.[14]

Privacy rights have also been under threat in Western countries. From 9/11 onwards, in Australia, the United States, the United Kingdom and other liberal democratic countries, the threat from terrorism resulted in a number of significant changes to legislation and practices of law enforcement and security agencies.[15] The net result of these reforms is that governments have given these agencies much greater powers to collect evidence and conduct surveillance, and to do so more proactively, in order to detect and counter elusive non-state threats such as terrorism and transnational crime. The impact of these changes has sparked debates about whether this more proactive collection of data from citizens who have not committed a crime is acceptable,[16] and on the ethics of information collection programs more generally.[17]

However, the use of Facebook data in the Cambridge Analytica affair has led to increased scrutiny of social media companies, and both the public and regulators are becoming more concerned about how internet companies use the large amount of personal information they obtain. Some companies are also trying to reduce the amount of data they collect. For example, in early 2020, Google announced that it will begin blocking third-party cookies (data from websites that track users' viewing history, often used to inform advertising) in its web browser, which will impact on the ability of companies such as Facebook to track users and offer tailored advertising. This is likely to affect Facebook's business model and significantly impact on earnings.[18] Further, Facebook's proposed introduction of a new cryptocurrency, Libra, has faced staunch resistance from regulators in the United States and Europe, who are concerned not only about privacy, but also about Libra's potential use in money laundering and in funding criminal activities, as well as its potential to impact on financial market stability.[19]

# Australian privacy law

In the federal system of government in Australia, privacy law exists at the Commonwealth and the state level; however, the most important piece of legislation on the subject is the *Privacy Act 1988* (Cth) (Privacy Act). The Privacy Act provides the principal mechanism for the protection of privacy in Australia; its preamble explaining that it is intended to implement Australia's international obligations in this area. The external affairs power[20] of the Australian Constitution enables the Parliament to make laws relating to Australia's

13  Australian National University, *Incident Report on the Breach of the Australian National University's Administrative Systems* (ANU, 2019).
14  Australian Signals Directorate, *About ASD*. Available: <https://www.asd.gov.au/about>.
15  Seumas Miller and Ian Gordon, *Investigative Ethics* (Wiley Blackwell, 2014).
16  Georg Mascalo and Ben Scott, *Lessons from Summer of Snowden* (Open Technology Institute, 2013).
17  Adam Henschke, *Ethics in an Age of Surveillance* (Cambridge University Press, 2017).
18  David Swan, 'Privacy Crackdown a Blow to Facebook's Business Model', *The Australian*, 3 February 2020. This is discussed further in Chapter 8.
19  Richard Partington, 'How the Wheels Came Off Facebook's Libra Project', *The Guardian*, 19 October 2019. This is discussed further in Chapter 5.
20  Australian Constitution, s 51(xxix).

obligations under international treaties or agreements, customary international law or matters of international concern.[21] The preamble to the Privacy Act also refers to the following international instruments, which have influenced Australian law in this area:

- United Nations, *International Covenant on Civil and Political Rights (ICCPR)*[22]
- Organisation for Economic Co-operation and Development, *Guidelines on the Protection of Privacy and Transborder Flows of Personal Data* (OECD Guidelines)[23]
- Council of Europe, *Convention for the Protection of Individuals with regard to Automatic Processing of Personal Data.*[24]

While the Privacy Act was developed in response to Australia's obligations under the ICCPR, stating that it seeks 'to promote the protection of the privacy of individuals',[25] it also acknowledges that 'the protection of the privacy of individuals is balanced with the interests of entities in carrying out their functions or activities'.[26] This balancing approach between individual rights to privacy and other interests is apparent when considering law enforcement exemptions, which are discussed at length in Chapter 6. Major legal developments in Australian privacy law began with the commencement of the federal legislation in 1989. Since then, other developments include the establishment of the Office of the Privacy Commissioner in 2000, and subsequently, the Office of the Australian Information Commissioner in 2010. Further, the extension of the Privacy Act to the private sector as well as the public sector, which occurred in 2001, was a significant step. More recently, the introduction of the Australian Privacy Principles (APPs) in 2014, and of the data breach notification scheme in 2018, is also notable. These developments are summarised in Table 3.1.

**Table 3.1**    History of the Privacy Act[27]

| Reform | Summary |
| --- | --- |
| 1989: Privacy Act | The *Privacy Act 1988* (Privacy Act) commenced in 1989, giving effect to Australia's international obligations and setting out 11 Information Privacy Principles for how Australian government agencies must handle personal information. |
| 1991: Credit reporting | The *Privacy Amendment Act 1990* came into effect to regulate the handling of consumer credit reports by credit-reporting bodies and credit providers. |
| 1994: Australian Capital Territory | ACT government agencies became bound by a version of the Privacy Act. |

21  *Koowarta v Bjelke-Petersen* (1982) 153 CLR 168.
22  16 December 1966, [1980] ATS 23 (entered into force generally on 23 March 1976), art 17.
23  (1980).
24  28 January 1981, Council of Europe, CETS No 108 (entered into force generally on 1 October 1985). This instrument is referred to in the second reading speech to the Bill; however, it is not binding on Australia.
25  *Privacy Act 1988* (Cth), s 2A(a); *International Covenant on Civil and Political Rights*, opened for signature 16 December 1966, 999 UNTS 171 (entered into force 23 March 1976).
26  *Privacy Act 1988* (Cth), s 2A(b).
27  Office of the Australian Information Commissioner, *History of the Privacy Act* (OAIC, 2019). Available: <https://www.oaic.gov.au/privacy/the-privacy-act/history-of-the-privacy-act/>.

| Reform | Summary |
|---|---|
| 2000: Office of the Privacy Commissioner | The Office of the Privacy Commissioner established and separated the Privacy Commissioner from the Human Rights and Equal Opportunity Commission. |
| 2001: Private-sector reforms | The *Privacy Amendment (Private Sector) Act 2000* extended coverage of the Privacy Act to some private-sector organisations, introducing 10 National Privacy Principles into the Privacy Act, which set standards for private-sector organisations. |
| 2010: Office of the Australian Information Commissioner | The Office of the Australian Information Commissioner (OAIC) established. |
| 2011: Norfolk Island | On 1 January 2011, the Privacy Act was extended to Norfolk Island government agencies by the *Territories Law Reform Act 2010*. |
| 2014: Major privacy reforms | The *Privacy Amendment (Enhancing Privacy Protection) Act 2012* introduced: <br><br> • the Australian Privacy Principles (APPs) (replacing the Information Privacy Principles and National Privacy Principles) <br> • new laws on codes of practice about information privacy (APP codes) and a code of practice for credit reporting (the CR code) <br> • new enforcement powers for the Information Commissioner. |
| 2014: ACT privacy reforms | The *Information Privacy Act 2014* (ACT) introduced new privacy laws for ACT public-sector agencies. (Prior to that, it adopted the Commonwealth legislation.) |
| 2018: The Notifiable Data Breaches scheme | The *Privacy Amendment (Notifiable Data Breaches) Act 2017* established the Notifiable Data Breaches scheme for all organisations and agencies with existing personal information security obligations under the Privacy Act. |

Section 6 of the Privacy Act defines three key terms. *Identification information* includes details such as a person's name, age, sex and address; *personal information* refers to information or an opinion about a person; while *sensitive information* includes information such as race, religion, sexual orientation, criminal record, and political associations or memberships. Sensitive information is also defined to include scientific information such as genetic and 'biometric information that is to be used for the purposes of automated biometric verification or biometric identification'.[28] Sensitive information must only be collected with the consent of the individual concerned,[29] unless the entity is an 'enforcement body' and there is a reasonable belief that 'the collection of the information is reasonably necessary for, or directly related to, one or more of the entity's functions or activities'.[30] Entities cannot use or disclose information collected for a particular purpose for a secondary purpose, without the consent of the individual[31] unless 'the use or disclosure of the information is reasonably

---

28  *Privacy Act 1988* (Cth), s 6(1) (definition of 'sensitive information', paras (d)–(e)).
29  Ibid, Schedule 1, cl 3.3(a).
30  Ibid, Schedule 1, cl 6.1. Section 6 defines 'enforcement body' as agencies that have an enforcement function, including the Australian Federal Police, the Integrity Commissioner, the Australian Criminal Intelligence Commission, the Immigration Department, and a police force or service of a state or a territory.
31  Ibid, Schedule 1, cl 6.1 (APP 6).

necessary for one or more enforcement related activities'.[32] Agencies with an enforcement function do not need consent, a warrant or a court order to collect and retain information such as photographs or biometric templates, or to disclose or share this information with other agencies.

Key terms are defined in the Privacy Act as follows:

## Section 6 Interpretation

*identification information* about an individual means:

**(a)** the individual's full name; or
**(b)** an alias or previous name of the individual; or
**(c)** the individual's date of birth; or
**(d)** the individual's sex; or
**(e)** the individual's current or last known address, and 2 previous addresses (if any); or
**(f)** the name of the individual's current or last known employer; or
**(g)** if the individual holds a driver's licence – the individual's driver's licence number.

*personal information* means information or an opinion about an identified individual, or an individual who is reasonably identifiable:

**(a)** whether the information or opinion is true or not; and
**(b)** whether the information or opinion is recorded in a material form or not.

*sensitive information* means:

**(a)** information or an opinion about an individual's:
    **(i)**    racial or ethnic origin; or
    **(ii)**   political opinions; or
    **(iii)**  membership of a political association; or
    **(iv)**   religious beliefs or affiliations; or
    **(v)**    philosophical beliefs; or
    **(vi)**   membership of a professional or trade association; or
    **(vii)**  membership of a trade union; or
    **(viii)** sexual orientation or practices; or
    **(ix)**   criminal record;

    that is also personal information; or

**(b)** health information about an individual; or
**(c)** genetic information about an individual that is not otherwise health information; or
**(d)** biometric information that is to be used for the purpose of automated biometric verification or biometric identification; or
**(e)** biometric templates.

---

32  Ibid, Schedule 1, cl 6.2(e). Section 6 relevantly defines 'enforcement related activity' as activities including the prevention, detection, investigation, prosecution or punishment of criminal offences, breaches of a law imposing a penalty or sanction, or the conduct of surveillance activities, intelligence-gathering activities or monitoring activities.

# Australian Privacy Principles

Schedule 1 to the Privacy Act provides details of 13 Australian Privacy Principles. The APPs establish how government, the private sector and not-for-profit agencies must manage personal information. The principles that relate to the notification of the collection of personal information, its use, and the circumstances in which it can be disclosed are most important.[33] Entities covered by the APPs must take reasonable measures to implement practices, procedures and systems that ensure the entity complies with the APPs, including making its policies available to anyone who requests them.[34] They must also allow for the anonymity of those whose data they hold, except where this is impractical or required under law.[35] Unless an exception applies, entities may only collect information that is necessary for the agency's functions and with the consent of the individual concerned.[36] If information is received in error, or an entity is not entitled to hold it, then it must be de-identified or destroyed as soon as it is practicable.[37] If an entity collects personal information about an individual, it must notify them that it has collected it, the purpose(s) for which it was collected, the consequences if it is not collected, whether it is required to be collected under Australian law, and whether it is likely to be disseminated overseas.[38] Information collected for one purpose cannot be used or disclosed for a secondary purpose, except, for example, if it is directly related to its primary purpose, or it could reasonably be expected to be disclosed for that purpose, or it is required by an enforcement agency or by law.[39] An entity cannot disclose personal information about an individual for direct marketing purposes, except, for example, where it would be reasonably expected or the person that it relates to has given consent.[40] Prior to disclosing personal information about an individual to an overseas recipient, an entity must take all reasonable steps to ensure that the recipient does not breach the APPs.[41] Entities may only use government identifiers, such as tax file numbers, as its own identifier of an individual if this is reasonably necessary, such as in fulfilling its legal obligations.[42] Entities must take reasonable steps to ensure that any personal information they collect is accurate and up-to-date.[43] Entities must ensure the security of personal information and protect it from loss, misuse, interference, unauthorised access, modification or disclosure.[44] They must also give

33  The APPs relate to the open and transparent management of personal information (APP 1), anonymity and pseudonymity (APP 2), collection of solicited personal information (APP 3), dealing with unsolicited personal information (APP 4), notification of the collection of personal information (APP 5), use or disclosure of personal information (APP 6), direct marketing (APP 7), cross-border disclosure of personal information (APP 8), adoption, use or disclosure of government-related identifiers (APP 9), quality, security, access to, and correction of, personal information (APPs 10–13).
34  APP 1.
35  APP 2.
36  APP 3.
37  APP 4.
38  APP 5.
39  APP 6.
40  APP 7.
41  APP 8.
42  APP 9.
43  APP 10.
44  APP 11.

the individual access to the information they hold about them on request, except in certain circumstances, such as where the request is vexatious or it would pose a serious threat to the life, health or safety of any individual, or to public health or public safety.[45] Finally, if the entity becomes aware that the information it holds about an individual is inaccurate, out-of-date or misleading, it must take steps to correct the information.[46] A brief summary of the APPs is also provided in Table 3.2.

**Table 3.2**    Overview of the Australian Privacy Principles[47]

| Principle | Title | Purpose |
|---|---|---|
| APP 1 | Open and transparent management of personal information | Ensures that APP entities manage personal information in an open and transparent way. This includes having a clearly expressed and up-to-date APP privacy policy. |
| APP 2 | Anonymity and pseudonymity | Requires APP entities to give individuals the option of not identifying themselves, or of using a pseudonym. Limited exceptions apply. |
| APP 3 | Collection of solicited personal information | Outlines when an APP entity can collect personal information that is solicited. It applies higher standards to the collection of sensitive information. |
| APP 4 | Dealing with unsolicited personal information | Outlines how APP entities must deal with unsolicited personal information. |
| APP 5 | Notification of the collection of personal information | Outlines when and in what circumstances an APP entity that collects personal information must tell an individual about certain matters. |
| APP 6 | Use or disclosure of personal information | Outlines the circumstances in which an APP entity may use or disclose personal information that it holds. |
| APP 7 | Direct marketing | An organisation may only use or disclose personal information for direct marketing purposes if certain conditions are met. |
| APP 8 | Cross-border disclosure of personal information | Outlines the steps an APP entity must take to protect personal information before it is disclosed overseas. |
| APP 9 | Adoption, use or disclosure of government related identifiers | Outlines the limited circumstances when an organisation may adopt a government-related identifier of an individual as its own identifier, or use or disclose a government-related identifier of an individual. |
| APP 10 | Quality of personal information | An APP entity must take reasonable steps to ensure the personal information it collects is accurate, up-to-date and complete. An entity must also take reasonable steps to ensure the personal information it uses or discloses is accurate, up-to-date, complete and relevant, having regard to the purpose of the use or disclosure. |

---

45  APP 12.
46  APP 13.
47  Office of the Australian Information Commissioner, *Australian Privacy Principles*. Available: <https://www.oaic.gov.au/privacy/australian-privacy-principles/australian-privacy-principles-quick-reference/>.

| Principle | Title | Purpose |
| --- | --- | --- |
| APP 11 | Security of personal information | An APP entity must take reasonable steps to protect personal information it holds from misuse, interference and loss, and from unauthorised access, modification or disclosure. An entity has obligations to destroy or de-identify personal information in certain circumstances. |
| APP 12 | Access to personal information | Outlines an APP entity's obligations when an individual requests to be given access to personal information held about them by the entity. This includes a requirement to provide access unless a specific exception applies. |
| APP 13 | Correction of personal information | Outlines an APP entity's obligations in relation to correcting the personal information it holds about individuals. |

## Oversight and investigation

The Office of the Australian Information Commissioner (OAIC) is a statutory agency within the Commonwealth Attorney-General's portfolio responsible for providing advice, reviewing complaints, conducting investigations and monitoring compliance in relation to the federal Privacy Act.[48] The OAIC has three functions: privacy law, freedom of information, and government information policy.[49] In 1989, the Privacy Commissioner, located within the Australian Human Rights and Equal Opportunity Commission (now the Australian Human Rights Commission, or AHRC), was responsible for administering the Privacy Act.[50] The Privacy Commissioner was separated from the AHRC in 2000,[51] and amalgamated with the OAIC in 2010. The present office combines the Australian Information Commissioner and Privacy Commissioner.[52] There have also been reductions in funding to the OAIC, so that it now has a relatively small staff allocation. Further, the Office is now located within the portfolio of the Attorney-General's Department, which is responsible for criminal justice policy, potentially leading to less independence.[53] The decrease in funding to the OAIC and

---

48 Office of the Australian Information Commissioner, *About Us*. Available: <https://www.oaic.gov.au/about-us/>.

49 Established under the *Privacy Act 1988* (Cth), Part IV, Division 2; *Freedom of Information Act 1982* (Cth), s 8F; and the *Australian Information Commissioner Act 2010* (Cth), Part 2, Division 3.

50 Office of the Australian Information Commissioner, *History of the Privacy Act*. Available: <https://www.oaic.gov.au/history-of-the-privacy-act>; Roger Clarke, *A History of Privacy in Australia* (8 January 2002). Available: <www.rogerclarke.com/DV/OzHistory.html>.

51 *Privacy Amendment (Office of the Privacy Commissioner) Act 2000* (Cth).

52 *Australian Information Commissioner Act 2010* (Cth), s 6. One person currently administers the statutory functions of the Australian Information Commissioner and the Privacy Commissioner. Leanne O'Donnell, 'Government Haste Lays Waste to Consultation' (2015) 25(23) *Eureka Street* 63, 65.

53 Richard Mulgan, 'The Slow Death of the Office of the Australian Information Commissioner', *The Canberra Times*, 1 September 2015. Funding was initially reduced within the 2014–15 Budget to coincide with the proposed abolition of the OAIC, although this decision was reversed in the 2015–16 and 2016–17 Budgets: Mary Anne Neilsen, 'Office of the Australian Information Commissioner: Reinstatement of Ongoing Funding' (Budget Review 2016–17, Parliamentary Library, Parliament of Australia, 2016).

Privacy Commissioner has arguably contributed to regulatory gaps in matters of privacy regulation in Australia.[54] Australian states and territories also have relevant legislation, and in most cases, information and privacy commissioners.[55] The complex nature of developing forms of technology, coupled with the way it is used by law enforcement and security agencies, and continuing developments within this area are a sign that the OAIC may need additional resources, specialisation and responsibilities in biometrics in order to effectively govern new developments.[56] In contrast with the United Kingdom, for example, which has a biometrics commissioner, the OAIC does not have a specific function or officer to oversee or regulate the collection, retention and use of specific types of specialised technical information, also contributing to a lack of regulation.[57]

## Australian privacy law in practice

Historically, commentators in Australia have criticised the exemptions to the Privacy Act as being too broad.[58] An Australian Law Reform Commission inquiry into the Privacy Act recommended that exemptions should only be permitted with compelling justification.[59] A key example of these exemptions are those made to the Privacy Act for the purposes of 'enforcement related activities' on the basis of balancing individual interests against those of collective security. It has been argued that the consequence of this balancing approach is that 'individual rights are invariably "traded off" against the community interests in preventing, detecting and prosecuting crime'.[60] The inclination for legislators to promote community

---

54  The position of the Independent National Security Legislation Monitor, a similar oversight position in regulating security legislation, was left vacant for an extended period of time with threat of abolition during key debates around the 2014 tranche of national security legislation as described above: Roger Gyles, 'INSLM Annual Report 2014–2015' (*Annual Report*, Independent National Security Legislation Monitor, 7 December 2015), 1. Available: <https://www.inslm.gov.au/sites/default/files/publications/inslm-annual-report-2015.pdf>.

55  For example, in New South Wales there is the NSW Information and Privacy Commission, and in Queensland the Queensland Office of the Information Commissioner: Office of the Australian Information Commissioner, *Privacy in Your State*. Available: <https://www.oaic.gov.au/privacy/privacy-in-your-state/>. State and territory privacy protection includes, for example: *Privacy and Personal Information Protection Act 1998* (NSW); *Information Privacy Act 2009* (Qld); *Personal Information Protection Act 2004* (Tas); and *Privacy and Data Protection Act 2014* (Vic).

56  During the 2016 Australian Federal Election campaign, the Australian Greens called for a similar expansion of regulatory oversight via a Digital Rights Commissioner, proposed within the framework of the Australian Human Rights Commission: Australian Greens, *A Digital Rights Commissioner*. Available: <http://greens.org.au/digital-rights-commissioner>.

57  See Victorian Law Reform Commission, *Surveillance in Public Places, Final Report No 18* (2010), Chapter 3. The Victorian Law Reform Commission conducted an inquiry into surveillance in public places, recommending that an independent regulator be established to provide oversight of public surveillance, and that the Victorian Parliament enact new laws promoting the responsible use of surveillance devices in public places. The report did not consider the surveillance practices of police and security agencies, instead recommending that they be considered separately, which has not occurred. This is related to the use of automated facial recognition technology integrated with CCTV in public places.

58  See, eg, Graham Greenleaf, '"Tabula Rasa": Ten Reasons Why Australian Privacy Law Does Not Exist' (2001) 24 *University of New South Wales Law Journal* 262, 264.

59  Australian Law Reform Commission, *For Your Information: Australian Privacy Law and Practice, Report No 108* (ALRC, 2008), 113.

60  Simon Bronitt and James Stellios, 'Telecommunications Interception in Australia: Recent Trends and Regulatory Prospects' (2005) 29 *Telecommunications Policy* 875, 887.

interests over the protection of individual privacy and the absence of a bill of rights may mean the Australian legal framework is unbalanced, and that statutory privacy protections in Australia are limited in comparison with Europe. Some commentators have argued that privacy rights are not being adequately protected by Australian legislators, in the context of a rapid advance in technologies that expand the sharing of personal information, and which are likely to lead to greater opportunities for it to be accessed without authorisation. Some have questioned whether a new approach is required, given the rate of technology advancement – stating that 'privacy seems a woefully inadequate tool to regulate the use of big data'.[61]

The main privacy concerns associated with new technology relate to the circumstances in which it is obtained, retained, stored and shared between agencies, and the overall purposes for which it is used by the private sector, governments, healthcare institutions, law enforcement and security agencies.[62] For example, healthcare and biometric information is 'privacy invasive', as it identifies individuals and can be used to link and connect information across datasets.[63] The extent of the privacy concerns depends on a number of factors, including whether the information is used for verification, identification or diagnosis, whether the data is identifiable, and whether information is stored in a centralised database or local device.[64] One major concern about the inadequacy of privacy protections is the potential for 'function creep', where the use of information obtained for a particular purpose is later used for other purposes for which consent was not obtained.[65] These types of considerations and potential privacy impacts are particularly relevant for new types of technology-derived data, such as biometric information, because many of them (fingerprints, faces, genetic information) are difficult or impossible to hide and alter, and are linked to an individual's physical existence.[66] Biometric technologies such as automated facial recognition technology (AFRT) can be used to locate and track individuals through widely implemented CCTV surveillance systems.

---

61  Melissa de Zwart, Sal Humphreys and Beatrix van Dissel, 'Surveillance, Big Data and Democracy: Lessons for Australia from the US and UK' (2014) 37 *University of New South Wales Law Journal* 713, 741.
62  Norberto Nuno Gomes de Andrade, Aaron Martin and Shara Monteleone, '"All the Better to See You With, My Dear": Facial Recognition and Privacy in Online Social Networks' (2013) 11 *IEEE Security & Privacy* 21.
63  Paul De Hert, 'Biometrics and the Challenge to Human Rights in Europe. Need for Regulation and Regulatory Distinctions'. In Patricio Campisi (ed), *Security and Privacy in Biometrics* (Springer, 2013), 369, 390.
64  For complete treatment of privacy issues presented by biometrics, see Patrizio Campisi, 'Security and Privacy in Biometrics: Towards a Holistic Approach'. In Patrizio Campisi (ed), *Security and Privacy in Biometrics* (Springer, 2013). These issues could be addressed in the design of biometric systems, policies and procedures and robust oversight of use.
65  Philip Brey, 'Ethical Aspects of Facial Recognition Systems in Public Places' (2004) 2 *Journal of Information, Communication and Ethics in Society* 97, 104–5.
66  Norberto Nuno Gomes de Andrade, Aaron Martin and Shara Monteleone, '"All the Better to See You With, My Dear": Facial Recognition and Privacy in Online Social Networks' (2013) 11 *IEEE Security & Privacy* 21, 22. Another technology that raises similar concerns and that was recently implemented in Australia is Automated Licence Plate Recognition (ALPR). Licence plate information is linked to the registered vehicle owner, including their identification, enabling tracking (through CCTV or electronic toll collection). There are similarities between AFRT and ALPR, including the use of technology for surveillance through the digitisation of routinely collected information, image recognition and database technology. See also Ian Warren et al, 'When the Profile Becomes the Population: Examining Privacy Governance and Road Traffic Surveillance in Canada and Australia' (2013) 25 *Current Issues in Criminal Justice* 565, where the authors argue that in relation to the introduction of ALPR in Australia, new technologies have resulted in a diminished requirement for reasonable suspicion and a lack of safeguards in relation to the collection and use of personal information.

An example of function creep in the context of biometric information is the development of a national database of facial templates, created using existing photographs submitted by citizens for the purpose of obtaining a driver's licence or passport. In this example, individuals consented to providing a photograph to obtain a passport, but did not consent to their biometric information being extracted from that image and being used for law enforcement, security or intelligence purposes. While photographs and government records have traditionally been a resource available for use in individual police investigations,[67] the digitisation, automation and integration of information on a scale facilitated by big data analytics and facial recognition technologies is a marked shift in the way that these photographs could be used, requiring a greater level of scrutiny and review. As is discussed in greater detail in Chapter 6, these examples are not theoretical. In 2019, the Australian government sought to introduce a national biometric database via inter-agency information-sharing agreements, rather than new Commonwealth legislation. This was to operate as a 'hub', rather than a centralised database, facilitating matching between state, territory and Commonwealth databases – an approach that would avoid scrutiny that might otherwise have occurred if new legislation for a central database were introduced.[68]

An Australian case that deals with similar subject matter is *Caripis v Victoria Police (Health and Privacy)*,[69] which was heard by the Victorian Civil and Administrative Tribunal (VCAT). Ms Caripis brought an action against Victoria Police seeking to destroy images that were taken of her at an environmental protest. The VCAT considered whether, by failing to destroy the footage, the Police contravened the *Information Privacy Act 2000* (Vic), which provided that '[a]n organisation must take reasonable steps to destroy or permanently de-identify personal information if it is no longer needed for any purpose'.[70] Victoria Police argued that the images were required for 'intelligence, planning and briefing for further protests, [and] evidence in case a complaint is made'.[71] The VCAT ultimately found that the retention of the protest footage was not an interference with Ms Caripis's privacy and Victoria Police was able to retain the images for future use.[72] The outcome in the *Caripis* case differed from that in relevant UK cases discussed later in this chapter. While Victoria also has a *Charter of Human Rights and Responsibilities Act 2006* (Vic), the tribunal found that 'no charter unlawfulness arises from retention of the footage',[73] as in Australia there is no court of human rights and limited human rights legislation.

Technology has resulted in an expansion of the application and use of a wide range of new technologies for enforcement agencies to use, including biometric information. In

---

67  Gary Edmond and Mehera San Roque, '*Honeysett v The Queen*: Forensic Science, Specialised Knowledge and the Uniform Evidence Law' (2014) 36 *Sydney Law Review* 323; Jake Goldenfein, 'Police Photography and Privacy: Identity, Stigma and Reasonable Expectation' (2013) 36 *University of New South Wales Law Journal* 256.

68  Monique Mann and Marcus Smith, 'Automated Facial Recognition Technology: Recent Developments and Approaches to Oversight' (2017) 40 *University of New South Wales Law Journal* 121.

69  [2012] VCAT 1472 (*Caripis*).

70  *Information Privacy Act 2000* (Vic), Schedule 1, para 4.2. This Act has since been repealed and replaced with the *Privacy and Data Protection Act 2014* (Vic).

71  *Caripis* [2012] VCAT 1472, [26].

72  Ibid, [101].

73  Ibid, [100].

addition to the retention of photographs, facial recognition technology has the potential for information sharing and integration with big data, thus enabling use for secondary or unanticipated purposes.[74] As discussed, in Australia, enforcement agencies or agencies with an enforcement function are exempt from the Privacy Act and individual privacy rights are balanced against collective security interests. The significant expansion in the collection and use of data by law enforcement means that the current privacy framework is at risk of becoming obsolete. Lachmayer and Witzleb have argued:

> Australians lack a constitutional right to privacy and the data protection provisions of the *Privacy Act 1988* (Cth) contain significant holes. The activities of the intelligence agencies are not subject to the Act and exemptions to the APPs give law enforcement agencies relatively free reign [sic] in designing their information handling practices as well as easier access to information held by other agencies.[75]

In light of the above, a re-evaluation of privacy protections in response to new technology, and additional oversight mechanisms, are necessary. The expansion of data collection and information sharing by law enforcement and security agencies has not been matched with an expansion in oversight and accountability.

## Data retention

The developments in data retention in Australia over the past five years merit particular attention. As would be expected, law enforcement and security agencies can access the communications of suspects if they are needed to investigate serious crimes. The *Telecommunications (Interception and Access) Act 1979* (Cth) (TIA Act) and the *Surveillance Devices Act 2004* (Cth) provide for the content of communications such as phone calls, emails and messages to be intercepted, or stored communications accessed, if a warrant has been obtained by a law enforcement or national security agency, the information is reasonably necessary, and access is undertaken by an officer carrying out their lawful duties.[76]

> The primary function of the TIA Act is to allow lawful access to communications and data for law enforcement and national security purposes, in a way that protects the privacy of people who use the Australian telecommunications network. Serious and organised criminals seeking to harm Australia's national security routinely use telecommunications services and communications technology to plan and carry out their activities. The TIA Act provides a legal framework for national security and law enforcement agencies to access the information held by communications providers that agencies need to investigate criminal offences and other activities that threaten safety and security. The access that may be sought under the TIA Act includes access to telecommunications data, stored communications that already exist, or the interception of communications

---

74 Daniel Neyland, 'Who's Who?: The Biometric Future and the Politics of Identity' (2009) 6 *European Journal of Criminology* 135, 152.
75 Konrad Lachmayer and Normann Witzleb, 'The Challenge to Privacy from Ever Increasing State Surveillance: A Comparative Perspective' (2014) 37 *University of New South Wales Law Journal* 748, 772.
76 TIA Act, s 7(2).

in real time. Each of the powers available under the TIA Act is explained below. The use of warrants related to these powers is independently overseen by the Commonwealth Ombudsman and equivalent state bodies.[77]

According to the Department of Home Affairs, in the 2018 financial year, 3524 interception warrants were issued, contributing to 2429 arrests, 5415 prosecutions and 3516 convictions. Interception warrants can only be obtained in association with the investigation of serious offences carrying a penalty of at least seven years' imprisonment, including murder, kidnapping, serious drug offences, terrorism, offences involving child pornography, money laundering, and offences involving organised crime.[78]

While a warrant is necessary to obtain the content of communications, law enforcement and other government agencies can access communication 'metadata' *without* a warrant. This development follows laws that came into effect in Australia in 2015 requiring telecommunications service providers to retain and store Australians' metadata for two years, in order to ensure that it is available for law enforcement and national security investigations. 'Metadata' refers to information such as the phone numbers involved in a communication, the location of the devices used, the date and time of the communication, and the length of the conversation. In relation to internet use, it includes Internet Protocol addresses of users' devices. Given how extensively most people currently use smartphones, this amounts to a very large amount of data being stored in relation to all citizens. Metadata can provide a detailed picture of an individual's life, even if the content of communications is not accessed, particularly when analysed over longer periods of time. It raises significant questions about the balance between individual privacy and the need for law enforcement agencies to effectively conduct investigations in relation to serious crime and terrorism.[79]

The legislation that facilitates metadata retention is the *Telecommunications (Interception and Access) Amendment (Data Retention) Act 2015* (Cth). It came into effect in October 2015, with telecommunications service providers given until April 2017 to develop infrastructure to retain customers' metadata for the two-year period and deliver it to government agencies upon request. Section 172 of the legislation states that disclosure of 'the contents or substance of a communication' is not permitted. Details of the kinds of metadata telecommunications service providers are required to retain are provided in s 187AA of the legislation:

## *Telecommunications (Interception and Access) Act 1979* (Cth)

### Section 187AA: Information to be kept

(1) The following table sets out the kinds of information that a service provider must keep, or cause to be kept, under subsection 187A(1):

---

77  Department of Home Affairs, *Telecommunications (Interception and Access) Act 1979 Annual Report 2017–18* (2018).
78  Ibid.
79  Rick Sarre, 'Metadata Retention as a Means of Combatting Terrorism and Organised Crime: A Perspective from Australia' (2017) 12 *Asian Journal of Criminology* 167–79.

| Kinds of information to be kept | | |
|---|---|---|
| **Item** | **Topic** | **Description of information** |
| 1 | The subscriber of, and accounts, services, telecommunications devices and other relevant services relating to, the relevant service | The following:<br>(a) any information that is one or both of the following:<br>   (i) any name or address information;<br>   (ii) any other information for identification purposes;<br>   relating to the relevant service, being information used by the service provider for the purposes of identifying the subscriber of the relevant service;<br>(b) any information relating to any contract, agreement or arrangement relating to the relevant service, or to any related account, service or device;<br>(c) any information that is one or both of the following:<br>   (i) billing or payment information;<br>   (ii) contact information;<br>   relating to the relevant service, being information used by the service provider in relation to the relevant service;<br>(d) any identifiers relating to the relevant service or any related account, service or device, being information used by the service provider in relation to the relevant service or any related account, service or device;<br>(e) the status of the relevant service, or any related account, service or device. |
| 2 | The source of a communication | Identifiers of a related account, service or device from which the communication has been sent by means of the relevant service. |
| 3 | The destination of a communication | Identifiers of the account, telecommunications device or relevant service to which the communication:<br>(a) has been sent; or<br>(b) has been forwarded, routed or transferred, or attempted to be forwarded, routed or transferred. |
| 4 | The date, time and duration of a communication, or of its connection to a relevant service | The date and time (including the time zone) of the following relating to the communication (with sufficient accuracy to identify the communication):<br>(a) the start of the communication;<br>(b) the end of the communication;<br>(c) the connection to the relevant service;<br>(d) the disconnection from the relevant service. |
| 5 | The type of a communication or of a relevant service used in connection with a communication | The following:<br>(a) the type of communication;<br>Examples: Voice, SMS, email, chat, forum, social media.<br>(b) the type of the relevant service;<br>Examples: ADSL, Wi-Fi, VoIP, cable, GPRS, VoLTE, LTE.<br>(c) the features of the relevant service that were, or would have been, used by or enabled for the communication.<br>Examples: Call waiting, call forwarding, data volume usage.<br>Note: This item will only apply to the service provider operating the relevant service: see paragraph 187A(4)(c). |

| Kinds of information to be kept | | |
| --- | --- | --- |
| Item | Topic | Description of information |
| 6 | The location of equipment, or a line, used in connection with a communication | The following in relation to the equipment or line used to send or receive the communication: (a) the location of the equipment or line at the start of the communication; (b) the location of the equipment or line at the end of the communication. Examples: Cell towers, Wi-Fi hotspots. |

It is also worth noting that there is some ambiguity over whether the Uniform Resource Locators (URLs) of websites visited are metadata.

> Put simply, metadata (in the context of web browsing) is what remains of a communication or document after its contents and substance is excluded. As a result, the legal definition of metadata is ambiguous; an oversight commentators suggest is surprising. In part, the ambiguity arises from conflicting views on what constitutes 'the content' of a communication. For example, one of the most contentious issues of the current Australian regime is whether URLs are metadata. If they are, then warrantless governmental access to individuals' web browsing history is possible. One view is that as URLs are user-generated, they are content. Another view – expressed by the Attorney-General's Department – is that metadata is 'information that allows a communication to occur'. As that is what URLs do, consequently they are not content. The issue is that some URLs can identify the substance of a communication. [80]

As noted above, metadata can be accessed without a warrant and there is a relatively low threshold for access. There is only a requirement that it be reasonably necessary for the enforcement of a law imposing a pecuniary penalty or for the protection of the public revenue.[81] Other circumstances include where it is reasonably necessary:

- for the enforcement of the criminal law[82]
- for the purposes of finding a person who the Australian Federal Police, or a Police Force of a State, has been notified is missing.[83]

At the time this legislation was first introduced in 2015, there was significant public debate. The Prime Minister at the time emphasised that metadata retention was needed to protect the community from harm.

> To help combat terrorism at home and deter Australians from committing terrorist acts abroad, we need to ensure our security agencies are resourced properly and have the powers to respond to evolving threats and technological change.[84]

---

80  Jaan Murphy, *Access to and Retention of Internet 'Metadata'* (Australian Parliamentary Library, 2014).
81  *Telecommunications (Interception and Access) Act 1979* (Cth), s 179(3).
82  Ibid, s 178(3).
83  Ibid, s 178A(3).
84  Prime Minister Tony Abbott, cited in Michelle Grattan, '$131 million for Companies' Metadata Retention in Budget Boost to Counter Terrorism', *The Conversation*, 12 May 2015. Available: <https://theconversation.com/131-million-for-companies-metadata-retention-in-budget-boost-to-counter-terrorism-41637>.

On the other hand, civil libertarians emphasised the risks of retaining such vast and detailed information on Australian citizens. One senator commented:

> Access to private communications records is already out of control in Australia, with telecommunications regulator the Australian Communications and Media Authority reporting 580,000 warrantless demands in the last financial year. Mandatory data retention simply adds warehouses full of new private information to this broken access regime … in the few years I have been working up close to the government, I have learned one important lesson: governments cannot be trusted; this government, the one before it, the one that will come after it.[85]

The increasing use of metadata by an expanding number of government agencies has also been highlighted as a concern in recent years. Initially, only 22 police and intelligence agencies could access metadata without a warrant; however, that list has grown to more than 80 agencies, including local councils, Australia Post, the RSPCA and even Greyhound Racing Victoria.[86] The number of requests for access has also grown. In the 2019 financial year, requests from the NSW Crime Commission increased 25 per cent to 2322; and requests from the Australian Securities and Investments Commission increased 11 per cent to 1898. By far the largest user of metadata is the Australian Federal Police, which made 23 337 requests in the 2018 financial year.[87]

The legislation states that a warrant is required if an agency requests information relating to a journalist. In 2019, it was reported that in the previous financial year, warrants had been sought in relation to journalists 58 times. This came to light after the Australian Federal Police conducted raids on individual journalists and the Australian Broadcasting Corporation in relation to news stories published about the activities of the Australian military that were based on classified information. This led to a great deal of public debate over press freedom in Australia, and to further scrutiny of the increasing scope of Australia's national security legislation, including metadata retention.[88]

## Data access

Australia was the first liberal democratic country to enact legislation that seeks to facilitate access by law enforcement and national security agencies to communications that have been encrypted. Encryption, the process of encoding messages so that their content can only be read by those that send and receive them, is widely used for privacy and security on the internet, ranging from banking transactions to messaging applications such as WhatsApp and Signal. However, encryption can also be used by criminals to communicate and carry out crime, preventing law enforcement agencies from investigating or obtaining critical

85  Scott Ludlam, 'Data Retention: We Need This Opposition to Oppose', *Australian Broadcasting Corporation News*, 27 February 2015.
86  Hannah Francis, 'Dozens of Government Agencies Request Access to Citizen Metadata Without Warrants', *Sydney Morning Herald*, 19 January 2016.
87  Yolanda Redrup, 'Experts Demand Increased Transparency in Metadata Surveillance Laws', *Australian Financial Review*, 23 July 2019.
88  Bevan Shields, 'Federal Police Accessed the Metadata of Journalists Nearly 60 Times', *Sydney Morning Herald*, 8 July 2019.

evidence. In 2018, the Australian Parliament enacted controversial world-first legislation to address this issue.

The *Telecommunications and Other Legislation Amendment (Assistance and Access) Act 2018* (Cth) seeks to prevent encryption being used to prevent law enforcement agencies from accessing the communications by requiring technology companies to provide reasonable assistance to access the content of communications facilitated on their platforms. Under the legislation, technology companies may be required to respond to the following:

- A technical assistance request (TAR): a request that they voluntarily assist law enforcement by providing the technical details about one of their products or services.
- A technical assistance notice (TAN): a requirement that they assist by decrypting a specific communication, or face a fine if they refuse.
- A technical capability notice (TCN): a requirement that they create a new function to enable police to access a suspect's data, or face a fine if they refuse.[89]

Prior to issuing a TAR or TAN, the decision-maker must be satisfied that the request or requirement is reasonable and proportionate and that compliance is practicable and technically feasible.[90] Prior to the legislation being enacted, an inquiry was conducted by the Parliamentary Joint Committee on Intelligence and Security. In addition to the privacy implications associated with this development, there were broader concerns expressed. Many stakeholders, and particularly the technology industry, explained the issues associated with creating vulnerabilities in their systems that would compromise their ability to provide their services to customers, and impact on the commercial viability of Australian companies in the international marketplace. Section 317ZG now expressly provides that companies 'must not be requested or required to implement or build a systemic weakness or systemic vulnerability'. However, there remain ongoing concerns for the sector in relation to this.

> As outlined in our submission, the claim that the proposed legislation will not compromise critical encryption systems or introduce any 'systemic weaknesses' into products does not stand up to scrutiny. Firstly, while the title of section 317ZG states that 'communications provider must not be required to implement or build a systemic weakness or systemic vulnerability etc' the actual wording contained within that clause is more narrowly targeted and, as noted by the IGIS [Inspector-General of Intelligence and Security] and others, does not apply to technical assistance requests. The analysis undertaken by numerous parties demonstrates that this clause does not, and almost certainly cannot, achieve its stated aim. Aside from numerous clauses within the Bill that appear to contradict section 317ZG, as outlined in our opening comments, it remains the case that leading academic institutions, such as MIT [Massachusetts Institute of Technology] have 'yet to identify a system design that would allow law enforcement the requested access without introducing systemic weaknesses or vulnerabilities' and major corporations such as Cisco hold that 'the law would result in the creation of backdoors'.[91]

89  Defined in *Telecommunications and Other Legislation Amendment (Assistance and Access) Act 2018* (Cth), s 317B.
90  Ibid, s 317JAA (TARs); s 317P (TANs); and s 317TAAA(6) (TCNs).
91  Francis Galbally, *Questions on Notice from Senetas Corporation*, Parliamentary Joint Committee on Intelligence and Security, Review of the Telecommunications and Other Legislation Amendment (Assistance and Access) Bill 2018 (Parliament of Australia, 2018).

# International perspectives

## Europe

Data protection law in Europe became harmonised with the Data Protection Directive 1995,[92] which was enacted into legislation in member states, such as the *Data Protection Act 1998* in the United Kingdom.[93] This framework was developed in the early 1990s, prior to the rapid expansion of the internet and the advent of smartphones and social media. A more recent development is the *General Data Protection Regulation* (GDPR),[94] which came into effect in 2018, binding all European Union (EU) member states to a comprehensive and modern instrument. The GDPR sought to bind companies that were not based in the EU to regulation where they held the data of EU citizens, and to allow companies that were based in one country but doing business throughout Europe to comply with harmonised regulation throughout the Union.

The GDPR was implemented following important cases that should be noted, such as *Google Spain v AEPD and Mario Costjea Gonzalez*,[95] also known as the 'right to be forgotten case'. It concerned a Spanish citizen, Sr Gonzales, who was subject to a debt recovery action by the government. A public auction was advertised in the newspaper *La Vanguardia* to recover the debt. After the auction, these details identifying his past public debt were indexed in Google, because a web search on his name brought up details of the public action, something he considered to affect his business reputation and standing in the community. A complaint was lodged with the data protection agency in Spain, and the Court of Justice of the European Union (CJEU) found that Google, in producing the search returns, controlled the data, rather than simply indexing data that was held by other parties. Under Article 12 of the Data Protection Directive 1995, individuals had a right to request erasure or rectification of their data. Lynskey (2015), writing in *Modern Law Review,* discusses the significance of the case.

> In Google Spain the Court was asked to determine what obligations – if any – EU data protection law imposes on search engines, in this instance Google, vis-à-vis individuals who seek to suppress information relating to them which is lawfully available online. The Court held that when a person is searched for by name in Google's search engine, Google is obliged to remove links to web pages from the results its search engine displays if the processing of this data is incompatible with the provisions of the Data Protection Directive. These links must be removed irrespective of whether the web pages themselves continue to be lawful. It has been this finding of the Court which provoked the most controversy, in particular because of the Court's failure to address its freedom of expression implications. At the heart of the matter is the divisive issue of default control over information: should individuals be entitled to control the

---

92  Directive 95/46/EC.
93  The status of EU-based human rights and other legislation such as the *Data Protection Act 1998* in the United Kingdom may change in the future, following 'Brexit' in 2020.
94  2016/679. The UK government created a new *Data Protection Act 2018* reflecting the GDPR.
95  Case 131/12, *Google Spain SL, Google Inc v Agencia Española de Protección de Datos and Mario Costeja González* [2014] ECR I-000.

dissemination of their personal data or should the claim that this information belongs in the public domain prevail?[96]

The finding of the CJEU resulted in debate with respect to whether this amounted to a form of censorship. The decision was attacked by newspapers and media organisations, and resulted in hundreds of thousands of requests being directed to Google to delist internet sites.

In 2018, the GDPR came into effect. While a detailed analysis of the GDPR is outside the scope of this text, its key elements should be noted, including:

- that data only be collected if it is necessary to do so[97]
- the need for clear and affirmative consent by the data subject[98]
- the erasure of data where storage is no longer necessary for the purpose it was initially collected for, or after consent is withdrawn by the data subject[99]
- the right to obtain rectification of inaccurate personal data[100]
- the right to transfer personal data to another service provider[101]
- the right not to be subject to a decision based solely on automated processing[102]
- the right of the data subject to be informed when their data is compromised.[103]

The GDPR also imposes burdens on controllers of information to ensure data is held securely and to implement data protection measures, including encryption. For example, Article 32 provides that:

Taking into account the state of the art, the costs of implementation and the nature, scope, context and purposes of processing as well as the risk of varying likelihood and severity for the rights and freedoms of natural persons, the controller and the processor shall implement appropriate technical and organisational measures to ensure a level of security appropriate to the risk, including inter alia as appropriate:

(a) the pseudonymisation and encryption of personal data
(b) the ability to ensure the ongoing confidentiality, integrity, availability and resilience of processing systems and services
(c) the ability to restore the availability and access to personal data in a timely manner in the event of a physical or technical incident
(d) a process for regularly testing, assessing and evaluating the effectiveness of technical and organisational measures for ensuring the security of the processing.[104]

A more recent case involving Google in the EU, the 2019 case *Google v Commission Nationale de l'informatique et des libertes (CNIL)*, related to Article 17 of the GDPR. The French privacy regulator took action seeking clarity regarding whether Google was required

---

96   Orla Lynskey, 'Control Over Personal Data in a Digital Age: *Google Spain v AEPD and Mario Costeja Gonzalez*' (2015) 78 *Modern Law Review* 522–34.
97   *General Data Protection Regulation*, art 6.
98   Ibid.
99   Ibid, art 17.
100  Ibid, art 16.
101  Ibid, art 20.
102  Ibid, art 22.
103  Ibid, art 34.
104  Ibid, art 32.

to remove search listings that contained false or damaging information about a person globally – Google had subsequently introduced a geoblocking feature preventing EU users from accessing delisted links. The CJEU found in favour of Google. The court concluded that:

> [C]urrently, there is no obligation under EU law for a search engine operator who grants a request for de-referencing made by a data subject, as the case may be, following an injunction from a supervisory or judicial authority of a Member State, to carry out such a de-referencing on all the versions of its search engine. However, EU law requires a search engine operator to carry out such a de-referencing on the versions of its search engine corresponding to all the Member States and to take sufficiently effective measures to ensure the effective protection of the data subject's fundamental rights. Thus, such a de-referencing must, if necessary, be accompanied by measures which effectively prevent or, at the very least, seriously discourage an internet user conducting a search from one of the Member States on the basis of a data subject's name from gaining access, via the list of results displayed following that search, through a version of that search engine outside the EU, to the links which are the subject of the request for de-referencing. It will be for the national court to ascertain whether the measures put in place by Google Inc. meet those requirements.[105]

Shifting focus now to the *European Convention on Human Rights* (ECHR), which includes an article addressing privacy rights, there have been several cases involving the retention of biometric information and photographs of individuals by police which have engaged this instrument. Privacy rights in relation to biometric information have been upheld in the European Union under Article 8 of the ECHR,[106] which states that 'everyone has the right to respect for his private and family life, his home and his correspondence'. In the most prominent of these cases, *S and Marper v United Kingdom*,[107] discussed in greater detail in Chapter 6, the European Court of Human Rights considered the indefinite retention of biometric information by UK police (specifically DNA profiles and fingerprints).[108] In *Marper*, the applicants argued that Article 8 was contravened by legislation enacted in the UK allowing the indefinite retention of biometric information after criminal proceedings had concluded and no conviction had been recorded. The court found in favour of the applicants, stating:

> [T]he blanket and indiscriminate nature of the powers of retention of the fingerprints, cellular samples and DNA profiles of persons suspected but not convicted of offences, as applied in the case of the present applicants, fails to strike a fair balance between the competing public and private interests and that the respondent State has overstepped any acceptable margin of appreciation in this regard. Accordingly, the retention at

---

105   Court of Justice of the European Union, *Judgment in Case C-507/17 Google LLC, successor in law to Google Inc v Commission nationale de l'informatique et des libertés (CNIL)*, 24 September 2019.

106   *Convention for the Protection of Human Rights and Fundamental Freedoms*, opened for signature 4 November 1950, 213 UNTS 221 (entered into force 3 September 1953).

107   [2008] ECHR 1581.

108   Including cellular samples, fingerprints and DNA profiles. Note that photographs or facial templates were not considered in this case.

issue constitutes a disproportionate interference with the applicants' right to respect for private life and cannot be regarded as necessary in a democratic society.[109]

In another UK case concerning the retention of photographs, *R (on the Application of Wood) v Metropolitan Police Commissioner*,[110] Wood, a media coordinator employed for the Campaign Against Arms Trade, challenged the retention of photographs taken by police at an annual trade fair. Although Wood had no criminal convictions and had never been arrested, police took photographs for intelligence purposes that could later be converted to 'spotter cards' intended to be stored on a searchable database. The Court of Appeal considered the facts of the case in light of Article 8, and found that as Wood had not committed a criminal offence, there was no basis to justify retention. A key factor in the court's decision in this case was the proportionality of the actions of the police, especially given that Wood had not committed a criminal offence.

In *R (on the Application of RMC) v Commissioner of Police of the Metropolis*,[111] RMC and FJ were arrested and photographed but not subsequently convicted of any offences. RMC and FJ unsuccessfully sought to have their photographs deleted from the Police National Computer. The applicants successfully challenged the decision, with the court finding that the policy on the retention of custody photographs was unlawful.[112] This case further affirmed that the retention of either biometric information or photographs of individuals who had been charged but not convicted of a criminal offence violated privacy rights established in the ECHR. The judge in this case emphasised that photographs can uniquely identify individuals, in a way similar to other biometrics including DNA and fingerprints, and there was no basis for distinguishing them from other forms of biometric information.

## United States

The United States Constitution provides some limited protections that are relevant to individual privacy in relation to use of their personal data by government. The Fourth Amendment is the main example of this, protecting against the collection of personal information by the government. It states:

> The right of the people to be secure in their persons, houses, papers, and effects, against unreasonable searches and seizures, shall not be violated, and no warrants shall issue, but upon probable cause, supported by oath or affirmation, and particularly describing the place to be searched, and the persons or things to be seized.[113]

It has been noted in the literature that this, rather antiquated, protection does not align with the conditions under which governments access personal data today. Data is now routinely stored in databases in order to administer services, and in accessing that data, the government is not limited by a concept that requires a 'search' or 'seizure'. Further, the Constitution does not protect an individual in relation to third parties such as banks or healthcare providers

---

109   European Court of Human Rights, *Application Nos 30562/04 and 30566/04*, 4 December 2008, [125].
110   [2009] 4 All ER 951.
111   [2012] 4 All ER 510 (*RMC*).
112   Ibid, 537, per Richards LJ at [58].
113   Fourth Amendment, United States Constitution.

when they provide personal information to the government. Commentators have noted that 'at best, the Fourth Amendment provides a judicially enforced warrant requirement against a limited group of law enforcement activities'.[114]

Interestingly, the free speech clause in the First Amendment of the Constitution actually safeguards the free flow of personal data, rather than personal privacy rights. It has been relied upon to narrow the scope of privacy laws. In the case *Sorrell v IMS Health Care*,[115] at issue was a law that prevented pharmacies from selling information that identified the prescriber without their consent. The Supreme Court invalidated the law, meaning that pharmacies could sell the information on the basis of the free speech clause, because it restricted 'free speech in aid of pharmaceutical marketing'.[116] The First Amendment may well continue to be a source of rights for those utilising data in other areas.

Regarding statutory protection of privacy rights in the United States, the laws are included in various statutes enacted by individual states, and lack an overarching framework or regulatory scheme.

> Unlike EU law, US law starts with a principle of free information flow and permits the processing of any personal data unless a law limits this action. There is also no requirement for the creation of statutory laws. When it does apply, moreover, US law does not protect the individual through an omnibus law. Rather, information privacy law takes the form of a patchwork that includes statutes as well as regulations at both the federal and state level. The initiation of legislative action also frequently requires the presence of ... convincing evidence of abusive data practices.[117]

Over the past decade, discussion of privacy and data security in the United States has focused on actions of the intelligence agencies. Digital surveillance is now central to law enforcement and national security work. This includes data obtained through monitoring phone calls, email, social media, internet traffic, CCTV, GPS and biometric tracking. Digital surveillance in the United States is facilitated chiefly by three major pieces of legislation:

- *Foreign Intelligence Surveillance Act 1978* (FISA)
- *Uniting and Strengthening America by Providing Appropriate Tools Required to Intercept and Obstruct Terrorism Act 2001* (USA PATRIOT Act)
- *Uniting and Strengthening America by Fulfilling Rights and Ensuring Effective Discipline Over Monitoring Act 2015* (USA FREEDOM Act).

FISA sets out the procedure for electronic surveillance of foreign agents, including US citizens, that are suspected of espionage or terrorism. It does not require a court order in order to spy on foreign agents; however, a warrant is necessary to spy on a US citizen – requiring probable cause that the subject is an agent of a foreign power. The PATRIOT Act, introduced following 9/11, expanded surveillance powers, allowing foreign intelligence information to be collected from US citizens as well as foreigners. A 2007 amendment to this legislation allowed the wiretapping of foreign communications that pass through communications networks in the United States, giving:

---

114    P Schwartz and KN Peifer, 'Transatlantic Data Privacy Law' (2017) 106 *Georgetown Law Journal* 115.
115    564 US 552 (2011).
116    Ibid.
117    P Schwartz and KN Peifer, 'Transatlantic Data Privacy Law' (2017) 106 *Georgetown Law Journal* 115.

the National Security Agency the right to collect such communications in the future without a warrant. But it goes further than that: It also would allow the monitoring, under certain conditions, of electronic communications between people on U.S. soil, including U.S. citizens, and people 'reasonably believed to be outside the United States,' without a court's order or oversight.[118]

The FISA Court has the power to make secret orders in relation to these activities. In 2006, through a creative interpretation of s 215 of the PATRIOT Act, it found that all phone records could potentially be relevant to a terrorism investigation. As a result, the National Security Agency (NSA) began requiring telecommunications companies to provide access to all their data. In 2013, following Edward Snowden's disclosures, vast data collection programs engaged in by the NSA in the United States were revealed, along with the participation of partner agencies such as the Government Communications Headquarters (GCHQ) in the United Kingdom and the Australian Signals Directorate (ASD) in Australia. The programs revealed included *PRISM*, involving the collection of internet communications from US internet companies; *Upstream/Tempora*, the collection of internet traffic from fibre-optic cables; and *XKeyscore*, a program that facilitated searching and analysis of the data obtained from the other programs.[119] There was a mixed response to Snowden's actions, and controversy over whether he should be viewed as a hero or a traitor.[120]

Following this development, the FREEDOM Act banned bulk collection of call records, but renewed, in a modified form, controversial parts of the PATRIOT Act that would otherwise have expired in 2015. The result of this was that vast numbers of call records continued to be collected. In 2019, the Executive sought to make permanent the ability of the NSA to collect call records, despite the fact that they said the capacity was not actually being used. While there are technical issues at present, technology could improve in the future, facilitating effective use.

> The National Security Agency has suspended the call detail records program that uses this authority and deleted the call detail records acquired under this authority ... This decision was made after balancing the program's relative intelligence value, associated costs, and compliance and data integrity concerns caused by the unique complexities of using these company-generated business records for intelligence purposes.[121]

It is clear that in the debate between individual privacy and national security in the United States, there are strong arguments on each side. The complex and top secret nature of the technologies deployed to analyse data records, the secrecy of courts interpreting the legislation, the complexity of the legislation itself, and the increasing weight given to arguments about terrorism following 9/11 have made this one of the most challenging areas of law and policy. The close cooperation between defence and security agencies in the United States, the United Kingdom and Australia in terms of infrastructure and intelligence

---

118 Ellen Nakashima and Joby Warrick, 'House Approves Wiretap Measure', *Washington Post*, 5 August 2007.
119 'The NSA Files', *The Guardian*. Available: <https://www.theguardian.com/us-news/the-nsa-files>.
120 Nate Fick, 'Was Snowden a Traitor or a Hero, Perhaps a Little of Both', *Washington Post*, 19 January 2017.
121 Charlie Savage, 'Trump Administration Asks Congress to Reauthorize NSA's Deactivated Call Records Program', *New York Times*, 15 August 2019.

sharing means that there will be implications for these countries. The public debate on metadata retention in the United States provides an opportunity to reflect on Australian law in this area that was discussed earlier in the chapter.

# Conclusion

Privacy law is an important area of the legal system that raises important questions about the balance that must be set between community and individual interests in liberal democracies. Technology continues to advance rapidly, and consumers are eager to utilise new ways of improving their lives. However, privacy can often be a trade-off in the absence of appropriate regulation. The development of privacy law and policy usually lags behind the development of technology itself.

The growing amount of data that is being produced is of great value to businesses in order to inform marketing, and to governments in formulating policy and enforcing laws. A review of the privacy law in Australia, along with a brief comparison with Europe and the United States, reveals that EU law and human rights frameworks are relatively more developed and better placed to respond to emerging technologies that have implications for individual privacy. Developments in the United States have exposed the diminution of privacy rights, particularly in the national security domain, and constitutional protections are not as extensive as those that have been established in Europe's human rights instruments. Australia lacks a federal charter of rights, and while some aspects of international human rights instruments, such as the ICCPR, have been integrated into Australian law, protections are weaker than in Europe, and some may consider that these have been eroded further with the enactment of the recent data retention and access laws.

# 4

LAW,
TECHNOLOGY
AND
HEALTHCARE

# Introduction

Technology offers a means of developing new therapies to treat human illness and has great potential to reduce suffering and increase living standards around the world. For this reason, there is a large investment in research and development for new pharmaceuticals and medical devices, and the healthcare sector is rich with new forms of technology and legal issues associated with them. Fields such as genomics, the study of the genome, are providing a more detailed understanding of human health, ranging from cardiovascular diseases to cancer, along with improved methods of prevention and treatment. Assisted reproductive technologies are giving couples who would otherwise not have been able to have children the opportunity to do so, and allowing serious conditions to be identified earlier during, or even prior to, a pregnancy. Stem cell technologies will lead to replacement organs and body parts in coming decades, and already form the basis of treatments for serious conditions such as leukaemia and myeloma. Artificial intelligence is already transforming areas of medicine such as radiology and pathology: screening images for disease and other abnormalities under the supervision of doctors, saving time and improving access to healthcare for patients in rural and remote areas. As with other technologies discussed throughout this text, law and regulation will play an important role in ensuring that benefits are promoted, while associated risks are managed to reduce the prospect of harm to patients and the wider community.

The chapter is divided into four parts. The first will consider fundamental issues underlying law, technology and healthcare, including autonomy, consent, confidentiality and biobanks. The second will focus on genomics, including databases and information security, genomic property rights and developing issues in the field. The third will examine reproductive technology, including assisted reproductive technologies and preimplantation genetic diagnosis. The final part of the chapter will consider developing healthcare technologies, including human cloning, stem cell technology, and the rapidly developing areas of nanotechnology and artificial intelligence software in medical screening and diagnostics. There will also be consideration of public health surveillance technology in the context of the COVID-19 pandemic. It is worth noting that the ethical theories discussed in Chapter 2 are particularly relevant to the issues of law and technology discussed in relation to healthcare.

# Fundamental issues

## Autonomy and consent

The discipline of healthcare law came to prominence in the 1970s, prompted by an expansion in medical negligence litigation and the capacity of the law to play a role in regulating the ethical relationship between doctors and their patients.[1] Common law principles in this field focus on the doctor–patient relationship – setting out the limits of what is permissible with respect to patients' bodies. Patient autonomy is an important ethical principle of clinical practice.[2] It does not mean that patients are solely responsible for making decisions, but

---

1    Ian Freckelton, 'The Emergence and Evolution of Health Law' (2013) 29 *Law in Context* 74.
2    Sheila McLean, *Autonomy Consent and the Law* (Routledge, 2010); for case law on the issue, see, eg, *Rogers v Whittaker* (1992) 175 CLR 479.

rather that they should make a decision that is 'an informed and free decision made by someone with the capacity to make such a choice'.[3] While a competent patient has the right to refuse medical treatment, no matter how adverse the outcome of that decision for the patient,[4] they cannot demand to receive treatment that their doctor believes is not clinically indicated.[5] Greater focus on patient autonomy can be viewed as a shift away from medical paternalism, where patients accept medical advice without critical reflection. It has likely been advanced more recently with the greater availability of medical information for consumers that is available through the internet, leading to increased participation in the decision-making process in relation to their treatment.

The historic Australian case *Rogers v Whittaker*[6] was an important decision in relation to the disclosure of 'material risks' by doctors to their patients. The respondent had been almost completely blind in her right eye since nine years of age. At the age of 47, she was referred to Dr Rogers for surgery. He advised that he could operate on the eye to remove scarring and possibly restore sight to that eye. However, following the operation, not only was there no improvement to her right eye, but she developed inflammation and other issues (sympathetic ophthalmia, a 1:14 000 risk) in her left eye, leading to a complete loss of sight in the left eye which left her almost completely blind. Dr Rogers had not advised his patient of this risk. The High Court held that the doctor's failure to advise and warn of risks inherent in the operation constituted a breach of duty.

> [T]he law should recognise that a doctor has a duty to warn a patient of a material risk inherent in the proposed treatment; a risk is material if, in the circumstances of the particular case, a reasonable person in the patient's position, if warned of the risk, would be likely to attach significance to it, or if the medical practitioner is or should reasonably be aware that the particular patient, if warned of the risk, would be likely to attach significance to it.[7]

In response to concerns about a personal injury litigation and insurance crisis, restrictive legislative reforms in Australia were implemented in the early 2000s, which have limited the ability of people injured as a result of medical treatment to seek redress.[8] In response to similar issues in the United Kingdom, a mediation service has been used successfully there to settle cases before they reach court, as well as a state-backed indemnity scheme to reduce rising insurance premiums.[9]

Prior to a doctor treating a patient, it is vital that the patient provide valid consent. Consent authorises a doctor to undertake an action that they would not have otherwise been permitted to undertake, and if it is not obtained, could lead to liability to an action in battery or negligence. Consent must be given freely and voluntarily. It must not be given by coercion or when under the influence of medication.[10] Consent must also relate to the

---

3  Margaret Bazier and Emma Cave, *Medicine, Patients and the Law* (5th ed, Penguin, 2011).
4  See, eg, *Brightwater Care Group v Rossiter* (2009) 40 WAR 84.
5  See, eg, *R (Burke) v General Medical Council* [2005] EWCA Civ 1003.
6  *Rogers v Whittaker* (1992) 175 CLR 479.
7  Ibid, 490.
8  Thomas Faunce, 'Disclosure of Material Risk as Systems Error Tragedy: Wallace v Kam (2013) 87 ALJR 648; [2013] HCA 19' (2013) 21(1) *Journal of Law and Medicine* 53.
9  See, eg, 'Medical Negligence: There are No Winners', *The Lancet*, 26 May 2018.
10  See, eg, *Beausoleil v The Sisters of Charity* (1964) 53 DLR (2d) 65.

act performed. In cases where a patient consents to one surgical procedure, but wakes up to find that another has been performed by mistake, the surgeon will be liable for battery.[11] Sufficient information must be given to the patient to enable them to decide whether to consent to the treatment. If the information used as a basis for their decision is incorrect, the consent may later be invalidated. However, if the patient broadly understands the nature of a procedure (as opposed to the 'precise physiological processes'), that is sufficient.[12]

Consent can only be provided by a person who is competent to provide it. There is a presumption that adults of sound mind are competent. 'Competency' refers to a person's capacity to receive information, consider it, apply it to their situation, and make a decision that they are then able to communicate.[13] According to what has been termed 'Gillick competence',[14] children with sufficient maturity, such as those aged 12–15 years, who understand the nature of the treatment to be provided, can give their consent.

## Confidentiality

Health information is very often sensitive, and most people would prefer that their medical diagnoses and treatments are handled with a degree of privacy. However, there is also a need to provide patients with a right to access information about themselves and for information to be used by other treatment providers, and in some cases in a de-identified form in research projects.

Skene (2004) discusses the rationale for confidentiality from three perspectives. From an ethical perspective, maintaining confidentiality in relation to a patient's medical record respects their autonomy. Second, if a patient knows that what they discuss with their doctor is confidential, they are more likely to be frank about what they divulge, and this is beneficial for their treatment. Finally, from a public policy perspective, it is in society's interest that patients receive the best possible medical care, and for that to take place and medical conditions to be diagnosed accurately, frank disclosure by the patient is necessary.[15]

Two exceptions to the duty of confidence that a doctor owes to their patient are consent and public interest. Consent must be expressly given, or implied, such as when a referral is made from a general practitioner to a specialist. The public interest exception arises where the disclosure of confidential information is necessary to protect other members of the public from harm.[16]

In *Breen v Williams*,[17] the patient had a breast implant procedure and requested her medical records from her surgeon in order to participate in class action litigation. When her surgeon responded that he would release the records if she indemnified him from liability arising from the surgery, she commenced legal action to access the records. The High Court determined that creating a new legal right that enabled patients to access their medical

---

11  See, eg, *Chatterton v Gerson* [1981] QB 432.
12  *R v Mental Health Act Commission; Ex parte X* (1991) 9 BMLR 77, 87.
13  *Re C (adult: refusal of medical treatment)* [1994] 1 All ER 819.
14  *Gillick v West Norfolk and Wisbech Area Health Authority* [1986] AC 112; endorsed in Australia in
    *Secretary, Department of Health and Community Services v JWB and SMB* (1992) 175 CLR 218, 239.
15  Loane Skene, *Law and Medical Practice: Rights, Duties, Claims and Defences* (2nd ed, Lexis Nexis,
    2004), 256.
16  See, eg, *W v Egdell* [1990] Ch 359; *Duncan v Medical Practitioners Disciplinary Committee* [1986] 1
    NZLR 513.
17  (1996) 43 ALD 481.

records was too significant a change to be made by the courts and should be left for the legislature.

> In a democratic society, changes in the law that cannot logically or analogically be related to existing common law rules and principles are the province of the legislature. From time to time it is necessary for the common law courts to re-formulate existing legal rules and principles to take account of changing social conditions. Less frequently, the courts may even reject the continuing operation of an established rule or principle. But such steps can be taken only when it can be seen that the 'new' rule or principle that has been created has been derived logically or analogically from other legal principles, rules and institutions. In the present case, it is not possible, without distorting the basis of accepted legal principles, for this Court to create either an unrestricted right of access to medical records or a right of access, subject to exceptions. If change is to be made, it must be made by the legislature.[18]

The government subsequently amended the *Privacy Act 1988* (Cth),[19] extending that legislation to cover information disclosed in doctor–patient consultations.[20] The Office of the Australian Privacy Commissioner can investigate potential breaches of privacy and apply to the Federal Court for enforcement, such as the payment of compensation.[21] As discussed in Chapter 3, the Privacy Act established the Australian Privacy Principles, a number of which relate to health information.

According to APP 3, an entity must not collect sensitive information about an individual unless they give their consent, or it is reasonably necessary for, or directly related to, the agency's functions or activities. APP 6 provides that an entity can only use or disclose personal information for a purpose for which it was collected, unless an exception applies. The exceptions include consent; where they would reasonably expect the entity to use or disclose their personal information; the use or disclosure is required by a court order; or the entity reasonably believes that the use or disclosure is reasonably necessary for one or more enforcement-related activities. APP 11 requires that reasonable steps are taken to protect personal information it holds from misuse, unauthorised access, modification or disclosure. This includes physical security, information technology security and destruction. APP 12 requires entities that hold personal information about an individual to give the individual access to that information on request, subject to grounds for a valid refusal. This can include where it would pose a serious threat to the life, health or safety of any individual; would have an unreasonable impact on the privacy of other individuals; or where authorised by the *Freedom of Information Act 1982* (Cth).

The My Health Record (MyHR) system (otherwise known as a Personally Controlled Electronic Health Record [PCEHR] or an eHealth record) is an online summary of a person's health information that allows doctors, hospitals and other healthcare providers to view health information. The *My Health Records Act 2012* (Cth) limits the collection, use and disclosure of

---

18   Ibid, 509.
19   Section 6(1) provides that 'health information' means information or an opinion about the health or disability of an individual; expressed wishes about the future health services; health services provided; organ donation; and genetic information.
20   Similar amendments were also made to state legislation around Australia. See, eg, *Health Records and Information Privacy Act 2002* (NSW). APP 12 also covers access to information.
21   *Privacy Act 1988* (Cth), ss 36 and 55A.

information in the record and seeks to improve the flow of patient data to improve treatment. Andrews et al (2014) surveyed the Australian population, finding that trust, perceived risks, and privacy concerns influenced attitudes towards the MyHR system, but that take-up was increasing over time.[22] In 2019, following the introduction of an opt-out system in January of that year, it was reported that only 9 per cent of Australians with a MyHR had ever accessed it. It was also reported that only 42 per cent of private diagnostic pathology and radiology practices, and 33 per cent of private hospitals, were connected to the service.[23]

## Biobanks

Biobanks are databases that store human tissue, genetic information and health-related information. They can be operated by governments, universities, hospitals, research institutes or companies. In Australia, there is no coordinated approach to regulation and it has been suggested that a national approach would be more effective.[24] The *National Statement on Ethical Conduct in Human Research* requires a governance model to be adopted to address the 'collection, storage, use and disposal of human tissue in research'.[25] The legal issues raised by biobanking include consent, privacy, confidentiality and property rights in the context of prospective commercialisation. Some authors have argued that consent should be required not only when the tissue or data is first included in the biobank, but on an ongoing basis and be 'dynamic' in nature, with participants engaged and updated about research being conducted and any associated risks.[26] One of the world's largest biobanks, the UK Biobank, which holds medical data and blood samples from 500 000 volunteers for the purpose of genetic testing, provides regular updates to all participants on how their data is being used on an ongoing basis. As information exchange becomes easier to facilitate and more globalised over the next decade, due to technology advances, this issue will grow in importance.[27]

As technology has developed that has the potential to utilise human tissue for therapeutic purposes, the question of ownership, control and property rights has become more significant. The concept of 'property' is usually understood in terms of rights: the right to use, sell and exclude others from use. It can include personal property, real property (land) and intellectual property. A person can allow someone else to have possession of their property but still retain ownership of it, a concept known as bailment. A person can also abandon property, relinquishing their rights to it, and it may be claimed by another

22  Lynda Andrews, Randike Gajanayake and Tony Sahama, 'The Australian General Public's Perceptions of Having a Personally Controlled Electronic Health Record' (2014) 83 *International Journal of Medical Informatics* 889–900.

23  Dana McCauley, 'Australians Shun My Health Record with only 9 per cent Ever Logging In', *Sydney Morning Herald*, 22 December 2019.

24  Anne-Marie Farrell, 'Biobanks'. In *Health Law: Frameworks and Context* (Cambridge University Press, 2017), 258.

25  National Health and Medical Research Council, *National Statement on Ethical Conduct in Human Research* (2018). Available: <https://www.nhmrc.gov.au/about-us/publications/national-statement-ethical-conduct-human-research-2007-updated-2018>.

26  Jane Kaye et al, 'Dynamic Consent: A Patient Interface for Twenty-First Century Research Networks' (2015) 23 *European Journal of Human Genetics* 141.

27  See, eg, Edwina Light et al, 'Disruption, Diversity, and Global Biobanking' (2019) 19 *American Journal of Bioethics* 45.

person who finds it.[28] The traditional legal position is that the human body, and parts of it, cannot be the subject of property interests, except in special circumstances. One of these circumstances is the work/skill exception – a person may acquire property rights over human tissue through the application of lawful work or skill.[29]

More recent cases in this area have arisen in relation to stored semen. In *Bazley v Wesley Monash IVF Pty Ltd*,[30] a widow sought to prevent a fertility clinic from destroying her husband's sperm samples following his death. The court held that, in these circumstances, the semen was the property of the deceased prior to his death, after which it became the property of his legal representative, his widow. In *Roblin v Public Trustee for the Australian Capital Territory*,[31] this right was extended to a widow in a scenario where the sperm was extracted following the husband's death.

Property rights have been recognised by courts in relation to human tissue used in medical research, likely influenced by the policy benefits of promoting scientific research. There have been a number of influential cases in the United States, where a large proportion of medical technology originates. In *Moore v Regents of the University of California*,[32] a patient sued researchers who had removed tissue from Moore's spleen during treatment and subsequently developed it into a valuable cell line with therapeutic applications. The court found that the patient's loss of property rights in his tissue was sufficient for a tortious claim in conversion. In *Washington University v Catalona*,[33] a researcher sought to move a tissue bank of thousands of samples to another university when he took up a new position. Despite the support of the patients who donated the samples, the court found that Washington University owned the samples and the patients and the researcher had no right to determine where the samples would be held.

Advances such as stem cell technology and 3D printing are likely to lead, in the coming decades, to the capacity to create organs for transplantation.[34] The Human Tissue Acts in Australia deal with blood, tissue and organ donation for medical and research purposes.[35] They were developed following a 1977 Australian Law Reform Commission (ALRC) report.[36] In Australia, human organs and tissue can be donated through a gift relationship,[37] but it is illegal to sell or trade in these products, irrespective of whether the donor is alive

28  For a detailed discussion of property rights in healthcare, see, eg, Imogen Goold, *Persons, Parts and Property: How Should We Regulate Tissue in the 21st Century?* (Hart, 2014).
29  See, eg, *Doodeward v Spence* (1908) 6 CLR 406; *R v Kelly and Lindsay* [1998] 3 All ER 741; *Roche v Douglas* (2000) 22 WAR 331.
30  [2011] 2 Qd R 207.
31  (2015) 10 ACTLR 300.
32  793 P 2d 479 (1990).
33  437 F Supp 2d 985 (2006).
34  Satyajit Patra and Vanesa Young, 'A Review of 3D Printing Techniques and the Future in Biofabrication of Bioprinted Tissue' (2016) 74 *Cell Biochemistry and Biophysics* 93–8.
35  See, eg, *Transplantation and Anatomy Act 1978* (ACT), s 6; *Human Tissue Act 1983* (NSW), s 4. This legislation differentiates between *tissue* – an organ, or part of a human body or a substance extracted from or from a part of the human body; and *regenerative tissue* – tissue which after injury or removal is replaced in the body of a living person through natural processes of growth and repair. The legislation does not cover access, storage and transfer of human tissue. Reproductive tissue is also not covered by this legislation, and the relevant law on that will be discussed later in the chapter.
36  Australian Law Reform Commission, *Human Tissue Transplants* (ALRC Report 7) (AGPS, 1977).
37  See, eg, Richard Titmuss, *The Gift Relationship: From Human Blood to Social Policy* (George Allen & Unwin, 1970).

or deceased.[38] The rationale for this includes the negative influence of commodifying the human body and the related potential for donor exploitation.[39] The issue of presumed consent regimes is an interesting one. For example, Wales changed its law to presume that people who have not recorded an organ donation decision on a register do not object to the donation of their organs.[40] The Welsh model is known as 'deemed consent' and includes a 'soft opt-out' where families are given the opportunity to refuse.[41] In Australia, consent is not presumed; however, those people who wish to can register their donation decision on the Australian Organ Donor Register.[42]

# Genomics

Recent advancements in genomics promise unprecedented individual and public health benefits, including improved diagnosis and treatment of some of the most serious health conditions, including cancer, heart disease and inherited genetic diseases. *Genomics* refers to the holistic study of all of an organism's genes (their genome). It can be contrasted with the more established field of *genetics,* which refers to the study of single genes and how related traits or conditions are passed on to following generations.[43] Since the early 1990s, genomics has become increasingly important in understanding medical conditions and behavioural traits, raising a range of ethical questions about how the information it generates should be used.[44] Interest in the field grew rapidly during the completion of the Human Genome Project (between 1990 and 2003) undertaken by the US Department of Energy and the National Institutes of Health to locate and sequence all human genes. The genome comprises introns and exons: *exons* are the parts of the genome that code for specific proteins, while *introns* are the non-coding regions of genes. The genome itself is made up of *DNA* (deoxyribonucleic acid), held within the nucleus of all cells in the human body – discovered in its distinctive double helix form by Watson and Crick in 1953.[45]

It has become clear more recently that there is a complex interaction between genes and the environment. The field of *epigenetics* is the study of the modification of gene expression

---

38  See, eg, *Transplantation and Anatomy Act 1978* (ACT), s 44; *Human Tissue Act 1983* (NSW), s 32.

39  See, eg, Nuffield Council on Bioethics, *Human Bodies: Donation for Medicine and Research* (NCB, 2011).

40  See, eg, Ana Manzano, 'Organ Donation: Does Presumed Consent Work?', *The Conversation*, 20 November 2015. Available: <https://theconversation.com/organ-donation-does-presumed-consent-work-49478>.

41  Ibid.

42  Australian Government, Organ and Tissue Authority. Available: <www.donatelife.gov.au/registering-be-donor>.

43  The World Health Organization explains the difference between *genomics* and *genetics*. 'Genetics is the study of heredity[,] while genomics is defined as the study of genes and their functions, and related techniques. The main difference between genomics and genetics is that genetics scrutinizes the functioning and composition of the single gene[,] whereas genomics addresses all genes and their inter relationships in order to identify their combined influence on the growth and development of the organism': World Health Organization, *Human Genomics in Global Health* (2020). Available: <https://www.who.int/genomics/geneticsVSgenomics/en/>.

44  National Human Genome Research Institute, *What is the Human Genome Project?* (2019). Available: <https://www.genome.gov/human-genome-project/What>.

45  James Watson and Francis Crick, 'Molecular Structure of Nucleic Acids: A Structure for Deoxyribose Nucleic Acid' (1953) 171 *Nature* 737.

and trait variations that result from chemical interactions that can activate or deactivate genes, and how the environment influences whether genes are activated. Further, many diseases and traits are a result of the interaction of hundreds of genes, making them difficult to understand and develop treatments for, even with the advanced forms of gene therapy currently being developed.[46]

Genomics has revolutionised the field of clinical medicine, enabling the emergence of precision healthcare – tailoring treatment to each individual's genetic make-up. Whole-genome sequencing (WGS) and whole-exome sequencing (WES) have been shown to substantially enhance the diagnostic rate of rare diseases (from 6 per cent with traditional genetic testing to 50 per cent with WES), as well as being cost effective.[47] There is presently a great deal of interest and investment in genomics-informed healthcare, both in government and in the private sector, with the volume of information that can be derived from the human genome and applied to clinical medicine and public health in a range of contexts expanding rapidly. Further research in genomics has great potential to improve the effectiveness of medical treatment. Potential public health benefits that derive from genomics and the linkage of this form of information as its availability increases include new or improved interventions to prevent and treat disease, and better understanding of the number of people in a country or region that are predisposed to specific diseases, leading to improved public health planning.

## Testing, privacy and discrimination

The availability of genetic information has increased, with the commercial market in direct-to-consumer health testing, ancestry testing and paternity testing increasing rapidly, raising questions relating to data security, consent, privacy and ownership.[48] These ethical and associated legal issues became widely discussed in Australia following the ALRC's 2003 report, *Essentially Yours*,[49] which has influenced legal development through the implementation of some of the recommendations. Genetic testing is widely undertaken in medicine. For decades, newborns have been tested for conditions such as cystic fibrosis; and more recently, predictive testing for conditions that have a genetic element, such as certain cancers, is available through clinicians and online. The lack of regulation around these is concerning and raises a wide range of issues, including test accuracy, privacy and data security, and the advisability of consumers receiving complex genetic data about themselves without the benefit of a doctor to explain it to them and provide reassurance and advice.[50] As discussed further in Chapter 6, this data has even been accessed by law enforcement and

---

46  See, eg, Annalisa Roberti et al, 'Epigenetics in Cancer Therapy and Nanomedicine' (2019) 11 *Clinical Epigenetics* 81.

47  Elizabeth Palmer et al, 'Integrating Exome Sequencing into a Diagnostic Pathway for Epileptic Encephalopathy: Evidence of Clinical Utility and Cost Effectiveness' (2018) 6 *Molecular Genetics and Genomic Medicine* 186–99.

48  Tia Moscarello, Brittney Murray, Chloe Reuter and Erin Demo, 'Direct-to-Consumer Raw Genetic Data and Third-Party Interpretation Services: More Burden than Bargain? (2019) 21 *Genetics in Medicine* 539–41.

49  Australian Law Reform Commission, *Essentially Yours: The Protection of Human Genetic Information in Australia* (ALRC Report 96, 2003).

50  Andelka Phillips, 'Reading the Fine Print When Buying Your Genetic Self Online: Direct-to-Consumer Genetic Testing Terms and Conditions' (2017) 37 *New Genetics and Society* 273–95.

has led to the resolution of serious crimes, the most prominent example being the 'Golden State Killer' case in the United States, where the suspect was found to be responsible for at least 13 murders.[51]

Genetic information is significant information conveying details not only about an individual, but also potentially about their family. For this reason, it is protected under privacy legislation in Australia and categorised as sensitive information within the Privacy Act and APPs. Its disclosure is authorised where 'the organisation reasonably believes that the use or disclosure is necessary to lessen or prevent a serious threat to the life, health or safety of another individual who is a genetic relative of the first individual'.[52]

'Genetic discrimination' refers to discrimination against a person on the basis of their genetic predisposition to a characteristic or disease, and is particularly relevant in employment and insurance contexts. The *Disability Discrimination Act 1992* (Cth) includes in its definition of disability 'a disability that may exist in the future (including because of a genetic predisposition to that disability)'.[53] This inclusion protects against discrimination in employment contexts; however, the situation with regard to insurers is less clear due to an exemption in this legislation that allows insurers to discriminate if it is reasonable in the circumstances – for example:

(f) the discrimination is based upon actuarial or statistical data on which it is reasonable for the first-mentioned person to rely; and is reasonable having regard to the matter of the data and other relevant factors; or

(g) in a case where no such actuarial or statistical data is available and cannot reasonably be obtained – the discrimination is reasonable having regard to any other relevant factors.[54]

A 2018 federal parliamentary inquiry into the life insurance industry recommended a ban on the use of predictive genetic test results; however, to date, it has not been implemented.[55]

## Genomic databases

There is wide variation around the world in the regulatory approaches to genomic databases. Even in developed countries such as Australia, the United Kingdom and the United States, legislation is outdated and has not been developed to respond to modern aspects of genomic research.[56] Data analytics and machine learning are rapidly growing fields due to the vast and expanding amount of data available, and there are strong medical, economic and policy motives for it to be utilised.

The Human Genome Organisation's *Imagined Futures* document outlines likely future issues associated with data security, privacy and trust.[57] Considerations associated with

51  Chris Phillips, 'The Golden State Killer Investigation and the Nascent Field of Forensic Genealogy' (2018) 36 *Forensic Science International: Genetics* 186.

52  *Privacy Act 1988* (Cth), s 16B(4).

53  Ibid, s 4.

54  *Disability Discrimination Act 1992* (Cth), s 46(1)(f)–(g).

55  Parliamentary Joint Committee Services on Corporations and Financial Services, *Life Insurance Industry* (27 March 2018).

56  Michelle Taylor-Sands and Chris Gyngell, 'Legality of Embryonic Gene Editing in Australia' (2018) 26 *Journal of Law and Medicine* 356–73.

57  Benjamin Capps et al, *Imagined Futures: Capturing the Benefits of Genome Sequencing for Society* (HUGO Committee on Ethics, Law and Society, 2013).

storing genomic data in repositories include consent to data inclusion, how data can be used, and the threats of human error, hacking and the interoperability of different storage formats. More recently, the Global Alliance for Genomics and Health[58] has engaged in the development of standards and frameworks for genomic data sharing internationally, and the Nuffield Council on Bioethics has identified scientific developments related to crime and security as a key issue on the horizon for the field.[59] From a public health perspective, data from populations can be integrated with other population and personal health data, as well as a wide range of data about such diverse arenas as economics, the environment and consumer behaviour, to inform public health interventions, targeting and expenditure. The All of Us initiative in the United States, which plans to sequence the genomes of a million Americans, is an early step towards databases that will enable this level of integration.[60]

The collection of genomic information from a growing range of sources has a wide range of potential applications and implications. It has potential security benefits, such as using DNA profiling in the prevention, investigation and prosecution of crime. Another application is the use of big data analytics to generate important health information. Both developments give rise to concerns about individual privacy rights, discrimination, ownership of personal data, data integration and profit motive, to the extent that private companies obtain genomic information. Such concerns are particularly important in the absence of democratic accountability. The 'surveillance state' and social credit system established in China provide an extreme possible development, but it demonstrates how imperative it is for countries such as Australia to responsibly regulate the development and security of genomic databases and their integration with other forms of data. Big data analytics adds a new dimension to the risks of genomic databases. A prominent recent example is law enforcement agencies accessing commercial ancestry databases to identify suspects in cases involving serious offences.[61]

It is important that governments examine the ethical and legal issues arising from the rapid growth of collections of human genomic data and its integration with other data sources. This should build on established ethical and legal principles already identified, such as: respect for persons, human rights, participation of those with morally relevant interests, and accountability to ensure that appropriate regulation and policy is developed, internationally.[62] Australian regulators must collaborate with those in other countries such as the United Kingdom and the United States, given the globalised nature of information exchange. They should also examine potential combined uses of personal genomic data, biometric data, big data analytics and machine learning analytic tools for public health and security contexts to ensure that governance arrangements are effective, given the increasing applications of genomic information, spanning clinical care, research, direct-to-consumer health and ancestry screening. Examining the potential for integration with other relevant

58  Global Alliance for Linked Genomics and Health, *Enabling Responsible Linked Genomic Data Sharing for the Benefit of Human Health* (2019). Available: <https://www.ga4gh.org>.

59  Nuffield Council on Bioethics, *Horizon Scanning Workshops* (2019). Available: <http://nuffieldbioethics.org/future-work/horizon-scanning-workshops>.

60  Greg Feero et al, 'Precision Medicine, Genome Sequencing, and Improved Population Health' (2018) 319 *Journal of the American Medical Association* 1979–80.

61  Thomas May, 'Sociogenetic Risks: Ancestry DNA Testing, Third-Party Identity and Protection of Privacy' (2018) 379 *New England Journal of Medicine* 410–12.

62  Nuffield Council on Bioethics, *The Collection, Linking and Use of Data in Biomedical Research and Health Care: Ethical Issues* (2015).

biometric and non-biometric information, such as financial data, social security records, personal health app data, and facial recognition templates, will also be important. Potential theft of genomic information by state and non-state actors is described in the literature, as are calls for further work to examine best practice in relation to the protection of genomic data and the harmonisation of laws internationally that govern the generation of, access to and sharing of this information.[63]

## Property rights in genes

As discussed earlier in the chapter, in relation to the cases *Moore v Regents of the University of California*[64] and *Washington University v Catalona*,[65] courts have held that a person's discarded or donated tissue ceases to be their property once scientists undertake work to isolate cell lines or create a research biobank. In the case *Greenburg v Miami Children's Hospital Research Institute Inc*,[66] the court held that the tissue provided by a patient was not their property and the gene responsible for their disease (the Canavan gene) that was identified by scientists, and later patented, was the property of the scientists and the hospital. In *Association for Molecular Pathology v Myriad Genetics Inc*,[67] the US Supreme Court rejected biotechnology company Myriad Genetics' right to patent diagnostic tests for the BRCA1 and BRCA2 gene mutations that form a basis for identifying those at risk of developing breast and ovarian cancer. The court found that merely identifying a gene was not a basis for a patent: 'genes and the information they encode are not patent eligible … simply because they have been isolated from the surrounding genetic material'.[68]

In Australian litigation, *D'Arcy v Myriad Genetics Inc*,[69] the High Court determined that claims to isolated gene sequences of the BRCA1 breast cancer gene were not patentable. This result overturned a decision of the Federal Court, in light of the US Supreme Court decision the previous year. The High Court stated in relation to the subordinate court's decision:

> Myriad submitted, as the Full Court had held, that its claims are for a product. To assess patentability, it said, they must be construed in the same way as any other claim for an invention which is a product. The product was 'a chemical compound [which] has no counterpart in nature.' That characterisation of the claims superficially accords with their form.
>
> The approach taken by the Full Court and urged by Myriad involves an apparently straightforward characterisation based on the formal terms of the patent identifying the isolated nucleic acids as products which, notwithstanding their derivation from naturally occurring DNA, have been brought into existence by human artifice and, in that sense, 'made'. So characterised, and without further inquiry into the breadth of the claims or their substance, they could be seen to fall comfortably within principles attracting characterisation as a manner of manufacture. None of the purposive or policy factors mentioned earlier in these reasons need be considered on that approach …

63 Kavita Berger and Phyllis Schneck, 'National and Transnational Security Implications of Asymmetric Access to and Use of Biological Data' (2019) 7 *Frontiers in Bioengineering and Biotechnology* 21–5.
64 793 P 2d 479 (1990).
65 437 F Supp 2d 985 (2006).
66 262 D Supp 2d 1064 (2003).
67 133 S Ct 2107 (2013).
68 Ibid 2120.
69 (2015) 258 CLR 334.

Ms D'Arcy submitted that none of the chemical, structural or functional differences between isolated nucleic acids and nucleic acids in the cellular environment, relied upon by Myriad, plays any part in the definition of the invention as claimed in each of the claims. She invoked the observation of the plurality opinion of the Supreme Court of the United States in *Myriad* directed to a common feature of the claims in issue in that case and the claims in issue in this case:

> Myriad's claims are simply not expressed in terms of chemical composition, nor do they rely in any way on the chemical changes that result from the isolation of a particular section of DNA. Instead, the claims understandably focus on the genetic information encoded in the BRCA1 and BRCA2 genes.

That characterisation, so far as it emphasises the focus of the claims on genetic information, is applicable to the claims in this case and, contrary to the view of the Full Court, should be accepted.[70]

The High Court found that the isolated gene sequences were not a 'manner of manufacture' within section 18(1)(a) of the *Patents Act 1990* (Cth):

> Although it may be said in a formal sense that the invention as claimed, referring to isolated nucleic acids, embodies a product created by human action, that is not sufficient to support its characterisation as a manner of manufacture. The substance of the invention as claimed and the considerations flowing from its substance militate against that characterisation. To include it within the scope of a 'manner of manufacture' involves an extension of that concept, which is not appropriate for judicial determination. Further, to include this class of claim within that concept would not contribute to coherence in the law as was the case in *Apotex*. Nor do Australia's international obligations and the differently framed patent laws of other jurisdictions, which were referred to earlier in these reasons, support the conclusion that this class of claim should fall within the concept.
>
> The invention as claimed in Claims 1 to 3 does not meet the requirement of s 18(1)(a) and the appeal should be allowed.[71]

# Future issues

The expanding use of genomic data raises a number of wider ethical concerns relating to individual privacy, autonomy and democratic accountability. Most states around the world permit the taking of genetic data at arrest, including of juveniles in some states, and not all have mechanisms for the subsequent destruction of those samples and resulting data if the arrestee is not charged.[72] In 2019, the Trump Administration in the United States proposed using genetic testing on detained, undocumented immigrants as a way of determining family relationships.[73] However, fundamental ethical and legal principles must be maintained, notwithstanding the undoubted and increasing benefits to security and public health that genomic databases provide.

---

70  Ibid, [86], [87] and [90].
71  Ibid, per majority judgment of French CJ, Kiefel, Bell and Keene JJ at [94]–[95] (footnotes omitted).
72  See, eg, in the United States, Federal Bureau of Investigation, *CODIS – NDIS Statistics July 2019* (2019). Available: <https://www.fbi.gov/services/laboratory/biometric-analysis/codis/ndis-statistics>.
73  Axios, *Trump Admin Proposes DNA Testing on Detained, Undocumented Immigrants* (30 August 2019). Available: <https://www.axios.com/undocumented-immigrants-dna-testing-dhs-doj-detained-871679cc-c863-4998-917c-e4f8c68063c9.html>.

As will be discussed in Chapter 6, DNA identification has a history of successful use in the criminal justice system to investigate serious crime. Databases utilising (non-coding) genomic information were established around the world by the early 2000s, and forensic techniques in this area continue to expand.[74] DNA is now widely used as an identifier in security contexts. Law enforcement agencies have integrated databases where one identifier is linked to others (eg DNA identification–fingerprint identification–photographs–intelligence reports). So, a person's DNA can be linked to these other forms of information about them, and vice versa, if a suspect's identity was not otherwise known.[75]

DNA databases have proven highly effective in the identification of offenders and the prosecution of serious crimes such as murder and sexual assault, as well as in exonerating innocent persons previously convicted of crimes.[76] However, universal forensic databases that include the DNA profiles of an entire jurisdiction, irrespective of whether those included have been convicted – or even suspected – of committing any crime, could unjustifiably compromise individual privacy and autonomy. Further, the capacity to link or integrate genomic information with other data sources adds to these concerns. For instance, biometric facial image templates can be used, in conjunction with digital images sourced from CCTV, phone GPS data, and internet history, to provide an increasingly complete picture of an individual's movements and lifestyle which could be linked to genomic information.[77]

A range of ethics and policy challenges will arise in the future in this area in relation to genomic data being collected or provided for one purpose, such as greater understanding of personal health, but at a later point in time being used for other purposes. These include potential conflicts:

- between securing public goods and individual rights – for example, with informed consent in relation to the collection of genomic information, and with privacy and autonomy rights in relation to access and use of individuals' data
- between using data collected for health purposes in population-wide genomic databases for forensic purposes in law enforcement or national security purposes
- between securing financial gain at the expense of individual rights in the private sector, particularly in the absence of effective and timely regulation.

More extensive utilisation of genomic information and databases will lead to greater risks, or greater implications of existing risks, due to more information being held. These include:

- data security breaches
- use of information for unauthorised purposes
- genetic discrimination
- sale of data without consent[78]
- increased surveillance through the integration genomic and other data sets
- the potential for pre-emptive incarceration to occur on the basis of genomic status.

---

74  See, eg, Marcus Smith, *DNA Evidence in the Australian Legal System* (Lexis Nexis, 2016).

75  Australian Criminal Intelligence Commission, *Annual Report 2017–18: National Information and Intelligence Sharing Services* (2018). Available: <www.acic.gov.au/publications/annual-reports/australian-criminal-intelligence-commission-annual-report-2017-18>.

76  Seumas Miller and Ian Gordon, *Investigative Ethics* (Wiley Blackwell, 2014).

77  Marcus Smith, Monique Mann and Gregor Urbas, *Biometrics, Crime and Security* (Routledge, 2018).

78  Melanie Evans, 'DNA Data Shared in Ways Patients May Find Surprising', *Wall Street Journal*, 12 August 2019. Available: <https://www.wsj.com/articles/deals-give-drugmakers-rights-to-dna-data-11565607602>.

While there are existing ethical guidelines and regulations relating to the use of genomic information and databases in clinical practice, for commercial purposes, in criminal investigation and in other contexts, there are significant gaps where these areas overlap. There is a need to review, update and develop ethical guidelines, law and policy governing the use of linked genomic databases, including those relating to privacy, ownership, data sharing, and use by third parties such as private companies and government agencies.

# Assisted reproductive technology

Approximately one in six couples around the world experience infertility.[79] Assisted reproductive technologies (ARTs), including in vitro fertilisation (IVF), have revolutionised treatment of the condition and are now widely used around the world. 'ART' refers to a wide range of treatments that seek to improve the chances of achieving a pregnancy – each directed at different causes of infertility. These are now briefly explained to ensure the following regulatory discussion is clear. In Australia, tens of thousands of women have received ART treatment – equivalent to one in 25 children born in Australia.[80] These figures continue to rise, meaning that the technology is likely to be more widely utilised in coming years, and the associated issues will become increasingly prevalent. This discussion will consider the regulation of ART, including the prohibition of cloned and hybrid human embryos, pre-implantation genetic diagnosis, mitochondrial donation, egg freezing and surrogacy. Key terms are explained in Box 4.1.

## BOX 4.1   KEY TERMS IN REPRODUCTIVE TECHNOLOGY

*Artificial insemination* is used to overcome mechanical difficulties with intercourse or where semen has been frozen – for example, prior to cancer treatment. Semen is inserted into the uterus at the time of ovulation.

*Donor eggs* are used where eggs are of low quality, such as due to age, there is a history of miscarriage, or there is a high chance of a genetic condition being passed on. In this case, hormone medications are prescribed to stimulate the production of eggs, which are retrieved and placed together with sperm from the female's partner or donor. Once the embryos have formed, one is inserted into the uterus. In rare cases where donor eggs and sperm are required, *donor embryos* can also be used.

*Donor insemination* is used in cases where a male does not produce sperm, or there are abnormalities with it, or there is a high chance of a genetic condition being passed on; or by single women or women in same-sex relationships.

*Intra-cytoplasmic sperm injection* (ICSI) is similar to IVF, but is specifically undertaken to address problems with the male's sperm. The main difference is that ICSI involves directly injecting a single sperm into individual eggs to achieve fertilisation.

---

79   Marcia Inhorn and Pasquale Patrizio, 'Infertility Around the Globe: New Thinking on Gender, Reproductive Technologies and Global Movements in the 21st Century' (2015) 21 *Human Reproductive Update* 411–26.

80   Katie Harris et al, *Assisted Reproduction Technology in Australia and New Zealand 2014* (University of New South Wales, 2016).

*In vitro fertilisation* is used in a number of circumstances to assist with achieving a pregnancy. In this approach, eggs are collected, together with a partner's or donor's sperm, and placed in a culture dish to allow fertilisation. If this takes place, the embryo is placed into the female's uterus.

*Mitochondrial DNA* exists outside of a nucleus in the mitochondrion, the component of cells responsible for energy production. This DNA is passed maternally through the egg cell.

*Non-invasive prenatal testing* (NIPT) is undertaken to detect genetic abnormalities such as Down syndrome (also called trisomy 21). It is a blood test that examines foetal DNA present in the blood of a pregnant woman.

*Oocyte* – a female germ cell involved in reproduction, otherwise referred to as an egg.

*Pre-implantation genetic diagnosis* is a technique used as part of IVF to reduce the risk of passing on genetic conditions. It can be used in single-gene (also known as Mendelian) disorders to identify embryos not affected by the 'faulty' gene, or to determine whether embryos have the correct amount of genetic material. In this process, embryos are first generated through IVF or ICSI, and one or two cells are then removed and screened for a genetic condition. Those found not to be affected are transferred to the female's uterus.

*Surrogacy* involves a woman (known as the surrogate) carrying an embryo for another person or couple with the intention of giving the baby to them at birth.

In Australia, ART is regulated at both the state and federal level. The *Prohibition of Human Cloning for Reproduction Act 2002* (Cth) (PHCR Act) and the *Research Involving Human Embryos Act 2002* (Cth) set out the Australian position, which is reflected in the states' and territories' mirror legislation.[81] Small divergences in the legislation of the states and territories have emerged over time. Under this legislation, even if it were technologically possible, it is prohibited for anyone to reproduce by creating a clone of themselves. The *Research Involving Human Embryos Act* provides that ART treatment can only be undertaken in a licensed facility.[82] The Reproductive Technology Accreditation Committee (RTAC) is responsible for accreditation. RTAC requires that all ART centres be fully compliant with the *National Health and Medical Research Council Ethical Guidelines on the Use of ART in Clinical Practice and Research 2017* (NHMRC Guidelines). The NHMRC notes that:

> There are different views held in the Australian community about the status attributed to a human embryo. To different individuals the same embryo can be seen as a living human entity in the earliest stage of development, a potential life, or a group of cells.[83]

The NHMRC Guidelines have also set out nine principles to inform law and policy relating to the use of ART in Australia. They emphasise respect for the autonomy of all relevant parties involved and the potential implications of using this complex technology. The guiding principles state:

81  See, eg, *Human Cloning and Embryo Research Act 2004* (ACT); *Human Cloning for Reproduction and Other Prohibited Practices Act 2003* (NSW).

82  Section 10.

83  National Health and Medical Research Council, *Ethical Guidelines on the Use of Assisted Reproductive Technology in Clinical Practice and Research* (NHMRC, 2017), 21.

1. ART activities must be conducted in a way that shows respect to all involved.
2. The interests and wellbeing of the person who may be born as a result of an ART activity must be an important consideration in all decisions about the activity.
3. ART activities must be undertaken in a manner that minimises harm and maximises the benefit to each individual or couple involved in the ART activity, any persons who may be born as a result of the activity, and any other child within the family unit who may be affected by that birth.
4. Decision-making in the clinical practice of ART must recognise and take into account the biological connections and social relationships that exist or may be formed as a result of the ART activity.
5. Decision-making in the clinical practice of ART must recognise and respect the autonomy of all relevant parties, promoting and supporting the notion of valid consent as a fundamental condition of the use of ART.
6. Decision-making in the clinical practice of ART must recognise that social relationships and social context may affect an individual's or a couple's decision-making and be sensitive to cultural and spiritual differences.
7. Processes and policies for determining an individual's or a couple's eligibility to access ART services must be just, equitable, transparent and respectful of human dignity and the natural human rights of all persons, including the right to not be unlawfully or unreasonably discriminated against.
8. The provision of ART must be underpinned by policies that support effective and efficient practices that minimise interventions not supported by evidence of successful clinical outcomes.
9. The provision of ART must be transparent and open to scrutiny, while ensuring the protection of the privacy of all individuals or couples involved in ART and persons born, to the degree that is protected by law.[84]

# Pre-implantation genetic diagnosis

Pre-implantation genetic diagnosis (PGD) is a form of screening undertaken on the genetic material of an embryo, prior to the implantation, in order to identify whether any medical disorders are present. In the context of IVF treatment, prospective parents would then decide whether or not to use an embryo if it does have a genetic defect. PGD should be distinguished from non-invasive prenatal testing (NIPT). This involves a blood test of a pregnant woman that tests cell-free foetal DNA in maternal blood. In can detect a range of chromosomal disorders, including Down syndrome, and abnormalities relating to the sex-determining chromosomes. In the future, this technique may become obsolete as foetal genome screening becomes more widely available – which itself brings with it issues such as consent and privacy of the unborn foetus. Current issues with NIPT include social pressure to act on the results of tests and terminate abnormal pregnancies.[85]

There are a number of ethical and legal issues of note that are associated with PGD. One is the potential for 'designer babies', where embryos are selected or designed for particular characteristics, such as favourably perceived aesthetic, sporting or intellectual attributes, and how this should be regulated.[86] A further issue is sex selection. The use of PGD for sex selection on a

---

84  Ibid, 20.
85  Isabel Karpin, 'Protecting the Future Well' (2016) 25 *Griffith Law Review* 71.
86  See, eg, James M Kemper, Christopher Gyngell and Julian Savulescu, 'Subsidizing PGD: The Moral Case for Funding Genetic Selection' (2019) 16 *Journal of Bioethical Inquiry* 405.

medical basis, such as to prevent the transmission of a sex-linked genetic condition, is accepted practice.[87] However, the NHMRC Guidelines prohibit sex selection for non-medical reasons, and this has meant that clinics in Australia cannot offer this service and maintain their accreditation. Legislation also prohibits the practice. In Victoria, the *Assisted Reproductive Treatment Act 2008* (Vic) only allows it to take place at the discretion of the Patient Review Panel.[88] In *JS and LS v Patient Review Panel*,[89] a couple argued that they should be allowed to access the technique as they had lost a previous child and wanted to replace that child with one of the same sex. They argued that one reason they should be granted permission was that the experience had been psychologically traumatic for them. The Panel rejected their request, noting that they had not sufficiently addressed a key element of the legislation – namely, whether the actions would promote the wellbeing of the child that would be born. A third potential application of PGD is to conceive a child that is a compatible tissue donor for an existing child that requires the tissue for treatment of a medical condition. The NHMRC Guidelines state that this should only be permitted in the case of siblings. A child born in these circumstances is referred to as a 'saviour sibling'.[90] Finally, and most contentiously, there are cases where parents wish to select a child with the same disability as themselves or an existing child, such as blindness or deafness. This is not permitted under the NHMRC Guidelines or legislation.[91]

According to the Guidelines, PGD may only be used in three circumstances. These are to:

- select against genetic conditions, diseases or abnormalities that would severely limit the quality of life of the person who would be born
- select an embryo with compatible tissue for subsequent stem cell therapy intended for a parent, sibling or other relative
- increase the likelihood of a live birth.[92]

The Guidelines state that PGD 'may not be used to preferentially select in favour of a genetic condition, disease or abnormality that would severely limit the quality of life of the person who would be born'.[93] They acknowledge that it is not possible to specify a list of the genetic conditions in which it is acceptable for PGD to be used, but provide a set of criteria for assessing ethical acceptability. These include the impact the condition is likely to have, and the circumstances of the parents, such as:

- current evidence and expert opinion on the impact of the condition, disease or abnormality on the quality of life of the person who would be born, including the anticipated symptoms, age-of-onset and the degree/spectrum or severity of the condition, disease or abnormality
- the concerns of the intended parent(s) about their ability to care for a person born with the condition, disease or abnormality
- the availability and accessibility of therapies or interventions to reduce the severity, delay onset or minimise the impact of the condition, disease or abnormality

87  NHMRC Guidelines, 8.13.
88  *Assisted Reproductive Treatment Act 2008* (Vic), s 28(2)(b).
89  [2011] VCAT 856.
90  Sandra Samardzic, 'Saviour Siblings – Current Overview, Dilemmas and Possible Solutions?' (2019) 12 *Medicine, Law & Society* 89.
91  See, eg, Isabel Karpin, 'Choosing Disability: Preimplantation Genetic Diagnosis and Negative Enhancement' (2007) 15 *Journal of Law and Medicine* 89.
92  NHMRC Guidelines, 8.15.1.
93  Ibid, 8.15.2.

- the limitations of the technology, including the likelihood of false positive and false negative results
- the experiences of individuals and families living with the condition, disease or abnormality
- the potential for stigma to influence the perceived impact of the condition, disease or abnormality on the quality of life of the person who would be born
- the extent of social support available to the intended parent(s) and to the person who would be born.[94]

## Mitochondrial donation

In 2015, the United Kingdom legalised the use of technology that allows embryos to be created that are combined with donor mitochondria (the part of the cell that produces energy). This enabled the treatment of previously incurable forms of debilitating mitochondrial disease, which causes severe disability.[95] The treatment involves taking the nuclear genetic material from the mother and inserting it into a donor egg that has had all genetic material except the mitochondrial DNA removed. The embryo is then fertilised and placed in the mother's uterus and the child will then have the genetic material of three people: the mother, the female mitochondrial donor and the father.[96]

Despite the fact that mitochondrial disease affects approximately one in 500 births, mitochondrial donation is currently prohibited in Australia because it would contravene the PHCR Act.

A person commits an offence if:

**(a)** the person intentionally creates or develops a human embryo by a process of the fertilisation of a human egg by a human sperm outside the body of a woman; and
**(b)** the human embryo contains genetic material provided by more than 2 persons.[97]

In 2018, the Australian Senate Community Affairs References Committee recommended that the government begin taking steps towards legalising mitochondrial donation as part of its inquiry, *Science of Mitochondrial Donation and Related Matters*.[98] It also recommended that, in the interim, the Australian government should negotiate with the UK government to facilitate Australian patients being treated in that jurisdiction:

> The committee notes the strong potential of mitochondrial donation to address the debilitating effects of inheriting mitochondrial disease. The committee recommends that public consultation be undertaken regarding the introduction of mitochondrial donation to Australian clinical practice. To facilitate this consultation, the committee further recommends the Australian Government prepare a consultation paper, including

94  Ibid, 8.18.5.
95  Zosia Kmietowicz, 'UK Becomes First Country to Allow Mitochondrial Donation' (2015) 350 *British Medical Journal* 1103.
96  Rosa Castro, 'Mitochondrial Replacement Therapy: The UK and US Regulatory Landscapes' (2016) 3 *Journal of Law and the Biosciences* 726.
97  Section 13.
98  Senate Community Affairs References Committee, *Science of Mitochondrial Donation and Related Matters* (Parliament of Australia, 2018).

options for legislative change that would be required. The Minister for Health should seek advice from the National Health and Medical Research Council on the most appropriate timing and format for this consultation.[99]

The committee recommends, noting the need for community consultation and scientific review, the urgency of treatment for current patients and the small number of patients seeking this treatment, that the Australian Government initiate dialogue with the relevant authorities in the United Kingdom to facilitate access for Australian patients to the United Kingdom treatment facility as an interim measure.[100]

## Oocyte preservation and surrogacy

Oocyte freezing technology, using a technique known as *vitrification,* has made it possible to freeze eggs (in addition to sperm and embryos). Egg freezing for social reasons, such as waiting to have children until a person finds an appropriate partner, is financially secure, or is at a convenient point in their career, is now possible.[101] Some employers, such as Google, offer to pay for their employees to freeze their eggs, as part of their health insurance package.[102] Given the costs associated with the technology, it may be difficult for many to access egg freezing without the assistance of an employer or insurer. However, as with many areas of technology, these costs are likely to decrease over time. Surrogacy, involving a woman carrying to term a foetus to which she is not biologically related, is also possible and becoming more common. Commercial surrogacy, involving a fee arrangement, is prohibited throughout Australia, but altruistic surrogacy, where no payment is exchanged, is legal.[103] One exception is the Northern Territory, which does not have any laws governing surrogacy but is in the process of law reform in this area.[104]

# Developing forms of health technology

The technologies dealt with in this part of the chapter include biotechnology, nanotechnology, artificial intelligence and public health surveillance. Biotechnology is an area of biology that utilises living organisms to make products, encompassing recombinant gene technology, also known as gene editing. 'Nanotechnology' refers to the convergence of biology and engineering to create extraordinarily small devices, pharmaceuticals and other products. Artificial intelligence employs algorithms to analyse data and make decisions – a digital recreation of human intelligence. It is being applied in areas of medicine such as pathology to diagnose disease in images of human tissue. A summary of key terms in these areas is provided in Box 4.2.

 99  Ibid, Recommendation 1.
100  Ibid, Recommendation 4.
101  Vinney Gunnala and Glenn Schattman, 'Oocyte Vitrification for Elective Fertility Preservation' (2017) 29 *Current Opinion in Obstetrics and Gynecology* 59.
102  Christine Ro, 'The Workplaces that Will Pay for Surrogacy', *British Broadcasting Corporation*, 12 September 2019.
103  See, eg, *Surrogacy Act 2010* (NSW); *Assisted Reproductive Treatment Act 2008* (Vic).
104  See, eg, Government of the Northern Territory, *A Conversation about Surrogacy in the Northern Territory: Discussion Paper* (NT Government, 2019).

## BOX 4.2  KEY TERMS IN BIOTECHNOLOGY

*Artificial gametes* are artificial sperm and egg cells that have been made from embryonic stem cells or adult cells.

*Artificial intelligence* refers to the development of computer systems that can perform tasks that involve decision-making in a manner usually associated with human cognitive function.

*Biotechnology* is the application of biological systems or living organisms to make or modify products.

A *chimera* is a single organism composed of two different sets of DNA. This can occur when a mother is carrying twins and one twin dies early in the pregnancy, and the surviving twin takes on some of its cells. It can also occur during bone marrow transplants.

*Cloning* refers to the production of genetically identical copies of a biological entity. Researchers have cloned individual genes, cells and entire organisms, such as sheep and monkeys.

*CRISPR* (Clustered, Regularly Interspaced, Short Palindromic Repeats) is short for CRISPR/Cas9. It is an enzyme that can be used to cut strands of DNA. This technology has allowed gene editing to become more efficient, and may lead to cures for genetic diseases such as cystic fibrosis.

*Hybrid* refers to an organism that is a result of combined genetic material from two species. Research in this field has been directed at the prospect of using animals for human organ transplants.

*Induced pluripotent stem cells* (iPS) are adult cells, such as skin cells or blood cells, that have been genetically reprogramed to a state equivalent to an embryonic stem cell by being forced to express genes and other factors that maintain the properties of embryonic stem cells. Tissues that are derived from iPS will be a match to the cell donor and can be used to avoid immune rejection.

*Nanotechnology* refers to the study of materials and products at scales below 100 nanometres.

*Somatic cell nuclear transfer* (SCNT) is the process of creating an embryo by combining the nucleus of a body cell with an egg cell that has had its nucleus removed.

*Stem cells* are human cells that have the ability to develop into many different types of cells, such as skin cells or muscle cells. Embryonic stem cells from unused embryos are pluripotent and can develop into any kind of cells. Adult stem cells can usually only develop into cells of the same kind; however, scientists have developed the ability to reprogram them in the laboratory.

## Gene editing

CRISPR (Clustered, Regularly Interspaced, Short Palindromic Repeats) is a gene editing technique that has recently been developed in association with the Cas9 DNA-cutting enzyme. The capacity to cut-and-paste DNA has enormous scientific potential, including the capacity to correct and improve genes.

> CRISPR's greatest contribution will surely be the sheer pace, depth, and breath [sic] of applications and findings it permits ... consideration of the public good deserve[s] far greater consideration in making sure that these rapid advances become shared benefits

[for] scientific, clinical, and patient and family associations, governmental agencies, and interdisciplinary policy institutes.[105]

From a legal and ethical perspective, the most contentious aspect of CRISPR/Cas9 is its potential impact in the field of assisted reproductive technology. It has the potential to edit the genetic material in embryos that contain mutations associated with diseases such as cystic fibrosis. As was discussed in the previous section, this raises issues such as a parent's right to select a child with a particular genetic make-up, eugenics and the nature of the human race itself. The CRISPR/Cas9 technology is so complex and powerful that it could change the human genome in unforeseeable ways. If these changes are passed on to future generations, there are potential implications for the human race as a whole that need to be considered.[106] The Committee on Ethics, Law and Society (CELS) of the Human Genome Organisation (HUGO) on CRISPR/Cas9 is continuing to work through the ethical, legal and social issues of this technology.

The regulatory landscape in this area is still developing. In 2019, it was announced that the Australian government will not regulate gene-editing techniques in plants, animals and human cell lines in cases where new genetic material is not introduced.[107] This follows a decision in 2018 by the US Department of Agriculture which excluded gene-edited plants from regulatory oversight altogether. In contrast with this approach, the Court of Justice of the European Union ruled in 2018 that it would define any form of gene-edited crops as genetically modified organisms and place them under stringent regulation.[108] Given the implications of this technology, it is important that governments work together to develop consistent approaches around the world.

## Cloning and stem cell technology

The field of cloning and stem cell technology has been an important area of scientific advancement over the past 25 years. A major breakthrough was the cloning of Dolly the sheep from an adult sheep cell in 2007 at the University of Edinburgh in Scotland. Since that time a range of other animals have been cloned (including monkeys) and the technique may have an important role to play in saving endangered species.[109]

The United States prohibited human cloning for reproductive purposes in 1997, and this was followed by equivalent Australian legislation in 2002. The *Prohibition of Human Cloning for Reproduction Act 2002* (Cth) prohibits 'placing a human embryo clone in the human body or the body of an animal',[110] as well as the creation of hybrids and chimeras,[111] and indeed

105  John Mulvihill et al, 'The International Human Genome Organisation Committee of Ethics, Law and Society: Ethical Issues of CRISPR Technology and Gene Editing through the Lens of Solidarity' (2017) 122 *British Medical Bulletin* 17, 23.

106  Adam Cribbs and Sumeth Perera, 'Science and Bioethics of CRISPR-Cas9 Gene Editing: An Analysis Towards Separating Facts and Fiction' (2017) 90 *Yale Journal of Biology and Medicine* 625.

107  Smriti Mallapaty, 'Australian Gene-Editing Rules Adopt "Middle Ground"' *Nature*, 23 April 2019.

108  Ibid.

109  The research that produced Dolly also discovered that adult cells can be reprogramed into induced pluripotent stem cells. Regarding cloning, see, eg, Dennis Normile, 'These Monkey Twins Are the First Primate Clones Made by the Method that Developed Dolly', *Science*, 24 January 2018.

110  *Prohibition of Human Cloning for Reproduction Act 2002* (Cth), s 9.

111  Ibid, ss 17 and 18.

any forms of genetic modification that are inheritable.[112] A licensing scheme has been introduced regarding cloning for research purposes.[113] The *Research Involving Human Embryos Act 2002* (Cth) (RIHE Act) provides further details of the licensing system, related offences, and the monitoring and reporting processes.

Scientists have sought to use embryonic stem cells in research, due to their potential to develop new treatments for serious diseases. Under this legislation, it is permissible to harvest embryonic stem cells from embryos that had been created using ART and were excess to needs; however, it remains prohibited to create an embryo using IVF for the purpose of scientific research. In 2007, when cloning techniques became more advanced, it became possible to create pluripotent stem cells using somatic cell nuclear transfer (SCNT). The legislation allows SCNT embryos to be used for research purposes, but the PHCR Act states that these cannot be developed beyond 14 days and only enucleated human egg cells may be used for this purpose.

A person commits an offence if the person intentionally develops a human embryo outside the body of a woman for a period of more than 14 days, excluding any period when development is suspended.[114]

The advancements that enable the development of induced pluripotent stem cells (iPS) from adult skin cells avoid the destruction of an embryo as part of the process. The potential exists for this to lead to human cloning, the development of entire organs, and the possibility of two men or two women having an offspring that is genetically related to both of them. Under the PHCR Act, cloning remains an offence in the following situations:

**(3)**  A person commits an offence if the person intentionally places an embryo in the body of a woman knowing that, or reckless as to whether, the embryo is a prohibited embryo.

**(4)**  In this section:

'*prohibited embryo*' means:

**(a)**  a human embryo created by a process other than the fertilisation of a human egg by human sperm; or ...

**(f)**  a human embryo that contains a human cell (within the meaning of section 15) whose genome has been altered in such a way that the alteration is heritable by human descendants of the human whose cell was altered.[115]

If researchers wanted to create an embryo via iPS for the purpose of research, this may be permissible if they were licensed under s 22 of the PHCR Act, and the relevant sections of the RIHE Act.

---

112   Ibid, s 15.
113   Ibid, ss 22–23C.
114   Ibid, s 14. Section 18 of the PHCR Act makes it is an offence to create a hybrid embryo, and s 22 requires a licence to be obtained for the conduct of these activities, as provided by Division 4 of the RIHE Act. The NHMRC Embryo Research Licensing Committee reports on this to Parliament on a six-monthly basis: National Health and Medical Research Council, *Embryo Research Licensing Committee: Reports to Parliament* (2020). Available: <https://www.nhmrc.gov.au/research-policy/embryo-research-licensing/embryo-research-licensing-committee-reports-parliament>.
115   Section 20(3), (4)(a) and (f).

A distinct recent issue in relation to stem cells is the advertisement by entrepreneurial doctors of experimental stem cell treatments for a wide range of medical conditions for which there is no proven therapeutic benefit. In 2019, a Sydney-based cosmetic medicine practitioner was disqualified from practice following the death of a patient after a liposuction procedure.[116] The purpose of the procedure was to obtain adipose-derived stem cells with the scientifically unsupported objective of treating her advanced dementia.

> According to the NSW Deputy Coroners' Report, Dr Bright had removed approximately 500 mL of fat from Mrs Drysdale's flanks and buttocks on the day of the intervention. This tissue was then 'processed' in the clinic's laboratory to derive '1.5 billion stem cells' for subsequent intravenous administration later that day. In the immediate postoperative period, Mrs Drysdale was noted to be drowsy and hypotensive. Even though Mrs Drysdale was being monitored and administered medications to assist in her recovery, she continued to deteriorate and died at her nursing home less than 3 hours after being discharged …
>
> What makes her death so profoundly tragic, however, is that it occurred as a complication of an intervention for which there is no scientific support. While there are some preclinical data and (weak) evidence from clinical trials to suggest that autologous adipose-derived mesenchymal stem cells may have some benefit for the treatment of arthritis and other joint or muscular injuries, there is *no* published scientific research that indicates *any* benefit for patients with dementia.[117]

Further regulation in this area of the law is needed to prevent desperate patients being taken advantage of and risking their lives for treatment that has no chance of improving their condition.

## Nanotechnology

'Nanotechnology' refers to the convergence of the fields of biology and engineering to create devices that are extraordinarily small (one billionth of a metre), the size of individual atoms or molecules. The term 'nanoscale' refers to a size range of between approximately 1 and 100 nanometres. Nanotechnology is used in a range of industries, including cosmetics and food production, but has the potential to revolutionise the healthcare sector.[118]

Nanotechnology is a rapidly developing area of investment, research and development for pharmaceutical companies and in the future is likely to be combined with gene therapy to create personalised medical treatments.[119] Nanoscale devices have the potential to enter human cells and interact with DNA and proteins, allowing for more efficient diagnosis and treatment of disease. For example, it may be possible to engineer more specific cancer therapies that target only malignant cells, leading to more effective treatments with less impact on the patient.[120] Some current examples are listed in Table 4.1.

---

116   Tamra Lysaght et al, 'The Deadly Business of an Unregulated Global Stem Cell Industry' (2017) 43 *Journal of Medical Ethics* 744.
117   Ibid, 746.
118   Ian Kerridge, Michael Lowe and Cameron Stewart, *Ethics and Law for the Health Professions* (Federation Press, 2013), 1121–2.
119   Thomas Faunce and Tim Vines, 'Biotechnology and Nanotechnology Regulation in Australia'. In Ben White, Fiona McDonald and Lindy Willmott (eds), *Health Law in Australia* (Thomson Reuters, 2014).
120   Anna Cattaneo et al, 'Nanotechnology and Human Health: Risks and Benefits' (2010) 30 *Journal of Applied Toxicology* 730.

**Table 4.1**   Examples of Therapeutic Goods Administration-approved 'nano' medicines[121]

| Commercial name | Active Ingredient | Indication |
| --- | --- | --- |
| AMBISOME® | Amphotericin B | Fungal infections |
| CAELYX® | Doxorubicin | Cancer |
| ABRAXANE® | Albumin-bound paclitaxel | Cancer |
| RISPERDAL CONSTA® | Risperidone | Schizophrenia |

The rise of nanotechnology raises a number of issues, such as patient and environmental safety, access to nanotechnology products in the context of some uncertainty about longer-term impacts.[122] Because this technology has many applications in a range of industries, there is no single agency responsible for regulating nanotechnology, but responsibility is shared across several, including the National Industrial Chemicals Notification and Assessment Scheme (NICNAS), which regulates industrial chemicals and cosmetics; the Australian Pesticide and Veterinarian Medicines Association (APVMA) in relation to pesticides or veterinary medicines; the Therapeutic Goods Administration (TGA), which regulates medicines and medical devices; and Food Standards Australia New Zealand (FSANZ), which regulates foods and food packaging.

The nanotechnology industry in Australia will continue to develop, and more specific regulation will be required to balance innovation with public health and safety. There have been proposals in the literature for a regulatory framework with specific legislation providing for a combination of public-sector and industry regulation, public education, and mandatory disclosure of the use of nanotechnology in products.[123]

# Artificial intelligence

Artificial intelligence (AI) is becoming an important tool in clinical medicine. Medicine generates a large amount of complex data, and AI can potentially replace doctors for screening and diagnosis in image- and data-based disciplines. AI incorporates automation to perform monotonous tasks, simplify complex procedures, and gain new diagnostic information using data integrated from laboratory tests and medical imaging. Digital pathology incorporates computer-assisted diagnosis and AI to improve accuracy and efficiency. Studies in the field of pathology have demonstrated positive results. Van et al found digital pathology to be better than traditional microscopy for taking measurements and equivalent in diagnostic accuracy.[124] A study examining the use of AI for quantitative image analysis found that the best-performing AI algorithm outperformed 11 pathologists when analysing whole-slide images from breast cancer biopsies.[125]

---

121   Therapeutic Goods Administration, *Regulation of Nanomedicines* (Australian Government, 2016).
122   Robert Sparrow, 'Revolutionary and Familiar, Inevitable and Precarious: Rhetorical Contradictions in Enthusiasm for Nanotechnology' (2007) 12 *NanoEthics* 57.
123   Shahriar Hossain et al, 'Nanotechnology and its Medical Applications: Revisiting Public Policies from a Regulatory Perspective in Australia' (2017) 6 *Nanotechnology Reviews* 3.
124   Simone Van Es, 'Digital Pathology: Semper ad Meliora' (2019) 51 *Pathology* 1.
125   Babak Bejnordi et al, 'Diagnostic Assessment of Deep Learning Algorithms for Detection of Lymph Node Metastases in Women with Breast Cancer' (2017) 318 *Journal of the American Medical Association* 2199.

In radiology, AI algorithms facilitate automation of many aspects of image analysis. The availability of large amounts of medical imaging data has also proven useful for AI-based training processes. Current research in this field has focused on comparison between algorithms and the performance of expert radiologists. However, these studies may not take into consideration the patient's clinical history, physical examination findings, laboratory results, population and racial demographics, and the inherent subjectivity of interpretations, rending them unreliable.[126] A recent study by McKinney et al found an AI system capable of outperforming six radiologists in breast cancer prediction. The system was used to interpret mammograms in order to identify breast cancer at early stages of the disease, demonstrating great potential for the use of AI in breast cancer screening.[127] In ophthalmology, AI has been applied to diabetic retinopathy, glaucoma and age-related macular degeneration. Algorithms may also provide patients with greater access to screening, diagnosis and monitoring of major ocular diseases in primary and remote health settings.[128]

It is important also to consider the challenges of implementing AI technology alongside the potential benefits of its application in clinical practice, particularly in the context of an increasing number of AI companies in the market, with an expanding capability to process the large amounts of data being generated by digital imaging. First, there are challenges in integrating AI systems into clinical care due to the difficulties in quantifying precisely how algorithms arrive at decisions – this is known as 'black box' data processing. Clinical diagnoses are often complex and require contextual knowledge and experience; diagnostic patterns in medicine can be variable and difficult for AI algorithms to interpret. For this reason, the oversight of clinicians will be crucial in verifying the accuracy and safety of these applications, in order to encourage their integration into routine clinical practice over time. At present, the costs associated with AI systems are a further limiting factor for many practices, and for the healthcare system more broadly; however, these will reduce over time.

From a legal perspective, the question of who will be responsible in the case of a misdiagnosis or other error involving the application of AI technology in clinical practice remains uncertain. Courts will need to determine what clinicians and hospitals are required to do in order to satisfy their duty of care when AI technology is used to make diagnoses or inform their clinical decisions. Clinicians, hospitals, software companies and algorithm developers may all be potentially liable. Given the complexity of AI, determining what went wrong will likely be difficult, and as AI technology provides information to assist rather than replace clinicians in making decisions, it may be unlikely a court would find the developer of the algorithm or software solely liable.

There are three approaches to liability: the clinician/hospital being responsible, the algorithm/software company being responsible, or a shared approach to liability among all parties. The first would focus on whether the clinician acted in accordance with a practice widely accepted by peer professional opinion;[129] the second would focus on whether the

126   Peter Savadjiev et al, 'Demystification of AI-Driven Medical Image Interpretation: Past, Present and Future' (2019) 29 *European Radiology* 1616.

127   Scott McKinney, Marcin Sieniek and Shravya Shetty, 'International Evaluation of an AI System for Breast Cancer Screening' (2020) 577 *Nature* 89.

128   Avinah Varadarajan et al, 'Deep Learning for Predicting Refractive Error from Retinal Fundus Images' (2018) 59 *Investigative Ophthalmology and Visual Science* 2861.

129   See, eg, *Civil Liability Act 2002* (NSW), s 50; *Civil Liability Act 2003* (Qld), s 22; *Wrongs Act 1958* (Vic), s 59.

algorithm operated within acceptable limits; and the third would avoid assigning fault to a specific person or entity – with each bearing some responsibility for the outcome. The latter approach would address the difficulties in ascertaining how a particular diagnosis was arrived at, but may mean that the AI system would require a form of malpractice insurance to pay claims.[130]

In a regulatory context, these technologies are referred to as software as a medical device (SaMD). The complexity of AI systems and the pace at which AI is being incorporated into several specialties means it is difficult to regulate it adequately using existing law and policy frameworks. The traditional model of regulation for medical devices administered by the TGA is based on pre-market evaluation of a static product, in contrast with AI technology, which applies adaptive techniques that develop over time. The TGA has already acknowledged that the Australian regulatory framework 'may not be well structured to address the potential public health risks posed by SaMD products', and in 2019, conducted a consultation process as part of its review of the existing framework, along with regulators in overseas jurisdictions such as the United States and the European Union.[131] The regulatory framework for the use of AI in healthcare is still developing.

Due to the difficulty in identifying the exact reasoning process an algorithm undertakes, and the fact that they will make specific, individualised predictions and recommendations, adapting and becoming more complex as they incorporate more data, it is not feasible to use clinical trials (the usual approach the TGA would use to evaluate medical devices and pharmaceuticals) as a process to ensure quality and safety. A collaborative approach is most likely to be adopted for the regulation of AI technologies. These would incorporate a review of data quality and validation prior to clinical use, in association with ongoing monitoring involving clinicians, hospitals, specialist colleges and insurance companies, under the oversight of the TGA, and a requirement that all diagnoses made by AI systems are reviewed by a clinician.

The use of AI in clinical practice is rapidly advancing, with great potential to improve efficiency in coming decades, as long as the technology is carefully regulated, and operated under the supervision of clinicians.[132] The associated legal and regulatory challenges are complex and will need to be addressed in coming years. They will require the collaboration of clinicians, hospitals, technology companies, insurers and regulators to ensure clinicians can incorporate the best available technology to determine the most appropriate clinical approach in partnership with patients.

## Public health surveillance

The coronavirus (COVID-19) pandemic had a massive global impact, with millions of infections and deaths, and a severe contraction in economies around the world. While most infected individuals only experienced mild respiratory illness, for the elderly and those

---

130    Ibid.

131    Therapeutic Goods Administration, *Regulation of Software, Including Software as a Medical Device* (2019); Federal Drug Administration, *FDA Selects Participants for New Digital Health Software Precertification Pilot Program* (2017). See, also, W Nicholson Price, 'Artificial Intelligence in Health Care: Applications and Legal Issues' (2017) 14 *Scitech Lawyer* 10–13.

132    Rachael Heath Jeffery and Marcus Smith, 'Artificial Intelligence in Ophthalmology: Current Applications and Emerging Issues' (2020) 48 *Clinical and Experimental Ophthalmology* 526.

with underlying medical conditions, it was life threatening.[133] As governments implemented biosecurity powers to force compliance with business closures and social distancing measures, technology was deployed to ensure the law was followed, and to aid in conducting contact tracing of those who contracted the disease. The use of phone metadata to geo-locate individuals and track their movements took place in liberal democracies as the seriousness of the pandemic intensified. Phone applications subsequently introduced by governments in a number of countries communicated with surrounding phones via Bluetooth to record other persons that an individual had been in contact with.[134]

In May 2020, the Australian government announced it was implementing a smartphone application and promoted it as having a low impact on individual privacy.[135] The government did not require citizens to download the application, but initially stated that 10 million people would need to download it in order for it to function effectively.[136] It sought to incentivise its use by highlighting that if this take-up was achieved, social restrictions could be safely eased: 'We need that tool so that we can open up the economy … that's why it's so important.'[137] In less than a month over 6 million people had downloaded the app.[138]

The technology did not use metadata or GPS, but communicated with surrounding phones using Bluetooth, recording those (with the application) that had been in close proximity for a minimum time period. The data was held for 21 days and then deleted. It therefore did not monitor an individual's location: only their phone's relationship to other phones, as it is irrelevant where a person was when they were in close proximity to another person that subsequently tested positive for COVID-19, only that they were at some point close enough to be infected. The data was only decrypted and accessed by public health officials once a person tested positive – and then only consisted of the phone numbers of others they had been in close proximity to, enabling them to be contacted and tested.[139] The functionality of the Bluetooth application was an issue and depended on whether the phone was locked or unlocked; whether the communicating phones utilised Android or iOS operating systems; and the degree of interference between the phones, such as the number of people standing between them.[140] For instance, after a month of use, and despite ongoing updates to address these issues, the Australian Bluetooth application was only performing at a moderate level (25–50 per cent) with regard to locked phones using iOS.[141]

133  World Health Organization, *Coronavirus Disease (COVID-2019) Situation Reports* (2020). Available: <https://www.who.int/emergencies/diseases/novel-coronavirus-2019/situation-reports>.
134  Ariel Bogle, 'Will the Government's Coronavirus App COVIDSafe Keep Your Data Secure? Here's What the Experts Say', *Australian Broadcasting Corporation News*, 27 April 2020.
135  Ibid.
136  Ibid.
137  'The Main Points from Scott Morrison's Latest Coronavirus Update', *Australian Broadcasting Corporation News*, 1 May 2020. Available: <https://www.abc.net.au/news/2020-05-05/morrison-key-points-on-coronavirus-economic-response/12217026>.
138  '6 Million People Have Now Downloaded the COVIDSafe Tracing App', *Australian Broadcasting Corporation News*, 24 May 2020. Available: <https://www.abc.net.au/news/2020-05-24/coronavirus-australia-live-news-covid-19-latest/12280370>.
139  Ariel Bogle, 'Will the Government's Coronavirus App COVIDSafe Keep Your Data Secure? Here's What the Experts Say', *Australian Broadcasting Corporation News*, 27 April 2020.
140  Ariel Bogle, 'COVIDSafe App Tests Revealed iPhone Performance Issues at Launch that Weren't Shared with the Public', *Australian Broadcasting Corporation News*, 17 June 2020.
141  Ibid.

In addition to new applications, the COVID-19 pandemic also brought to light another use for existing metadata: contact tracing and public health order enforcement. Almost as soon as governments implemented social isolation and distancing requirements, smartphone metadata was being used around the world to track the location of individuals who had been diagnosed with COVID-19. While few examples are discussed on the public record, it was reported that police in South Australia accessed the metadata of tourists known to be infected with COVID-19, to identify where in the city they had visited, and people they may had been in contact with. The same systems were used to access metadata for this purpose as were used in a criminal investigation if a threshold is met regarding suspicion of a serious offence. The police stated that COVID-19 placed the community at risk of life-threatening consequences and that this warranted access to metadata: 'In this case, we think there's a genuine risk to public safety, and certainly there's community concern about this, so it's one of the occasions we elected to use it.'[142]

In South Korea, the government went further, relaying individuals' metadata information to the community in public health announcements. The government sent text messages to citizens residing in a specific locality – for instance: 'A woman in her 60s has just tested positive. Click on the link for the places she visited before she was hospitalised.'[143] Such messages may have allowed individuals to be identified.

# Conclusion

This chapter has addressed the legal and regulatory considerations associated with a broad range of technological developments across the healthcare sector. The discussion of technologies in this field was organised into three broad areas: genomics, reproductive technology and developing healthcare technologies. A range of legal issues were covered by the discussion. Confidentiality, privacy and data security are key considerations when dealing with genomic and other forms of health information, particularly given the rate at which it is being generated and utilised. Reproductive technologies, including cloning and stem cell technologies that are associated with the modification of human genetic information, have significant implications for the human race. Careful regulation is therefore vital to ensure that, in coming decades, the potential for harm does not outweigh the benefits of new technologies, such as treating infertility with ART and stem cell therapy. Finally, AI technologies can improve efficiency and increase access to healthcare, yet it remains important that human clinicians oversee automated diagnostic and screening and that, as far as possible, decision-making processes are transparent and auditable.

---

142   Malcolm Sutton, 'Phone Tracking Used to Follow Movements of Chinese Couple with Coronavirus in Adelaide', *Australian Broadcasting Corporation News*, 6 February 2020.

143   Nemo Kim, 'More Scary than Coronavirus: South Korea's Health Alerts Expose Private Lives', *The Guardian*, 6 March 2020.

# 5

LAW, TECHNOLOGY AND COMMERCIAL TRANSACTIONS

# Introduction

The internet, social media, smartphones and encryption have radically changed the way goods are bought, sold and advertised. In doing so, they have opened up new markets and increased economic opportunities, enabling advertising to reach a global and more targeted audience. Individuals can start an online business or take on a second job more easily than ever before. Technology has disrupted many areas of the economy. Digital currencies, such as Bitcoin, have facilitated encrypted online transactions without the need for processing by a third party such as a bank. Blockchain technology has enabled contracts to be executed online instead of requiring a hard copy to be signed by the parties as a means of verifying an agreement. Online businesses have emerged to disrupt traditional models in a range of sectors, including transportation, where ride-sharing apps have challenged taxis; accommodation, in the form of apps used to book private homes or rooms for short stays; and online clothing retailers that can offer substantially reduced prices with minimal rent and staffing costs. Developments such as these raise a number of legal and regulatory issues; for example, digital currencies may increase opportunities for fraud and create challenges for law enforcement agencies investigating online distributors of illegal drugs. In considering the issues associated with law, technology and commerce, this chapter begins with a discussion of digital currencies, and then proceeds to examine online markets and services, electronic contracting, and changes brought by new technology for professional services and other businesses. Emerging issues such as anti-competitive practices are also discussed.

# Digital currencies

In contrast with traditional currency, digital currencies allow payments to be made directly to another person online, anywhere in the world. The best-known cryptocurrency is Bitcoin. Launched in 2009, Bitcoin facilitates peer-to-peer transactions, without the need for bank processing, using blockchain technology to record transactions and ownership.

> This is essentially technology that connects groups of transactions ('blocks') together over time (in a 'chain'). Each time a transaction occurs, it forms part of a new block that is added to the chain. As a result, the block-chain provides a record (or database) of every bitcoin transaction that has ever occurred, and it is available for anyone to access and update on a public network (this is often referred to as a 'distributed ledger'). The integrity of the Bitcoin system is protected by 'cryptography', which is a method of verifying and securing data using complex mathematical algorithms (or codes). This makes the system very difficult to corrupt.
>
> Bitcoin transactions are verified by other users of the network, and the process of compiling, verifying and confirming transactions is often referred to as 'mining'. In particular, complex codes need to be solved to confirm transactions and make sure the system is not corrupted. The Bitcoin system increases the complexity of these codes as more computing power is used to solve them. A new block of transactions is compiled approximately every ten minutes. 'Miners' want to solve the codes and process transactions because they are rewarded with new bitcoins.[1]

---

1    Reserve Bank of Australia, *Cryptocurrencies* (2020). Available: <https://www.rba.gov.au/education/resources/explainers/cryptocurrencies.html>.

Cryptocurrencies have disrupted the financial system, presenting a number of challenges for regulators, including from the perspectives of taxation, fraud, money laundering and use in association with criminal activity. Many people became aware of the criminal use of Bitcoin in relation to the underground 'Silk Road' website that came to prominence in allowing illicit drugs and other commodities to be bought using the cryptocurrency.

> In February of 2011, Ross William Ulbricht, who went by the nom de guerre of 'Dread Pirate Roberts,' founded the site 'Silk Road.' Ulbricht, a former Penn State graduate student and amateur programmer with a strong libertarian and anarchist bent, dreamt of an online marketplace where people would be able to buy and sell narcotics and other illicit items, without governmental interference. While the users of a Darknet site can use Tor and Virtual Private Networks to obscure and hide their identities, they had no way of exchanging anonymous payments among themselves … Ulbricht got around this conundrum by using bitcoin as a payment method. Bitcoin addresses do not require a bank account, ID, social security number or name, and are free to open and maintain. Bitcoin's decentralized ledger – the blockchain – provided a way to verify that payments had been received or sent. By using bitcoin, the only identifying information for a narcotics transaction would be the address of the receiver, a problem solved by using an anonymous P.O. box. Ulbricht would act as an escrow service between buyer and seller, and would profit from commissions taken from every transaction.[2]

This activity came to the attention of authorities, and Ulbricht was arrested in a Federal Bureau of Investigations (FBI) sting operation in 2013. By this time, it was estimated that Silk Road had a turnover of more than US$1 billion. Millions of bitcoins associated with Silk Road were seized, and the site was taken down. After a protracted criminal prosecution, Ulbricht was sentenced to life imprisonment and failed to overturn his conviction and sentence on appeal. One of the officers involved in the investigation of Silk Road was later convicted of the theft of over US$800 000 worth of its bitcoin holdings along with money laundering and obstruction.[3]

In 2014, a major bitcoin trading exchange known as 'Mt. Gox' collapsed following hacking attacks in which US$460 million worth of the cryptocurrency was allegedly stolen. The former head of the exchange pleaded not guilty to data manipulation and embezzlement charges in Japan in 2017, but was convicted of the former.[4]

Australian agencies have moved to regulate cryptocurrencies and a Senate inquiry into 'digital currency' provided a report on the issue in 2015.[5] The Australian Taxation Office (ATO) considers cryptocurrencies for capital gains purposes where their purchase value exceeds $10 000.

---

2   David Adler, 'Silk Road: The Dark Side of Cryptocurrency', *Fordham Journal of Corporate & Financial Law* (blog: 21 February 2018).

3   United States Department of Justice (Media release, 31 August 2015), 'Former Silk Road Task Force Agent Pleads Guilty to Money Laundering and Obstruction'. Available: <https://www.justice.gov/opa/pr/former-silk-road-task-force-agent-pleads-guilty-money-laundering-and-obstruction>.

4   'Former Mt. Gox Bitcoin Exchange Boss Pleads Not Guilty', *British Broadcasting Corporation News*, 11 July 2017. Available: <https://www.bbc.com/news/technology-40561420>.

5   Senate Economics References Committee, *Digital Currency* (Parliament of Australia, 2015).

> Where you use bitcoin to purchase goods or services for personal use or consumption, any capital gain or loss from disposal of the bitcoin will be disregarded (as a personal use asset) provided the cost of the bitcoin is $10,000 or less.[6]

The Australian Securities and Investments Commission (ASIC) considers that cryptocurrencies are not financial products under the *Australian Securities and Investments Commission Act 2001* (Cth) or the *Corporations Act 2001* (Cth). However, ASIC does provide consumer advice in relation to cryptocurrencies, emphasising that the exchange platforms they are sold on are not regulated, and that if these are hacked or fail, consumers will have no legal recourse; that they are not guaranteed by banks or governments; and that they are 'highly speculative, as values can fluctuate significantly over short periods of time'.[7] There have been many examples in Australia and in other countries of pyramid schemes associated with purported investments in cryptocurrencies that have defrauded consumers out of large sums of money.[8]

The anonymity afforded by cryptocurrencies is a major concern for regulators. In 2018, digital currency exchange providers in Australia were required to comply with the anti-money laundering/counterterrorism financing (AML/CTF) legislation. This followed a number of parliamentary and government reviews and public consultation processes, and recommendations of the intergovernmental Financial Action Task Force (FATF) which sets standards and promotes regulatory measures to address potential threats to the integrity of the international financial system.

> AML/CTF regulation of digital currency businesses was also recommended by the Senate Economics References Committee in August 2015 and the Productivity Commission in September 2015 in the context of broader reviews related to digital currency and business set up, transfer and closure respectively. Regulating digital currency exchange providers is consistent with FATF's guidance on a risk-based approach to digital currencies.[9]

The *Anti-Money Laundering and Counter-Terrorism Financing Amendment Act 2017* (Cth) amends the *Anti-Money Laundering and Counter-Terrorism Financing Act 2006* (Cth) to extend the coverage of the legislation to include digital currencies and regulates digital currency exchanges (DCEs). DCEs are required to enrol on a register that is maintained by the Australian Transaction Reports and Analysis Centre (AUSTRAC). This approach seeks to mitigate the risk of money laundering and to ensure that service providers know who their customers are. The legislation requires DCEs to implement an AML/CTF program, maintain records, and report transactions in certain circumstances. The legislation defines 'digital currency' in section 5 and establishes a register in the following way:

6   Australian Taxation Office, *Tax Treatment of Cryptocurrencies* (2020). Available: <https://www.ato.gov.au/general/gen/tax-treatment-of-crypto-currencies-in-australia–specifically-bitcoin/>.

7   Australian Securities and Investments Commission, *Cryptocurrencies* (2020). Available: <https://www.moneysmart.gov.au/investing/investment-warnings/virtual-currencies>.

8   Jordan Hayne, 'Bitcoin Investment Scam Steals Tens of Thousands from Couple as Cryptocurrency Losses Grow', *Australian Broadcasting Corporation News*, 4 July 2019.

9   Cat Barker, 'Anti-Money Laundering and Counter-Terrorism Financing Amendment Bill 2017', *Australian Parliamentary Library Bills Digest No. 47*, 2017–18.

## Section 5 Definitions

*[D]igital currency* means:

**(a)** a digital representation of value that:
   **(i)**  functions as a medium of exchange, a store of economic value, or a unit of account; and
   **(ii)** is not issued by or under the authority of a government body; and
   **(iii)** is interchangeable with money (including through the crediting of an account) and may be used as consideration for the supply of goods or services; and
   **(iv)** is generally available to members of the public without any restriction on its use as consideration; or
**(b)** a means of exchange or digital process or crediting declared to be digital currency by the AML/CTF Rules;

but does not include any right or thing that, under the AML/CTF Rules, is taken not to be digital currency for the purposes of this Act.

## Section 76B Digital Currency Exchange Register

**(1)** The AUSTRAC CEO must maintain a register for the purposes of this Part, to be known as the Digital Currency Exchange Register.

**(2)** The AUSTRAC CEO may maintain the Digital Currency Exchange Register by electronic means.

**(3)** The Digital Currency Exchange Register is not a legislative instrument.

**(4)** The AML/CTF Rules may make provision for and in relation to the following:

   **(a)** the correction of entries in the Digital Currency Exchange Register;

   **(b)** the publication of the Digital Currency Exchange Register in whole or part, or of specified information entered on the Digital Currency Exchange Register;

   **(c)** any other matter relating to the administration or operation of the Digital Currency Exchange Register.

The value of the bitcoin, the most widely used cryptocurrency, has been decreasing as more digital currencies are launched and enter the market. Trading in the currency has decreased, while the trend for online marketplaces to accept more traditional payment methods is another factor. While the use of bitcoin to purchase legal goods online is decreasing, its use to purchase illegal items, such as drugs, as well as in perpetrating fraud and cybercrime, has increased substantially.

> The amount of cryptocurrency spent on so-called dark net markets, where stolen credit card information and a wide array of illegal drugs can be purchased with Bitcoin, rose 60 percent to reach a new high of $601 million in the last three months of 2019. Bitcoin played a crucial role in the recent growth of so-called ransomware attacks, in which hackers steal or encrypt computer files and refuse to give them back unless a Bitcoin payment is made.[10]

---

10  Nathaniel Popper, 'Bitcoin Has Lost Steam: But Criminals Still Love It', *New York Times*, 28 January 2020.

In 2019, Facebook proposed the introduction of a new cryptocurrency, Libra, which would be expected to have a large take-up due to its association with the social networking site. This proposal has faced a high degree of resistance from regulators in the United States and Europe, concerned not only about privacy, but about the stability of financial markets, money laundering and the currency's potential use to fund criminal activities.[11] Over the coming decade, digital currencies are likely to cause further disruption by changing how companies buy and sell products, are funded and are financially managed. Cryptocurrencies have the potential to disrupt the financial system as it currently exists.

> Digital currencies like Bitcoin and Libra, Facebook's planned offering, bypass central banks and could undermine their control of the monetary system. One solution is for central banks to get into the digital currency business themselves … As with cash, people can use digital currencies to pay other people directly, without a bank in the middle. But unlike cash, digital currencies allow person-to-person transactions to take place online. Such a system could be more efficient, but also risky … Commercial banks might become superfluous and fail, leaving central banks to become, in effect, giant retail banks. But they have no experience dealing with millions of individual customers and could be overwhelmed. If a central bank collapsed, so would the monetary system.[12]

There are various approaches to the regulation of digital currencies around the world. This will have implications for national and global economies as these currencies inevitably become more widely utilised, with jurisdictions that do not currently accept their legitimacy likely to do so over time. The Organisation for Economic Co-operation and Development (OECD) recognises that new technology has great potential to positively impact on social welfare and economic growth. Further, the Group of Twenty (G20) is supportive of digital currencies and their capacity to decentralise economies and enable people to transact directly on a global basis without large corporate intermediaries.[13] Jia and Zhang (2018) describe regulatory approaches to cryptocurrencies in three ways – as liberalised, prohibitory or prudential – and, of course, this greatly influences where companies establish their business.[14] In the first category are the United States, where the Securities and Exchange Commission has approved share issuance using digital currencies; Germany; South Korea; and the United Kingdom, where a recent Office of Science report emphasised the benefits that blockchain can provide in the public sector and promoted its take-up and regulation by government.[15] Other countries, such as Vietnam and Ecuador, have banned cryptocurrencies altogether.

---

11  Richard Partington, 'How the Wheels Came Off Facebook's Libra Project', *The Guardian*, 19 October 2019.

12  Jack Ewing, 'Climate Change Could Blow Up the Economy: Banks Aren't Ready', *New York Times*, 23 January 2020.

13  Julie Maupin, 'The G20 Countries Should Engage with Blockchain Technologies to Build an Inclusive, Transparent, and Accountable Digital Economy for All', Policy Brief, *G20 Insights*, 16 March 2016, 2–3.

14  Kai Jia and Falin Zhang, 'Between Liberalization and Prohibition: Prudent Enthusiasm and the Governance of Bitcoin/Blockchain Technology'. In Malcolm Campbell-Verduyn (ed), *Bitcoin and Beyond: Cryptocurrencies, Blockchains, and Global Governance* (Routledge, 2018), 88.

15  Zhuling Chen, 'How Should We Regulate Blockchain? It Depends on Which Country You Ask', *Fortune*, 25 June 2018; UK Government Chief Scientific Adviser, 'Distributed Ledger Technology: Beyond Block Chain'.

China initially had one of the largest bitcoin exchanges in the world, but then banned the technology, blocked access to bitcoin exchanges, and directed bitcoin mining companies to exit the industry. The reason for this became clear in late 2019 as it announced plans to launch its own cryptocurrency and passed laws 'facilitating the development of the cryptography business and ensuring the security of cyberspace and information'.[16] This recent development by the Chinese government is likely to significantly boost the cryptocurrency sector in general by increasing the stability and credibility of the technology. The more widely this technology is used, the more secure and robust the sector will become.

# Smart contracts

While Bitcoin was the first application of blockchain technology to be widely adopted, there are other applications that have the potential to be just as influential in the future. Smart contracts are a leading example. They enable contracts to be automatically executed by embedding computer code in a blockchain platform in order to implement an agreement between parties, rather than having it drafted by a lawyer and enforced by a court.[17] The most widely used blockchain platform for smart contracts is currently Ethereum, which employs a peer-to-peer network to validate conditions that initiate the automated execution of the contract.[18] Etherium was launched in 2015 and is described as 'a global, open-source platform for decentralized applications' where people can 'write code that controls digital value'.[19] The code written into the blockchain technology actually guarantees the performance of the agreement.

> Some actions that may be automatically executed through smart contracts include the calculation of interest, transfer of payment for goods and storage of records. Ethereum also allows the automation of complex, multi-party agreements: loan financing with the buyer, seller and lender all having a stake in the platform; distribution by a company of its shares and dividends; and even the provision of public services to constituents.[20]

Governments around the world are establishing their own platforms that major companies will feel comfortable utilising routinely for major transactions. In 2018, the Commonwealth Scientific and Industrial Research Organisation (CSIRO), IBM and the law firm Herbert Smith Freehills formed a consortium to establish a national platform that will be known as the Australian National Blockchain (ANB), to enable businesses and companies to use

---

16 Anthony Cuthbertson, 'China Bans Anti-Blockchain Sentiment as it Prepares for Launch of State Cryptocurrency', *The Independent*, 30 October 2019.

17 This builds upon the widespread acceptance of electronic signatures for commercial transactions, as reflected in the *United Nations Convention on the Use of Electronic Communications in International Contracts (Electronic Communications Convention)* (2005) GA res 60/21; and the *Electronic Transactions Act 1999* (Cth), s 8(1) of which provides: 'For the purposes of a law of the Commonwealth, a transaction is not invalid because it took place wholly or partly by means of one or more electronic communications.'

18 William Mougayar, *The Business Blockchain: Promise, Practice, and Application of the Next Internet Technology* (Wiley, 2016), 21.

19 <https://ethereum.org/>.

20 Arvin Razon, 'Liberalising Blockchain: An Application of the GATS Digital Trade Framework' (2019) 20 *Melbourne Journal of International Law* 125.

the network to digitally manage contracts, exchange data, and conduct authentication and quality assurance processes. The government also acknowledges that smart contracts 'hold the potential to be used with AI [artificial intelligence] and advanced analytics to help ensure regulatory compliance or provide new business insights'.[21] The platform will become operational with a pilot in 2020.

> The platform will represent a significant new piece of infrastructure in Australia's digital economy. The ANB will soon invite regulators, banks, law firms and other Australian businesses to participate in the pilot, which is expected to start before the end of the year. Should the Australian pilot be successful, the consortium intends to roll out the technology to other markets beyond Australia.
>
> For the legal industry, success depends on the promise of transparency and auditability for all participants. The ANB will allow organisations to digitally manage the lifecycle of a contract, not just from negotiation to signing but also continuing over the term of the agreement, with transparency and permissioned-based access among all parties in the network, by using blockchain-based smart contracts to trigger business processes and events. These contracts contain smart clauses which have the ability to record external data sources, such as Internet of Things (IoT) device data and self-execute if specified contract conditions are met.[22]

It is still relatively early days in the development and evolution of smart contracts, and while they will undoubtedly become much more widely used in the future, there are a number of legal considerations that will need to be worked through currently and as they begin to be more widely used. National infrastructure, such as the ANB, will be a considerable resource in addressing some of the potential problems, such as confidentiality, security and privacy issues – although these can never be completely mitigated and there is still the potential for any system to be compromised by unauthorised access. It will assist with governance and regulatory compliance, but new legislation and regulations will need to be developed and enacted to address problems that may arise. A pilot project, along with analysis of international experiences, should be effective in terms of identifying how these should be framed and addressed.

There is a range of legal issues that can be anticipated and will require clarification if smart contracts are to become the dominant form of contracting. First, given that these contracts are effectively written in computer code, consideration will need to be given to how the terms should be interpreted, and a new body of case law developed to address this point.[23] Second, given that smart contracts effectively execute themselves when specified events occur, this raises the question of how these contracts could be unwound or adjudicated if it became necessary, for example, due to a mistake or unconscionable conduct; or varied if a

21   CSIRO, *New Blockchain-Based Smart Legal Contracts for Australian Businesses* (2018). Available: <https://www.csiro.au/en/News/News-releases/2018/New-blockchain-based-smart-legal-contracts>.

22   Australian National Blockchain, *A New Digital Backbone for Business* (2020). Available: <https://www.australiannationalblockchain.com/>.

23   Michel Cannarsa, 'Interpretation of Contracts and Smart Contracts: Smart Interpretation or Interpretation of Smart Contracts?' (2018) 26(6) *European Review of Private Law* 773–85.

dispute arose.[24] Finally, in the event that a contract required analysis to determine a dispute, complex expert evidence would be required to investigate and understand the terms of the contract, and translate that into language – something that is likely to be highly complex and difficult for a court to adjudicate.[25]

# Online markets and services

In the 2020 financial year, there has been mounting pressure placed on retail stores from more competitively priced online marketplaces. This trend was accelerated by the COVID-19 pandemic and has become increasingly apparent as a string of high-profile chains have collapsed in Australia and the United Kingdom.[26] Factors such as weaker consumer spending and rising costs have also contributed; however, the shift to online spending has been a key factor, and online sales now amount to approximately 20 per cent of all retail sales.[27]

It is not only the retail sector that has experienced pressures from the shift to online markets. Technology-facilitated work has displaced workers from traditional careers, impacting on a range of sectors. The pressure on the taxi industry from the rise of Uber is a classic example and has been described as the flagship of the new economy. However, recent research has found that Uber has created new business in the market and only reduced the income of taxi drivers by approximately 10 per cent, while increasing the number of self-employed drivers by 50 per cent. Berger et al (2018) found:

> The higher hourly earnings among self-employed drivers suggest that capacity utilization, in terms of the time spent in the car with a passenger, has increased with Uber, as its platform allows for better matching between drivers and passengers. But for traditional taxi drivers the effect has been the opposite, with a decline in the amount of time they have a passenger in their vehicle even in one of the sharing economy's most exposed industries, traditional jobs have not been displaced … The effects are complex; while some have seen a loss in income, Uber has created more jobs than it has destroyed, demonstrated by the staggering expansion of self-employment following its introduction.[28]

However, a separate issue raised by the emergence of Uber and other applications in recent years is the challenge of regulating these new applications that are being developed and taken up at a rapid rate. Regulators in London recently revoked Uber's licence after finding 'widespread instances of unauthorised drivers using the ride-hailing app to pick up customers'.[29] This development has raised concerns about the ability to police, monitor and control the behaviour of people that use the platform, and about the consequences

24 Guido Governatori et al, 'On Legal Contracts, Imperative and Declarative Smart Contracts, and Blockchain Systems' (2018) 26(4) *Artificial Intelligence and Law* 377–409.
25 Matthew McMillan and Ken Wong 'Blockchain and Smart Contracts: The Dawn of the Internet of Finance?' (2016) 35(2) *Communications Law Bulletin* 24.
26 Sue Mitchell, 'More Collapses to Come in Retail's Killing Season', *Australian Financial Review*, 4 February 2020; Julia Kollewe and Sarah Butler, 'High Street Crisis: Which Big Names Closed Stores in the Past Year?', *The Guardian*, 8 January 2020.
27 Ibid.
28 Thor Berger, Chinchih Chen and Carl Frey, 'Drivers of Disruption? Estimating the Uber Effect' (2018) 110 *European Economic Review* 197.
29 'Uber Loses London Licence Amid Fake Drivers Scandal', *The Australian*, 27 November 2019.

for the maintenance of public safety. Sexual assaults have been reported by users of both taxi and ride-sharing services, but research indicates that the use of Uber reduces the risk of victimisation where alternative transport options are scarce.[30] In 2018, the first pedestrian death caused by an experimental Uber vehicle operating in autonomous or 'self-driving' mode was reported. The experimental program was suspended pending safety investigations, which indicated that a combination of imperfect 'machine perception' of pedestrian behaviour (a woman walking her bicycle across a dark road) and inadequate 'human oversight' (the human operator of the autonomous vehicle was streaming a video on her cell phone at the time of the collision) was responsible.[31]

In New South Wales, the *Point to Point Transport (Taxis and Hire Vehicles) Regulation* came into effect in late 2017 in an attempt to regulate this new sector. Authorised service providers, including taxi and ride-share operators, must comply with a common code of safety designed to eliminate or minimise as far as is practicable all safety risks to passengers. Booking service providers also have a duty of care to ensure the health and safety of their drivers.[32] In other countries, litigation involving ride-share operators has largely revolved around whether their drivers have employee status and corresponding legal rights, whether they compete unfairly with traditional taxi and hire car services, and the safety of passengers and their private data.[33]

Analogous disruption occurred in relation to accommodation booking services such as Airbnb. Widely used as an alternative to hotel accommodation, such services allow private property owners to let rooms or houses through an app. As with ride-sharing services, there is a rating system, but the onus falls largely on property owners to screen out undesirable guests. There have been reports of Airbnb properties being seriously damaged by large groups after being rented, with the platform introducing restrictions to avoid its listings being used as 'party houses' after a mass shooting at such a gathering in California in 2019.[34]

Such examples serve to highlight the risks that can accompany a relatively deregulated business environment. Whereas in the past, transportation and accommodation services tended to be dominated by fewer but more closely regulated providers, the emergence of peer-to-peer transactions facilitated by social media and smartphone apps has resembled a largely anarchic environment with limited opportunities for state control.

> The virtual world is defined primarily by social, rather than physical, constraints. Social constraints can take the form of law, but also operate through norms, as well as market forces. While law and Lessig's concept of architecture do regulate actors in the virtual world, these constraints are in many ways less important than norms and market forces. Laws without enforcement are simply ignored, and architectures are hacked and

---

30  Jiyong Park et al, 'Offender or Guardian? An Empirical Analysis of Ride-Sharing and Sexual Assault', *KAIST College of Business Working Paper Series No. 2017–006; Fox School of Business Research Paper No. 18–010.*

31  'Why Uber's Self-Driving Car Killed a Pedestrian: It Was the First Fatal Accident of its Kind', *The Economist*, 29 May 2018.

32  New South Wales Government, Transport Commissioner, Point to Point, Frequently Asked Questions. Available: <https://www.pointtopoint.nsw.gov.au/frequently-asked-questions>.

33  Peter Pelzer et al, 'Institutional Entrepreneurship in the Platform Economy: How Uber Tried (and Failed) to Change the Dutch Taxi Law' (2019) 33 *Environmental Innovation and Societal Transitions* 1.

34  'Airbnb Moves to Ban "Party Houses" after Five Die in Halloween Shooting at California Rental', *Australian Broadcasting Corporation News,* 4 November 2019.

repurposed to serve the ends of users. The lack of practical resort to the state as an effective arbiter of disputes and enforcer of judgments suggests that the virtual world is anarchic.[35]

As the above quote indicates, the architecture of online platforms itself constrains user behaviour, as Lawrence Lessig observed some two decades ago (see Chapter 2). This means that communities of users will explore the possibilities within each such platform and, through information sharing, establish some semblance of ground rules. Supplemented by social norms, market forces and the threat of legal sanctions, this helps to establish boundaries on what is considered acceptable online behaviour. The risk of financial loss is always a strong motivator, as seen with market responses to destructive behaviour by users of online accommodation booking services. Similar observations apply to online commentary that becomes defamatory, as discovered by some social media users.

# Anti-competitive behaviour

The growth of online markets and advertising has led to new dynamics of competition and the emergence of some anti-competitive practices. Internet advertising has proved to be vulnerable to various forms of manipulation, such as 'click fraud'. Search engines such as Google introduced a Pay-Per-Click (PPC) mechanism in the early 2000s which allowed more targeted advertising to potential online shoppers, where search entries are matched by algorithms to advertising that reflects what a consumer appears to be most interested in. For example, a search for holiday packages will have the result that online ads appearing on the search page, and even on other pages visited by the same person, will offer various holiday options and deals. Advertisers pay search engines per click on their ad or search result link, on the basis that this type of advertising is likely to be more effective in translating into a sale than less targeted strategies. This model has been so successful that it constitutes the bulk of Google's revenue. However, most businesses only have a limited budget for online advertising, and an unscrupulous competitor can cause financial loss by repeatedly clicking on a rival's ads without this generating a sale. By the mid-2000s, a new industry of 'click fraud' detection services had emerged, but other forms of manipulation persist, including the hijacking of links to direct browsers to other sites.[36]

In mid-2019, the Australian Competition and Consumer Commission (ACCC) published a voluminous report on digital platforms, summarising the competition issues as follows:

> Businesses looking to advertise their services and products, on the other hand, have largely benefited from the rise of the digital platforms. For many advertisers, digital platforms have provided a cheaper and more targeted way of reaching consumers who spend an increasing amount of their time online, particularly on the websites and apps controlled by the two major digital platforms in Australia: Google and Facebook. Advertisers have always sought to use information collected on potential audiences to target their advertising, but the granularity and immediacy of the targeting ability

---

35  Gabriel Michael, 'Anarchy and Property Rights in the Virtual World: How Disruptive Technologies Undermine the State and Ensure that the Virtual World Remains a "Wild West"', *SSRN Working Paper* (1 March 2013).

36  Nir Kshetri and Jeffrey Voas, 'Online Advertising Fraud' (2019) 52 *Computer* 58.

of digital platforms and the volume and scope of information that digital platforms have access to is a substantial step-change in the ability of advertisers to target their intended audience. However, this too has not been without complexities. Where Google's and Facebook's business users are also their competitors, there are questions about whether there is a level playing field, or whether they have the ability to give themselves advantages by favouring their own products. As Google and Facebook continue to expand into adjacent markets through acquisitions and organic expansion, these risks increase.[37]

Recommendations arising from the ACCC's report include compelling Google and Facebook to disclose their algorithms and business methods to regulators, with the latter given increased powers to monitor and counter anti-competitive behaviour.

# Professional and government services

The growth of online commerce extends to services for the third-party storage of commercial and private data, such as cloud computing services. These enable large amounts of data to be stored and retrieved efficiently, alleviating the need for and cost of storage by the data owners.

> Storage 'virtualization' makes it possible for a user to have access to what appears to be a single file or document while the relevant data are stored in a physically distributed fashion across different pieces of hardware (e.g. a Storage Area Network or SAN), with specialized software managing storage and retrieval. The intention is that users not be concerned with the details of physical storage as this is handled automatically for them … Cloud service providers often employ various, in some cases proprietary, systems to manage large-scale distributed data storage and retrieval across different hardware, including distributed file systems and distributed databases.[38]

The legal regulation of cloud computing is essentially contractual, though the often multi-jurisdictional nature of the agreements and services provided tends to produce difficulties for public authorities such as data protection regulators and law enforcement agencies. As discussed in greater detail in Chapters 7 and 10, investigators face difficulties in obtaining and executing appropriate warrants to obtain access to data stored in another jurisdiction, or in a distributed system across multiple jurisdictions.[39]

Professional service firms and businesses are also adapting their practices to integrate new communications technologies and AI systems into their workplaces.[40] Similarly, some

---

37  Australian Competition and Consumer Commission, *Digital Platforms Inquiry: Final Report* (26 July 2019).
38  Christopher Millard (ed), *Cloud Computing Law* (Oxford University Press, 2013), 8.
39  See also Ned Schultheis, 'Warrants in the Clouds: How Extraterritorial Application of the Stored Communications Act Threatens the United States Cloud Storage Industry' (2015) 9 *Brooklyn Journal of Corporate, Financial & Commercial Law*.
40  This can include videoconferencing, website portals and online messaging services to communicate with clients and colleagues, as well as artificial intelligence software to assist with analysis and drafting, such as Beagle and ROSS Intelligence: speech by Morry Bailes, 'The Law and Legal Technology – Our Changing Work Practices' Law Council of Australia, Australian Young Lawyers' Conference, Sydney, 20 October 2017.

services provided by government, such as social security payments, are being automated using AI systems. The professional education sector has also changed, with web-based subject materials and tutorials, as well as email and online discussion forums being widely used to discuss learning materials and cases, in addition to face-to-face learning styles. Digital learning begins the development of skills that graduates can go on to use in the workplaces of the future, while also offering more efficient and flexible options for studying and combining part-time study and work.

For law firms, this includes incorporating new technologies to undertake legal analysis and drafting, and particularly in communicating with colleagues and clients. The importance of technology to collaboration in modern legal practice will continue to make communicating with clients and other parties faster and more efficient. Today, the legal profession is moving to videoconferencing, website chat, online portals and smart documents to communicate with clients and colleagues and complete work.[41] These approaches will make professional practice more efficient, but also more competitive, blurring traditional working hours and geographically extending the legal marketplace.

New technologies will reduce the range of human skill sets, as AI becomes more advanced, meaning that legal knowledge in itself will not be sufficient.[42] This evolving workplace culture is likely to place even greater emphasis on effective communication, teamwork and innovation as fundamental skills in their own right that add value to the practice as more mundane tasks are performed by technology. Platforms such as Lex Machina[43] are already becoming part of trial preparation for civil litigation, as well as in criminal law. Based on court decisions that have been made in the past, legal analytics platforms can provide an indication of the likelihood that a particular judge will allow specific evidence to be adduced, grant bail or convict for a specific offence in a criminal trial or grant an order in a civil trial – as well as how long the hearing is likely to take. It can also assess an opposing counsel's level of experience and likely approach. The company providing the software states that their program mines litigation data to reveal insights

> ... about judges, lawyers, parties, and the subjects of the cases themselves, culled from millions of pages of litigation information ... you can easily view how likely a judge is to find infringement of a patent, fair use of a trademark or a Securities Act violation.[44]

Technology Assisted Review (TAR), which can be used in discovery to process voluminous information, has been used in the United States since 2012 and Australia since 2016.[45] It has proven to be faster, more efficient and more accurate than manual document reviews and uses machine learning to identify patterns in data. A lawyer codes a set of documents, labelling them as relevant, irrelevant, privileged etc, and the AI system then applies this

---

41  Ibid.
42  The Council of Australian Law Deans (CALD) includes effective communication skills, and the capacity to work well with others as skills within their threshold academic standards for legal education. CALD, *Learning and Teaching Academic Standards Project Bachelor of Laws Learning and Teaching Academic Standards Statement* (2010).
43  Lex Machina, *Legal Analytics Platform* (2019). Available: <https://lexmachina.com/legal-analytics/>.
44  Ibid.
45  Peter J Pizzi, 'Towards a Synthesis of Judicial Perspectives on Technology-Assisted Review' (2015) 82 *Defence Counsel Journal* 309; *McConnell Dowell Constructors (Australia) Pty Ltd v Santam Ltd (No 1)* (2016) 51 VR 421.

model to a large set of documents and identifies whether they share associated characteristics and should be flagged for review by the lawyer.[46]

Software is now available to draft legal documents such as contracts and wills, populated with template answers provided by the client. A wide range of legal services is now provided in this way, from patent applications to appeals of government decisions and fines. An associated area of rapid growth is the use of chatbots in association with neuro-linguistic programming (NLP), as well as document drafting software to generate a letter or legal document.[47]

AI will significantly change many professions. As was discussed in Chapter 4, it is having an impact in other professions such as medicine, where it is used to analyse large volumes of complex data, particularly in relation to screening and diagnosis in image- and data-based disciplines. In pathology and radiology, it has proven able to outperform medical specialists in some specialised diagnostic tasks.[48] The impact on manual labour and more routine professions will be even more profound as these types of work are more easily automatable.

> [A]nalysis of the impact of automation and AI on work shows that certain categories of activities are technically more easily automatable than others. They include physical activities in highly predictable and structured environments, as well as data collection and data processing, which together account for roughly half of the activities that people do across all sectors in most economies. The least susceptible categories include managing others, providing expertise, and interfacing with stakeholders. The density of highly automatable activities varies across occupations, sectors, and, to a lesser extent, countries. Our research finds that about 30 percent of the activities in 60 percent of all occupations could be automated – but that in only about 5 percent of occupations are nearly all activities automatable. In other words, more occupations will be partially automated than wholly automated.[49]

With increased automation of decision-making come interesting questions about accountability, transparency and responsibility. Where a decision is made by a program to cancel a social security benefit, for example, what recourse does a citizen have? In Australia, this question was brought into focus with the deployment by the federal Department of Human Services of an automated debt recovery system which sent hundreds of thousands of debt notices to social security recipients, many of which were challenged. In 2020 the government announced it was ending the system and more than $700 million in debts raised would be paid back.[50] In particular, the automated decision was found to be 'not a validly issued notice for the purpose of s 1229 of the *Social Security Act 1991* (Cth) because the decision-maker could not have been satisfied that a debt was owed in the amount of the

---

46  Bolch Judicial Institute, *Technology Assisted Review (TAR) Guidelines* (2019).
47  Michael Legg and Felicity Bell, *Artificial Intelligence and the Legal Profession* (Law Society of New South Wales, 2018).
48  Babak Bejnordi et al, 'Diagnostic Assessment of Deep Learning Algorithms for Detection of Lymph Node Metastases in Women with Breast Cancer' (2017) 318 *Journal of the American Medical Association* 2199.
49  McKinsey Global Institute, *The Promise and Challenge of the Age of Artificial Intelligence* (2018).
50  Georgia Hitch, 'Scott Morrison Apologises for "any hurt or harm" Caused by Robodebt Scheme', *Australian Broadcasting Corporation News*, 11 June 2020. A $1.2 billion settlement of litigation was announced in November 2020: Matthew Doran, 'Federal Government ends Robodebt class action with settlement worth $1.2 billion', *Australian Broadcasting Corporation News*, 16 November 2020.

alleged debt'.[51] An inquiry being conducted by the Australian Human Rights Commission has received submissions generally supporting the view that proper regulation of AI decision-making must take into account the following principles:

- transparency regarding the use of AI to make or support a decision about an individual, including notification of that use to the individual concerned
- trust, including in relation to how personal data being collected may be used in future in AI-informed decision-making
- fairness, including by avoiding bias and discrimination in the development and use of AI technologies, and for private entities to be proactive in their monitoring and evaluation of algorithms
- mitigation of risk, including through the design and management of AI technologies, such as identifying potential bias in a data source
- responsibility, including by ensuring AI technologies are developed and used for social good.[52]

As was the case in the medical profession, due to the difficulty in identifying the exact reasoning process an algorithm undertakes, new models of regulation and legal responsibility will need to be developed as use of these technologies becomes more widespread. It is likely that responsibility will be shared more widely among the developers of the technology, the companies using them and insurers.

Ethics principles being developed by the Australian government for the use of AI in industry include the following: 'Those responsible for the different phases of the AI system lifecycle should be identifiable and accountable for the outcomes of the AI systems, and human oversight of AI systems should be enabled.'[53] Such an approach helps to ensure that where problems occur, those affected still have legal rights of recourse.

# Robotics and regulation

The industrial use of robotic technology raises similar regulatory challenges. For a long time, robots were more prevalent in science fiction than in real life, but their use is increasing.

> Robots are nowadays a matter of fact for professional users, as witnessed by robots exploring the surface of Mars, repairing oil pipes deep in the ocean, performing surgical operations in hospitals, defusing or firing bombs in the battlefields, performing manufacturing tasks in factories – just to name a few applications. However, robots are also becoming popular in people's daily lives, for so-called non-professional users. We can see robots at work in homes doing household tasks, such as cleaning sitting rooms, preparing and cooking food, mowing the lawn or playing games with students and children. In addition, in many cities, public transportation means are becoming increasingly robotic, e.g. with driverless undergrounds and metro systems. Automobiles too are endowed with new capabilities such as adaptive cruise control, lane-keeping systems, emergency braking systems, electronic stability control, intelligent parking

---

51  *Amato v Commonwealth*, Federal Court Registry consent orders (27 November 2019).
52  Australian Human Rights Commission, *Human Rights and Technology: Discussion Paper* (December 2019).
53  Australian Government, Department of Industry, Science, Energy and Resources, *AI Ethics Principles* (2020).

assist systems; and developments in fully autonomous vehicles, such as the Google car, are speeding up. Thus, robots are becoming increasingly prevalent in daily, social, and professional life.[54]

Given this increasing level of interaction between humans and machines, which in the medical field extends to the use of computerised prosthetics (the 'cyborg' scenario), questions of regulation include the following:

> Are our existing normative frameworks adequate to deal with developments in robotics? Can new robotic technologies, particularly if they feature increasing levels of autonomic behaviour, be regulated within existing legal and ethical frameworks, and if not, should existing laws be made more generic so that provisions also encompass robotic technologies, or should we rather aim for sui generis laws for robots? And are fundamental assumptions underlying regulatory frameworks, such as a very generic distinction between 'things' and 'humans', sustainable in the longer term, if (bio)robotic applications are increasingly built into human bodies? These are some of the more general and fundamental questions that the development of robotics raise[s].[55]

To some extent, regulatory approaches such as worker safety provisions extend without great elaboration to robotic production facilities. For example, an Australian Capital Territory work safety regulation dealing with industrial robots provides:

## Industrial robots

**(1)** This section applies to a person with management or control of an industrial robot or other remotely or automatically energised plant at a workplace.

**(2)** The person must not direct or allow a worker to work in the immediate vicinity of the plant if it could start without warning and cause a hazard, unless suitable control measures are in place to control the risks to health and safety.[56]

As can be seen, legal responsibility is simply placed on a person with management and control functions within the workplace, with potential vicarious liability also extending to the overall employer.[57] In more complex situations – for example, where an AI-controlled robotic device such as a driverless car is involved – there may be arguments for more inventive solutions. It has been argued, for example, that where a robot is equipped with sufficient capacity to make 'moral choices', there may be utility in imposing legal liability directly on the machine so as to create a more inclusive regulatory framework.

> If we were to live in a world in which smart robots could both make and act on their moral decisions, it would be important to clarify the scope of actions that those robots

---

54  Ronald Leenes et al, 'Regulatory Challenges of Robotics: Some Guidelines for Addressing Legal and Ethical Issues' (2017) 9(1) *Law, Innovation and Technology* 1.
55  Ibid, 2.
56  *Work Health and Safety Regulation 2011* (ACT), reg 221, with maximum fine of $6000 for an individual and $30 000 for a corporate entity.
57  ACT law already includes offences of industrial manslaughter, relating to employers and senior managers, which could apply in the case of a fatal event involving workplace machinery: *Crimes Act 1900* (ACT), Part 2A.

are prohibited, permitted, or obligated to undertake. A criminal code for robots helps reduce such ambiguities by providing a minimum set of moral standards to which all smart robots must adhere. These minimum standards should not be left to the whims of each robot manufacturer or trainer but should be decided by the society collectively. Collective decision making helps prevent a possible race to the bottom, in which robot manufacturers compete against each other to make the most self-interested robot. Imagine the designer of an autonomous car advertising: 'This car will not care how much harm it causes to others as long as you are safe!' Fearing for their lives, consumers scramble to shop for the most aggressive car possible, even though they might be content with a more cooperative vehicle if everybody opts for the same.[58]

As noted earlier in this chapter, there have already been fatalities caused by driverless cars, though it appears that the main shortcoming to date has been poor human supervision in tests. In the event that this technology becomes more routine on our roads, the resolution of legal liability disputes in the case of death, injury and damage may require new approaches. For example, product liability rather than vehicular (driver) negligence might apply to vehicle manufacturers, and state liability may attach to jurisdictions that license the use of driverless vehicles on public roads.

Autonomous vehicles can also occupy the skies. These can range from satellites, which once sent into orbit follow a predetermined path with no further human navigation, to unmanned aircraft including drones, also known as Unmanned Aerial Vehicles (UAVs). While these technologies have been developed in the context of space research, aeronautics and military programs, their adoption for commercial purposes is increasing rapidly. Privately owned telecommunications satellites, which now number in the hundreds, have been regulated since the mid-1960s.[59] More recently, drones have been used for commercial purposes such as aerial filming, and for food and consumer goods deliveries. Since then, trials of drone deliveries have been undertaken in numerous locations around the world, including in Canberra, with mixed reactions from residents.[60]

Drone flights are regulated by aviation authorities such as the Civil Aviation Safety Authority (CASA), which has issued standard operating conditions. These include:

> You can only fly one drone at a time, and that drone can't go any higher than 120 metres – that's 400 feet or about the length of a football field. Drones may be aircraft, but they can't fly anywhere near major airports. You must fly at least 5.5 kilometres away from a controlled airport, which generally have a control tower at them.[61]

An emerging array of commercial drone services includes not only deliveries, but aerial support for construction and farming, wildlife management, and even aerial taxis currently

---

58  Ying Hu, 'Robot Criminals' (2019) 52 *University of Michigan Journal of Law Reform* 487, 502–3.
59  Pamela Meredith and Franceska Schroeder, 'Privately-Owned Commercial Telecommunications Satellites: Licensing and Regulation by the Federal Communications Commission' (1990) 27(1) *California Western Law Review* 107.
60  Jake Evans, 'Google's Drone Delivery Trial Could be Under Threat from Group of Angry Australian Residents', *Australian Broadcasting Corporation News*, 9 March 2019.
61  Civil Aviation Safety Authority, *Drone Safety Rules*. Available: <https://www.casa.gov.au/drones/rules/drone-safety-rules>.

being trialled by Uber in the United States and Australia.[62] As with driverless cars, despite some early failures in ensuring public safety, the commercial imperative of introducing ever more advanced transport systems in crowded cities suggests that unmanned aerial commuters may become a common sight in the near future.

# Conclusion

This chapter has examined the way technology continues to change the commercial sector, retail, contracting, finance, and the way law firms and other companies integrate the latest communications and AI innovations into their business. Market forces promote creativity, and new ideas and the substantial financial rewards available to those that develop new technology platforms have led to rapid developments and societal change, particularly over the past two decades. The impact of ride-sharing applications on the taxi industry is just one prominent example, while the growth of online shopping and the automation of careers that have for decades been performed by humans are other examples of technology shaping the commercial sector and society more broadly.

Blockchain technology, applied to cryptocurrencies and smart contracts, has moved beyond the point where it presents an alternative option, only used in niche markets or by technology companies, to the stage where advanced economies such as Australia and China are investing in and developing major infrastructure to ensure stability and long-term growth of blockchain in the business sector. This will require further legislation and guidelines to be developed in coming years, and the corresponding expansion of case law to adjudicate disputes involving smart contracts. The commercial sector is a vital and central part of society, and it is important that the legal system continue to develop to ensure new developments can be implemented, and that these are regulated and integrated with the existing legal framework.

---

62   Matthew Marino, 'Uber Air's Flying Taxi Trial Could Open up New Possibilities for Air Travel in Australia', *Australian Broadcasting Corporation News*, 6 December 2019.

# 6

# LAW, TECHNOLOGY AND THE CRIMINAL JUSTICE SYSTEM

# Introduction

For over a century, the field of forensic science has been applying contemporary technology to the investigation of crime. The imperative to identify offenders, particularly in relation to serious offences, has meant that governments are willing to invest in new technologies to achieve this objective. Fingerprinting, first developed in the late 19th century to identify individuals based on the unique patterns on the fingertips, led the way as one of the earliest means of identifying people, and is still used today in a digitised format.

Other technologies that have been adapted and developed to assist law enforcement include video surveillance and DNA evidence. Current applications in information technology provide the basis for a range of techniques such as facial recognition, data system integration and analytics. However, it is important that the potential for inaccuracies, sample contamination, hacking and human error is borne in mind, and that potential impacts on individual rights are weighed against the benefits. Further, safeguards are needed to protect individual rights, including privacy and autonomy, as technology provides increasingly accurate and efficient tools to monitor behaviour and investigate crimes.

This chapter focuses on the use of identification technologies in the criminal justice system in three areas. It begins with general considerations regarding the use of technology in identifying suspects. This is followed by a detailed look at historical developments, impact on investigations, databases, and evidentiary issues in relation to three of the most widely used technologies: fingerprint identification, DNA identification and facial recognition. Other relevant technologies are discussed elsewhere in the text, such as telecommunications metadata in Chapter 3 and cybercrime investigations in Chapter 10.

# Technology-based identification

'Biometric identification' refers to the measurement of physical features of the human body, including patterns of the skin; blood vessel networks; parts of the eye, such as the retina or iris; and facial appearance, taking account of the distance between features. It can also include behavioural traits, such as gait or voice characteristics; and biodynamics, such as the pattern of keystroke typing.[1] For the purpose of individual identification in a security or law enforcement context, a biometric feature must not only be a physical feature able to be measured; it must also be sufficiently distinctive to function as a unique identifier that is capable of being rapidly verified. It is important that biometrics are 'measurable, robust and distinctive physical characteristics or personal traits that can be used to identify an individual'.[2] Biometrics must not change significantly over time. They must be stable through ageing, injury or environmental changes,[3] and must be convertible into a digital format that can be integrated within a database to be stored, searched and matched. Biometric identification also requires automatic identification that is non-invasive and can occur in real time.

Biometric identification can be contrasted with other means of identification and access, such as keys, identification cards and passwords that provide access to a building, computer,

---

1   Marcus Smith, Monique Mann and Gregor Urbas, *Biometrics, Crime and Security* (Routledge, 2018), 2.
2   John Woodward et al, *Biometrics: A Look at Facial Recognition* (RAND, 2003).
3   Ibid, 1.

network, smartphone or bank account. A key distinction between biometric identification and other methods is that it is a part of the person, rather than an object carried on the person, or a password they must remember. A succinct definition is that rather than being something that an individual *knows* or *has*, it is something that they *are*.[4] Biometric systems involve an enrolment stage, acquiring the individual's biometric data and generating a template that can be stored in a database; and a matching stage, the comparison with a reference template, or all templates held on a database.[5]

When selecting which physical trait to use for biometric identification there are a number of considerations to take into account. Each trait will be suitable in different contexts. There are seven criteria that have been accepted as key indicators of suitability, known as the seven pillars of biometrics:

- universality
- distinctiveness
- permanence
- collectability
- performance
- acceptability
- resistance to circumvention.[6]

In comparison with these criteria, certain biometrics have features that make them more or less suitable in particular circumstances. For instance, fingerprint identification may be preferable to gait analysis on the basis of accuracy, as it is more distinctive and permanent. If it is only possible to identify a suspect from a distance, gait analysis would be preferred, because it can be assessed from a greater distance. In cases where a large number of people must be processed quickly at close proximity (such as immigration control in an airport), fingerprint identification would be more appropriate.

In broad terms, there are three applications of biometrics. The most straightforward approach is *one-to-one verification* of identity, which seeks to determine whether an individual is who they purport to be. In this case, a live profile is provided by the individual and compared with a template stored in the computer system or identification document, such as a passport or licence. This is commonly used for physical access to a smartphone, or building, or when transiting through immigration checkpoints. The second of these (and most common in a criminal investigation context) is *one-to-many searching*, where a biometric profile is compared with a database to identify the individual through a direct or partial match. This results in a computer-generated likelihood that two or more profiles are from the same individual. This approach is generally used in a criminal investigation, such as when a DNA profile is obtained from biological material located at a crime scene and the police seek to identify an unknown suspect. The third approach is *screening*, such as the use of biometrics to identify an individual on a watch-list, combining CCTV and facial

4   Richard Hopkins, 'Introduction to Biometrics and Large Scale Civilian Identification' (1999) 13 *International Review of Law, Computers and Technology* 337.
5   Ibid.
6   Anil Jain, Arun Ross and Sharath, Pankanti, 'Biometrics: A Tool for Information Security' (2006) 1 *IEEE Transactions on Information Forensics and Security* 125.

recognition technology. Screening suspects is more difficult from a technical standpoint than the first two examples, but an approach that is likely to become more common as technical capabilities improve.[7]

Like other areas of government and business, law enforcement has become increasingly digitised. There have been significant increases in data stores and the efficacy of managing and interrogating data.[8] In the 1980s, law enforcement agencies maintained paper-based file and index systems that required a large amount of storage space and were inefficient to search. In comparison with contemporary methods, there was less scope for inter-jurisdictional information sharing. Advances in technology, especially digitisation, over the past 40 years have facilitated the exchange and dissemination of information among state, national and international agencies, as well as integration between the multiple national databases.[9]

Law enforcement agencies use databases to store and compare information about crime scenes, individuals and registration details, not only biometric identification.[10] These range from basic record management, to complex analytical software systems that inform cross-jurisdictional criminal investigations[11] and strategic intelligence priorities.[12] Because this form of information is not usually discussed publicly, it is difficult to quantify the impact it has had on investigations. However, as will be discussed, DNA identification has been associated with the successful prosecution of many high-profile offences. There is ongoing debate in the literature over the extent to which these databases do in fact improve productivity, communication and management, in light of the additional administrative work and associated maintenance costs.[13]

Many national databases have been established around the world. In the United States, the Federal Bureau of Investigation (FBI) is responsible for developing and maintaining national information systems. These include the National Instant Criminal Background Check System, the National Integrated Ballistics Information Network and the Combined DNA Index System.[14] In the United Kingdom, the Home Office and the Association for Police and Crime Commissioners manage police information systems.[15] These include the Police National Computer (the national fingerprint and identity platform database), the National Ballistics Intelligence Service and the National DNA Database. The United Kingdom has created a Commissioner for the Retention and Use of Biometric Material to provide

---

7   Yingzi Du, *Biometrics: From Fiction to Practice* (Pan Stanford, 2013).
8   James Byrne and Gary Marx, 'Technological Innovations in Crime Prevention and Policing: A Review of the Research on Implementation and Impact' (2011) 20 *Journal of Police Studies* 39.
9   Marcus Smith, Monique Mann and Gregor Urbas, *Biometrics, Crime and Security* (Routledge, 2018), 2.
10  Sean Varano et al, 'Police Information Systems'. In Joseph Schafer (ed), *Policing 2020* (Federal Bureau of Investigation, 2007).
11  Maryke Nuth, 'Taking Advantage of New Technologies: For and Against Crime' (2008) 24 *Computer Law and Security Report* 437.
12  Jerry Ratcliffe, *Intelligence-Led Policing* (Willan Publishing, 2008).
13  Christopher Koper, Cynthia Lum and James Willis, *Realizing the Potential of Technology in Policing* (George Mason University Press, 2015).
14  Federal Bureau of Investigation, *Criminal Justice Information Services* (2017). Available: <www.fbi.gov/about-us/cjis>.
15  Association of Police and Crime Commissioners, *PCCs to Establish Ground-Breaking National Police ICT Company* (2015). Available: <www.apccs.police.uk/latest-news/pccs-to-establish-ground-breaking-national-police-ict-company/>.

protection from disproportionate law enforcement action, and limits on the application of surveillance and counterterrorism powers.[16]

The Australian Criminal Intelligence Commission seeks to assist law enforcement agencies throughout Australia by increasing information sharing and strategic intelligence about serious crime.[17] It maintains databases of DNA and fingerprint profiles, ballistics information, cybercrime reports, firearm and vehicle ownership, and persons of interest.[18] India operates the largest biometric database in the world, currently holding 700 million citizens' iris and fingerprint templates, and a range of demographic information. This information is included on a national identity card, known as an Aadhaar card, which can be used by police in criminal investigations, and is now required when a complainant reports a crime to police.[19]

The most important function of law enforcement databases is to improve the efficiency and effectiveness of investigations. A study by Chan (2001) investigating the extent to which information databases implemented in the 1990s had modified the practice of policing found that they enabled police to cope with a larger volume of information and to share it more effectively.[20] This study is supported by more recent research indicating that it improves the investigative process by assisting information flow.[21] Conversely, Hekim et al (2013) examined the use of police databases for criminal investigative purposes in 233 law enforcement agencies, and found no significant relationship between case clearance rates and the use of police databases.[22]

Issues that impact the effectiveness of police information systems include poor implementation, inadequate training and under-utilisation.[23] Other factors that have been identified include inaccurate data, siloed information and poor search capabilities. A further observation is that law enforcement agencies often have a conservative culture, which may impede change, with accountability requirements a leading contributor to resistance.[24] Over time, new generations of police and improved systems are likely to see the use of biometrics and other data become increasingly important.

A further recent development in the criminal justice system is judges' use of automated decision-making in determining sentences. The COMPAS (Correctional Offender Management Profiling for Alternative Sanctions) risk assessment tool uses historic data to make inferences regarding which defendants are at risk of re-offending, particularly in relation to violent offences. Courts in the United States have upheld the use of this technology in relation to the

---

16  See <https://www.gov.uk/government/organisations/biometrics-commissioner>.

17  Australian Criminal Intelligence Commission. Available: <www.acic.gov.au/our-services/biometric-and-forensic-services>.

18  Ibid.

19  Sinjini Mitra and Mikhail Gofman, *Biometrics in a Data Driven World: Trends, Technologies, and Challenges* (Taylor and Francis, 2016).

20  Janet Chan, 'The Technological Game: How Information Technology is Transforming Police Practice' (2001) 1 *Criminal Justice* 139.

21  Christopher Koper, Cynthia Lum and James Willis, *Realizing the Potential of Technology in Policing* (George Mason University Press, 2015).

22  Hakan Hekim, Serdar Gul and Bahadir Akcam, 'Police Use of Information Technologies in Criminal Investigations' (2013) 9 *European Scientific Journal* 221.

23  Christopher Koper, Cynthia Lum and James Willis, *Realizing the Potential of Technology in Policing* (George Mason University Press, 2015).

24  Janet Chan, 'Changing Police Culture' (1996) 36 *British Journal of Criminology* 109.

right to due process under the US Constitution: *State of Wisconsin v Loomis*.[25] However, in making this finding, the court emphasised that reliance on the technology is only permitted if the decision is not fully delegated to the system and there remains some human consideration of the factors involved.[26] Issues with this approach include a lack of transparency – the company that produces the tool considers the algorithm a trade secret.[27] Further issues have been raised in the literature.

> Unless the humans involved in these processes have a deep understanding of the legal context in which a decision is made, systems may fail in practice to meet the standard of equality before the law. The COMPAS system is an example of software that does not meet the needs of a fair criminal justice process – lack of transparency in a tool that relies on a large set of often legally irrelevant inputs prevents a defendant from having sufficient opportunity to participate in the court's findings on dangerousness, which is a crucial component of the ultimate decision. The fact that the tool has more 'false positives' in the African-American community than among white people is further evidence that humans are exercising insufficient control over the machine learning process to ensure that it operates appropriately.[28]

There are some basic evidentiary requirements of technology-based evidence in the courtroom that will be briefly addressed. Biometric identification evidence in a criminal case provides an alternative to traditional eyewitness identification. While it does not quite fall within the definition of identification evidence, it can be admissible as a form of circumstantial evidence. A biometric fingerprint or DNA match is not considered identification evidence because it is usually based not on what a person making an assertion saw, heard or perceived, but on later forensic analysis by a person who was not a witness to the events in question.[29] It is treated as a form of circumstantial evidence, as noted by the judge in *R v Pfennig (No 2)*: 'DNA evidence is not direct evidence going to the guilt of the accused. I treat it as circumstantial evidence to be considered alongside all of the other evidence in the case.'[30]

Biometric identification evidence is presented as expert opinion evidence, such as through a forensic analyst's report or witness testimony from the specialist who conducted the biometric analysis. There are three general requirements for admissibility of biometric identification. These are that the evidence be: *relevant* in the proceeding, based on *specialised knowledge* and not be *unfairly prejudicial*.

For biometric identification to be relevant in the proceeding, it must have the capacity to help resolve factual issues in the trial, such as the identity of an offender. For example, s 55 of the *Evidence Act 1995* (Cth) provides that 'the evidence that is relevant in a proceeding is evidence that, if it were accepted, could rationally affect (directly or indirectly) the assessment of the probability of the existence of a fact in issue in the proceeding'.[31] Section 56 of the UEL provides that relevant evidence is admissible, subject to other provisions.

---

25   881 NW 2d 749 (2016).
26   Ibid, [56].
27   Ibid, [144].
28   Monika Zalnieriute, Lyria Bennett Moses and George Williams, 'The Rule of Law and Automation of Government Decision-Making' (2019) 82 *The Modern Law Review* 425, 452.
29   Australian Law Reform Commission, *Uniform Evidence Law* (ALRC 102, 2005), [13.25].
30   [2016] SASC 171, [31].
31   Uniform Evidence Legislation (UEL) applies in the Commonwealth, ACT, NSW, Northern Territory, Tasmanian and Victorian jurisdictions.

Biometric identification must be presented by an expert who has specialised knowledge based on training, study or experience in the applicable field.

> If a person has specialised knowledge based on the person's training, study or experience, the opinion rule does not apply to evidence of an opinion of that person that is wholly or substantially based on that knowledge.[32]

A judge must exclude biometric identification evidence from the trial 'if its probative value is outweighed by the danger of unfair prejudice to the defendant'.[33] They also have the discretion to exclude evidence considered to have been obtained improperly, due to impropriety, or in contravention of a law.[34]

# Fingerprint identification

The classification of fingerprints, as it is understood today, is historically associated with the work of Sir Francis Galton (1822–1911) and Sir Edward Henry (1850–1931), who systematically organised thousands of individual fingerprints into a searchable database on the basis of their characteristic architecture, providing a method to classify and match fingerprints. Fingerprinting has been routinely used by police in criminal investigations since 1900,[35] and manual fingerprint databases were established by law enforcement agencies around the world by the mid-20th century.[36]

Human fingerprints are unique, universal and do not change over time. In addition to these characteristics, their easy accessibility made them attractive for biometric identification. The formation of fingerprints occurs during foetal development as a result of the formation of nerves beneath the skin. They serve the functional purpose of assisting with grip when handling objects. Each fingerprint is unique, not only among all people, but also between all fingers of the same person. In contrast with DNA, they are unique between identical twins.[37] Approximately 4 per cent of the population have fingerprints that cannot be used for biometric identification. This is caused by a range of factors, commonly through injuries, such as burns, or many years of manual labour. Therefore, biometric fingerprint databases cannot achieve universal coverage of an entire population. To address this, systems often combine multiple biometric profiles. However, their easy accessibility and cost-effectiveness have made fingerprints the most widely used contemporary form of biometric identification, accounting for more than half of the biometric market worldwide.[38]

Fingerprints are a series of ridges and valleys on the surface of the skin. These form patterns that allow fingerprints to be classified into *loops* (60 per cent), *whorls* (35 per cent) and *arches* (5 per cent) – at least one of which is present in every fingerprint. There

32  UEL, s 79.
33  Ibid, s 137.
34  Ibid, s 138.
35  Jeremy Gans, 'A Tale of Two High Court Forensic Cases' (2011) 33 *Sydney Law Review* 515.
36  Rory Allen et al, 'Fingerprint Identification Technology'. In James Wayman, *Biometric Systems: Technology, Design and Performance Evaluation* (Springer, 2005).
37  Anil Jain, Arun Ross and Salil Prabhakar, 'An Introduction to Biometric Recognition' (2004) 14 *IEEE Transactions on Circuits and Systems for Video Technology* 1.
38  Damien Dessimoz and Christophe Champod, 'Linkages between Biometrics and Forensic Science'. In Anil Jain et al, *Handbook of Biometrics* (Springer, 2006), 425–59.

are several key features: the *core* refers to the centre of a pattern; the *delta*, a point where multiple ridges deviate; and the *minutiae*, the point where a ridge ends or bifurcates.[39]

Initially, a card-based system was used by law enforcement agencies to store and compare individual fingerprints. The manual comparison of cards within a large collection was burdensome and time consuming. In the latter half of the 20th century, technology advancements that enabled computer technology to digitally retrieve and match fingerprint data increased the system's efficiency and accuracy, along with its potential applications. There are now large automated fingerprint databases, managed by law enforcement agencies, that only require human input at the final stage to distinguish between highly similar fingerprints in a list of close matches.[40]

Digital biometric fingerprint recognition compares the unique combination of patterns on individuals' fingerprints through an automated process. An optical scanner is used to illuminate the fingerprint ridges and convert the resulting image into a digital format. An algorithm filters out distortions caused by factors such as sweat or dirt, and further enhances the definition of the ridges in the image. In most digital systems in use today, between 10 and 100 minutiae are used by the algorithm to create the digital template.[41] There are four steps in converting a fingerprint to the digital template: the fingerprint is scanned; minutiae points are identified and mapped; and finally, the map is converted to data and stored in a database.

The concept of fingerprint identification has been widely accepted for over a century and has become established as a primary means of personal identification. The digitisation of fingerprints and the efficiency offered by automated biometric technology has been quickly integrated into practice by law enforcement and border security agencies around the world.

## Databases

The Automated Fingerprint Identification Systems currently used by law enforcement were developed in the late 1990s and have a search function that determines the correlation between two or more fingerprints, based on nominated scoring criteria. In one-to-many searches, the system produces a list of fingerprints in the database with the closest match, and a human expert makes a final determination on whether the fingerprints of the suspect and database templates belong to the same individual.[42] Law enforcement databases include two subsystems: a 10-print identification system comprising a set of fingerprints obtained through an arrest; and those obtained under less controlled conditions, from crime scenes or physical evidence.[43]

These subsystems enable fingerprint databases to conduct the following four types of searches:

39  Andrew Jackson and Julie Jackson, *Forensic Science* (Pearson, 2008), 89.
40  Kenneth Moses et al, 'Automated Fingerprint Identification Systems'. In Department of Justice, *Fingerprint Sourcebook* (National Institute of Justice, 2010).
41  Damien Dessimoz and Christophe Champod, 'Linkages between Biometrics and Forensic Science'. In Anil Jain et al, *Handbook of Biometrics* (Springer, 2006), 425–59.
42  Robert Milne, *Forensic Intelligence* (CRC Press, 2013).
43  Kenneth Moses et al, 'Automated Fingerprint Identification System'. In Department of Justice, *Fingerprint Sourcebook* (National Institute of Justice, 2010).

- *print-to-print searches:* conducted to verify the identity of a suspect through a comparison of fingerprints obtained from a suspect against fingerprints stored in the database
- *mark-to-print searches:* conducted in order to compare a fingerprint obtained from a crime scene, or other physical evidence, against fingerprints held within the database
- *print-to-mark searches:* used to determine whether an individual is linked to other crime scenes by comparing their fingerprints against all the fingerprints held within the database, but in instances where previous searches have failed
- *mark-to-mark searches:* used to determine whether a fingerprint obtained from a crime scene or physical evidence is connected with other prints held within the database.[44]

In the United States, the Integrated Automated Fingerprint Identification System was established in 1999 as a national fingerprint database, and was operated by the FBI until 2014 when it was integrated into a new biometric identification service, known as the Next Generation Identification (NGI) system. The NGI is linked to biographical information about the individuals included in the database, such as their address, social security data and criminal history; as well as their links to persons of interest and intelligence relevant to investigations and operations across many jurisdictions throughout the country.[45] It has multimodal biometric functionality, adding several stages of advanced capability and enhancing the accuracy and scope of the system. The NGI links fingerprint data to other biometrics, including iris and facial recognition templates, and also enables text-based searches for tattoos.[46]

In the United Kingdom, the national database is known as IDENT1, developed as a joint venture between the Home Office and the defence technology company Northrop Grumman. Its computing infrastructure comprises over 1000 workstations and approximately 500 fingerprint scanning units, providing a link between 57 law enforcement agencies across England, Wales and Scotland, and integration with criminal record and intelligence holdings on the Police National Computer.[47] An evaluation of the national fingerprint database in the United Kingdom, which analysed how police in five jurisdictions obtained fingerprint evidence in volume crime, such as burglary and motor vehicle thefts, found that the system provided a greater capacity to identify suspects and greater efficiency in reaching case outcomes than would otherwise have been possible.[48]

The Australian fingerprint database has operated since 2001 and is known as the National Automated Fingerprint Identification System (NAFIS). Operated by the Australian Criminal Intelligence Commission (ACIC), it provides Australian law enforcement agencies, including the Department of Immigration and Border Protection, with a centralised automated search and matching capability. The NAFIS enables near real-time fingerprint uploads and matching

---

44  Ibid.
45  Federal Bureau of Investigation, *Integrated Automated Fingerprint Identification System* (2019). Available: <www.fbi.gov/about-us/cjis/fingerprints_biometrics/iafis/iafis>.
46  Federal Bureau of Investigation, *NGI Officially Replaces IAFIS* (2019). Available: <https://www.fbi.gov/services/cjis/cjis-link/ngi-officially-replaces-iafis-yields-more-search-options-and-investigative-leads-and-increased-identification-accuracy>.
47  Northrop Grumman, *IDENT1 Automated Fingerprint System, United Kingdom* (2019). Available: <www.homelandsecurity-technology.com/projects/ident1-automated-fingerprint-system-northrop-grumman-uk/>.
48  Richard Saferstein, *Criminalistics: An Introduction to Forensic Science* (Pearson Education, 2015).

from individuals and crime scenes.[49] A Biometric Identification System was scheduled to replace NAFIS in mid-2017. It sought to improve police agencies' access to provide integration between fingerprints and other forms of biometrics, including facial images. However, the project was not successfully completed and was disbanded after $34 million of the $52 million budget had been spent. A review conducted by the Australian National Audit Office identified problems with the governance and management of the project,[50] and it is expected that the Australian government will seek to implement a new form of the integrated system by 2025.

The digitisation of fingerprint identification through automated databases has led to a significant number of positive identifications and linkages between individuals and physical evidence at crime scenes. Data published in annual reports of the ACIC indicates a dramatic increase in the use of biometric fingerprint identification by law enforcement agencies in Australia over the past decade. In the 2007–08 financial year, there were 298 790 searches for fingerprints on the national database, resulting in 31 219 identifications.[51] By the 2018–19 financial year, this number had increased substantially. Ten years later, there are more than five times as many searches being conducted (1 647 519), resulting in three times as many matches (99 524). By 2019, NAFIS held more than 10 million fingerprint records.[52]

## Evidentiary issues

Courts around the world have admitted fingerprint evidence in criminal trials for more than a century. In 1912, the Australian High Court observed:

> Signatures have been accepted as evidence of identity as long as they have been used. The fact of the individuality of the corrugations of the skin on the fingers of the human hand is now so generally recognised as to require very little, if any, evidence of it, although it seems to be still the practice to offer some expert evidence on the point. A fingerprint is therefore in reality an unforgeable signature.[53]

The expert witness providing evidence in these cases is often the forensic scientist who collected and compared the relevant fingerprints in the investigation.[54] As discussed above, the process of comparison often involves an automated database, accompanied by manual confirmation; or manual comparison of digital photographs of fingerprints collected at a crime scene[55] with the purpose of establishing that two fingerprints are from the same person.

Fingerprint comparison does not rely on calculating the probability of a match, but on the expert's judgement in making a visual comparison – which introduces a capacity for

49  Australian Criminal Intelligence Commission, *Biometric and Forensic Services* (2019). Available: <www.acic.gov.au/our-services/biometric-and-forensic-services>.
50  Australian National Audit Office (ANAO), *The Australian Criminal Intelligence Commission's Administration of the Biometric Identification Services Project* (Australian Government, 2019).
51  CrimTrac, *Annual Report 2013–2014* (Australian Government, 2014).
52  Australian Criminal Intelligence Commission, *Annual Report 2018–19* (Australian Government, 2019), 42.
53  *Parker v The King* (1912) 14 CLR 681, 683 (Griffith CJ), cited in *R v Mitchell* [1997] ACTSC 93.
54  See, eg, the cases of *R v Regan* [2014] NSWDC 118; and *DPP v Watts* [2016] VCC 1726; or *R v Trewin* [2018] ACTSC 109, 245.
55  *R v Trewin* [2018] ACTSC 109, 248.

error.[56] The following extract indicates how fingerprint comparison evidence is adduced by the prosecution in a criminal case.

> The real strength of the Crown case lay in the fingerprint evidence. Ms Lam, a crime scene investigator, attended the scene at about 4.45 pm. She found a number of fingerprints, including some left on the television set, and both photographed them and took tape lifts from them. Mr Comber, a fingerprint expert, gave evidence that he had compared a fingerprint lifted from the television set with a fingerprint identified as that of the accused on the National Automated Fingerprint Identification System ('NAFIS'). He found that the two prints had both been made by the middle finger of the same left hand. There was no challenge to Mr Comber's methodology or as to the accuracy of this conclusion. I found him to be an impressive witness and accepted his evidence. It was not suggested that the fingerprint obtained from NAFIS had been incorrectly attributed to the accused and I was satisfied beyond reasonable doubt that the print had been left on the television set when touched by the accused.[57]

While match probabilities are not involved in fingerprint comparisons, two prints are compared on the basis of numerous 'characteristic points'.[58] The more points that are compared, and the greater the similarity between them, the more persuasive is any conclusion drawn regarding a person's identity. The expert witness may not need to describe all of the details of the matching process, and the defence will have the opportunity to cross-examine the expert to test the basis of their finding.

Fingerprint evidence forms part of the circumstantial case against the defendant. The probative value of a fingerprint match is assessed in the context of all the other evidence admitted in the trial, including the explanation for how it came to be at the scene of the crime.[59]

The expert evidence requirements mean that a witness who conducted the comparison should be able to demonstrate how it provides a sound basis for their opinions.[60] If their explanation is inadequate, defence counsel can seek to have the opinion excluded, or ask for the jury to be cautioned in relation to the weight that should be accorded to it.[61] An appeal could also be lodged on the basis that the judge did not properly describe the fingerprint

---

56   Gary Edmond and Mehera San Roque, 'The Cool Crucible: Forensic Science and the Frailty of the Criminal Trial' (2012) 24 *Current Issues in Criminal Justice* 51.

57   *R v Millard* [2006] ACTSC 56, [15]. See also *R v Fitzgerald* [2005] SADC 118.

58   *JP v DPP (NSW)* (2015) 256 A Crim R 447, [36], referring to the case of *Bennett v Police* [2005] SASC 167 in which 'more than 20 characteristics … were common and identical'. In *JP*, the police witness claimed to have examined 35 comparison points but did not specify how many were considered to be a match with the defendant's prints, as opposed to the overall conclusion of identity.

59   For example, there have been cases where fingerprint evidence was sought to be excluded on the basis of allegations that police had forged the defendant's fingerprint: *Mickelberg v The Queen* (2004) 29 WAR 13.

60   Leading authorities on specialised knowledge under UEL, s 79(1) are *Makita (Australia) Pty Ltd v Sprowles* (2001) 52 NSWLR 705; *HG v The Queen* (1999) 197 CLR 414; and *Honeysett v The Queen* (2014) 253 CLR 122.

61   In *JP v DPP (NSW)* (2015) 256 A Crim R 447, the defence argued unsuccessfully that the expert had insufficiently explained the reasoning process they undertook. The judge noted at [43] that 'with fingerprint evidence it will often be the case that *"little explicit articulation or amplification"* of how the stated methodology warrants the conclusion that two fingerprints are identical will be required before it can be concluded that the second condition of admissibility under s 79(1) has been satisfied' (emphasis original), citing *Dasreef Pty Ltd v Hawchar* (2011) 243 CLR 588.

evidence when instructing the jury;[62] or that evidence of the database match implied that the defendant had a criminal history and was therefore unfairly prejudicial.[63]

# DNA identification

DNA identification is the most significant scientific advancement in the history of forensic science and has played a crucial role in many high-profile investigations around the world. The comparison between DNA profiles obtained from a crime scene, and a suspect or database, is widely used in cases involving serious crimes against the person, particularly homicide and sexual assault. While the fundamental technique was first established in the late 1980s, new techniques continue to be developed and applied to solve crimes where a database match is not available.[64] DNA evidence is used to link or exclude an individual from association with the crime scene (notwithstanding the potential for the evidence to have been planted, or other explanation).

DNA can be recovered from most biological material. At a crime scene, the forensic scientist must identify whether a sufficient amount of biological material is present to enable a sample to be taken. Measures must be taken to ensure that the biological material is properly preserved and not contaminated: such as wearing gloves and a mask over the nose and mouth. The sample collection must accord with standard procedure, and a chain of custody must be established.

Evidence obtained at a crime scene is analysed and then compared with biological material collected from a suspect. A sample from a suspect is usually obtained by pressing a cotton tip against the inside of the suspect's cheek, which painlessly removes mucosal cells (a buccal swab).[65] A match between a DNA profile obtained from a crime scene sample and a DNA profile obtained from a suspect provides strong support for the inference that the samples are from the same person. However, there are alternative hypotheses that can account for a match that must also be considered, such as whether the sample has been contaminated. DNA identification must therefore be considered in the context of the other evidence.[66]

An individual's genome is unique, although vast regions of the human genome are shared. By closely analysing the points that differ, DNA can be used as a form of identification. Repetitive parts of DNA within the genome, *short tandem repeats* (STRs), are the points of difference between individuals that are used by DNA profiling. A DNA profile is created by analysing the number of STRs that occur at specific locations in an individual's genome. The STRs used for DNA identification occur in *introns* (non-coding regions of the human genome): these regions do not code for specific genes and, based on current scientific understanding, do not provide health or any other information about the individual beyond their identity. *Exons* are the coding regions of the genome that, for example, code for

---

62  *Ghebrat v The Queen* (2011) 214 A Crim R 140.

63  To address this issue, the judge could warn the jury against making an adverse inference of this type. See, eg, the defence submission in *R v Ahola (No 6)* [2013] NSWSC 703, [3].

64  Marcus Smith, *DNA Evidence in the Australian Legal System* (Lexis Nexis, 2016).

65  John Butler, *Forensic DNA Typing* (Elsevier, 2005).

66  Jeremy Gans and Gregor Urbas, 'DNA Identification in the Criminal Justice System' (2002) 226 *Trends and Issues in Crime and Criminal Justice* 1.

eye or hair colour, or are associated with particular health conditions.[67] A DNA profile includes a gender designation and set of paired numbers. These numbers specify the STRs at approximately 20 points in the human genome and a sex indicator – for example: 'XY, 13,5 4,11 7,10 … '. The numbers are paired at each point because one STR is inherited from each of an individual's parents.

## Collection of DNA evidence

DNA identification was first applied to a criminal investigation in 1987 in the United Kingdom. Professor Alec Jeffreys was asked to analyse biological samples recovered from the crime scene where two children were murdered in Leicestershire, and to compare them with a sample of a suspect who had confessed to killing one of the victims. The DNA profiles actually established that the suspect's DNA did not match the sample recovered from the victim, and he was released. A screening of the men from three surrounding villages was undertaken, and it emerged that one man, Colin Pitchfork, had coerced another into providing a sample on his behalf. Pitchfork's DNA profile was matched to the one found at the crime scene and he was subsequently convicted.[68]

The process by which samples are collected by forensic investigators is critical, and while the scientific foundation of DNA identification is well established, human factors, either intentional or by error, may compromise the validity of the laboratory tests. For instance:

> A suspect's DNA profile might match the profile found at a crime scene as a result of tampering with the crime scene or subsequent substitution of DNA samples. This might occur where the actual offender, a police investigator, or another person deliberately leaves a suspect's genetic sample at the crime scene. Alternatively, it is possible that a suspect's sample might later be substituted for the actual crime scene sample to falsely implicate the suspect in the offence.[69]

Key questions for courts in DNA evidence cases include whether it was lawfully obtained, whether it was planted at the crime scene, whether there are untested samples that may be of significance to the case, whether the chain of custody was maintained, and whether the suspects' samples could have been mislabelled or contaminated.[70]

In recent years, more creative avenues for collecting DNA evidence have been documented. There have been several cases of police covertly obtaining evidence to enhance their investigations. These include police following a suspect into a restaurant and obtaining evidence from cutlery, after a suspect has left; or after they have observed a suspect spit on

---

67  A key technique used in DNA identification is *polymerase chain reaction* (PCR), developed in the 1980s, and enabling the rapid replication of a DNA sequence. PCR has enabled DNA identification to advance, both in terms of its power of discrimination and in its ability to obtain information from very small amounts of biological material. It is an enzymatic process that amplifies specific regions of DNA through cycles of heating and cooling: Randall Saki and Kary Mullis, 'Primer-Directed Enzymatic Amplification of DNA with a Thermostable DNA Polymerase' (1988) 239 *Science* 487.

68  Mark Jobling and Peter Gill, 'Encoded Evidence: DNA in Forensic Analysis' (2004) 5 *Nature Reviews Genetics* 739. The facts of the case are set out in the appellate decision: *R v Pitchfork* [2009] EWCA Crim 963.

69  Australian Law Reform Commission, *Essentially Yours: The Protection of Genetic Information in Australia* (ALRC 96, 2003), 1095.

70  Marcus Smith and Monique Mann, 'Recent Developments in DNA Evidence' (2015) 506 *Trends and Issues in Crime and Criminal Justice* 1.

the pavement.[71] In a high-profile case in the United States, Lonnie Franklin was convicted of 10 murders and numerous counts of sexual assault following the covert collection of his DNA from a pizza restaurant.[72] The same technique was used in the investigation of Bradley Edwards, arrested in 2016 in relation to three murders in Perth, Australia in the mid-1990s, known as the Claremont serial killings. Edwards was subsequently convicted of two of the three murders in September 2020.[73]

The most significant case involving the retention of DNA evidence in the United Kingdom is *R v Marper and S*.[74] In this case, provisions of the *Criminal Justice and Police Act 2001* (UK) were challenged on the basis of the right to privacy expressed in Article 8 of the *European Convention on Human Rights*.[75] Two individuals, including a 12-year-old child, were charged with separate offences: the child attempted to steal a bike; and the adult was charged with harassment of their partner, but they were later reconciled. Biological samples were obtained, and their DNA profiles created and included in the national DNA database. Following their acquittal, the South Yorkshire Police refused to destroy the biological samples and DNA profiles. The case was appealed to the House of Lords,[76] and then to the European Court of Human Rights. The court ruled in favour of Marper and S, finding that:

> ... the blanket and indiscriminate nature of the powers of retention of the fingerprints, cellular samples and DNA profiles of persons suspected but not convicted of offences, as applied in the case of the present applicants, fails to strike a fair balance between the competing public and private interests and that the respondent State has overstepped any acceptable margin of appreciation in this regard.[77]

The case did not focus on whether police had the legal right to obtain the evidence, but on whether the retention breached the privacy rights of the individuals concerned, under Article 8 of the Convention, as well as the right to fair and equal treatment under Article 14 of the Convention. In relation to DNA profiles, the case highlighted the apparently unfair distinction between individuals who had been suspected and charged with an offence but subsequently released without conviction; and those in the broader community who had never been suspected of committing, and never been charged with committing, a criminal offence.

Following the *Marper* ruling, the UK government responded with a number of policy changes. The DNA profiles of children under 10 were removed from the database, and

71  Amy Harmon, 'Lawyers Fight DNA Samples Gained on the Sly', *New York Times*, 3 April 2008.
72  Marcus Smith and Monique Mann, 'Recent Developments in DNA Evidence' (2015) 506 *Trends and Issues in Crime and Criminal Justice* 1.
73  Andrea Mayes, 'Claremont Killer Bradley Edwards Found Guilty of Jane Rimmer and Ciara Glennon Murders but not Sarah Spiers', *Australian Broadcasting Corporation*, 24 September 2020. Available: <https://www.abc.net.au/news/2020-09-24/claremont-killer-bradley-edwards-guilty-rimmer-glennon-murders/12426210>.
74  (2002) EWCA Civ 1275.
75  1. Everyone has the right to respect for his private and family life, his home and his correspondence; 2. There shall be no interference by a public authority with the exercise of this right except such as is in accordance with the law and is necessary in a democratic society in the interests of national security, public safety or the economic well-being of the country, for the prevention of disorder or crime, for the protection of health or morals, or for the protection of the rights and freedoms of others (1953).
76  *R v Marper and S* [2004] UKHL 39.
77  *S and Marper v United Kingdom* [2008] ECHR 1581.

legislative amendments were introduced that complied with the court's decision. Individuals convicted of a recordable offence will still have their DNA profiles retained indefinitely; however, under the amended legislation, the government has acted to:

- [destroy] all original DNA samples, including mouth swabs, as soon as they are converted into a digital database profile;
- [delete] the profiles of those arrested but not convicted of a serious violent or sexual crime after 12 years;
- [delete] the profiles of anyone arrested but not convicted of other offences after six years; and
- [remove] the profiles of young people arrested but not convicted, or convicted of less serious offences, when they turn 18.[78]

In the United States, under the *Justice for All Act of 2004*, DNA profiles can be included in the national database if a person is charged with an indictable offence, even if the charges are subsequently withdrawn; however, DNA profiles of arrestees could not be included. The *DNA Fingerprint Act of 2005* enabled an arrestee's profile to be uploaded to the database at the time of arrest. If the arrestee is not subsequently charged with an offence, the burden lies with the arrestee to file a court order stating that the charges have been dismissed.[79]

The Fourth Amendment of the US Constitution governs the legitimacy of government intrusion into the lives of private citizens, protecting the 'right of the people to be secure in their persons … against unreasonable searches and seizures'.[80] In order to be considered reasonable, a search needs to be supported by a warrant on the basis of 'probable cause': the reasonable belief that the individual has committed a crime. In the 2013 US Supreme Court case *Maryland v King*,[81] King was arrested on assault charges and his DNA profile collected and retained in the state DNA database. His DNA profile was later linked to an unsolved rape of which he was subsequently convicted. King argued that the DNA evidence should have been supressed because the Maryland DNA collection legislation violated the Fourth Amendment. While the Maryland Court of Appeals found the legislation was unconstitutional, and set aside the rape conviction, the Supreme Court overturned this decision and held that the collection and retention of DNA profiles in databases is a legitimate and constitutionally valid procedure for identifying arrestees.

Police in most jurisdictions can obtain forensic biological material from volunteers who consent to provide a sample. If a volunteer is a suspect, they have the right to refuse; however, even their behaviour in refusing the request can provide police with useful information about their guilt or innocence. As was discussed in relation to the Pitchfork case, the offender was apprehended after it became apparent that he had asked another man to provide a sample on his behalf.[82] Observing the behaviour and body language of those asked to provide a biological sample can be as important to the investigation

---

78  National DNA Ethics Group, United Kingdom, *Second Annual Report* (2009). Available: <https://www .gov.uk/government/publications/ndnad-ethics-group-2nd-annual-report>.
79  Privacy International, *The United States and the Development of DNA Data Banks* (2006). Available: <www.privacyinternational.org/article.shtml?cmd%5B347%5D=x-347-528471#_ftn25>.
80  Fourth Amendment, United States Constitution.
81  569 US 435 (2013).
82  Joseph Wambaugh, *The Blooding* (Bantam, 1989).

as the technology of DNA identification itself. There remain questions over whether this potentially infringes the fundamental privilege against self-incrimination, 'because it forces individuals who are reluctant to undergo DNA profile surveillance to reveal that reluctance to investigators'.[83] This issue would be considered by a court in determining whether the probative value of the evidence outweighed its prejudicial effect.

## DNA evidence in criminal trials

DNA evidence is a form of circumstantial evidence, insufficient for a conviction by itself, and usually comprising part of the prosecution's case. If an accused has a strong alibi, it is possible they will be found not guilty, despite the existence of DNA evidence. However, if other evidence demonstrates an association between an accused and a crime scene, the DNA evidence will be a significant aspect of the prosecution's case – supported by the other circumstantial evidence.[84]

Despite the fact that DNA evidence has been accepted as reliable for over 20 years, it is complex scientific evidence and the potential for the jury to misunderstand it may affect the assessment of its probative value. A match between a defendant's DNA profile and a crime scene sample is presented in court as a *match probability*: the probability that if another individual were selected from a population at random, they would have the same DNA profile. This can be potentially confusing in the context of a criminal trial if it is not explained and presented correctly, given the large numbers (in the billions) that are regularly quoted and the lack of scientific training of judges and jurors.

Empirical research indicates that the availability of DNA evidence increases the likelihood that a defendant will be convicted.[85] Research based on interviewing jurors at the conclusion of trials has raised questions about the capacity of jurors to understand and apply scientific evidence to facts presented in the courtroom.[86] Basic training on relevant scientific principles and interpretation issues for jurors could help ensure a sufficient level of understanding is present to inform effective decision-making.

A further important aspect of DNA identification is the opportunity it provides to evaluate the accuracy of convictions and acquittals, and to examine the causative factors involved. This is particularly so with older cases prior to the 2000s, when DNA technology became commonly used. Eyewitness error has been found to be the most prevalent factor contributing to wrongful conviction, and contributes to approximately 60 per cent of all wrongful convictions identified.[87] False confessions obtained under duress are also

---

83 Jeremy Gans, 'Something to Hide: DNA, Surveillance and Self-Incrimination' (2001) 13 *Current Issues in Criminal Justice* 168.
84 Mark Findlay and Julia Grix, 'Challenging Forensic Evidence? Observations on the Use of DNA in Certain Criminal Trials' (2002) 14 *Current Issues in Criminal Justice* 272.
85 Michael Briody, 'The Effects of DNA Evidence on Homicide Cases in Court' (2004) 37 *Australian and New Zealand Journal of Criminology* 252.
86 Mark Findlay and Julia Grix, 'Challenging Forensic Evidence? Observations on the Use of DNA in Certain Criminal Trials' (2002) 14 *Current Issues in Criminal Justice* 272.
87 Ronald Huff, 'Wrongful Convictions: The American Experience (2004) *Canadian Journal of Criminology and Criminal Justice* 107.

significant contributors.[88] Innocence projects have made good use of DNA evidence. The original Innocence Project, founded in 1992 at Cardozo Law School in New York, has been responsible for 367 post-conviction DNA exonerations (225 of which involved African Americans). It provides legal representation, undertakes research into the causes of wrongful conviction, contributes to law reform efforts, and seeks to raise awareness in the community. The work of innocence projects has led to the identification of flaws in earlier forms of scientific technology. For example, convictions obtained in cases using microscopic hair analysis were overturned when mitochondrial DNA identification became available and demonstrated that the hair samples presented at trial did not match the person convicted of the crime.[89]

In an Australian case, a 22-year-old named Farah Jama was released from prison after serving 18 months of a six-year prison sentence for rape. Despite the fact that DNA evidence was the only evidence that linked Jama to the crime, and he had an alibi, he was nonetheless convicted. It was later established that the match occurred following contamination at the forensic medicine centre where the samples were taken. Following the incident, a review of all cases involving DNA evidence over the previous five years was announced in Victoria, the state where this case occurred, and the use of DNA evidence at trial suspended while a review was undertaken. In the public debate that followed, comments were made to the effect that 'there is a strong case building for some kind of a warning to juries about not placing too much reliance on DNA evidence' and the need to 'guard against these sorts of errors being made in the future by overreliance on DNA evidence'.[90] In Western Australia in 2017, the leading forensic science expert in the state was sacked after systematically breaching protocols, casting doubt on the outcomes of more than 27 convictions for serious crimes.[91]

The risks associated with DNA evidence are not theoretical and these examples highlight the importance of appropriate scrutiny and avenues for review. In the United Kingdom, the Criminal Cases Review Commission (CCRC) was established in 1995 to determine whether the legal system was correctly convicting the guilty. This is an independent body established to conduct transparent, impartial and accountable investigations into suspected miscarriages of justice. It has the power to refer claims of wrongful conviction to the Court of Appeal, where there is a 'real possibility' that the conviction can be overturned on the basis of arguments not raised at trial, evidence not presented at trial, or other exceptional circumstances. Between 1997 and 2019, the CCRC referred 667 cases for review, and of those, 441 appeals against convictions were allowed.[92] There have been calls for a similar organisation to be established in Australia.[93]

---

88  Kathryn Campbell and Myriam Denov, 'Criminal Injustice: Understanding the Causes, Effects and Responses to Wrongful Conviction in Canada' (2005) 21 *Journal of Contemporary Criminal Justice* 224.
89  Innocence Project – About (2019). Available: <https://www.innocenceproject.org>.
90  Frank Vincent, *Inquiry into the Circumstances that Led to the Conviction of Mr. Farah Abdulkadir Jama* (Department of Justice, 2010).
91  Graeme Powell, 'Leading DNA Scientist Sacked, 27 Criminal Convictions in Doubt, WA Attorney-General Says', *Australian Broadcasting Corporation News*, 31 March 2017.
92  Select Committee on Home Affairs, *First Report: The Work of the Criminal Cases Review Commission* (1999).
93  See, eg, Bibi Sangha and Robert Moles, *Miscarriages of Justice: Criminal Appeals and the Rule of Law in Australia* (LexisNexis, 2015).

# Impact of DNA databases

DNA databases are digital collections of DNA profiles, stored in various categories such as offender profiles, suspect profiles and crime scene profiles; as well as associated information to identify the individuals they belong to, or details of the crime scene where they were collected. These databases have become very large, with most developed countries' databases holding millions of profiles. In 2020, the US National DNA Index System contains over 14 million offender profiles and 3.7 million arrestee profiles;[94] the UK National DNA Database has over 5.5 million individual profiles and over 600 000 crime scene sample profiles;[95] and the Australian National Criminal Investigation DNA Database contains more than 1.3 million DNA profiles.[96] Several countries share DNA profiles internationally when relevant. In 2014, the Australian government acknowledged that it had entered into a DNA profile-sharing program with the United Kingdom, the United States and Canada.[97]

Empirical evidence of the contribution of DNA to criminal investigations indicates that it has a positive impact on investigation outcomes. A large randomised study of the effect of DNA evidence in property crime investigations in the United States used traditional investigative techniques in treatment and control groups, with the treatment group incorporating DNA. The use of DNA evidence in the investigation of property offences resulted in twice as many suspects identified, arrests and cases accepted for prosecution. A comparison between DNA and fingerprint identification was also undertaken, finding that DNA was five times more likely than fingerprint evidence to result in the identification of a suspect.[98]

Previous Australian research has examined the impact of DNA evidence on court outcomes for homicide and sexual offences. Half of the cases utilised DNA evidence in court, while the other half were assigned as comparison-control cases. In sexual offence cases, DNA evidence was found to double the likelihood that a case reached court, and provided a 33-fold increase in the likelihood that a jury would find the offender guilty. In relation to homicide cases, those where DNA evidence was available were more than 14 times more likely to reach court, with juries 23 times more likely to convict if it was used.[99] There is strong empirical evidence supporting the use of DNA in criminal investigations, particularly with respect to serious offences against the person.

---

94   Federal Bureau of Investigation, *NDIS Statistics* (2019). Available: <https://www.fbi.gov/services/laboratory/biometric-analysis/codis/ndis-statistics>.

95   Home Office of the United Kingdom, *National DNA Database Statistics* (2019). Available: <https://www.gov.uk/government/statistics/national-dna-database-statistics>.

96   Australian Criminal Intelligence Commission, *Annual Report 2018–19* (2019). Available: <https://www.acic.gov.au/our-services/biometric-matching/national-criminal-investigation-dna-database>.

97   Michael Keenan, 'Minister Signs International DNA Exchange Pilot with United Kingdom' (Media release, 6 November 2014).

98   John Roman, *The DNA Field Experiment: Cost-Effectiveness Analysis of the Use of DNA in the Investigation of High-Volume Crimes* (Urban Institute, 2008).

99   Michael Briody, 'The Effects of DNA Evidence on Sexual Offence Cases in Court' (2002) 14 *Current Issues in Criminal Justice* 159; Michael Briody, 'The Effects of DNA Evidence on Property Offences in Court' (2006) 17 *Current Issues in Criminal Justice* 380.

# New forms of DNA identification

A range of new techniques in the field of DNA identification developed over the past decade increase the options available to investigators where they do not obtain a match on a database for the suspect's DNA profile. In some instances, these techniques extend beyond STR-based DNA profiling to actual analysis of coding regions of the genome. A further important general development is a reduction in the required time, as well as the size and cost of the equipment used, to undertake DNA profiling. Rapid DNA analysis is becoming more common, allowing DNA profiles to be created in an hour from a cheek swab in a police station.[100] Devices that can be connected to a smartphone and provide a DNA profile within 10 minutes have been developed and are expected to be widely available in a matter of years.[101] This is an important technological development that will contribute to DNA identification being considered a primary biometric identifier in the way that fingerprints and iris scans are today.

DNA profiles can demonstrate familial relationships on the basis of the number of shared STR markers between two or more profiles. For instance, a child would share some of each parent's STR markers, because half of a person's genetic code is received from each parent. *Familial searching* is a new application of DNA identification that is increasingly being used in criminal investigations. If a match cannot be established with any of the DNA profiles held on a database, partial matches may indicate familial relationships that police can then investigate using traditional lines of inquiry – for instance, whether a relative lives in the vicinity of the crime scene.[102] This technique has not been particularly controversial, as it uses the same method as traditional DNA profiling; however, it has been suggested that the potential implications for an individual's relatives should be made clear as part of gaining informed consent when obtaining a DNA sample.[103] The first publicised case of this technique successfully being used to secure a conviction in Australia occurred in 2017 in Adelaide.

> [T]he sharing of an allele at every locus between the crime stain and the candidate male relative yielded extremely strong support that the individual who had left the crime scene stain was a potential father or son of the person identified in the candidate list arising from the familial search. Police generated a list of relatives of the individual

100  Federal Bureau of Investigation, *Rapid DNA General Information* (2019). Available: <https://www.fbi.gov/services/laboratory/biometric-analysis/codis/rapid-dna>.
101  Matthew Chin, 'UCLA Researchers Make DNA Detection Portable, Affordable Using Cellphones' (Media release, 20 March 2017). Available: <http://newsroom.ucla.edu/releases/ucla-researchers-make-dna-detection-portable-affordable-using-cellphones>.
102  In England, familial searching has been used to identify a suspect who threw a brick from an overpass, killing a truck driver. DNA evidence obtained from the brick elicited a partial match that showed that the suspect who deposited their biological material on the brick had a brother who lived near the crime scene. This person was located, eventually confessing to the crime and being convicted of manslaughter: Henry Greely et al, 'Family Ties: The Use of DNA Databases to Catch Offenders' Kin' (2006) 34 *Journal of Law, Medicine & Ethics* 248.
103  See, eg, Marcus Smith and Gregor Urbas, 'Regulating New Forms of Forensic DNA Profiling under Australian Legislation: Familial Matching and DNA Phenotyping' (2012) 44 *Australian Journal of Forensic Sciences* 63.

identified by the search. One individual could be placed in the area around the time the incidents occurred and this person had a similar appearance to the identikit picture developed from the victims' description of the attacker. A DNA sample was obtained from this individual and matched the autosomal and Y-STR DNA profiles generated from the exhibits analysed previously. This person was subsequently arrested and ultimately pleaded guilty to the charges.[104]

Another relatively new technique is *DNA phenotyping*, which involves analysis of coding regions of the genome. This is more controversial than familial searching because it uses a different methodology to that permitted under most legislative regimes. DNA phenotyping can determine whether an individual has specific genes that are relevant to physically identifiable features, such as hair and eye colour, height, ethnic background, facial features, and also predisposition to medical and psychological conditions.[105] It is therefore used to obtain an indication of the suspect's likely physical appearance in cases where investigators cannot establish a DNA match on a database. In most jurisdictions around the world the technique remains unregulated, with the Netherlands one of the few countries where it is referred to in legislation – limiting this form of analysis to deriving externally visible traits.[106] From an ethical standpoint, there are limited privacy concerns in relation to externally visible traits such as eye and hair colour; however, concerns do arise when DNA phenotyping reveals medical conditions.[107] In the UK, police used DNA phenotyping to determine a suspect's race, which proved critical to the investigation of a prolific offender who committed numerous burglaries and rapes over a 20-year period.[108]

The third and most recently developed technique is the use of commercial ancestry databases to identify suspects of serious offences.[109] Unlike the other developing issues in DNA identification discussed, this technique involves the use of information not obtained for the purposes of an investigation, but freely submitted by members of the public to a commercial company to obtain information about their family background and genetic relatives, and who did not anticipate its use for law enforcement purposes. It raises significant questions about individual rights, and while this approach may be considered appropriate as a last resort in identifying the offender of serious offences, it would be concerning if it became used more widely.

The 'golden state killer' case in the United States is a prominent recent example of the use of this technique in identifying Joseph DeAngelo, who committed 13 murders and other

104 Damien Abarno et al, 'The First Australian Conviction Resulting from a Familial Search' (2019) 51 *Australian Journal of Forensic Sciences* S56, S58.

105 Manfred Kayser and Peter Schneider, 'DNA-Based Prediction of Human Externally Visible Characteristics in Forensics: Motivations, Scientific Challenges and Ethical Challenges' (2009) 3 *Forensic Science International: Genetics* 154.

106 Charles MacLean, 'Creating a Wanted Poster from a Drop of Blood: Using DNA Phenotyping to Generate an Artist's Rendering of an Offender Based Only on DNA Shed at the Crime Scene' (2013) 36 *Hamline Law Review* 357.

107 Marcus Smith and Gregor Urbas, 'Regulating New Forms of Forensic DNA Profiling under Australian Legislation: Familial Matching and DNA Phenotyping' (2012) 44 *Australian Journal of Forensic Sciences* 63.

108 Matthew Kopec, 'A New Use of "Race": The Evidence and Ethics of Forensic DNA Ancestry Profiling' (2014) 31 *Journal of Applied Philosophy* 237.

109 Thomas May, 'Sociogenetic Risks: Ancestry DNA Testing, Third-Party Identity and Protection of Privacy' (2018) 379 *New England Journal of Medicine* 410–12.

offences over a 12-year period.[110] Use of these and other techniques will continue to expand over coming years, including in new contexts. Despite ongoing technological advancements, it is important that DNA identification be considered as only one part of the overall evidence in a case.

## Evidentiary issues

DNA evidence is more discriminating than other biometric methods, but it can be susceptible to court challenges on the basis of sample contamination, or cause confusion for fact finders.[111] Compliance with forensic procedures legislation is a requirement for the admissibility of DNA evidence, and if this does not occur, the defence can challenge the integrity of samples on the basis that chain-of-custody requirements have not been observed. Cases such as *Jama* reinforce the need for compliance with forensic collection, storage and analysis protocols, as errors can be difficult to identify and correct at trial.[112]

Because a DNA profile can be obtained from just a small number of skin cells, it can be easily transferred through physical contact between persons or objects, and then onto other persons or objects – even through shaking hands. A person's DNA may therefore be found at a location where they have never actually been present. In order for the prosecution to be able to use the presence of DNA as proof of involvement in a crime, it may then be necessary to negate, beyond reasonable doubt, the possibility of this type of transference. This situation has arisen in several cases, such as *Hillier v The Queen*.[113] The defendant in that case was charged with the murder of his estranged partner. Part of the prosecution's evidence was that his DNA was found on the deceased's pyjamas. However, none of the expert witnesses at the trial were able to rule out the possibility that transference occurred through the couple's children, as they shared custody.

> There is nothing in the evidence to exclude the possibility that the children may have had some of the appellant's DNA transferred to their sleeves or other parts of their clothing when they hugged him at the end of a week spent in his care, and then subsequently hugged their mother in a similar manner. Nor is there any reason to suppose that DNA left on their clothing after contact with the appellant might not have been transferred to the deceased's pyjamas at some later stage when she had been handling that clothing.[114]

The murder conviction was quashed on this basis. On appeal it was overturned and a re-hearing of the appeal was ordered. This second appeal ordered a re-trial, at which the defendant elected to be tried by judge alone, rather than before a jury as in the first trial, and finally, Hillier was acquitted.[115]

110   Rebecca Gold, 'From Swabs to Handcuffs: How Commercial DNA Services Can Expose You to Criminal Charges' (2019) 55 *California Western Law Review* 491.

111   Marcus Smith and Monique Mann, 'Recent Developments in DNA Evidence' (2015) 506 *Trends and Issues in Crime and Criminal Justice* 1.

112   FHR **Vincent**, *Inquiry into the Circumstances that Led to the Conviction of Mr Farah Abdulkadir Jama* (**Victorian Government, Printer, 2010**).

113   *Hillier v The Queen* [2005] ACTCA 48.

114   Ibid, per Higgins CJ and Crispin P at [60].

115   The High Court appeal was *R v Hillier* (2007) 228 CLR 618, which was followed by re-heard appeal in *Hillier v The Queen* [2008] ACTCA 3; the final acquittal is unreported.

As has been discussed already, there is a question of whether juries are capable of understanding complex scientific information such as DNA evidence, and if they are required to evaluate it themselves, the forms in which it should be presented to facilitate their understanding. However, merely because it is complex does not mean it should not be heard.

> Juries are frequently called upon to resolve conflicts between experts. They have done so from the inception of jury trials. Expert evidence does not, as a matter of law, fall into two categories: difficult and sophisticated expert evidence giving rise to conflicts which a jury may not and should not be allowed to resolve; and simple and unsophisticated expert evidence which they can. Nor is it the law, that simply because there is a conflict in respect of difficult and sophisticated expert evidence, even with respect to an important, indeed critical matter, its resolution should for that reason alone be regarded by an appellate court as having been beyond the capacity of the jury to resolve.[116]

Another problem in this area that can occur is referred to as the 'CSI effect' referencing a television series featuring forensic science.[117] The issue here is that, even where experts accurately describe the limitations and confidence levels of their analysis, the jury may be overwhelmed by the scientific nature of the evidence and accord more weight than it warrants.

> The 'CSI effect' is a reference to the atmosphere of scientific confidence evoked in the imagination of the average juror by descriptions of DNA findings. As we have explained, as a matter of pure logic, the DNA evidence has little or no probative value. By virtue of its scientific pedigree, however, a jury will likely regard it as being cloaked in an unwarranted mantle of legitimacy – no matter the directions of a trial judge – and give it weight that it simply does not deserve. The danger of unfair prejudice is thus marked, and any legitimate probative value is, at best, small.[118]

# Facial recognition

Since the 19th century, law enforcement agencies have used photographs, and artist sketches based on eyewitness accounts, for the purposes of identifying unknown suspects. This historical approach forms the basis for contemporary facial comparison and digital facial recognition.[119] Facial mapping involves the review of photographic and CCTV images by an

---

116   *Velevski v The Queen* (2002) 76 ALJR 402, per Callinan and Gummow JJ at [182]. This case did not concern DNA evidence but, rather, knife wounds and expert opinion as to how they could have been inflicted. Although expert opinion evidence is largely governed by s 79 of the UEL, s 80 does allow specialised knowledge to be supplemented by 'common knowledge' as part of the expert's reasoning, as it provides: 'Evidence of an opinion is not inadmissible only because it is about: (a) a fact in issue or an ultimate issue, or (b) a matter of common knowledge.' Thus, an expert witness may 'have regard to matters that are within the knowledge of ordinary persons in formulating his or her opinion' (Gaudron J at [82]).

117   Jenny Wise, 'Providing the CSI Treatment: Criminal Justice Practitioners and the CSI Effect' (2010) 21 *Current Issues in Criminal Justice* 383.

118   *DPP v Wise (a pseudonym)* [2016] VSCA 173, [70]; *DPP v Paulino* (2017) 54 VR 109, per Weinberg JA at [24].

119   Tim Valentine and Josh Davis, *Forensic Facial Identification: Theory and Practice of Identification from Eyewitnesses, Composites and CCTV* (Wiley Blackwell, 2015).

expert, where the prosecution seeks to prove that the defendant is the individual depicted in the evidence. It can involve either a quantitative method, where measurements between facial features are compared, known as photo-anthropometry; or a qualitative method, which examines the similarities of facial features, known as morphological analysis.[120]

Digital facial recognition utilises an algorithm to map, digitise and compare the arrangement of facial features[121] – a similar process to that used for fingerprint recognition.[122] It facilitates the comparison of facial image photographs, such as those stored in databases or identification documents. The process has a number of steps: a digital photograph being taken, scaling and alignment to establish a baseline, template extraction, contour mapping of the position of individual facial features, and conversion to a digital template using an algorithm.[123]

In the matching process, pairs of digital templates are compared, deriving a numerical score as a probabilistic measure of likeness.[124] A threshold of similarity is established in the system for an identified match, and in a law enforcement context, a match is confirmed by a human decision-maker.[125]

Facial recognition can be used in verification and identification contexts. Verification is a type of one-to-one matching: for example, the comparison of faces with digital templates stored in identification documents or databases, such as passing through border crossings where a live face is compared with a digital template stored in a passport.[126] Identification involves one-to-many searching, where a database is searched to identify an unknown person. An example would be searching a database incorporating biometric driver licence photographs, to identify an unknown offender in CCTV footage or on social media. Verification has been described as 'targeted and public' in contrast with identification, described as 'generalised and invisible' surveillance to identify or track individuals.[127] Law enforcement can create watch lists and apply facial recognition to CCTV footage in a public location through existing street cameras or body-worn cameras, so they are informed when the system detects the person.[128]

120  Gary Edmond et al, 'Law's Looking Glass: Expert Identification Evidence Derived from Photographic and Video Images' (2009) *Current Issues in Criminal Justice* 337.

121  Karl Ricanek, 'Beyond Recognition: The Promise of Biometric Analytics' (2014) 47 *Computer* 87.

122  Andy Adler and Michael Schuckers, 'Comparing Human and Automatic Face Recognition Performance' (2007) 37 *IEEE Transactions on Systems, Man, and Cybernetics, Part B: Cybernetics* 1248.

123  Karl Ricanek and Chris Boehnen, 'Facial Analytics: From Big Data to Law Enforcement' (2012) 45 *Computer* 95.

124  Clare Garvie, Alvaro Bedoya and Jonathan Frankle, 'The Perpetual Line-Up: Unregulated Police Face Recognition in America' (2016) *Georgetown Law Center on Privacy and Technology Report* 9.

125  Lucas Introna and Helen Nissenbaum, 'Facial Recognition Technology: A Survey of Policy and Implementation Issues', *Department of Organisation, Work and Technology, Lancaster University Working Paper* (2010).

126  Phillip Brey, 'Ethical Aspects of Facial Recognition Systems in Public Places' (2004) 2 *Journal of Information, Communication and Ethics in Society* 97.

127  Clare Garvie, Alvaro Bedoya and Jonathan Frankle, The Perpetual Line-Up: Unregulated Police Face Recognition in America' (2016) *Georgetown Law Center on Privacy and Technology Report* 2.

128  Lucas Introna and Helen Nissenbaum, 'Facial Recognition Technology: A Survey of Policy and Implementation Issues', *Department of Organisation, Work and Technology, Lancaster University Working Paper* (2010).

The accuracy and sensitivity of facial recognition technology is still developing, particularly in non-standardised environments, such as when applied to moving subjects in uncontrolled conditions.[129] There is a greater risk of inaccuracy with live CCTV footage and large databases such as social media holdings.[130] For example, Grother et al (2017) examined the use of facial recognition in video surveillance with non-cooperative subjects, finding that accuracy was far less in comparison with a digital photograph in a controlled setting.[131] Non-stationary faces in video surveillance may be impacted by movement, magnification, depth of view, orientation and lighting conditions. Data compression for storage may also impact on quality and accuracy. Interoperability between systems and cameras may have an impact on facial recognition capabilities. Changes to an individual's face may also lead to false positive or negative matches, a particular susceptibility in contrast with DNA or fingerprint identification. These could include ageing, cosmetic surgery, make-up, or weight gain; and counter-surveillance methods, such as masks, can be used to nullify facial recognition applications in certain circumstances.[132]

## Applications

Developed countries around the world are working to establish facial recognition databases. At the federal level in the United States, the multimodal Next Generation Identification (NGI) system includes facial templates alongside a number of other biometrics.[133] The NGI is the largest police information system in the world, with more than 50 million photographs that can be searched.[134] In addition, the Department of Homeland Security collects digital photographs from all non-US citizens entering the country, which it shares with other government agencies, including its law enforcement partner countries Australia, Canada, New Zealand and the United Kingdom.[135] Approximately 30 jurisdictions in the United States permit law enforcement to conduct facial recognition searching of driver licence databases.

129   See, eg, Patrick Grother, George Quinn and Mei Ngan, *Face in Video Evaluation (FIVE): Face Recognition of Non-Cooperative Subjects* (National Institute of Standards and Technology, 2017).
130   Clare Garvie, Alvaro Bedoya and Jonathan Frankle, 'The Perpetual Line-Up: Unregulated Police Face Recognition in America' (2016) *Georgetown Law Center on Privacy and Technology Report*.
131   See, eg, Patrick Grother, George Quinn and Mei Ngan, *Face in Video Evaluation (FIVE): Face Recognition of Non-Cooperative Subjects* (National Institute of Standards and Technology, 2017).
132   Gabriel Samuels, 'Anti-Surveillance Clothing Unveiled to Combat Facial Recognition Technology', *The Independent*, 5 January 2017.
133   Federal Bureau of Investigation, *Next Generation Identification* (2019). Available: <https://www.fbi.gov/services/cjis/fingerprints-and-other-biometrics/ngi>; Federal Bureau of Investigation, *NGI Monthly Fact Sheet* (2019). Available: <https://www.fbi.gov/file-repository/ngi-monthly-fact-sheet/view>; Federal Bureau of Investigation, *Next Generation Identification: Implementing the Future of Identification and Investigative Services Flyer* (2019). Available: <https://www.fbi.gov/file-repository/next-generation-identification-ngi-flyer.pdf/view>. The Australian Criminal Intelligence Commission is developing a similar multi-modal database, known as the Biometric Identification Services (BIS).
134   United States Government Accountability Office, *Face Recognition Technology: FBI Should Better Ensure Privacy and Accuracy* (2016). Available: <https://www.gao.gov/products/GAO-16-267>.
135   United States Department of Homeland Security, 'DHS/NPPD/Privacy Impact Assessment-002 Automated Biometric Identification System (2015). Available: <https://www.dhs.gov/publication/dhsnppdpia-002-automated-biometric-identification-system-ident>.

There are estimates that facial recognition databases include more than 117 million American adults, which equates to approximately half of all American adults.[136]

In recent years there has been increasing public debate in relation to legislation drafted to implement facial recognition databases in Australia. All state governments now use biometric driver licence photographs, and SmartGate technology has been established at all international airports. There are plans to introduce a national facial recognition database that will enable federal agencies to share and search facial templates, including the Department of Foreign Affairs and Trade, the Department of Immigration and Border Protection, the Australian Federal Police, and the Australian Security Intelligence Organisation.[137] Half of the Australian population holds biometric passports. With driver's licences added to this, it is estimated that such a database would incorporate biometric facial templates of approximately 18 million people.[138] The Australian Human Rights Commission has recommended that there be a moratorium on the use of this technology.

> The Australian Government should introduce a legal moratorium on the use of facial recognition technology in decision making that has a legal, or similarly significant, effect for individuals, until an appropriate legal framework has been put in place. This legal framework should include robust protections for human rights and should be developed in consultation with expert bodies including the Australian Human Rights Commission and the Office of the Australian Information Commissioner.[139]

A key capability of automated facial recognition that can be expected to become increasingly widely used is the capacity to identify individual faces in a large crowd. It could be used to identify a terrorist suspect at a major public event, a known shoplifter in a department store, or a criminal suspect at an international airport. Most significantly, integrating facial recognition with CCTV systems enables real-time surveillance, identification and tracking of individuals through public places.[140] In 2016, police used the technology to scan the faces of over a million people attending the Notting Hill Carnival and have since used it at major European football matches.[141] Law enforcement agencies within the United States also use facial recognition from cameras on the street, in automatic teller machines, and on vehicles, drones and body-worn cameras – it can potentially be integrated with any type of live video surveillance.[142] Recent developments in China provide insights into how the use of facial recognition and other biometrics by governments may advance without democratic accountability. In China, the government uses facial recognition and gait analysis systems

136   Clare Garvie, Alvaro Bedoya and Jonathan Frankle, 'The Perpetual Line-Up: Unregulated Police Face Recognition in America' (2016) *Georgetown Law Centre on Privacy and Technology Report*.

137   Monique Mann and Marcus Smith, 'Automated Facial Recognition Technology: Recent Developments and Approaches to Oversight' (2017) 40 *University of New South Wales Law Journal* 121.

138   Department of Foreign Affairs and Trade, *Annual Report 2010–2011* (2011).

139   Australian Human Rights Commission, *Discussion Paper on Human Rights and Technology* (2020), Proposal 11. Available: <www.tech.humanrights.gov.au/consultation>

140   Kelly Gates, *Our Biometric Future: Facial Recognition Technology and the Culture of Surveillance* (New York University Press, 2011).

141   Darren Boyle, 'Police to Scan 1 Million People with New Automatic Facial Recognition Software in Bid to Beat Crime at Notting Hill Carnival', *The Daily Mail*, 27 August 2016.

142   Clare Garvie, Alvaro Bedoya and Jonathan Frankle, 'The Perpetual Line-Up: Unregulated Police Face Recognition in America' (2016) *Georgetown Law Centre on Privacy and Technology Report*.

to identify individuals in public places who are suspected of committing minor crimes, such as jaywalking.[143] This plays a key role in the social credit system, which rewards and punishes citizens on the basis of compliance with behavioural norms. Facial recognition is used in concert with other automated data capabilities such as GPS data, internet use and financial transactions. Those with low social credit scores may be restricted from travelling and excluded from private schools, among other sanctions.[144]

Another important application of facial recognition is the analysis of images drawn from the internet, and in particular social media. Law enforcement utilise images from Facebook, Twitter, LinkedIn, Google and dating sites. Facebook has hundreds of billions of photographs on its site, and the number is increasing by more than five billion images a month.[145] The site uses facial recognition technology to tag photographs with users' names, and to link images to personal profiles,[146] regardless of whether that person has their own Facebook account or consented to Facebook storing their digital facial template.[147] This development was challenged in a number of European countries. Facebook subsequently disabled the facial recognition tagging feature in Europe, deleted stored biometric information previously collected, and suspended the creation of new facial templates without prior active consent.[148]

## Evidentiary issues

With regard to law enforcement investigations and prosecutions, facial recognition technology is primarily used as an intelligence method and has not yet been tested in the courtroom. Comparing still images to establish identity typically involves an image taken from a crime scene and a comparable one of a criminal defendant. This process will be similar to matching, but with greater potential for inaccuracies in facial recognition. It is likely to become an important form of identification evidence, and courts will build upon the current approach to existing facial mapping techniques.

In some instances, this visual comparison can be undertaken by a jury without the assistance of an expert witness. Indeed, courts have previously stressed that allowing witnesses to offer their opinions of similarity may usurp the role of the jury.[149] However,

---

143   Xaio Qiang, 'The Road to Digital Unfreedom: President Xi's Surveillance State' (2019) 30 *Journal of Democracy* 1.

144   Matthew Kugler, 'How Should We Think About Biometric Privacy Harms?' (2018) 18 *Northwestern University Pritzker School of Law Public Law and Legal Theory Series* 25.

145   Karl Ricanek, 'Beyond Recognition: The Promise of Biometric Analytics' (2014) 47 *Computer* 87.

146   Anna Bunn, 'Facebook and Face Recognition: Kinda Cool, Kinda Creepy' (2014) 25 *Bond Law Review* 35.

147   Ibid.

148   Monique Mann and Marcus Smith, 'Automated Facial Recognition Technology: Recent Developments and Approaches to Oversight' (2017) 40 *University of New South Wales Law Journal* 121.

149   *Smith v The Queen* (2001) 206 CLR 650, in which a High Court majority observed: 'Because the witness's assertion of identity was founded on material no different from the material available to the jury from its own observation, the witness's assertion that he recognised the appellant is not evidence that could rationally affect the assessment by the jury of the question we have identified. The fact that someone else has reached a conclusion about the identity of the accused and the person in the picture does not provide any logical basis for affecting the jury's assessment of the probability of the existence of that fact when the conclusion is based only on material that is not different in any substantial way from what is available to the jury.'

facial mapping does involve technical skill that in many cases will go beyond what a lay jury is able to do, and applies a scientific approach to eyewitness identification.

An illustrative Australian case involving this type of evidence was the murder trial arising from the disappearance of a British tourist in the Northern Territory.[150] The evidence included a photographic image obtained from a security camera at a highway truck stop, which a facial mapping expert called by the prosecution compared with photographs of the defendant. The judge allowed the evidence to be admitted,[151] but on appeal it was held that the facial mapping evidence should not have been allowed to draw a conclusion about identity; it should only have been used to assist the jury to ascertain physical similarities.

> [T]he technique employed by Dr Sutisno did not have a sufficient scientific basis to render the results arrived at by that means part of a field of knowledge which is a proper subject of expert evidence. However the evidence given by Dr Sutisno was capable of assisting the jury in terms of similarities between the person depicted in the truck stop footage and the appellant. It was evidence that related to, and was admissible as, demonstrating similarities but was not admissible as to positive identity.[152]

Similar evidence was considered in the *Honeysett* case, where the opinion of the expert identified the appellant.

> Although the offender covers his head and face with a cloth (what looks like a T-shirt) … the knitted fabric is elastic and adheres closely to the vault of his skull (braincase). This shows that his hair is short and does not distort the layout of the fabric. The shape of the head is clearly dolichocephalic (long head, elongated oval when viewed from the top) as opposed to brachycephalic (short head, nearly spherical) … His skull vault is dolichocephalic when viewed from the top. Comparison of lateral (side) and front views of his head also indicates the head … is long but narrow. His skin is dark, darker than that of persons of European extraction, but not 'black'.[153]

The expert in *Honeysett* asserted that there was a 'high degree of anatomical similarity' between the offender and the appellant, 'strengthened by the fact that he was unable to discern any anatomical dissimilarity between the two individuals'.[154] This evidence was allowed to be heard by the jury, which convicted the appellant. On appeal, the court held that the evidence fell within the 'training, study or experience' of the expert witness.[155] The

---

150  Jeremy Gans, 'Much Repented: Consent to DNA Sampling' (2007) 30 *University of New South Wales Law Journal* 579.

151  *R v Murdoch (No 4)* (2005) 195 FLR 421, per Martin CJ at [207]–[208]. DNA aspects of the case are discussed in two articles by Jeremy Gans, 'The Peter Falconio Investigation: Needles, Hay and DNA' (2007) 18 *Current Issues in Criminal Justice* 415 and 'Catching Bradley Murdoch: Tweezers, Pitchforks and the Limits of DNA Sampling' (2007) 19 *Current Issues in Criminal Justice* 34.

152  *Murdoch v The Queen* (2007) 167 A Crim R 329, [300]. Despite this ruling, however, the conviction was upheld as it was amply supported by other evidence. A special leave application to the High Court was unsuccessful: *Murdoch v The Queen* [2007] HCATrans 321.

153  *Honeysett v The Queen* (2014) 253 CLR 122, [14]–[17].

154  Ibid.

155  *Honeysett v The Queen* (2013) 233 A Crim R 152 (Macfarlane JA, Campbell J and Barr AJ agreeing).

appeal went to the High Court for further consideration, which agreed that the expert's opinion was not sufficiently based on his expertise in anatomy:

> Professor Henneberg's knowledge as an anatomist, that the human population includes individuals who have oval shaped heads and individuals who have round shaped heads (when viewed from above), did not form the basis of his conclusion that Offender One and the appellant each have oval shaped heads. That conclusion was based on Professor Henneberg's subjective impression of what he saw when he looked at the images. This observation applies to the evidence of each of the characteristics of which Professor Henneberg gave evidence …
>
> Professor Henneberg's opinion was not based wholly or substantially on his specialised knowledge within s 79(1). It was an error of law to admit the evidence.[156]

While facial mapping has been accepted as a form of evidence, there have been some reservations about the strength of the expert opinions, and as to whether it is a field of 'specialised knowledge'. Commentators such as Edmond and San Roque take the following position:

> We contend that too much weak, speculative and unreliable opinion is allowed into criminal proceedings … The problems with the contested image comparison evidence in *Honeysett* are representative of widespread problems with forensic science evidence more broadly.[157]

When digital facial recognition comes to be adduced as evidence in criminal trials, a body of case law will develop, evaluating its strengths and weaknesses and that of the experts who inform the court about it. It will continue to be important for courts to challenge the scientific basis and accuracy of the application of new technologies to investigations and prosecutions in the criminal justice system.

## Conclusion

This chapter has examined the use of identification technology in the criminal justice system generally, and through a focus on the three most widely used technologies: fingerprint identification, DNA identification and facial recognition. The discussion provides an indication of the impact technology has had on the criminal justice system, and how this will continue to develop. In just a century, this field has advanced from classifying patterns on the fingertips, to establishing a suspect's identity and physical appearance from a drop of their blood, to creating national databases of biometric facial templates that can be integrated with CCTV systems.

There are broader considerations associated with these developments that must also be taken into account. Despite the strong scientific basis of these technologies, there remains the potential for system failure, hacking, human errors, sample contamination, and the like,

156  *Honeysett v The Queen* (2014) 253 CLR 122, per French CJ, Kiefel, Bell, Gageler and Keane JJ at [43]–[46]. The appellant's conviction was ordered to be quashed and a new trial allowed.
157  Gary Edmond and Mehera San Roque, '*Honeysett v The Queen*: Forensic Science, "Specialised Knowledge" and the Uniform Evidence Law' (2014) 36 *Sydney Law Review* 324.

that can have dire consequences for individuals and undermine confidence in the criminal justice system if they are not properly scrutinised. An individual's biometrics are permanent and cannot be changed as a password can, meaning there are more significant implications associated with the security of this information. The role of contaminated DNA evidence in the 2008 *Jama* case is a salient reminder of the potential negative outcomes that can occur.

It is also important that safeguards are established to protect individual rights, including privacy and autonomy, as technology provides increasingly accurate and efficient tools to monitor behaviour and investigate crimes. Liberal democracies such as Australia, the United Kingdom and the United States must ensure they utilise the latest technology to prevent crime in a way that does not create a surveillance state. The following chapter on cybercrime will continue this discussion, examining the most recent forms of technology-based crime, followed by the challenges it presents for investigation and prosecution.

# 7

# CYBERCRIME

# Introduction

One of the more challenging intersections of law and technology is the use of computers and associated systems to commit criminal offences. While terminology varies, the neologism *cybercrime* is widely used to refer to a range of offending that involves computers as targets (eg hacking); as instruments (eg online fraud and forgery); or as incidental to the commission of a crime (eg using the internet to plan or organise a more conventional crime).[1] As noted in Chapter 2, some cybercrimes are essentially the same as their 'terrestrial' counterparts, but adopt modern technology for their commission (ie 'old wine in new bottles'), while others represent significantly newer forms of criminality. Examples of the former might include cyberstalking and online fraud, where the message is much the same but the means of communication is more efficient; while the latter might include distributed denial-of-service (DDoS) attacks against websites.

The focus for this chapter will be on crimes involving unauthorised access, modification and impairment of computers and data, as well as the use of these methods to commit fraud or similar financially motivated crimes. The extension of these topics into cyberterrorism and cyberwarfare will also be considered. All of these three areas are relevant to Chapter 10, which explores jurisdictional law enforcement and regulatory challenges.

# Computer hacking

The term 'hacker' is popularly used to describe those who engage in illegal computer intrusions, usually using a variety of tools and techniques not readily available to ordinary computer users. While early hackers were largely motivated by idle curiosity, the motivations of modern-day hackers tend to be to create damage and/or accrue financial gain. To some extent, this form of cybercrime also has associations with sophisticated or organised crime, at least insofar as more effective criminal enterprises usually involve a number of offenders organised according to their specialised skills.

In order to understand the legal definition of computer hacking, it is necessary to appreciate its development in society more broadly. The societal evolution of computer hacking has been described as follows:

> A few decades ago, the terms 'hacker' and 'hacking' were known only to a relatively small number of people, mainly those in the technically specialised world of computing. Today they have become 'common knowledge' … It is this widely accepted sense of hacking as 'computer break-in', and of its perpetrators as 'break-in artists' and 'intruders', that structures most media, political and criminal justice responses.[2]

As the following example indicates, historically, computer hacking was associated with teenagers using their developing computer skills to find vulnerabilities in websites and

---

1   Russell Smith, Peter Grabosky and Gregor Urbas, *Cyber Criminals on Trial* (Cambridge University Press, 2004), Chapter 2; see also Gregor Urbas, *Cybercrime: Legislation, Cases and Commentary*, 2nd edn (LexisNexis, 2020).

2   Majid Yar, 'Computer Hacking: Just Another Case of Juvenile Delinquency?' (2005) 44(4) *Howard Journal of Criminal Justice* 387, 389–90.

information systems. Their exploits can cause enormous damage and expense, as shown by the example of 'Mafiaboy' who, aged just 15 and still at school in Canada in 2000, launched a sophisticated denial-of-service attack that brought down the websites of major corporate entities including Amazon, CNN, Dell, eBay and Yahoo! In view of his age, he was sentenced to a period in youth detention on more than 50 charges. As an adult, this reformed former offender became a 'white hat' hacker, assisting corporate clients to find and repair vulnerabilities in their systems before internal intrusion by malicious actors, or 'black hat' hackers, could occur. For completeness, 'gray/grey hat hackers' are those who discover weaknesses but offer these to any paying customer, regardless of which side they are on.[3]

Data security has become a far more significant issue for government, and the community as a whole, as greater volumes of data are generated and used in novel ways. Instances of large-scale data breaches involving Australian institutions, governments and businesses are becoming more common. More recently, hacking by state actors has gained prominence.[4] These are hackers that are financially backed or employed by foreign governments, and the information sought is usually associated with a political motive. Indicators that a state actor is involved include the target and the level of sophistication and resources involved. It has been suggested that a number of recent attacks on the Australian Parliament were conducted by foreign governments.[5] The Australian National University data breach, made public in 2019 and which involved data relating to 200 000 people extending over a 19-year period, is believed to have been perpetrated by a sophisticated state actor seeking information about government employees who may have previously studied at the institution.[6]

## Malware

Malicious software, or 'malware', is used both to infect individual computers and to create larger compromised networks such as botnets.[7] Malware is often self-propagating and may actively seek out and steal personal and financial data, such as account login credentials. It is thus a vital tool for cybercriminals, particularly those interested in creating serious harm or gaining financial rewards from their exploits.[8] An early example of the creation of malware was the 'Love Bug' virus or worm that infected millions of computers around the world in mid-2000. After being traced to the Philippines, a suspect was arrested but he could not be successfully prosecuted as the country had no adequate offences relating to the creating and use of malware.[9] This gap was quickly remedied with the passage of legislation that included

---

3   Gregor Urbas, *Cybercrime*, 2nd edn (LexisNexis, 2020), 20.
4   Daniel Miller, 'The Cyber Attack on Parliament was Done by a "State Actor"', *Australian Broadcasting Corporation News*, 20 February 2019.
5   Ibid.
6   Australian National University, 'Incident Report on the Breach of the Australian National University's Administrative Systems', 2 October 2019. Available: <https://www.anu.edu.au/news/all-news/anu-releases-detailed-account-of-data-breach>.
7   Article 6 of the *Convention on Cybercrime* deals with misuse of devices, including computer programs, and covers the use of malware to commit other crimes such as hacking and fraud.
8   Australian Institute of Criminology, 'Malware: Viruses, Worms, Trojan Horses' (2006) *High Tech Crime Brief* 10.
9   Susan Brenner, 'Cybercrime Investigation and Prosecution: The Role of Penal and Procedural Law' (2001) 8(2) *Murdoch University Electronic Journal of Law*.

'hacking and cracking' offences, as well as the introduction of computer viruses.[10] Countless and more sophisticated varieties of malware have been created in the ensuing decades, with the computer security industry playing a major role in finding technical countermeasures and assisting law enforcement in identifying those responsible.[11]

In legal terms, developers of malware may be held liable not only for their own criminal exploits, but also as accessories to the crimes of others to whom they sell or make available their products. For example, in 2018 a United States citizen, Taylor Huddleston, was sentenced to 33 months in prison for aiding and abetting computer intrusions committed by customers to whom he sold malware that he had developed and sold online.[12]

> According to court documents, Huddleston developed, marketed, and distributed two products that were extremely popular with cybercriminals around the world. The first is the 'NanoCore RAT,' a type of malware that is used to steal information from victim computers, including sensitive information such as passwords, emails, and instant messages. The NanoCore RAT even allowed users to surreptitiously activate the webcam on the victim computers in order to spy on the victims. Huddleston's NanoCore RAT was used to infect and attempt to infect tens of thousands of computers.[13]

There are many online marketplaces where malware, hacking tools, stolen data and cybercrime services can be bought, sold or exchanged. Some of these operate relatively openly, while others are found in the 'dark web' beyond the reach of standard search engines, where access is gained through sharing of links between users and via anonymised browsers such as Tor (short for 'The Onion Router'). Despite these efforts at secrecy, however, such sites are not entirely beyond law enforcement discovery and disruption.

> In recent years, the Dark Web's anonymity and low barriers to entry have attracted scores of criminals to Dark Web markets, including those trafficking in child pornography, illicit firearms, illegal drugs, murder-for-hire, and human trafficking. Sophisticated hackers also frequent Dark Web forums for the newest malware or stolen data, and might use the Tor network to host botnet command-and-control infrastructure that is more resistant to disruption and take-downs. Despite the many challenges the Dark Web poses, law enforcement around the world have successfully disrupted criminals operating in the cyber underground by de-anonymizing users engaging in illegal activity; seizing their websites, domains, servers, and ill-gotten gains; and criminally prosecuting them.[14]

A type of malware used to extort money from individuals, businesses and organisations is known as 'ransomware'. It typically infects a computer and encrypts its files, followed by

---

10  *Electronic Commerce Act of 2000* (Republic Act No 8792, June 2000), s 33.
11  See, eg, Microsoft, 'Global Threat Activity' (2020). Available: <https://www.microsoft.com/en-us/wdsi/threats>.
12  Huddleston was convicted under the *Computer Fraud and Abuse Act* (CFAA) 18 USC §1030(a)(5)(A).
13  United States Department of Justice, 'Arkansas Man Sentenced to Prison for Developing and Distributing Prolific Malware', 23 February 2018. Available: <https://www.justice.gov/opa/pr/arkansas-man-sentenced-prison-developing-and-distributing-prolific-malware>.
14  United States Department of Justice, *Report of the Attorney-General's Cyber Digital Task Force* (2018), 71–2.

a demand for payment in order to unlock the files. Victims of such attacks often have no realistic alternative but to comply with the demand, in the hope that access to data will be restored. The effects of a ransomware attack can be very serious.

Targets of ransomware attacks include businesses, universities and government departments. In 2018, a pair of suspects in Iran were identified by the Federal Bureau of Investigation (FBI) in relation to an attack, though it was conceded that they were out of the reach of that country's law enforcement system unless they travelled to the United States.[15] Those behind malware attacks range from individual hackers through to criminal syndicates and even, if reports of attribution are accurate, governments. For example, the 'WannaCry' malware that caused ransomware attacks across the world in 2017 was attributed by some to North Korea.[16]

A different kind of harm often associated with politically motivated attacks is 'website defacement', where a company or institution's site is altered to contain obscenities or slogans. Such an attack may be an example of 'hacktivism' or, where serious damage results, may approach a form of politically motivated terrorism.[17]

Although followers of these groups may have considered that what they were doing was engaging in lawful protest, or at least unlikely to have legal consequences, this is not a safe assumption. It has been reported that participants in Australia have been identified and ordered to pay fines as punishment for their offences.[18] Despite the name 'Anonymous', they were not anonymous. Issues of investigation, jurisdiction and prosecution are discussed further in Chapter 10.

## Legislative provisions

The leading international agreement is the Council of Europe's *Convention on Cybercrime*. The Convention has been ratified by a number of non-European countries, including Australia, the United States, Canada and Japan, that recognise the global nature of cybercrime and the need to share evidence and collaborative law enforcement approaches. The legal characterisation of computer hacking as a criminal offence varies across jurisdictions, but core concepts involve unauthorised (ie illegal or otherwise prohibited) access to computers and data, modification of data, and impairment of computer functions or databases.

Article 1 of the Convention defines key terms, while Articles 2–5 outline the relevant substantive criminal law offences required for member states.[19]

15  'FBI Charges Men in 2016 Ransomware Attack on University of Calgary', *Canadian Broadcasting Corporation News*, 28 November 2018. Available: <https://www.cbc.ca/news/canada/calgary/samsam-ransomware-attack-university-calgary-1.4924568>.
16  'Cyber-Attack: US and UK Blame North Korea for WannaCry', *British Broadcasting Corporation News*, 19 December 2017. Available: <https://www.bbc.com/news/world-us-canada-42407488>.
17  Dorothy Denning, 'Activism, Hacktivism and Cyberterrorism: The Internet as a Tool for Influencing Foreign Policy'. In John Arquilla and David Ronfeldt (eds), *Networks and Netwars: The Future of Terrorism, Crime and Militancy* (Rand Corporation, 2001).
18  Sarah Whyte, 'Meet the Hacktivist Who Tried to Take Down the Government', *Sydney Morning Herald*, 14 March 2011.
19  Council of Europe, *Convention on Cybercrime*, Treaty No 185, opened for signature in Budapest on 23 November 2001 (hence, often referred to as the 'Budapest Convention').

# Convention on Cybercrime

### Section 1: Substantive criminal law

*Title 1: Offences against the confidentiality, integrity and availability of computer data and systems*

### Article 2: Illegal access

Each Party shall adopt such legislative and other measures as may be necessary to establish as criminal offences under its domestic law, when committed intentionally, the access to the whole or any part of a computer system without right. A Party may require that the offence be committed by infringing security measures, with the intent of obtaining computer data or other dishonest intent, or in relation to a computer system that is connected to another computer system.

### Article 3: Illegal interception

Each Party shall adopt such legislative and other measures as may be necessary to establish as criminal offences under its domestic law, when committed intentionally, the interception without right, made by technical means, of non-public transmissions of computer data to, from or within a computer system, including electromagnetic emissions from a computer system carrying such computer data. A Party may require that the offence be committed with dishonest intent, or in relation to a computer system that is connected to another computer system.

### Article 4: Data interference

Each Party shall adopt such legislative and other measures as may be necessary to establish as criminal offences under its domestic law, when committed intentionally, the damaging, deletion, deterioration, alteration or suppression of computer data without right.

A Party may reserve the right to require that the conduct described in paragraph 1 result in serious harm.

### Article 5: System interference

Each Party shall adopt such legislative and other measures as may be necessary to establish as criminal offences under its domestic law, when committed intentionally, the serious hindering without right of the functioning of a computer system by inputting, transmitting, damaging, deleting, deteriorating, altering or suppressing computer data.

The term 'illegal access' in Article 2 is clarified in the Explanatory Report accompanying the *Convention on Cybercrime*, which treats unauthorised intrusions as a gateway offence for others such as the alteration or destruction of computer data.

> 'Illegal access' covers the basic offence of dangerous threats to and attacks against the security (i.e. the confidentiality, integrity and availability) of computer systems and data. The need for protection reflects the interests of organisations and individuals to manage, operate and control their systems in an undisturbed and uninhibited manner. The mere unauthorised intrusion, i.e. 'hacking', 'cracking' or 'computer trespass', should in principle be illegal in itself. It may lead to impediments to legitimate users of systems and data and may cause alteration or destruction with high costs for reconstruction. Such intrusions may give access to confidential data (including passwords, information about the targeted system) and secrets, to the use of the system without payment or even encourage hackers to commit more dangerous forms of computer-related offences, like computer-related fraud or forgery.[20]

---

20  Council of Europe, *Explanatory Report to the Convention on Cybercrime*, Treaty No 185, opened for signature in Budapest on 23 November 2001.

Unauthorised access to a computer or computer system, or to data held in a computer or system, may occur when an 'outsider' such as a remote hacker gains access by guessing or using an algorithm to find or 'crack' passwords or other protective measures. Attempting to log in without valid credentials will usually result in a message stating that the person making the attempt is not authorised to enter the system, but lack of authorisation extends to the situation where a valid password or other credential is guessed or used by someone other than the true owner or trustee (eg an employee) of that information. Thus, authorisation is not merely a technical matter defined in relation to a computer system, but involves legal or organisational controls on who is entitled to have access to computers, systems and data. In particular, unauthorised access may also be obtained by an 'insider' who is given access to a computer system but then (mis)uses that access to find information beyond the scope of authorisation.

For example, the main computer fraud offence in the *Computer Fraud and Abuse Act* of the United States refers to 'exceeds authorized access', which is defined as follows:

> ... to access a computer with authorization and to use such access to obtain or alter information in the computer that the accesser is not entitled so to obtain or alter.[21]

US court cases on this provision clarify that lack of authorisation may be demonstrated by reference to documents such as 'terms of service, a computer access policy, a website notice, or an employment agreement or similar contract' or, possibly, by considering any ulterior motives involved in the use of access granted by an employer to an employee.[22] For example, in the case of *United States v Nosal*, several employees of an executive search company had used their login access to download company data that they intended to use in setting up a rival business. Once they had resigned, their login access was revoked, but one member of the group, David Nosal, had continued to work as a contractor under a non-competition agreement. The group then asked a former assistant of Nosal to provide her login credentials, as she was still employed at the company, which they used to continue their access to the company's data. Nosal was charged with violations under the 'exceeds authorized access' provisions of the *Computer Fraud and Abuse Act*, based on his conduct while an employee, but those charges were initially dismissed. In an amended indictment, he was charged with being an accessory to the unauthorised access by his accomplices to the company data using his former assistant's credentials. A jury found him guilty on these and several other charges, and subsequent appeals were unsuccessful, with the higher courts holding that only the employer company could authorise anyone to have access (and not, for example, the assistant who shared her login credentials) and rejecting Nosal's argument that he could not be convicted of hacking offences unless he had circumvented some kind of 'technological access barrier' (eg by getting through a firewall by masking access location).[23]

---

21   US Code Title 18 (*Computer Fraud and Abuse Act of 1986*), §1030: Fraud and related activity in connection with computers, sub-s (e)(6).

22   United States Department of Justice, Computer Crime and Intellectual Property Section (CCIPS), Criminal Division, *Prosecuting Computer Crimes* (Office of Legal Education, 2015), 5–11.

23   *United States v Nosal (II)*, 828 F.3d 865 (2016). See, eg, 'Ninth Circuit Affirms Conviction of a Former Employee Who Used Another Employee's Password' (2017) 130 *Harvard Law Review* 1265.

In Australia, the *Criminal Code Act 1995* (Cth), s 477.1 prohibits unauthorised access to computers and data, including gaining access in order to commit or facilitate other offences.[24] This would cover, for example, hacking into a database to obtain personal and financial details to be used in committing fraud, whether online or otherwise. Further, one federal Australian offence prohibits the use of a telecommunications network (not requiring that such use be itself unauthorised) with intent to commit or facilitate a serious offence under Australian or even foreign law.[25] Such a broad offence potentially encompasses any criminally motivated use of the internet, and thus goes well beyond 'hacking' offences involving unauthorised access, modification and impairment. For example, this offence has been used to prosecute individuals who have obtained stolen credit card numbers online in order to facilitate fraud, or been involved in 'muling' (ie allowing online bank accounts to be used by a third party to launder money).[26]

Turning to unauthorised modification and impairment, these concepts relate to the alteration of computer data without the consent of the rightful owner or controller of the data, and the potential damage to computers, data and systems that may result. The *Convention on Cybercrime* has articles covering both data interference and system interference, recognising that not only the integrity of data but also the computer systems and related infrastructure supported by computers, such as transport and telecommunications, are at risk from attacks. While individual hacks may result in the deletion or alteration of data, this may also be achieved by the combined force of a multitude of compromised computers, such as where a 'botnet' is created that allows its controller to launch a DDoS attack on a target.[27] Botnets are also used to transmit millions of unsolicited messages, or 'spam', or to disseminate illegal content such as child exploitation material so as to hide its actual origin.[28] A botnet may be centralised, using a level or command-and-control server operated by its controller; or it may be decentralised, using peer-to-peer (P2P) connections to achieve greater concealment.

# Online fraud

A substantial proportion of online criminal activity involves various 'scams' designed to alleviate victims of some of their finances.[29] Such crimes may involve hacking or malware, but most often just rely on deceptive communications, such as 'phishing'. These emails, often delivered in bulk as spam, are designed to find credulous victims who will give up at least some of their personal and financial details through replying, if not falling for the scam entirely.[30] The internet plays a key role in facilitating such frauds, whether through email, social media or other communications. Few users have not received such items as

---

24  Similar offences exist in the United Kingdom. See, eg, *Computer Misuse Act 1990* (UK), ss 1 and 2.
25  *Criminal Code Act 1995* (Cth), s 474.14, where a 'serious offence' is one punishable by at least five years' or life imprisonment: s 473.1.
26  See *DPP v Carpenter* [2019] VCC 1453.
27  Meiring de Villiers, 'Distributed Denial of Service: Law, Technology and Policy' [2007] *University of New South Wales Law Research Series* 3.
28  Kim-Kwang Raymond Choo, 'Zombies and Botnets' (2007) *Trends & Issues in Crime and Criminal Justice* No 333 (Australian Institute of Criminology).
29  See Metropolitan Police, United Kingdom, *The Little Book of Big Scams* (4th ed). Available: <https://www .met.police.uk/SysSiteAssets/media/downloads/central/advice/fraud/met/the-little-book-of-big-scams.pdf>.
30  Australian Competition and Consumer Commission, ScamWatch, 'Phishing' (2020).

the 'Nigerian 419' email, so-named in reference to the section of the Nigerian Criminal Code dealing with fraud (though the origins of such emails may be in any country).[31] The scam works as follows:

* You receive a contact out of the blue asking you to 'help' someone from another country transfer money out of their country (eg Nigeria, Sierra Leone or Iraq).
* The request includes a long and often sad story about why the money cannot be transferred by the owner. This typically involves some type of conflict or inheritance and they may want to move the money straight into your account.
* You are offered a financial reward, such as a share in the amount, for helping them access their 'trapped' funds. The amount of money to be transferred, and the payment that the scammer promises to you if you help, is usually very large.
* They will claim that a bank, lawyer, government agency or other organisation requires some fees to be paid before the money can be moved. The scammer will often ask you to make payments for the fee via a money transfer service.[32]

Also known as 'advance fee fraud', this type of scam is lucrative to the extent that victims are willing to pay a smaller amount of money in the expectation of a much larger return. Variants include inheritance, prizes, lottery winnings, uncollected tax refunds or other unexpected windfall offers.[33] As offenders are usually located in other countries, and this is where any money is sent to, recovery and prosecution are difficult. Dealing with the consequences of losses through such frauds can involve not only criminal but also family law (as marriages and other relationships can suffer or fail) and inheritance law (due to estate losses).[34] Other tragic cases have involved 'romance scams' where fraudsters pose as eligible romantic partners and engage with vulnerable targets through dating sites, again with the aim of developing their trust and alleviating victims of their money.[35] For example, a woman in Northern Ireland was recently reported to have sent £300 000 to pay a scammer with whom she had developed an online relationship, purportedly so that his children could be educated in the United Kingdom.[36] And in an Australian case, a woman from Western Australia was killed after she travelled to Africa in an attempt to meet her online love interest.[37]

Online fraud often involves the use of false identities, or the misuse of someone's real identity. In the case of romance scams, the identity of the online romantic partner is usually a construct aided by pictures of a model and a sympathetic life story designed to create an emotional bond as well as physical attraction. Victims are often elderly people who

---

31  Federal Bureau of Investigation (FBI), United States, 'Nigerian Letter or "419" Fraud' (2020).

32  Australian Competition and Consumer Commission, ScamWatch, 'Nigerian Scams' (2020).

33  Russell Smith, Michael Holmes and Philip Kaufman, 'Nigerian Advance Fee Fraud' (1999) *Trends & Issues in Crime and Criminal Justice* No 121 (Australian Institute of Criminology); and Stuart Ross and Russell Smith, 'Risk Factors for Advance Fee Fraud Victimisation' (2011) *Trends & Issues in Crime and Criminal Justice* No 420 (Australian Institute of Criminology).

34  See, eg, the Queensland case of *SDJ v FWR* [2008] QSC 256 where a husband lost around A$800 000 to a Nigerian scam, resulting in separation and property distribution proceedings.

35  Australian Competition and Consumer Commission, ScamWatch, 'Dating and Romance' (2020).

36  'Romance Scam: NI Woman Loses £300,000 Online', *British Broadcasting Corporation News*, 17 October 2019. Available: <https://www.bbc.com/news/uk-northern-ireland-48750019>.

37  Government of Western Australia, WA ScamNet, 'Death of WA Romance Fraud Victim' (2020).

have lost a life partner through death or divorce. Prolonged communications between the victim and the partner (who typically is unable to make a physical meeting for a variety of reasons) inevitably lead to requests for money or financial support. In some cases, dating websites facilitate expensive chats, and even arrange flights paid for by the victim.[38] Some people whose pictures or identity have been used for these scams, such as military officers posing in uniform, find themselves embroiled in strangers' romantic adventures without their knowledge (until contacted by an admirer who claims to have been chatting online with them).[39] More often, scam victims never find out whether the person they think they met online exists at all. Contact usually stops with the willingness or ability to make payments.

More sophisticated scams include the creation and use of forged or altered documentation. This can be in the form of fake invoices, letters of demand, loan or mortgage documents, or websites or online content purporting to be from a legitimate agency or business, but actually linking to a criminal operation. Fake or 'spoof' websites abound, such as illegitimate login pages for online banking, and these play on customers' inability or lack of time to notice minor variations in URL addresses. In some cases, the fake is quite indistinguishable from the original.

The *Convention on Cybercrime* has articles dealing with computer-related forgery and fraud:

## Convention on Cybercrime

### Section 1: Substantive criminal law

*Title 2: Computer-related offences*

Article 7: Computer-related forgery

Each Party shall adopt such legislative and other measures as may be necessary to establish as criminal offences under its domestic law, when committed intentionally and without right, the input, alteration, deletion, or suppression of computer data, resulting in inauthentic data with the intent that it be considered or acted upon for legal purposes as if it were authentic, regardless [of] whether or not the data is directly readable and intelligible. A Party may require an intent to defraud, or similar dishonest intent, before criminal liability attaches.

Article 8: Computer-related fraud

Each Party shall adopt such legislative and other measures as may be necessary to establish as criminal offences under its domestic law, when committed intentionally and without right, the causing of a loss of property to another person by:

a.  any input, alteration, deletion or suppression of computer data;
b.  any interference with the functioning of a computer system,

with fraudulent or dishonest intent of procuring, without right, an economic benefit for oneself or for another person.

---

38  Shaun Walker, 'The Men Who Go to Ukraine Looking for a Wife then Fly Home Alone and Broke', *The Guardian*, 7 April 2014.

39  See US Army Criminal Investigation Command, 'Online romance scam information', which states that 'Army CID receives hundreds of allegations a month from victims who state they got involved in an online relationship with someone, on a legitimate dating website or other social media website, who claims to be a U.S. Soldier'. Available: <https://www.cid.army.mil/romancescam.html>.

Articles 7 and 8 deal with specific types of computer-related forgery and fraud involving the alteration of data, as opposed to the mere use of computer technology to commit crimes of dishonesty such as through phishing. However, the requisite criminal offences will usually be found in traditional forgery and fraud offences that pre-date modern telecommunications. Only a few jurisdictions have computer-specific fraud offences, an example being the following provision in the Criminal Code of Tasmania:

## Computer-related fraud

A person who, with intent to defraud –

(a) destroys, damages, erases, alters or otherwise manipulates data stored in, or used in connection with, a computer; or

(b) introduces into, or records or stores in, a computer or system of computers by any means data for the purpose of –

   (i) destroying, damaging, erasing or altering other data stored in that computer or that system of computers; or

   (ii) interfering with, interrupting or obstructing the lawful use of that computer or that system of computers or the data stored in that computer or system of computers; or

(c) otherwise uses a computer –

**is** guilty of a crime.[40]

One case involved the theft of a laptop, among other items, during a house break-in, where the laptop was subsequently used by the offender to access the householder's bank account, alter personal information relating to it, change the online banking facility to telephone banking and transfer large sums from the account into the offender's own account.[41] Another case concerned an employee of a car dealership who caused other (innocent) employees to direct payments to his own accounts at different banks, disguising the account details and also making fraudulent electronic journal entries to conceal the fact that funds were missing.[42]

In the United States, the older offence of 'wire fraud' may apply to online scams, but there are also specific offences under the *Computer Fraud and Abuse Act of 1986* (the name itself indicating the concern of the legislators to address computer-facilitated fraud).[43] An example of a complex crime involving both external hacking and fraud is that alleged to have been committed by a Ukrainian extradited to the United States. The Department of Justice alleges that he, with co-conspirators, hacked into various bank accounts, email servers and email accounts, in order to steal money and engage in unauthorised stock dealings. As part of the activity, it is alleged that they took over the email accounts of bank clients regularly engaged in stock trading, and used false emails with genuine electronic

---

40 *Criminal Code Act 1924* (Tas), Chapter XXVIIIA – Crimes Relating to Computers, s 257B.

41 *Brown v Tasmania* [2008] TASSC 33. A total of 57 offences of dishonesty, including 30 counts of computer-related fraud, resulted in sentence on guilty pleas of five years in prison, reduced to three on appeal.

42 *Hodgetts v Tasmania* (2018) 29 Tas R 310. The misappropriation of over A$700 000 over four years resulted in a sentence of five years' imprisonment, upheld on appeal.

43 United States Department of Justice, Computer Crime and Intellectual Property Section (CCIPS), Criminal Division, *Prosecuting Computer Crimes* (Office of Legal Education, 2015), 26–7.

signatures to deceive the banks into releasing many thousands of dollars of funds into accounts the criminals controlled.[44]

The use of 'spam' emails is not itself criminalised in many jurisdictions, but countries such as Australia and the United States have enacted legislation under which companies can be fined large amounts of money for failing to comply with regulatory prohibitions on the automated harvesting of emails, sending of unsolicited bulk commercial messages, and using deceptive headers or sender details in such messaging. In Australia, the relevant legislation is the *Spam Act 2003* (Cth); while the United States has enacted the *Controlling the Assault of Non-Solicited Pornography And Marketing (CAN-SPAM) Act of 2003*. The former has civil penalties only, while the latter includes some criminal offences for the fraudulent use of spam. Despite these legal restrictions, it is estimated that over half of all online message traffic is spam, generated using botnets.[45]

## Identity theft

More recently, legislatures have addressed identity fraud and theft as specific types of crime. The conceptual difference (though terminology varies) is that identity theft involves the use for criminal purposes of another real person's identification details; while identity fraud uses the details of a real person, a dead person or a fictitious person in order to deceive someone in order to obtain a benefit or cause a loss. There may thus be more than one victim – the person (if any) whose identity is misused, and the victim(s) of any fraud perpetrated using that identity.[46] For example, X's stolen identity details may be used to obtain a credit card from Y (a finance company), which is then used to order goods from Z (an online vendor). The credit history of X will be compromised, and the cost of the goods will be borne by Y and/or Z.

In 1998, the United States enacted the *Identity Theft and Assumption Deterrence Act*, which made it a federal crime to 'knowingly transfer or use, without lawful authority, a means of identification of another person with the intent to commit, or to aid or abet, any unlawful activity that constitutes a violation of federal law, or that constitutes a felony under any applicable state or local law'.[47] The *Identity Theft Penalty Enhancement Act of 2004* established penalties for aggravated identity theft, which is using the identity of another person to commit felony crimes, including immigration violations, theft of another's Social Security benefits, and acts of domestic terrorism.[48]

Clearly, there is money to be made from identity crime, and personal and financial details are routinely offered for sale on online markets. These may be as simple as names and dates of birth, or may include addresses, bank account details, credit card numbers and

---

44  United States Department of Justice, 'Alleged Cybercriminal Charged with Unauthorized Computer Intrusion, Wire Fraud, Securities Fraud and Other Crimes', 21 November 2019. Available: <https://www.justice.gov/usao-edny/pr/alleged-cybercriminal-charged-unauthorized-computer-intrusion-wire-fraud-securities>.

45  Adrienne LaFrance, 'The Internet is Mostly Bots', *The Atlantic*, 31 January 2017.

46  See Bert-Jaap Koops et al, 'A Typology of Identity-Related Crime' (2009) 12(1) *Information, Communication and Society* 1.

47  Amending US Code Title 18 §1028.

48  This requires the court to sentence a convicted aggravated identity theft offender to a minimum of two years for a general offence and five years for a terrorism offence: US Code Title 18 §1028A.

expiry dates (sometimes with additional security numbers) and medical records. Purchasers can use these details to perpetrate various frauds by using an existing identity or building a false one.

Criminal marketplaces operating largely on the 'dark web' (not accessible to ordinary search engines) have been the subject of some law enforcement and media attention, at least since the emergence of 'Silk Road' and similar sites promoting sales of illicit drugs.[49] This site was shut down by the FBI and other law enforcement agencies in 2013, its creator and main operator were prosecuted, and nearly US$50 million was recovered through the forfeiture of bitcoins, a digital currency widely used on such 'crypto markets'.[50] In 2017, a larger online market called 'AlphaBay', which traded drugs, card and identification details, and other illicit goods, was also closed down by law enforcement.

> The Justice Department today announced the seizure of the largest criminal marketplace on the Internet, AlphaBay, which operated for over two years on the dark web ... Around the time of takedown, there were over 250,000 listings for illegal drugs and toxic chemicals on AlphaBay, and over 100,000 listings for stolen and fraudulent identification documents and access devices, counterfeit goods, malware and other computer hacking tools, firearms and fraudulent services. Comparatively, the Silk Road dark web marketplace, which was seized by law enforcement in November 2013, had reportedly approximately 14,000 listings for illicit goods and services at the time of seizure and was the largest dark web marketplace at the time.[51]

An Australian connection with AlphaBay emerged with media reports that the Medicare health card details of three former Australian Federal Police (AFP) commissioners were discovered to be available for sale on the site, along with hundreds of other similar card details of other Australians. It is speculated that the data of such high-profile identities are not necessarily more lucrative as targets for identity crime, but provide online sellers 'a way of advertising, that they could get anybody's details, which evidently they can'.[52] In view of the difficulties of responding to identity crimes after they have occurred, many police forces and government agencies have adopted a crime prevention approach, providing educational material and advice to reduce the likelihood of victimisation.[53]

Another innovative approach is by way of assistance to victims of identity crime, who often face lengthy and frustrating delays in showing that they have not been involved in disputed transactions and in restoring their credit histories. In the United Kingdom, a partnership between government, business and law enforcement called CIFAS (which

---

49  James Martin, 'Lost on the Silk Road: Online Drug Distribution and the "Cryptomarket"' (2014) 14(3) *Criminology and Criminal Justice* 351.

50  Federal Bureau of Investigation, 'Ross Ulbricht, the Creator and Owner of the Silk Road Website, Found Guilty in Manhattan Federal Court on All Counts', 5 February 2015. Available: <https://www.fbi.gov/contact-us/field-offices/newyork/news/press-releases/ross-ulbricht-the-creator-and-owner-of-the-silk-road-website-found-guilty-in-manhattan-federal-court-on-all-counts>.

51  United States Department of Justice, 'AlphaBay, the Largest Online "Dark Market," Shut Down', 20 July 2017. Available: <https://www.justice.gov/opa/pr/alphabay-largest-online-dark-market-shut-down>.

52  Paul Farrell, 'Medicare Card Details of Former Australian Federal Police Commissioners Available on Dark Web', *Australian Broadcasting Corporation News*, 17 December 2019.

53  See, eg, Australian Federal Police (AFP), 'Identity Crime'. Available: <https://www.afp.gov.au/what-we-do/crime-types/fraud/identity-crime>.

stands for 'Credit Industry Fraud Avoidance System') offers both protective registration for individuals at risk of victimisation (including registration of deceased individuals by their relatives or executors) and victims of impersonation markers used to alert organisations and businesses in order to carry out further checks to ensure when dealing with known or suspected victims of identity crime.[54] The US Federal Trade Commission has a dedicated help service to enable reporting by victims and the creation of individual recovery plans.[55] In Australia, s 375.1 of the *Criminal Code Act 1995* (Cth) allows victims of identity crimes to apply for a court certificate, which they can use in restoring their creditworthiness and other affairs.

Recent estimates of the cost of identity crime to Australia by way of direct and indirect losses are in the order of A\$2.2 billion annually.[56] In the United States, total direct losses such as out-of-pocket expenses from identity crime were estimated at US\$17.5 billion in 2016.[57] Such losses do not include factors such as time taken to deal with financial institutions to restore creditworthiness, reputational damage, emotional stress and strained relationships.

## Card skimming

Card skimming is one of the main ways in which criminals acquire people's identification and financial details for use in fraudulent transactions. The process of 'skimming' is simply reading the card's details using a device like those found in shops, restaurants and fuel stations, and then using those details either to create a fake 'cloned card' that can be used at an automated teller machine (ATM) or to purchase goods online or by phone. Credit cards used to pay restaurant bills are particularly susceptible to being skimmed if taken away from the table to be processed, as it is easy for a dishonest staff member to quickly skim the card using a portable device as well as processing the genuine payment. Small readers can also be used at other retail payment points, or may be hidden inside ATMs, fuel bowsers or other machines accepting card payments. More sophisticated ATM skimming operations also use small hidden cameras to read personal identification numbers (PINs) as they are being keyed in by customers.[58]

Police and prosecution services regularly report instances of card skimming and ATM interference, such as the following case in Queensland and Victoria. The following summary from the Commonwealth Director of Public Prosecutions provides an indication of the scale and international nature of these offences.

> Between April 2009 and August 2015, Scott used card-skimming equipment on ATMs at the Gold Coast, Sunshine Coast and Melbourne to dishonestly obtain the bank card numbers and personal identification numbers of individuals who used the compromised machines.

54  Information Commissioner's Office, 'Identity Theft' (2020). Available: <https://ico.org.uk/your-data-matters/identity-theft/>.
55  United States Federal Trade Commission, 'Report Identity Theft and Get a Recovery Plan' (2020). Available: <https://www.identitytheft.gov/>.
56  Australian Government, Department of Home Affairs, 'Identity Crime and Misuse in Australia' (2016).
57  United States Bureau of Justice Statistics, 'Victims of Identity Theft, 2016' (2019).
58  Russell Smith, 'Plastic Card Fraud'. In *Trends and Issues in Crime and Criminal Justice* (Australian Institute of Criminology, 1997), 71.

On a hard drive seized from Scott's residence, police located more than 100 hours of video recordings of ATM keypads that captured individuals entering their PINs, as well as documents containing bank card numbers recovered from card readers used in the skimming, and PINs identified from the video footage. In total, Scott obtained at least 2,150 PINs and 1,200 bankcard numbers.

During the same period, Scott transferred, or caused to be transferred by 15 other people at his direction, proceeds of the card skimming offending totalling $557,176.94 to 68 recipients in Bulgaria, Germany and France, via 147 Western Union or bank transfers. Including transfer fees, the total amount of proceeds of crime that Scott dealt with in relation to those transfers was $565,320.28.

On 5 March 2018, Scott was sentenced to seven years' imprisonment with a non-parole period of three years and six months.[59]

Some offenders work alone or in small groups, while others are part of international card-skimming syndicates. The international dimension is reflected in the fact that those arrested are often not the principal organisers, who may be located in another country from where ATMs are being compromised, and thus more difficult to bring to justice. However, international law enforcement cooperation can help to overcome jurisdictional barriers.

In the absence of law enforcement or other warrants (discussed in more depth in relation to computer data and electronic communications in Chapter 10), such interception is generally prohibited, along with the use and trade in related surveillance and interception devices.[60]

# Cyberterrorism

The capacity to exploit computer technology for harmful purposes is not limited to criminals, but is available also to terrorist groups and nation states. While not always mentioned in the context of cybercrime, it is useful to consider hacking and associated activities on a spectrum, with motivations varying from technical curiosity, destructive desires and financial greed to political or ideological reasons. The latter is most closely associated with terrorist actors, who also use the online environment to organise, plan, recruit and finance their operations. Some also engage in online and other financial crimes to raise money. The ability to launch cyber operations against targets is also shared by governments, with some military forces having well-developed cyberwarfare capabilities, with dedicated units and training programs. There is already a degree of cyber conflict going on between various countries, with the capacity to escalate to full-fledged cyberwarfare in the future.

The term 'cyberterrorism', although widely used, is somewhat contested by analysts.

> Few terms in contemporary conventional discourse are used as loosely as 'cyber' and 'terrorism'. Not surprisingly, their use together is hardly a guarantor of conceptual rigour. To some, the term 'cyber' is synonymous with digital technology generally. This

59   Commonwealth Director of Public Prosecutions (CDPP), *Annual Report 2017–18*, 'Case Study: Card Skimming on the Gold Coast'. Available: <https://www.cdpp.gov.au/publications/2017-18-annual-report-0>.

60   See, eg, in Australia, *Criminal Code Act 1995* (Cth), s 474.4 (Interception Devices); *Surveillance Devices Act 2004* (Cth); and *Telecommunications (Interception and Access) Act 1979* (Cth).

is increasingly unhelpful given the pervasiveness of digital technology in contemporary society. As kitchen appliances increasingly become 'wired,' almost everything will be digital. For present purposes, let us use the term cyber to refer to those technologies commonly referred to as the internet and the world wide web.

The term terrorism has been grossly abused, and means many things to many people. To some, it has almost become synonymous with anything evil. Since the cold war, the adage 'one person's terrorist is another's freedom fighter' has become hackneyed … Today, the term is used to refer to an act or threat of violence to create fear and/or compliant conduct in a victim or wider audience for the purpose of achieving political ends.[61]

Nonetheless, legal prohibitions that emanate from both criminal law and anti-terrorism law result in interesting intersections. For example, hacking into protected databases to obtain militarily sensitive information and then passing this on to a terrorist group clearly implicates both cybercrime and national security offences. Such was the conduct of a citizen of Kosovo named Ardit Ferizi.

[Ferizi] was detained in Malaysia in 2015 and consented to his extradition to the United States, where he pled guilty to three offences: accessing a protected computer without authorisation in order to get personal information details of some 1,300 US military personnel, providing material support to the Islamic State of Iraq and the Levant (ISIL) which is a designated terrorist organisation, and obtaining information in order to provide material support to ISIL. He was sentenced to 20 years in prison, with the Assistant Attorney General for National Security stating: 'This case represents the first time we have seen the very real and dangerous national security cyber threat that results from the combination of terrorism and hacking.'[62]

In the United Kingdom, a computer expert who had set up what was probably the first English-language jihadist website in the world in the late 1990s, shut down soon after the 9/11 attacks in the United States, spent around eight years fighting extradition to that country. Finally, after the European Court of Human Rights ruled that there was no legal impediment to his extradition given assurances by the United States that he would not face the death penalty, he was extradited and pleaded guilty in 2013 to charges of conspiracy and providing material support to terrorism. Despite being sentenced to over 12 years in prison, taking into account the time he spent in custody in the United Kingdom before being extradited, he was returned there after serving only two years in a US prison facility.[63]

In Australia, Faheem Lodhi was convicted and sentenced to 20 years in prison in 2006 for collecting documents from the internet and other sources which included information about making explosives and maps of the Australian electricity grid, as well as what was described as a 'jihadi CD'. Although no terrorist attack eventuated, the prosecution was

61 Peter Grabosky and Michael Stohl, 'Cyberterrorism' (2003) 82 *Australian Law Reform Commission Reform Journal* 8.
62 United States Department of Justice, 'ISIL-Linked Kosovo Hacker Sentenced to 20 Years in Prison' (23 September 2016). Available: <https://www.justice.gov/opa/pr/isil-linked-kosovo-hacker-sentenced-20-years-prison>.
63 Dominic Casciani, 'Cyber-Jihadist Babar Ahmad Released', *British Broadcasting Corporation News*, 19 July 2015. Available: <https://www.bbc.com/news/uk-33585959>.

able to show that the documents were connected with preparation for such an act, which is an offence under Criminal Code provisions introduced soon after the 9/11 attacks.[64] The definition of 'terrorist act' under these provisions is itself noteworthy, as it includes reference to acts threatening or seriously interfering with electronic systems, including information and telecommunications systems.[65]

Turning to applicable cybercrime offences, the Criminal Code offence of using a telecommunications network with intent to commit or facilitate a serious offence under Australian or foreign law is available in relation to terrorist offences (which qualify as serious).[66] For example, use of the internet to download plans and instructions for a terrorist attack, whether it eventuates or not, would fall within such an offence as well as preparatory terrorism offences.[67] So would using social media to advocate, recruit or solicit finances for a terrorist organisation.[68] Other offences prohibit the use of such networks, including the internet and social media, to make a threat of death or serious injury, or a hoax threat, or to 'menace, harass or cause offence'.[69] Further discussion of the misuse of social media is provided in Chapter 8.

# Cyberwarfare

Turning finally to cyberwarfare, relations between nation states are less clearly regulated by domestic criminal law, but some aspects of cybercrime are reflected in responses to state-sponsored hacking, espionage, and attacks on security and energy infrastructure. At the outset, caution needs to be exercised in relation to the 'attribution problem', whereby it may appear that an attack emanates from a particular country or is supported by a foreign government, but this is generally beyond the ability of civil society actors such as academics and the media to verify or disprove.

In 2014, shortly before the Thanksgiving holiday in the United States, the Sony Pictures Entertainment company headquartered in Culver City in California found itself under cyber attack. Files were infected with destructive malware, computer screens were taken over by a red skeleton and warning messages using the name 'Guardians of Peace', and over the following months the personal emails, salaries and even medical records of around 6000 Sony employees were made public. Four unreleased Sony movies were posted to the internet. Investigations progressively focused on North Korea, which had expressed strong

---

64  Gregor Urbas, 'Cyberterrorism and Australian law' (2005) 8(1) *Internet Law Bulletin* 1; sentencing decision at *R v Lodhi* (2006) 199 FLR 364 (Whealy J).

65  *Criminal Code Act 1995* (Cth), s 100.1, where a 'terrorist act' is one that is done with the intention to coerce a government or a sector of society, causing or threatening to cause specified serious harm, and motivated by a political, religious or ideological cause; but not falling within an exemption for non-violent political protest.

66  *Criminal Code Act 1995* (Cth), s 474.14, discussed above.

67  Similarly to the facts in *R v Lodhi* (above), though in that case jihadi material was handwritten from online sources rather than downloaded; only the terrorism offences were prosecuted in that case.

68  Terrorist organisations are found in Division 102 (Terrorist Organisations) of the Criminal Code, where a 'terrorist organisation' is defined as '(a) an organisation that is directly or indirectly engaged in preparing, planning, assisting in or fostering the doing of a terrorist act; or (b) an organisation that is specified by the regulations for the purposes of this paragraph ... ' where around 20 such groups have been specified thus far.

69  *Criminal Code Act 1995* (Cth), ss 474.14, 474.15 and 474.17.

disapproval of an upcoming Sony Pictures movie which portrayed the assassination of the North Korean leader, Kim Jong-un. Official sanctions against North Korea were intensified by the Obama administration in 2015, and by mid-2018 the Department of Justice had finalised its investigations with the announcement of a criminal complaint charging a North Korean national with involvement in both the Sony Pictures hack and the dissemination of WannaCry ransomware that spread around the world in 2017. The wording of the complaint made clear that the North Korean government was alleged to have been responsible for the actions of the named national and his co-conspirators.

> The complaint alleges that Park was a member of a government-sponsored hacking team known to the private sector as the 'Lazarus Group,' and worked for a North Korean government front company, Chosun Expo Joint Venture (a/k/a Korea Expo Joint Venture or 'KEJV'), to support the DPRK government's malicious cyber actions. The Conspiracy's malicious activities include the creation of the malware used in the 2017 WannaCry 2.0 global ransomware attack; the 2016 theft of $81 million from Bangladesh Bank; the 2014 attack on Sony Pictures Entertainment (SPE); and numerous other attacks or intrusions on the entertainment, financial services, defense, technology, and virtual currency industries, academia, and electric utilities.[70]

Recognition of the need for the laws of war to encompass and regulate state responses to cyber attacks led to the *Tallinn Manual on the International Law Applicable to Cyber Warfare* being published in 2013 (updated in 2017).[71] The manual is the cooperative product of experts in international law and other disciplines, intended to guide governments and policymakers in formulating appropriate rules for the use of their cyber capabilities. Interestingly, the dominant view of cyber attacks appears to be that they can amount to the use of force if they are functionally equivalent to a conventional attack (eg in destroying transport or communications infrastructure) and that 'a state can respond to a non-cyber violation with a cyber countermeasure, and to a cyber violation with a non-cyber countermeasure'.[72]

A spectacular example of a state-sponsored cyber countermeasure to a non-cyber threat is the Stuxnet malware, reportedly developed by the United States and Israel specifically to attack and incapacitate Iranian nuclear facilities, which came to the world's attention a decade ago.

> In 2010, several independent technology researchers discovered a new virus that had invaded computer systems around the world. While viruses in many forms have been around since the early days of the Internet, this virus caught the attention of experts because it displayed unique functions and a level of sophistication never seen before. Dubbed 'Stuxnet,' this worm demonstrated a number of interesting qualities, including a specific attack vector that was limited to certain computers operating in a rather unique

---

70  United States Department of Justice, 'North Korean Regime-Backed Programmer Charged with Conspiracy to Conduct Multiple Cyber Attacks and Intrusions', 6 September 2018. Available: <https://www.justice.gov/opa/pr/north-korean-regime-backed-programmer-charged-conspiracy-conduct-multiple-cyber-attacks-and>.

71  Michael Schmitt (ed), *Tallinn Manual 2.0 on the International Law Applicable to Cyber Operations* (2017).

72  Eric Talbot Jensen, 'The Tallinn Manual 2.0: Highlights and Insights' (2017) 48 *Georgetown Journal of International Law* 735.

fashion. While the worm rapidly distributed itself around the globe, infecting tens of thousands of computers, its purpose remained a mystery. While early reports suggested that this worm was intended to disrupt satellite telecommunications and other computer controlled infrastructure systems, no direct link between the virus' functions and those specific systems was established. However, after several months it became apparent that the virus had a specific geographic target: Iran. A disproportionate number of infected computer systems were located in that country. While the virus appeared around the world, no discernible damage was reported to have occurred elsewhere.

Eventually, as the computer code contained in the virus was deciphered, it became evident that it was designed as a weapon, targeting a specific nuclear 'research' facility in the state of Iran. The virus – Stuxnet – was a weapon that disrupted the operation of gas centrifuges used to make highly enriched uranium, an essential component in the creation of nuclear weapons. Within months, the virus succeeded in damaging or destroying more than nine hundred centrifuges, setting back Iran's uranium enrichment program by several years.[73]

The legal position surrounding the use of cyber attacks against a state opponent remains unclear. While some legal scholars regard the international law of armed conflict as ill-adapted to deal with conflict in cyber rather than terrestrial space, it has been suggested that such an attack can rise to the level of 'armed attack' for the purposes of international law, making it more significant than a 'kinetic' attack. Schmitt has developed a six-part test for determining whether a cyber attack rises to the level of an armed attack under international law:

Economic and political coercion can be delimited from the use of armed force by reference to various criteria. The following number among the most determinative:
***Severity:*** Armed attacks pose the threat of injury, death, damage or destruction to a much greater degree than economic or political coercion.
***Immediacy:*** The negative consequences of an armed attack are more immediate, while economic or political coercion are less so.
***Directness:*** The consequence of an armed attack is more closely linked to the attack than is the case with economic or political coercion.
***Invasiveness:*** In an armed attack, the harmful event 'usually crosses into the target state, whereas in economic warfare the acts generally occur beyond the target's borders' with the former resulting in a greater intrusion on the rights of the targeted state and greater international instability.
***Measurability:*** The consequences of an armed attack are more easily measured than are the consequences of economic or political force.
***Presumptive legitimacy:*** The application of violence is generally deemed illegitimate, whereas economic or political force is deemed presumptively lawful.[74]

---

73  John Richardson, 'Stuxnet as Cyberwarfare: Applying the Law of War to the Virtual Battlefield' (2011) 29(1) *Journal of Computer and Information Law* 1.
74  Michael N Schmitt, 'Computer Network Attack and the Use of Force in International Law: Thoughts on a Normative Framework' (1999) 37 *Columbia Journal of Transnational Law* 885, 914–15.

While the United Nations is working towards a multilateral legal framework on cyberspace, the development of an international treaty appears some years away.[75] In the absence of a UN treaty on cybercrime generally, aside from the complexities of cyberwarfare, instruments such as the Council of Europe's *Convention on Cybercrime* occupy the field. Its provisions on illegal access and interception, and data and system interference, all refer to acts done 'without right'. There is a plausible argument that retaliatory acts such as 'defensive hacking' do not breach the prohibitions so long as they are done under lawful authority. Apart from the use of defence powers, it is unclear to what extent such techniques are permitted, for example, in ordinary law enforcement, but recent reports on Australian and US efforts in counterterrorism indicate that defensive hacking is being used with effect:

> The Australian Signals Directorate (ASD) is one of the nation's most secretive organisations and is tasked with intercepting foreign communication and cyber warfare. The United States drafted a team of 20 from within ASD to join a top-secret mission, called Operation Glowing Symphony, aimed at hacking into Islamic State's propaganda computer network. The Australian team included hackers, or 'offensive cyber operators' as they're officially called, counter terrorism experts, linguists, intelligence experts and technical specialists. The team spent four months preparing for a cyber-attack on Islamic State, during which they spied on the terror group's propaganda unit members.[76]

In practical terms, the legality of such measures is unlikely to be tested in open court, given the unlikelihood of its targets making a complaint to Australian or US law enforcement and prosecution authorities.

# National security

Given the demands on states and public authorities to safeguard the security of their citizens, (which includes critical infrastructure such as telecommunications, finance and transport systems), it is to be expected that some level of surveillance is necessary in order to predict and prevent, as well as respond to, cyberthreats. As discussed in Chapter 3, perennial and heated political debates focus on what level of surveillance is acceptable, and what forms this should take so as to involve minimal intrusions into citizens' privacy and civil liberties generally.[77] Such debates are made more complex by the fact that non-state actors such as large corporations (particularly those offering internet searching and social media services) already acquire massive amounts of information on their customers and others through the use of 'big data' analysis as well as details of internet searches, browsing habits and online purchases. Societal responses to these diverse intrusions into what some consider private

---

75  United Nations, Office for Disarmament Affairs, 'The Application of International Law in Cyberspace: State of Play', 25 October 2018.

76  Stephanie Borys, 'Australian Cyber Soldiers Hacked Islamic State and Crippled its Propaganda Unit – Here's What We Know', *Australian Broadcasting Corporation News*, 18 December 2019.

77  A useful touchstone is John Stuart Mills' 'harm principle', according to which intrusions into citizens' liberty are only justifiable in order to prevent harm to others (see Chapter 2), coupled with restraints of proportionality and appropriate levels of oversight – for example, through the use of judicial warrants to authorise surveillance.

spaces are by no means settled or clear, particularly as many people appear to be willing to post so much of their personal life online.

Legal frameworks around national security and surveillance vary across countries, but a joint information-sharing program between the United States and the United Kingdom was instituted at the end of the Second World War, which Australia, Canada and New Zealand later joined to form the 'Five Eyes Alliance'.[78] This and related regulatory frameworks in each country ensure a reasonable degree of commonality in approaches, although the degree of legal protection of privacy does vary. For example, the United States and Canada have constitutionally protected privacy rights, while in Australia the common law applies but lacks a clear tort of privacy invasion.[79] As has been discussed, an insight into the extent of state surveillance was provided in 2013 by the revelations of former National Security Agency (NSA) contractor Edward Snowden. Telecommunications laws in Australia require internet service providers (ISPs) and other telecommunications operators to retain metadata relating to communications for two years. These laws have particular relevance to the investigation of cybercrime, as offenders in this area are usually sophisticated and utilise technologies such as encryption to mask their crimes, meaning that barriers to enforcing laws in this area may face technological challenges, in addition to complex legal challenges.

There is now widespread use of encryption and cloud storage. Digital communications platforms increasingly include encryption options, which make it virtually impossible for either ISPs or law enforcement to decipher the meaning of data even if access can be provided. A notable example occurred in relation to a 2015 mass shooting attack in San Bernadino, California, suspected to be an act of terrorism. As the two shooters died in the incident, investigators worked to reconstruct their plans and motives from their histories and communications, but faced a barrier when one of the shooters' mobile phone could not be unlocked due to security settings that included encryption. The FBI requested that the phone's maker, Apple, assist in disabling the phone's security, which Apple refused to do based on its policy of not undermining the security and consumer privacy features of its products. The matter was partway into litigation when the FBI announced that, assisted by an unnamed third party (believed by many to be a foreign security service), it had been able to unlock the phone, and the legal proceedings were discontinued.[80] In addition to encryption issues, the case also raised the issue of cloud storage, as early attempts by investigators to change the password on the shooter's cloud storage account using the phone had the effect of making an auto-backup of the phone's contents to the cloud account impossible. The complexity of the role of technology companies in such investigations is significant.

> Both sides – law enforcement officials and privacy hawks – argue in absolute terms
> that obscure the many different layers of the debate. The truth is that the larger
> question is not just about 'encryption,' but rather envelopes multiple layers of the
> global information infrastructure implicated by the massive shift of personal and

---

78  Corey Pfluke, 'A History of the Five Eyes Alliance: Possibility for Reform and Additions' (2019) 38 *Comparative Strategy* 302.

79  See United States Constitution, Fourth Amendment; *Canadian Charter of Rights and Freedoms*, ss 7 and 8; and Australian Law Reform Commission (ALRC), *Serious Invasions of Privacy in the Digital Era* (DP80, 2014).

80  Joel Ruben et al, 'FBI Unlocks San Bernardino Shooter's IPhone and Ends Legal Battle with Apple, For Now', *Los Angeles Times*, 28 March 2016.

business records into the 'cloud.' Cloud infrastructure is mostly controlled by private corporations, including behemoths such as Google and Microsoft, which enter into contractual relationships with their users. The privacy issue, then, is not only about the traditional relationship between individuals and the government. It is more directly about the quasigovernmental role of these large cloud providers.[81]

The move by some providers towards encryption by default, and especially 'end-to-end' encryption which precludes readability of messages (including picture and sound) by anyone other than the sender and recipient, including the ISP, is (not surprisingly) seen by many governments as a dangerous development that will virtually end the possibility of law enforcement and national security access to encrypted communications. Ministers from Australia, the United States and the United Kingdom are joining forces to urge messaging application providers such as Facebook not to embrace end-to-end encryption, in the interest of law enforcement and national security investigations. An open letter states:

> Companies should not deliberately design their systems to preclude any form of access to content, even for preventing or investigating the most serious crimes. This puts our citizens and societies at risk by severely eroding a company's ability to detect and respond to illegal content and activity …[82]

The resolution of this standoff between governments and private corporations is likely to shape the evolution of online platforms for years to come in relation to cybercrime, and national security more broadly.

# Conclusion

This chapter has discussed the use of computers to commit crime, and the legal regime that has been developed internationally, and in Australia, over the past 20 years in response. It has considered hacking, online fraud, cyberterrorism, cyberwarfare and national security. Advancements in information and technology and the internet have provided the opportunity for criminals to undertake new forms of criminal activity. The globalised nature of the internet, and technologies such as encryption, make this a challenging area of the law to regulate, investigate, enforce and prosecute. The relationship between cybercrime, terrorism and national security will continue to develop, and new applications of cybercrime will no doubt emerge in the future. The following chapters will continue to build on the themes that have been introduced here, beginning with the regulation of the internet as it relates to social media and communications.

---

81  David Odperbeck, 'Encryption Policy and Law Enforcement in the Cloud' (2017) 49 *Connecticut Law Review* 713, 716.

82  United States Department of Justice, 'Attorney General Barr Signs Letter to Facebook from US, UK, and Australian Leaders Regarding Use of End-to-End Encryption', 3 October 2019. Available: <https://www .justice.gov/opa/pr/attorney-general-barr-signs-letter-facebook-us-uk-and-australian-leaders-regarding-use-end>.

# 8

## SOCIAL
## MEDIA AND
## COMMUNICATIONS

# Introduction

Social media and electronic communications dominate modern life. Workplaces have been transformed by email, teleconferencing and an array of new applications, along with our homes and social lives. Fewer people today go to a travel agent to book flights, subscribe to newspaper delivery, or even watch free-to-air television. All of this can be done more conveniently and with greater individual choice and control online, often guided by social media applications to channel information, in ways not mediated or filtered as in the past. Social relationships have changed along the way, with many people now exchanging texts rather than speaking face-to-face or by phone.

For all of the convenience, however, there are costs. The absence of face-to-face contact increases the risk of fraud, not only affecting consumer purchases and investments, but also physical and emotional safety, as in the 'romance scam' cases explored in Chapter 7. Cyberstalking and cyberbullying have exploded due to the multiplier effect of social media and telecommunications.

Legislators have revised existing laws and enacted new provisions, whether criminal, civil or regulatory. This chapter examines a range of new laws to address problems such as 'sexting' and 'revenge porn'; and legal responses to emerging challenges such as social media advertising and electoral manipulation through 'fake news'. Whether these laws can make much difference in shaping social norms is open to question, particularly given the small proportion of cases that can be processed by traditional criminal and civil justice systems.

There are many social media applications; this discussion will focus on the most familiar services, such as YouTube, Facebook, Twitter and Instagram. The use of social media is so widespread, numbering in the billions of users, that these companies exert significant force in aiding or resisting regulatory attempts by governments to exert some control through legislation. Thus, they can be seen as 'co-regulators' of a complex technical and social domain. Following a discussion of social media and the regulation of providers, the chapter will discuss online defamation, vilification and incitement to violence; cyber harassment, stalking and bullying; and illegal and offensive content.

# Social media

To distinguish social media websites and platforms from those on which content is merely posted by an agency or business with no facility for interaction, a definition of the term 'social media' should include the following features:

- It enables users to post self-generated content, such as text, photos and videos.
- It allows users to create profiles and engage with others, such as by posting comments, counterpoints, or endorsements eg using 'likes'.
- It enables users to form networks, linking those with similar interests, viewpoints or goals.[1]

---

1    Jonathan Obar and Steven Wildman, 'Social Media Definition and the Governance Challenge: An Introduction to the Special Issue' (2015) 39(9) *Telecommunications Policy* 745.

Social media enables collaborations to form in a relatively unstructured and non-hierarchical way, in the form of 'grassroots' movements or projects. An early example is the online encyclopaedia *Wikipedia*, which allows members of the public to add to and edit entries, thus harnessing in a historically unprecedented way the 'wisdom of the crowd'.[2] This relative lack of central control over content also enables false entries to be made, which can persist until corrected by moderators or other contributors. Examples include false reports of the death of politicians and celebrities, obscene content posted on entries about presidential candidates, and nonsensical material for presumed entertainment value. The phenomenon of creating fake 'grassroots' movements is arguably not a new form of propaganda, but the online version has acquired the noteworthy name of 'astroturfing'.

> Astroturfing is the simulation of a political campaign which is intended to manipulate the target audience. Often, the purpose of such a campaign is not clearly recognizable because a political effort is disguised as a grassroots operation … the first inklings of astroturfing emerged in the early twentieth century. However, astroturfing has also spread to the Internet and is seen, in this context, as a coordinated campaign 'where messages supporting a specific agenda are distributed via the Internet. These messages employ deception to create the appearance of being generated by an independent entity'.[3]

The term 'fake news' has recently gained traction as a description of deliberately false or heavily biased media reports, especially in the context of political discussion.[4] To outward appearances, such reports may seem credible, indeed indistinguishable from reports published by reputable news sources, but consumers are rarely in a position to establish the provenance of material that flashes across their social media pages to establish veracity. Fake news can be defined as:

> … fabricated information that mimics news media content in form but not in organizational process or intent. Fake-news outlets, in turn, lack the news media's editorial norms and processes for ensuring the accuracy and credibility of information … It is particularly pernicious in that it is parasitic on standard news outlets, simultaneously benefiting from and undermining their credibility.[5]

Current examples of misleading information or 'fake news' circulating on social media are not difficult to find, such as in relation to the COVID-19 pandemic, and often rely on automated dissemination using botnets.

> [T]he analysis identified co-ordinated efforts to promote a particular coronavirus conspiracy theory – that it was engineered as a bioweapon by China. With this narrower scope, the method to identify co-ordination was expanded from one second to one minute and so likely captures fully automated bot accounts as well as more hybrid automated-human accounts and perhaps some fully human accounts operating in close

2   Aniket Kittur and Robert Kraut, 'Harnessing the Wisdom of Crowds in Wikipedia: Quality through Coordination', *Proceedings of the 2008 ACM Conference on Computer Supported Cooperative Work* 37.

3   Kenneth Henrie and Christian Gilde, 'An Examination of the Impact of Astroturfing on Nationalism: A Persuasion Knowledge Perspective' (2019) 8 *Social Sciences* 38.

4   Regina Rini, 'Fake News and Partisan Epistemology' (2017) 27(2) *Kennedy Institute of Ethics Journal* 43.

5   David Lazer et al, 'The Science of Fake News' (2018) 359 *Science* 1094.

co-ordination. A co-retweet network of 2,903 accounts and 4,125 links or co-retweets between them was identified. Within this network, the top 30 clusters were analysed manually to identify group identities within each cluster.[6]

Not only can misleading information be posted on social media; so, too, can harmful content. Soon after YouTube's introduction in 2005, as a site where members of the public could post their own videos, concerns emerged about the phenomenon of 'happy slapping' which involved the filming of random attacks on unsuspecting individuals or fights between young people in public places. In 2006, three Google executives found themselves charged under Italian privacy protection laws, with a Milan court initially holding them liable for not expeditiously removing a video showing a disabled student being verbally and physically abused by other students, one of whom had filmed the incident.[7] Although overturned on appeal, the decision raised difficult questions about who might be responsible for objectionable content finding its way onto social media, and how content could be filtered without imposing a centralised censorship regime on an otherwise free avenue of expression.[8]

# Regulating social media

The regulation of social media providers centres on whether they should be viewed simply as conduits for users' content, with no responsibility for policing it, or be required to cooperate with law enforcement and regulators in ensuring a level of safety and propriety for their customers. Are these services more like the post office, which simply delivers the mail without opening letters and parcels, or more like a publisher, with both the means and responsibility for checking content that may be inaccurate, offensive and harmful? The answer is to a large extent still under construction, as governments around the world confront the logistics of holding large multinational companies such as Google and Facebook to demanding legal standards.

A good starting point is to consider what can broadly be labelled 'safe harbour' provisions under legislation, which shield online providers from civil and criminal liability except in specified circumstances. Perhaps the most well-known is s 230 of the *Communications Decency Act 1996* in the United States, which precludes civil claims such as defamation against providers for content, by providing: '(c)(1) No provider or user of an interactive computer service shall be treated as the publisher or speaker of any information provided by another information content provider.' At the same time, s 230(c)(2) protects from civil liability claims any action taken in good faith to block or remove material considered to be 'obscene, lewd, lascivious, filthy, excessively violent, harassing, or otherwise objectionable, whether or not such material is constitutionally protected'. Finally, the obligations of providers are set out.

---

6   Timothy Graham et al, *Like a Virus: The Coordinated Spread of Coronavirus Disinformation* (Australia Institute, 2020).
7   Giovanni Sartor and Mario Viola de Azevedo Cunha, 'The Italian Google-Case: Privacy, Freedom of Speech and Responsibility of Providers for User-Generated Contents' (2010) 18(4) *International Journal of Law and Information Technology* 356; Eric Pfanner, 'Italian Appeals Court Acquits 3 Google Executives in Privacy Case', *New York Times*, 22 December 2012.
8   Majid Yar, 'A Failure to Regulate? The Demands and Dilemmas of Tackling Illegal Content and Behaviour on Social Media' (2018) 1(1) *International Journal of Cybersecurity Intelligence and Cybercrime* 5.

A provider of interactive computer service shall, at the time of entering an agreement with a customer for the provision of interactive computer service and in a manner deemed appropriate by the provider, notify such customer that parental control protections (such as computer hardware, software, or filtering services) are commercially available that may assist the customer in limiting access to material that is harmful to minors. Such notice shall identify, or provide the customer with access to information identifying, current providers of such protections.[9]

Although the intent of the legislation was to include both protections and responsibilities for online providers, particularly in relation to blocking of offensive material, court decisions applying s 230 have largely turned on the 'safe harbour' from civil liability for the day-to-day operations in good faith of online platforms.[10] This and subsequent similar court decisions over the next decade meant that it was largely through political pressure, rather than legal actions, that the main social media providers such as Google and Facebook took any active steps to locate and remove illegal and offensive content.

In Australia, similar 'safe harbour' provisions exist for online service providers, but an array of statutory obligations imposes specific reporting and monitoring obligations nonetheless. This approach leaves unclear to what extent online providers are required actively to seek out prohibited content so as to block and report it, but Australian regulators have pointed to a different piece of legislation, which provides that carriage service providers must 'do the provider's best to prevent telecommunications networks and facilities from being used in, or in relation to, the commission of offences against the laws of the Commonwealth or of the States and Territories'.[11] In practice, responsible online service providers will work with law enforcement either on request or under their own policies. Further discussion of provider obligations with respect to material infringing intellectual property rights, such as copyright, is found in Chapter 9.

Social media remains a primarily self-governing industry in many jurisdictions. In the absence of regulatory governance imposed by external authorities, evaluation and removal of offending content is up to social media providers, as well as the community of social media users. Platforms such as Facebook publish policies outlining kinds of content or use that are considered unacceptable, such as violence and incitement, promotion of criminal groups or activities, and fraud or deception.[12] In June 2020, Facebook updated its Coordinating Harm and Publicizing Crime policy, committing to prohibiting 'people from facilitating, organizing, promoting, or admitting to certain criminal or harmful activities targeted at people, businesses, property or animals'.[13]

9   *Communications Decency Act*, 47 USC §230 (Protection for private blocking and screening of offensive material), paras (c)(1) and (2), and (d).
10  *Jane Doe v America Online Inc* 783 So2d 1010 (2001).
11  *Telecommunications Act 1997* (Cth), s 313(1). Section 313(3), which allows blocking of internet content at the request of law enforcement agencies, was the subject of a parliamentary inquiry which reported in 2015. Available: <https://www.aph.gov.au/Parliamentary_Business/Committees/House/Infrastructure_and_Communications/Inquiry_into_the_use_of_section_313_of_the_Telecommunications_Act_to_disrupt_the_operation_of_illegal_online_services>.
12  Facebook, *Community Standards*. Available: <https://www.facebook.com/communitystandards/>.
13  Ibid.

This concern is also reflected in YouTube's Transparency Report, which provides data on the number and breakdown of videos removed after being flagged for attention.

> YouTube relies on teams around the world to review flagged videos and remove content that violates our Community Guidelines; restrict videos (e.g., age-restrict content that may not be appropriate for all audiences); or leave the content live when it doesn't violate our guidelines.[14]

Figures for the January–March 2020 period indicate that 6 million videos were removed, the majority through automated flagging, and smaller numbers through user or non-government or government agency flagging, as outlined in Table 8.1.

**Table 8.1**   YouTube content removal, January–March 2020[15]

| Removal reason | Removal amount (videos) |
| --- | --- |
| Spam, misleading and scams | 2 263 383 |
| Child safety | 1 482 109 |
| Nudity or sexual | 873 351 |
| Violent or graphic | 699 651 |
| Harmful or dangerous | 304 133 |
| Promotion of violence and violent extremism | 258 908 |
| Hateful or abusive | 107 174 |
| Other | 86 189 |
| Harassment and cyberbullying | 36 110 |

Despite such measures, it is questionable whether self-regulation is an adequate response to the importance of social media in the dissemination of news and other information globally.[16] However, the response of trying to fit social media within a more traditional governance regime developed over many decades for public media such as newspapers, radio and television may also have unintended consequences.[17] Without committing to either of the labels of 'platform' or 'publisher', the role of social media in providing a linkage between users and content makes it accurate to describe them as 'intermediaries'.

> By calling them intermediaries, let's recognise that social media platforms are fundamentally in the middle – that is, they mediate between users who produce content and users who might want it. That makes them similar to not only search engines and ISPs, but also traditional media. They too face a regulatory framework designed to oversee how they mediate between producers and audiences, between speakers and

14   YouTube, *Community Guidelines Enforcement*. Available: <https://transparencyreport.google.com/youtube-policy/removals?hl=en>.

15   Ibid.

16   Philip Napoli, 'Social Media and the Public Interest: Governance of News Platforms in the Realm of Individual and Algorithmic Gatekeepers' (2015) 39(9) *Telecommunications Policy* 751.

17   Terry Flew et al, 'Internet Regulation as Media Policy: Rethinking the Question of Digital Communication Platform Governance' (2019) 10(1) *Journal of Digital Media and Policy* 33.

listeners. Social media platforms are not only in the middle between user and user, and user and public but between citizens and law enforcement, policymakers, and regulators charged with governing their behaviour.[18]

The role of intermediaries in relation to law enforcement investigations is further discussed in Chapter 10.[19]

As noted in Chapter 1, Facebook has come under the scrutiny of regulators in several countries over its management of user data following inquiries into its relationship with data-mining operations such as Cambridge Analytica, and has been fined or is in the process of being investigated by privacy agencies. The Australian Information Commissioner has commenced legal proceedings against Facebook, and in April 2020 obtained leave from the Federal Court to serve documents.[20] The key allegation is that Facebook has breached Australian privacy law by allowing third parties to harvest the personal information of hundreds of thousands of Australian Facebook users without their consent, along with those in other countries, which was disclosed to groups including Cambridge Analytica.[21]

# Online defamation, vilification and incitement to violence

## Defamation

Defamation is a civil cause of action that arises when someone unjustifiably publishes negative information about another, which harms that person's reputation. Defences include that the information was true or at least published in good faith (eg media reporting based on information available at the time of reporting), or was fair comment made in the public interest (eg criticism of a public official made without malice).[22] With the advent of online discussion and posts (often with little or no moderation), and especially social media, it is easy to publish comments that may prove to be defamatory.

An early example of online defamation was the case of *Dow Jones and Co Inc v Gutnick*.[23] The publisher of *The Wall Street Journal* and weekly finance magazine *Barron's* was sued by Gutnick over an allegedly defamatory story linking his charity to tax evasion and market

---

18    Tarleton Gillespie, Chapter 14: 'Regulation of and by Platforms'. In Jean Burgess et al (eds), *The Sage Handbook of Social Media* (Sage, 2018).

19    See also Gregor Urbas, 'Old Wine, Opaque Bottles? Assessing the Role of Internet Intermediaries in the Detection of Cybercrime'. In Lennon Chang and Russell Brewer (eds), *Criminal Justice and Regulation Revisited: Essays in Honour of Peter Grabosky* (Routledge, 2018).

20    Office of the Australian Information Commissioner, 'Statement on Facebook Proceedings' (Media release, 22 April 2020). Available: <https://www.oaic.gov.au/updates/news-and-media/statement-on-facebook-proceedings/>.

21    *Australian Information Commission v Facebook Inc* (2020) 144 ACSR 88.

22    The tort of defamation varies across jurisdictions in its scope and defences. In Australia, the offence of criminal defamation still exists in some states but is rarely prosecuted: see, eg, s 365 of the *Criminal Code 1899* (Qld) and s 529 of the *Crimes Act 1900* (NSW); see also *Williams v Spautz* (1992) 174 CLR 509.

23    *Dow Jones and Co Inc v Gutnick* (2002) 210 CLR 575; see also Richard Garnett, '*Dow Jones and Company Inc v Gutnick*: An Adequate Response to Transnational Internet Defamation?' (2003) 4(1) *Melbourne Journal of International Law* 1.

manipulation activities by others. This story appeared in those print media in late 2000 and was also posted to the website wsj.com, which was available to subscribers around the world, including in the Australian state of Victoria, where Gutnick lived. The legal proceedings mainly concerned the question of jurisdiction and appropriate forum – that is, whether a plaintiff residing in Australia could sue an American publisher of online content available worldwide in an Australian court and under Australian defamation law, which is more plaintiff-friendly than US law. The High Court unanimously ruled that he could, noting in reference to the defendant:

> If people wish to do business in, or indeed travel to, or live in, or utilize the infrastructure of different countries, they can hardly expect to be absolved from compliance with the laws of those countries. The fact that publication might occur everywhere does not mean that it occurs nowhere.[24]

In another case involving an Australian plaintiff, the actress Rebel Wilson successfully sued the publishers of print and online stories defaming her as a liar, which resulted in a multi-million dollar award of damages for the loss of international acting opportunities, the amount being later reduced on appeal.[25]

These cases convey that anybody who posts online should take care not to defame others, wherever they may be located, as unwelcome legal consequences may follow. A more recent example is the case of a lawyer in South Australia who, in 2019, brought defamation proceedings after a woman posted a one-star Google review in late 2018, with extensive negative comments about him in both English and Chinese. The lawyer, from Hong Kong and with clients largely drawn from the Chinese-speaking community in Adelaide, claimed that he lost around 80 per cent of his business after the review was published online. Google removed the review on the lawyer's request, but the woman posted a further two similar reviews under false names. The lawyer claimed that the woman was never a client of his, which she disputed in the later posts, but the court found for the plaintiff lawyer and awarded damages of A$750 000 and costs against the defendant.[26]

Many internet users who insult others, such as school bullies and online trolls, lack the financial resources to be suitable defendants in defamation proceedings. Moreover, they may use online names that conceal their real identities, so that proving who is behind a post may be difficult. However, an online publisher that allows such posts to be displayed to the world may well be both identifiable and liable. Whether a search engine that links to sites containing allegedly defamatory material is a publisher for the purposes of defamation law has been a contested issue, but a leading Australian decision indicates that it can be.[27] On appeal, it was noted that:

24  Per Callinan J at [186]. After this decision, further international litigation was attempted but the case was settled for an undisclosed sum. Defamation legislation introduced since, such as the *Defamation Act 2005* (NSW), s 32, includes a defence for 'innocent dissemination' that is applicable to internet service providers.
25  *Wilson v Bauer Media Pty Ltd* [2017] VSC 521; *Bauer Media Pty Ltd v Wilson (No 2)* (2018) 56 VR 674.
26  *Cheng v Lok* [2020] SASC 14. Eugene Bosivert, 'Adelaide Lawyer Gordon Cheng Wins $750,000 Defamation Judgment over Bad Google Review', *Australian Broadcasting Corporation News*, 7 February 2020.
27  *Trkulja v Google Inc* [2015] VSC 635.

In the context of the web, and defamation, proceedings have been brought against the operators of –

(1) search engines;

(2) blogging sites;

(3) Facebook site(s);

(4) YouTube site(s);

and also against –

(5) internet service providers ('ISPs'); and

(6) forum hosts of varying descriptions.

Relatively infrequently, however, have proceedings been brought against the authors of webpages, or the makers of comments posted in discussion forums and on bulletin boards, blogs, or Facebook users. That is so even when the identity of the author is apparent or is perhaps ascertainable. Presumably, it is an entity of the kind commonly sued which is thought to be worth powder and shot. The fact that proceedings are commonly brought against such entities has thrown up distinct problems in defamation law.[28]

Where the identity of a defamatory poster is unknown to the potential plaintiff, discovery proceedings may assist to identify him or her. In a Federal Court ruling in February 2020, Google was ordered to disclose information that ultimately helped him to identify a poster using the online handle 'CBsm 23' and who allegedly defamed a Melbourne dentist.[29] It has been reported that this ruling will allow a class action against similar platforms that allow anonymous reviews of businesses to be posted, where such reviews are defamatory and cause financial losses.[30] And in another proceeding involving alleged defamatory reviews about an Australian lawyer, legal action has been taken against Google to force the disclosure of the identity of an online reviewer who the plaintiff suspects is really a competitor in the legal community.[31]

## Vilification and incitement

Online vilification includes negative comment directed not only against individuals, but whole groups within society. Racial vilification, as well as abuse on the basis of religion, gender and sexuality, regrettably abounds on websites and in social media. White supremacist and neo-Nazi sites can easily be found, along with material condemning those perceived to transgress social, moral or religious taboos. At the extremes, online 'hate speech' is considered to inflame and contribute to real-world crimes, ranging from violent assaults to acts of terrorism.[32]

Balancing legitimate freedom of expression against the protection of minorities within society is a difficult task, but again guidance can be derived from the 'harm principle' that helps to define liberalism (discussed in Chapter 2). Contemporary debates tend to focus on what kind and level of harm is sufficient to merit interference by the state, particularly

---

28 *Google Inc v Trkulja* (2016) 342 ALR 504, [227]–[228].

29 *Kabbabe v Google LLC* [2020] FCA 126; see also *Smith v Jones* [2020] NSWDC 262, a case involving malicious and defamatory Google reviews posted about a solicitor.

30 Leo Shanahan, 'Google Faces Class Action Suit over Incognito Reviews', *The Australian*, 17 February 2020.

31 Danny Tran, 'Gangland Lawyer Zarah Garde-Wilson Launches Court Action to Unmask Google Reviewer', *Australian Broadcasting Corporation News*, 20 February 2020.

32 Abbee Corb, 'Online Hate and Cyber-Bigotry: A Glance at Our Radicalized Online World'. In Nathan Hall et al (eds), *Routledge International Handbook on Hate Crime* (Routledge, 2015).

in the form of criminal sanction. While some criminal offences for vilification exist, other laws impose aggravated sentences for hate-motivated crimes, or include such acts within statutory definitions of unlawful discrimination.[33]

While the Council of Europe's *Convention on Cybercrime* does not itself address racial vilification, this is covered by its additional protocol requiring signatories to criminalise dissemination over a computer system of racist and xenophobic material, and posting of racist or xenophobic threats and insults.[34] The protocol has fewer signatories than the Convention itself, partly due to the concern that countries (including the United States) have with balancing cybercrime laws against constitutional free speech protections.[35]

Incitement to violence is a criminal act in most jurisdictions, whether this occurs online or otherwise, but fewer countries have laws prohibiting content that depicts or describes violent acts. Content regulation in countries such as Australia, Canada, the United Kingdom and the United States is generally achieved through classification systems and conditions on broadcasting and other telecommunications licensing schemes, rather than criminal offences. However, some more extreme material has come to be prohibited, with responsibility increasingly falling on social media providers to remove the material expeditiously, or face substantial fines for failure to do so.

The mass shooting of dozens of people in two mosques in Christchurch, New Zealand in early 2019 was live-streamed on Facebook by the offender, who had also posted his intentions and beliefs on online forums before the attacks.

> [T]he world got a terrible reminder of how flawed existing social-media policies and algorithms are for policing violent and offensive content. In the days before the shooting, the perpetrator apparently boasted of his plans and posted an online manifesto. He then broadcast the horrific act live on Facebook. The attack left 49 people dead and dozens more injured. Over the past 18 months, following harassment and fake-news scandals, social-media companies have invested heavily in content moderators. But this did little to stop video of the shooting from spreading. Not only was the live stream reportedly up for 20 minutes, but the resulting video was then reposted on YouTube, with some clips remaining up for over an hour.[36]

In response, the Australian government announced new laws relating to 'abhorrent violent material' which is defined as audio and/or visual material that records or streams acts and is produced by a person involved in the acts, being acts of terrorism, murder, torture, rape or kidnap. However, the offences that were enacted do not target these acts directly (as they

---

33 In Australia, for example, websites denying the Holocaust have been found to be in breach of the *Racial Discrimination Act 1975* (Cth): see *Jones v Toben* (2002) 71 ALD 629.

34 Council of Europe, *Additional Protocol to the Convention on Cybercrime, concerning the Criminalisation of Acts of a Racist and Xenophobic Nature Committed through Computer Systems* (entry into force, March 2006).

35 Irene Nemes, 'Regulating Hate Speech in Cyberspace: Issues of Desirability and Efficacy' (2002) 11(3) *Information and Communications Technology Law* 193; Jessica Henry, 'Beyond Free Speech: Novel Approaches to Hate on the Internet in the United States' (2009) 18(2) *Information and Communications Technology Law* 235. Note that Australia is also not a signatory, while Canada has signed but not ratified the protocol.

36 Will Knight, 'The Mass Shooting in New Zealand Shows How Broken Social Media Is', *MIT Technology Review*, 15 March 2019.

are already criminalised under existing laws) but impose criminal liability on content and hosting services, including social media providers, for failure to notify and expeditiously remove such content, as determined by the eSafety Commissioner.[37] This approach signifies a shift in the legal position of internet and social media providers.

Key terms of this new legislative regime are defined as follows:

## 474.31 Abhorrent violent material

(1) For the purposes of this Subdivision, *abhorrent violent material* means material that:

    (a) is:

        (i) audio material; or

        (ii) visual material; or

        (iii) audio-visual material;

        that records or streams abhorrent violent conduct engaged in by one or more persons; and

    (b) is material that reasonable persons would regard as being, in all the circumstances, offensive; and

    (c) is produced by a person who is, or by 2 or more persons each of whom is:

        (i) a person who engaged in the abhorrent violent conduct; or

        (ii) a person who conspired to engage in the abhorrent violent conduct; or

        (iii) a person who aided, abetted, counselled or procured, or was in any way knowingly concerned in, the abhorrent violent conduct; or

        (iv) a person who attempted to engage in the abhorrent violent conduct.

(2) For the purposes of this section, it is immaterial whether the material has been altered.

(3) For the purposes of this section, it is immaterial whether the abhorrent violent conduct was engaged in within or outside Australia.

## 474.32 Abhorrent violent conduct

(1) For the purposes of this Subdivision, a person engages in *abhorrent violent conduct* if the person:

    (a) engages in a terrorist act; or

    (b) murders another person; or

    (c) attempts to murder another person; or

    (d) tortures another person; or

    (e) rapes another person; or

    (f) kidnaps another person.[38]

---

37 *Criminal Code Act 1995* (Cth), ss 474.30–474.45, added by the *Criminal Code Amendment (Sharing of Abhorrent Violent Material) Act 2019* (Cth) with effect from 5 April 2019. Further provisions, ss 474.46–474.48, were added with effect from 19 September 2019 to prohibit online incitement of trespass to agricultural land – for example, during protests – under the *Criminal Code Amendment (Agricultural Protection) Act 2019* (Cth).

38 *Criminal Code Act 1995* (Cth), ss 474.31 and 474.32(1), with sub-ss (2)–(7) defining the selected offences constituting 'abhorrent violent conduct' in greater detail.

The provisions go on to set out the obligations of internet service providers, content service providers and hosting service providers, where 'content service' includes social media providers.[39] Obligations include reporting abhorrent violent material to police, and expeditiously removing or ceasing to host the material if it is reasonably capable of being accessed within Australia. Penalties for failure to comply with these obligations can amount to millions of dollars or a sum of 10 per cent of annual turnover for corporate entities.[40] Defences are provided for law enforcement and other official dealings in such information, as well as journalistic and research uses, and the implied freedom of political communication is preserved.[41]

# Cyber harassment, stalking and bullying

## Cyber harassment

An enormous amount of vitriol appears to flow from online anonymity, which can be observed on almost every comments page of public websites. In social media, the more familiar term is 'trolling', which ranges from seemingly genuine contributions that nonetheless subvert conversations, to outright abuse.[42] Online harassment may target an individual, a group or an entire race, ethnicity, religion or sexual orientation. Surveys of internet users suggest that women are more likely than men to be trolled, and that at least one in three have experienced some level of harassment online, with impacts on health, safety and workplace productivity.[43] However, legal recourse is often difficult as most offenders are anonymous. Where an offender can be identified, and is within jurisdiction, there are several laws that can be used to prosecute. Under Commonwealth law, the following section relating to online harassment is applicable.

### 474.17 Using a carriage service to menace, harass or cause offence

**(1)** A person commits an offence if:

  **(a)**  the person uses a carriage service; and

  **(b)**  the person does so in a way (whether by the method of use or the content of a communication, or both) that reasonable persons would regard as being, in all the circumstances, menacing, harassing or offensive.

Penalty: Imprisonment for 3 years.[44]

The meaning of 'offensive' is explicated in an earlier provision:

---

39  Ibid, s 474.30, defining 'content service' and 'hosting service'.
40  Ibid, ss 474.33 and 474.34.
41  Ibid, ss 474.37 and 474.38.
42  Hannah Barton, 'The Dark Side of the Internet'. In Irene Connolly et al (eds), *An Introduction to Cyberpsychology* (Routledge, 2016).
43  The Australia Institute, 'Online Harassment and Cyberhate Costs Australians $3.7b' (January 2019).
44  *Criminal Code Act 1995* (Cth), s 474.17(1). In 2018, an aggravated form of the offences was added as s 474.17A, with a five-year maximum where the commission of the offence involved the misuse of 'private sexual material', and a seven-year maximum if this was after civil penalty orders had already been made: see *Enhancing Online Safety (Non-Consensual Sharing of Intimate Images) Act 2018* (Cth).

## 474.4 Determining whether material is offensive

**(1)** The matters to be taken into account in deciding for the purposes of this Part whether reasonable persons would regard particular material, or a particular use of a carriage service, as being, in all the circumstances, offensive, include:

**(a)**   the standards of morality, decency and propriety generally accepted by reasonable adults; and

**(b)**   the literary, artistic or educational merit (if any) of the material; and

**(c)**   the general character of the material (including whether it is of a medical, legal or scientific character).[45]

A case applying these provisions in the Australian Capital Territory (ACT) Supreme Court dealt with the misuse of a webcam to transmit, without consent of a participant, sexual activity that was otherwise consensual. A military cadet surreptitiously used Skype to transmit live images from a sexual encounter he was having with a female cadet to his friends in an adjoining room.[46] Another case involved the deceptive use of a fictitious persona on social media accounts, including Facebook, to entice and then coerce victims into sexual encounters.[47] The provisions have also been applied in stalking and harassment cases.[48]

In the United Kingdom, prosecutorial guidelines were amended in 2016 to allow incitement charges to be brought against those trolling online.[49] In the United States, which has constitutionally protected free speech, online harassment and stalking can nonetheless constitute crimes against federal and state laws.[50]

# Cyberstalking

The term 'cyberstalking' has been used for the past two decades to delineate those varieties of stalking behaviour that utilise communications technologies such as the internet.

> Cyberstalking is analogous to traditional forms of stalking in that it incorporates persistent behaviours that instil apprehension and fear. However, with the advent of new technologies, traditional stalking has taken on entirely new forms through mediums such as email and the Internet. Thus, it becomes cyberstalking. Increasingly, cyberstalking is gaining the attention of the media and the public as the nature of the crime incorporates elements of new technology and threatening behaviours, which symbolise a new form of threat.[51]

---

45   *Criminal Code Act 1995* (Cth), s 473.4. Note that this standard also applies to the definition of 'child abuse material' under the Code, so that not every explicit image is prohibited (eg content in an online medical course).

46   *R v McDonald and Deblaquiere* (2013) 233 A Crim R 185 (27 June 2013; sentencing 23 October 2013). The conduct was found to constitute an offence under s 474.17 of the *Criminal Code Act 1995* (Cth), as well as an act of indecency under the *Crimes Act 1900* (ACT).

47   *R v Tamawiwy (No 4)* [2015] ACTSC 371.

48   *R v Simonetti* [2018] ACTSC 31; *R v Cartwright* [2018] ACTSC 132; *R v EP (No 3)* [2019] ACTSC 242.

49   Crown Prosecution Service, *Cybercrime – Prosecution Guidance* (2019). Available: <https://www.cps.gov.uk/legal-guidance/cybercrime-prosecution-guidance>.

50   Steven Hazelwood and Sarah Koon-Magnin, 'Cyber Stalking and Cyber Harassment Legislation in the United States: A Qualitative Analysis' (2013) 7(2) *International Journal of Cyber Criminology* 155.

51   Emma Ogilvie, 'Cyberstalking', *Trends and Issues in Crime and Criminal Justice* No 166 (Australian Institute of Criminology, 2000).

Given the prevalence of social media use, this must now be considered a frontline in harassment and stalking generally. Indeed, these are increasingly being seen as forms of domestic violence.[52] In some cases, offenders use access to a victim's social media accounts, or those of friends and relatives, even using location-tracking applications to monitor victims. For example, in a recent case in the state of Tasmania, an ex-boyfriend was able not only to track his victim's movements, but even to control the operation of her car using an application he had helped install.[53]

Stalking legislation, which was first introduced in many jurisdictions in the 1990s, has been amended to ensure that it encompasses electronic communications and the use of social media. For example, the stalking offence in the Australian Capital Territory includes interference with the stalked person's property, and sending electronic messages to the person, or about the person to anybody else.[54] A case in the ACT Supreme Court illustrates that online stalking behaviour can be both delusional and yet still be overwhelming and terrifying for the victim, where the defendant had not only persistently texted the victim despite her requests that he stop but had also sent hundreds of texts to a local radio station he thought was passing on messages to him from the victim through its selection of songs, which she only discovered after police were contacted.[55] A more recent ruling held that interference with property would extend to the use of a location-tracking application.[56] The eSafety Commissioner provides advice on 'technology-facilitated abuse', including tracking devices and remote controls.[57]

# Cyberbullying

Online harassment and stalking directed at children and teens by their peers is often referred to as 'cyberbullying'. Perhaps due to the fact that there is no geographical or temporal respite from online bullying – that is, it is ever-present, unlike more traditional schoolyard bullying – levels of depression and suicide among victims are a great concern.[58] The phenomenon of cyberbulling on social media was brought to public attention in the mid-2000s with the Lori Drew case, which involved a mother victimising her daughter's friend using a false identity.[59] Initially charged with hacking offences under the US *Computer Fraud and Abuse Act* (discussed in Chapter 7), based on the fact that her use of MySpace violated its terms

---

52  Andrew King-Ries, 'Teens, Technology, and Cyberstalking: The Domestic Violence Wave of the Future' (2011) 20 *Texas Journal of Women and the Law* 131.
53  Reis Thebault, 'A Woman's Stalker Used an App that Allowed Him to Stop, Start and Track Her Car', *The Washington Post*, 7 November 2019.
54  *Crimes Act 1900* (ACT), s 35 (Stalking).
55  *R v Henderson* [2009] ACTCA 20, [9].
56  *R v NO* (2018) 330 FLR 134, [48].
57  Office of the eSafety Commissioner, 'Domestic and Family Violence: What is Technology-Facilitated Abuse?'. Available: <https://www.esafety.gov.au/key-issues/domestic-family-violence>.
58  See, eg, Julian Dooley et al, 'Cyberbullying versus Face-to-Face Bullying: A Theoretical and Conceptual Review' (2009) 217(4) *Journal of Psychology* 182; Faye Mishna et al, 'Ongoing and Online: Children and Youth's Perceptions of Cyber Bullying' (2009) 31(12) *Children and Youth Services Review* 1222; Jim Wang et al, 'Cyber and Traditional Bullying: Differential Association with Depression' (2011) 48(4) *Journal of Adolescent Health* 415.
59  The case facts are described in detail in Nicholas Johnson, '"I agree" to Criminal Liability: Lori Drew's Prosecution under §1030(a) of the Computer Fraud and Abuse Act' (2009) *Illinois Journal of Law, Technology and Policy* 561.

of use, a jury convicted on a misdemeanour count rather than the felonies argued for by federal prosecutors, but this conviction was reversed on review. Subsequently, many states enacted laws targeting cyberbullying more directly, an example being legislated in North Carolina:

Except as otherwise made unlawful by this Article, it shall be unlawful for any person to use a computer or computer network to do any of the following:

**(1)** With the intent to intimidate or torment a minor:

    **a.** Build a fake profile or Web site;

    **b.** Pose as a minor in:

        **1.** An Internet chat room;

        **2.** An electronic mail message; or

        **3.** An instant message;

    **c.** Follow a minor online or into an Internet chat room; or

    **d.** Post or encourage others to post on the Internet private, personal, or sexual information pertaining to a minor.

**(2)** With the intent to intimidate or torment a minor or the minor's parent or guardian:

    **a.** Post a real or doctored image of a minor on the Internet;

    **b.** Access, alter, or erase any computer network, computer data, computer program, or computer software, including breaking into a password protected account or stealing or otherwise accessing passwords; or

    **c.** Use a computer system for repeated, continuing, or sustained electronic communications, including electronic mail or other transmissions, to a minor.

**(3)** Make any statement, whether true or false, intending to immediately provoke, and that is likely to provoke, any third party to stalk or harass a minor.

**(4)** Copy and disseminate, or cause to be made, an unauthorized copy of any data pertaining to a minor for the purpose of intimidating or tormenting that minor (in any form, including, but not limited to, any printed or electronic form of computer data, computer programs, or computer software residing in, communicated by, or produced by a computer or computer network).

**(5)** Sign up a minor for a pornographic Internet site with the intent to intimidate or torment the minor.

**(6)** Without authorization of the minor or the minor's parent or guardian, sign up a minor for electronic mailing lists or to receive junk electronic messages and instant messages, with the intent to intimidate or torment the minor.[60]

This comprehensive provision includes not only direct communications with a victim, but also a range of other acts that may be done with the purpose of harassment, including with the use of a false online profile, as occurred in the Lori Drew case. Another case in Canada, involving the suicide of Amanda Todd after being bullied into taking naked pictures, became a touchstone for reform in that country.[61]

---

60 *Criminal Law* (NC Gen Stat) §14-458.1, *Cyber-Bullying; penalty*, added by an *Act Protecting Children of this State by Making Cyber-Bullying a Criminal Offence Punishable as a Misdemeanour.*

61 Amanda Todd's story is presented on a tribute site, the Amanda Todd Legacy Society. At the time of writing, proceedings for the extradition of her tormentor from the Netherlands, an adult named Aydin Coban, had not yet been finalised. Available: <https://www.amandatoddlegacy.org/aydin-coban.html>.

An equally tragic case was the impetus for similar reform in Australia, in the form of a general offence of preparing to harm a minor online:

A person (the *first person*) commits an offence if:

(a) the first person does any act in preparation for doing, or planning to do, any of the following:

   (i)   causing harm to a person under 16 years of age;

   (ii)  engaging in sexual activity with a person under 16 years of age;

   (iii) procuring a person under 16 years of age to engage in sexual activity; and

(b) the first person is at least 18 years of age; and

(c) the act is done using a carriage service.

Penalty: Imprisonment for 10 years.

Example: A person misrepresents their age online as part of a plan to cause harm to another person under 16 years of age.[62]

The Criminal Code contains provisions prohibiting the online promotion of suicide, whether by way of material which 'directly or indirectly counsels or incites committing or attempting to commit suicide' or which 'promotes a particular method of committing suicide' or 'provides instruction on a particular method of committing suicide'.[63]

The Office of the eSafety Commissioner also has a role in relation to cyberbullying under its legislation. Reporting and removal powers apply to 'cyberbullying material' which is defined as material that 'would be likely to have the effect on the Australian child of seriously threatening, seriously intimidating, seriously harassing or seriously humiliating the Australian child'.[64] Social media services can join the enforcement scheme at varying levels, and are thus voluntarily subject to civil penalties for non-compliance with removal requirements as notified by the Commissioner.[65]

In New South Wales, recent amendments to domestic violence legislation following a young girl's suicide after being bullied online have expanded the definition of 'intimidation' to include cyberbullying:

'intimidation' of a person means –

(a) conduct (including cyberbullying) amounting to harassment or molestation of the person, or

**Note:** An example of cyberbullying may be the bullying of a person by publication or transmission of offensive material over social media or via email.

(b) an approach made to the person by any means (including by telephone, telephone text messaging, e-mailing and other technologically assisted means) that causes the person to fear for his or her safety, or

---

62 *Criminal Code Act 1995* (Cth), s 474.25C (Using a carriage service to prepare or plan to cause harm to, engage in sexual activity with, or procure for sexual activity, persons under 16), added by the *Criminal Code Amendment (Protecting Minors Online) Act 2017* (Cth). The provision also refers to child grooming preparations, in view of the case of teenager Carly Ryan who was murdered by a child groomer using a false persona to seduce her into an online relationship.

63 *Criminal Code Act 1995* (Cth), s 474.29A (Using a carriage service for suicide related material), though the provision clarifies that it does not prohibit public discussion of topics such as suicide law reform and euthanasia.

64 Parts 1–5 of the *Enhancing Online Safety Act 2015* (Cth).

65 Ibid.

**(c)** any conduct that causes a reasonable apprehension of injury to a person or to a person with whom he or she has a domestic relationship, or of violence or damage to any person or property.[66]

The offence of stalking or intimidation with intent to cause fear or harm, which includes both cyberbullying and cyberstalking, carries a maximum penalty of five years' imprisonment.[67]

# Illegal and offensive content

## Child exploitation material

Social media and other forms of online communication can facilitate the distribution of illegal and offensive content, such as child exploitation material.[68] Child exploitation material is prohibited under domestic laws and international agreements.[69] The production and distribution of such material attracts severe criminal penalties,[70] as does child solicitation or 'grooming' using online communications.[71] The use of webcams to groom or coerce children into participating in sexual activities is one of the more insidious developments of modern communications technology. Once a victim has sent a picture, there may be a form of 'sextortion' that involves the offender threatening to distribute images of the victim to family or friends, unless further images are provided.

Victims often feel an immense burden of shame and helplessness that can lead to compliance, or other tragic outcomes such as self-harm and suicide.[72] Although child exploitation also occurs in a range of other contexts, the infiltration of social media is used by offenders to locate and coerce victims.[73] Recent cases of sextortion used to produce child

---

66 *Crimes (Domestic and Personal Violence) Act 2007* (NSW), s 7, as amended by the *Crimes (Domestic and Personal Violence) Amendment Act 2018* (NSW), introduced into the NSW Parliament as 'Dolly's Law' in honour of the young victim.

67 The definition of 'stalking' also covers 'contacting or otherwise approaching a person using the internet or any other technologically assisted means': *Crimes (Domestic and Personal Violence) Act 2007* (NSW), s 8.

68 Jasmine Eggestein and Kenneth Knapp, 'Fighting Child Pornography: A Review of Legal and Technological Developments' (2014) 9(4) *Journal of Digital Forensics, Security and Law* 29.

69 See, eg, the *Combatting Child Sexual Exploitation Legislation Amendment Act 2019* (Cth), which replaced all references to 'child pornography' in the *Criminal Code Act 1995* (Cth) with 'child abuse material'.

70 Part 10.6 of the *Criminal Code Act 1995* (Cth) includes offences such as s 474.22 (Using a carriage service for child abuse material), s 474.22A (Possessing or controlling child abuse material obtained or accessed using a carriage service) and s 474.23 (Possessing, controlling, producing, supplying or obtaining child abuse material for use through a carriage service). Internationally, the Council of Europe's *Convention on Cybercrime* (also called the 'Budapest Convention') includes a provision relating to the illegality of online distribution of child pornography (Article 9); however, it does not deal with child procurement or grooming.

71 Part 10.6 of the *Criminal Code Act 1995* (Cth) includes offences such as s 474.26 (Using a carriage service to procure persons under 16 years of age), s 474.27 (Using a carriage service to 'groom' persons under 16 years of age) and s 474.27A (Using a carriage service to transmit indecent communication to persons under 16 years of age). Internationally, the Council of Europe's *Convention on Protection of Children against Sexual Exploitation and Sexual Abuse* ('Lanzarote Convention') deals with child procurement and grooming.

72 Mirjana Gavrilovic Nilsson et al, 'Understanding the Link between Sextortion and Suicide' (2019) 13(1) *International Journal of Cyber Criminology* 55.

73 *R v Tahiraj* [2014] QCA 353, [20]–[25] describe the events involving several victims. The offender was sentenced to a cumulative term of 12 years' imprisonment.

exploitation material have involved the use of Facebook, Snapchat and other social media, as well as online games such as Fortnite.[74] Offenders may also use social media to arrange meetings with their targets in person, in order to commit contact offences.[75]

Online child grooming came to public attention in early cases such as that involving an American marine, who in 2003 had befriended a 12-year-old British girl online and persuaded her to meet him in Manchester and travel to Paris. There he sexually assaulted her, and was later arrested in Germany shortly after the girl had flown back home. After being sentenced to four and a half years' imprisonment in the United Kingdom on charges of abduction and gross indecency, the marine was extradited to the United States where he was sentenced to a further 11 years for the sexual assault under that country's laws applying to military personnel overseas.[76] Partly in response to this case, the *Sexual Offences Act 2003* (UK) included a new 'grooming' provision, which makes it an offence for a person over 18 years old to meet with or travel to meet with a person aged under 16 years after communicating with that person with the intention of committing a sexual offence. The mental requirement is that the defendant did not reasonably believe that the person was aged 16 years or more. The maximum penalty for an indictable offence under this provision is 10 years in prison.[77]

Australia, Canada and the United States have similar offences, and a similar law enforcement approach to investigating online child grooming. In particular, police use the covert investigation technique of assuming the identity of a child online, sometimes a real child if alerted that an offender has been grooming a victim, but often a fictitious child identity created for the purpose of interacting with suspected offenders online.[78] The use of this and other investigative techniques in dealing with cybercrime is discussed further in Chapter 10. It can be noted, however, that the drafting of Australian child grooming offences deliberately facilitates the use of fictitious identities, as the offence may be committed even though there is no actual child involved, so long as the defendant believed that he or she was communicating with a person under the age of 16 years. This means that ancillary offences such as attempt do not need to be used.[79]

Prosecutions in some countries have been successful, under a variety of criminal laws, in relation to the use of webcam technologies to exploit children. In Australia, for example, paying customers have been found guilty under Commonwealth Criminal Code offences of

74  Jeffery Martin, 'Florida Man Found Guilty of Using Snapchat and Kik for Sextortion and Production of Child Pornography', *Newsweek*, 10 February 2019.
75  In Australia and Great Britain, the term 'child grooming' is more often used; while in Canada and the United States, 'child luring' is often used. The concept can be seen as preliminary to the procuring of a child for sex.
76  Gregor Urbas, 'Protecting Children from Online Predators: The Use of Covert Investigation Techniques by Law Enforcement' (2010) 26(4) *Journal of Contemporary Criminal Justice* 410.
77  *Sexual Offences Act 2003* (UK), s 15 (Meeting a child following sexual grooming etc). A new s 15A was added in 2017 to criminalise 'sexual communications' with a child (using the same age parameters as s 15) not requiring any actual or intended meeting or travel for a meeting. The maximum penalty is two years.
78  Gregor Urbas, 'Threat on the Net! Online Child Grooming in Australia' (2011) 103 *Precedent* 16.
79  *Criminal Code Act 1995* (Cth), s 474.27 (Using a carriage service to 'groom' persons under 16 years of age), where 'carriage service' is defined to include communications services such as phone or internet; and remaining subsections and related offences cover situations of grooming for someone else, procuring, and sexual activity with a child using a carriage service; see *R v Stubbs* (2009) 228 FLR 221.

using a carriage service to access, solicit and produce child abuse material and engaging in sexual activity with a child outside Australia.[80] In a recent development, a major Australian bank is alleged to have facilitated payments to the Philippines for webcam child exploitation by exercising lax scrutiny over its customers' use of LitePay, a service set up to allow simple remittance payments between the two countries and promptly shut down when allegations emerged of its misuse, along with millions of alleged breaches of anti-money laundering laws. Senior bank executives have either resigned or brought forward their retirement in response.[81]

## Intimate images

The widespread availability of smartphones has led to a significant proportion of the community engaging in 'sexting' with a current or prospective romantic partner. (Sexting is the taking of a naked, or semi-naked, picture of oneself and sending it to someone else.) However, there is a danger that such images will be shared with third parties without the consent of the subject, such as if the relationship ends acrimoniously. The non-consensual sharing of intimate images in order to hurt or retaliate against a former partner is colloquially referred to as 'revenge porn'.[82] New laws have been enacted in numerous jurisdictions to deal with this form of online abuse, recognising that consent is typically limited to the viewing of images by a romantic partner and does not extend to the onward distribution of the images.[83]

An associated problem is that the images created and distributed in sexting may well constitute 'child exploitation material' under statutory definitions, so that children may find themselves liable under criminal law for possession, production and distribution offences.[84] The legislative response, where reform has been undertaken, has been to provide some form of legal protection for children, while still maintaining the focus of criminal prohibition on adult offenders and those who engage in the malicious distribution of intimate images without consent. The state of Victoria, for example, enacted the following summary offences in 2014.

---

80 *Criminal Code Act 1995* (Cth), s 272.9 creates an offence of engaging in sexual activity with a child outside Australia, where 'sexual activity' is defined so that 'a person is taken to engage in sexual activity if the person is in the presence of another person (including by a means of communication that allows the person to see or hear the other person) while the other person engages in sexual activity' (Dictionary to the Code); while s 272.11 relates to persistent sexual abuse of a child outside Australia, requiring more than one occasion.

81 Michael Roddan, 'Westpac Philippines Probe into Child Exploitation Scandal', *The Australian*, 11 December 2019.

82 An Australian Senate inquiry into the 'Phenomenon Colloquially Referred to as "Revenge Porn"', which involves sharing private sexual images and recordings of a person without their consent, with the intention to cause that person harm' reported in February 2016 with legislative recommendations, some of which have been adopted. Available: <https://www.aph.gov.au/Parliamentary_Business/Committees/Senate/Legal_and_Constitutional_Affairs/Revenge_porn>.

83 Gregor Urbas and Kendra Fouracre, 'Legal Responses to Sexting: The Importance of Consent' (2013) 16(7) *Internet Law Bulletin* 171. The Victorian legislation is provided as an example below.

84 Michael Salter et al, 'Beyond Criminalisation and Responsibilisation: Sexting, Gender and Young People' (2013) 24(3) *Current Issues in Criminal Justice* 301.

## Distribution of intimate image

**(1)** A person (A) commits an offence if –

   **(a)**   A intentionally distributes an intimate image of another person (B) to a person other than B; and

   **(b)**   the distribution of the image is contrary to community standards of acceptable conduct.

### Example

A person (A) posts a photograph of another person (B) on a social media website without B's express or implied consent and the photograph depicts B engaged in sexual activity.

**(2)** A person who commits an offence against subsection (1) is liable to level 7 imprisonment (2 years maximum).

**(3)** Subsection (1) does not apply to A if –

   **(a)**   B is not a person under the age of 18 years; and

   **(b)**   B had expressly or impliedly consented, or could reasonably be considered to have expressly or impliedly consented, to –

      **(i)**   the distribution of the intimate image; and

      **(ii)**   the manner in which the intimate image was distributed.

## Threat to distribute intimate image

**(1)**   A person (A) commits an offence if –

   **(a)**   A makes a threat to another person (B) to distribute an intimate image of B or of another person (C); and

   **(b)**   the distribution of the image would be contrary to community standards of acceptable conduct; and

   **(c)**   A intends that B will believe, or believes that B will probably believe, that A will carry out the threat.

**(2)** A person who commits an offence against subsection (1) is liable to level 8 imprisonment (1 year maximum).

**(3)** For the purposes of this section, a threat may be made by any conduct and may be explicit or implicit.[85]

As can be seen from the example provided in the legislation under the distribution offence, the posting on a social media site of an intimate image of a person (of any age) without that person's consent is presumed to be 'contrary to community standards of acceptable conduct'. A defence is provided for consensual distribution if the subject is aged 18 years or more; but the legislation is silent on whether distribution of an intimate image of a person under 18 years with consent would ever be within community standards and thus not an offence under these provisions. Of course, this would be little comfort if the image still contravenes child exploitation material laws, so Victoria also modified its child abuse material offences to provide an exemption for self-produced child images and a defence for images of sexual activity between children not more than two years apart in age.[86] However,

---

85   *Summary Offences Act 1966* (Vic), ss 41DA and 41DB, added by the *Crimes Amendment (Sexual Offences and Other Matters) Act 2014* (Vic).

86   *Crimes Act 1958* (Vic), ss 51M and 51N, added by the *Crimes Amendment (Sexual Offences) Act 2016* (Vic).

these defences would not protect an adult in possession of the same images. For example, in a 2016 case the concerned partner of the mother of a teenage girl discovered that the girl had been sexting and took her phone, made copies of the images on it, and reported the matter both to her school and police. He was charged with and convicted of possession of child exploitation material, receiving a good behaviour bond.[87]

Most social media providers have policies encouraging the reporting of objectionable images, with the possibility that they will be removed from the platform if they contravene national laws, placing a burden of proof on the complainant. The following example is from Instagram's policy on exposed private information.

> **Reporting photos and videos that violate your privacy**
>
> If you believe a photo or video violates your privacy, you can report it to us. We'll remove posts that you report as unauthorized if this is required by relevant privacy laws in your country, as long as the reported content involves you, your child (under 13) or another person for whom you're the legal representative or guardian. Photos or videos involving anyone else will need to be reported by the individual themselves.[88]

In Australia, the Office of the eSafety Commissioner operates under legislation that allows it to require the removal of offending content that it identifies, or is reported by members of the public, supported by a civil penalty regime for non-compliance, established under the *Enhancing Online Safety Act 2015* (Cth).

> This scheme allows victims of image-based abuse to make a report (complaint or objection notice) to the eSafety Commissioner. In response to a report, we may take removal action and, in some cases, also take action against the person who shared, or threatened to share, an intimate image without consent. In recognition of the serious and harmful nature of image-based abuse, the civil penalties scheme offers victims relief by helping to get intimate images quickly removed. There are also a range of civil remedies to hold the person responsible for the image-based abuse accountable.[89]

Since 2017, the legislation includes provisions making it unlawful for a person who is ordinarily resident in Australia to post on social media and other online services any non-consensual intimate image of another person, with a civil penalty attached. Further civil penalties may apply to service providers, who are required by formal notice to remove the offending material within specified time frames, if they fail to comply.[90]

# Conclusion

In contemporary society, social media occupies an important position in many people's lives. It is becoming the dominant means by which people receive information and news, and interact with others, affecting communication both positively and negatively. Terms such

---

87  *DPP v Ortell* [2016] VCC 1459, per Patrick J.

88  Instagram, 'Exposed Private Information'. Available: <https://help.instagram.com/122717417885747>.

89  Office of the eSafety Commissioner: 'Civil Penalties Scheme'. Available: <https://www.esafety.gov.au/key-issues/image-based-abuse/take-action/civil-penalties-scheme>.

90  Part 5A of the *Enhancing Online Safety Act 2015* (Cth) was added by the *Enhancing Online Safety (Non-Consensual Sharing of Intimate Images) Act 2018* (Cth), with effect from 31 August 2018.

as 'trolling' and 'fake news' have acquired new significance in relation to the collection of personalised data online and the manipulation of information for a range of political ends. Social media channels provide a new means for people to communicate and interact, but are also used for harassment, stalking and exploitation, often in ways that seriously harm their victims, in both online and offline environments.

Legal responses vary from the application of existing civil and criminal laws to social media users, to the enactment of new laws imposing criminal, civil or regulatory sanctions on social media platforms. Examples of the former include defamation proceedings against online posters who damage business reputations, and prosecutions of others who post malicious and offensive material on websites. Examples of the latter include increased statutory obligations to report and remove offensive material, such as the 'abhorrent violent material' laws recently enacted in Australia and specifically applying to social media platforms.

For their part, social media providers have taken some steps to self-regulate, though largely maintaining their position that they are platforms rather than publishers, and therefore should not be governed by the same regimes that apply to media publication of information. Rather, they see themselves as conduits for the sharing of users' content, with few editorial responsibilities. Recent legal developments indicate that this position is increasingly unrealistic. The conflict between demands for a relatively free and uncensored internet, including social media services, and protection of the vulnerable against harmful content and behaviours, will continue to demand the attention of legislators and regulators as technology advances.

# 9

# INTELLECTUAL PROPERTY

# Introduction

Intellectual property involves the legal protection of inventions and other creative products. Its main categories are patents, copyright and trade marks, with related forms of protection also covering designs, circuit layouts, plant breeders' rights, domain names and trade secrets. Some intellectual property rights attach automatically to a novel invention or creation, while others require registration in a publicly administered system, depending on the jurisdiction. Protection is typically limited to a specified time, with extension possible in some systems. What is offered to creators is an incentive to make potentially beneficial advances available to the public, rather than be kept secret or for private use only, by way of a limited monopoly.

The exclusive right that is granted has a number of components, but the main benefit it confers is the opportunity to exploit economically the invention or creation under a statutory monopoly for the prescribed length of time, after which it becomes generally available to the public on equal terms. For example, a technical innovation in car design might be achieved by one manufacturer, and introduced to the market under patent as well as other forms of protection, but is able to be adopted by competitors after the protections lapse. Until then, competitors may seek to introduce comparable innovations, but if they do so by too closely copying or exploiting the original and protected version, they will be at risk of infringement claims. The enforcement of intellectual property rights thus depends heavily on actual or potential litigation, adding a layer of legal process to any registration requirements.

Not everybody seeks to protect their intellectual property. Small business innovators or creative individuals may not see it as affordable to pay for registration, and may have limited resources to pursue litigation even when their innovations are copied by others. Even larger businesses may choose to rely on the protection of their valuable information through employment contracts, non-disclosure agreements and corporate secrecy, rather than by revealing all to the public in exchange for a time-limited set of protections.

This chapter will not attempt a comprehensive study of the international and various domestic systems of intellectual property protection, for which suitable texts can instead be consulted; rather, it will focus on three principal areas in which the intersection of law of technology raises fundamental and contentious legal issues. First, there is the question of to what extent developments in computer software are patentable as inventions. The broad answer to this question is that, while mathematical and scientific discoveries are not generally considered to be appropriate subject matter for the grant of patent protection, their application to technological procedures can result in patentable inventions. This distinction gives rise to a host of public policy choices about how advances in computer-related technology are to be regulated for the greatest public benefit, which varies considerably across countries.[1]

A second area that is giving rise to rapid legal reform is the digitisation of creative content such as music and films, enabling easy sharing between consumers without regard to copyright protections. Recent decades have seen the emergence of numerous file-sharing sites, some of them subject to noteworthy civil and sometimes criminal proceedings, followed by the development of more legitimate online platforms for downloading music and films. The battle between the entertainment industry, online pirates, internet users and

---

1   The similarly contested topic of biotechnology and patentability is discussed in Chapter 4.

service providers has been a dominant theme of internet regulation, with widely accepted resolutions of respective rights and interests still to be definitively found. Interestingly, this ongoing saga involves not only the use of law to protect new technologies, but also of 'technological protection measures' to protect associated legal rights such as copyright.

The third area of focus will be on the protection of business products and goodwill through the use of trade marks, along with business name and domain name registration. Given the widespread adoption of online platforms for business, including payment portals, the misuse of identifying marks and names is associated not just with intellectual property infringement but with online fraud, as discussed in Chapter 7. The protection of databases under international and domestic laws will also be considered.

Finally, the enforcement of intellectual property rights, including both civil and criminal litigation, will be examined – in particular, the challenges of enforcing these rights in an online environment, and innovative legal responses. The emerging shift of responsibility for illegal content discussed in relation to internet and social media providers in Chapter 8 will be revisited in relation to copyright and trade mark infringement.

# Patents and computing technologies

The basic requirements for patenting any invention, including computer-related advances in the form of programs (ie 'software' as opposed to the 'hardware' comprising the physical components such as circuitry, storage devices and peripherals), are as follows:

> To be eligible for patent protection, an invention must meet several criteria. Among those, five are most significant in determining patentability: (i) the invention must consist of patentable subject matter; (ii) the invention must be capable of industrial application (or, in certain countries, be useful); (iii) it must be new (novel); (iv) it must involve an inventive step (be non-obvious); and (v) the disclosure of the invention in the patent application must meet certain formal and substantive standards. Since patent law is applicable to inventions in any field of technology without discrimination, to be patentable, software-related inventions and business method-related inventions must also comply with those requirements.[2]

Many national and regional patent regimes specifically exclude computational processes, business methods and computer programs from patentability. The *European Patent Convention*, for example, excludes scientific discoveries and mathematical methods as well as 'schemes, rules and methods for performing mental acts, playing games or doing business, and programs for computers'.[3] However, this exclusion is not as simple as it may appear. Software that embodies a 'technical solution' to a problem, such as a program to make a computer function more efficiently, may nonetheless be patentable. Such a solution is described as a 'computer-implemented invention' (CII).

> In the case of CII, software which does not solve a technical problem in a novel and non-obvious manner cannot be patented. However a process comprising a series of steps to solve a technical problem may be worthy of patent protection, even if the

---

2    World Intellectual Property Office, *Patenting Software* (2020).
3    European Patent Office, *European Patent Convention*, art 52(2)(c).

process is carried out using software. The process in question might control external hardware (like a robot arm or a GPS device) or just run purely internally within a computer (like software to improve memory access or compress data). For example, a systems engineer who invents a new way of load balancing on a network of computers (defining which computer will perform which task) can implement the invention entirely in software. If this way of load balancing is new and inventive, it can be protected by a patent, such that competitors will be prevented from using the invention unless they pay a fee to the patent's owner.[4]

The difficulty lies in deciding, in each case involving a patent claim for software, whether what is encapsulated through a computer program is essentially an (unpatentable) algorithm or a novel and inventive (patentable) process that solves a technical problem in a useful way.

An example might be a computerised algorithm employed within a steel mill to produce a better-quality product, or new software that allows a computer processor to process data more efficiently. In each case, a technical problem is solved through the use of software, which is in principle patentable, subject to other requirements such as novelty and inventiveness. But software deployed in a business setting to track movements in share prices so as to optimise transaction timing does not solve a technical problem in the requisite sense.

In Australia, the threshold question for patentability lies in the statutory requirement that a claimed invention be a 'manner of manufacture' within the meaning of the *Statute of Monopolies* dating from 1624.[5] This venerable formulation has been interpreted by a leading High Court authority as requiring that 'the method the subject of the relevant claims has as its end result an artificial effect falling squarely within the true concept of what must be produced by a process if it is to be held patentable'.[6] For computer software, it has been held that 'the courts look to the application of the program to produce a practical and useful result, so that more than "*intellectual information*" is involved', and further that:

> There must be more than an abstract idea; it must involve the creation of an artificial state of affairs where the computer is integral to the invention, rather than a mere tool in which the invention is performed. Where the claimed invention is to a computerised business method, the invention must lie in that computerisation. It is not a patentable invention simply to 'put' a business method 'into' a computer to implement the business method using the computer for its well-known and understood functions.[7]

---

4  European Patent Office, *Hardware and Software* (2020).

5  In Australia, intellectual property legislation is almost entirely in the Commonwealth jurisdiction, as s 51(xviii) of the Constitution gives the Commonwealth legislative power with respect to 'copyrights, patents of inventions and designs, and trade marks'. The *Patents Act 1990* (Cth), s 18(1), requires that a patentable invention be 'manner of manufacture within the meaning of section 6 of the Statute of Monopolies' in addition to the requirements of novelty, inventive step, usefulness and lack of secret use.

6  *National Research Development Corporation v Commissioner of Patents* (1959) 102 CLR 252, [25]. For a discussion of how genetic engineering creates a patentable 'artificial state of affairs', see Chapter 4 as well as the Australian Law Reform Commission (ALRC) report entitled *ALRC 99: Genes and Ingenuity: Gene Patenting and Human Health* (August 2004).

7  *Research Affiliates LLC v Commissioner of Patents* (2014) 227 FCR 378, [94]; *Commissioner of Patents v RPL Central Pty Ltd* (2015) 238 FCR 27, [96].

In 2020, the Full Federal Court held that a patent application relating to a 'digital advertising system and method' that linked website users to advertising based on their previous interactions was not a manner of manufacture but rather a 'marketing scheme'.

> [I]n our view nothing about the way that the specification describes the computer hardware or software indicates that either is any more than a vehicle for implementing the scheme, using computers for their ordinary purposes.[8]

A claimed invention must involve a level of 'technical innovation' rather than merely a 'business innovation' through the use of routine computing functions. An example of what is not patentable might be the application of 'blockchain' technology, which relies heavily on complex but known computing functions, to a new area of application; while something that could be patentable is a 'new improvement to the processing or storage architecture of a blockchain, or alterations to handle types of information or transactions that couldn't be previously recorded by the blockchain'.[9]

In the United States, after a long period of inconsistent decisions on the patentability of software, largely reflected in a split between the US Supreme Court and the US Court of Appeals for the Federal Circuit, a landmark case was decided in 2014. The case concerned patents that had been granted for a process designed to decrease 'settlement risk' in financial negotiations, by using a computer system as a third-party intermediary. In a unanimous decision, the nine-member US Supreme Court held the patents to be invalid as the computerisation of a new business method did not itself make the innovation a technical rather than conceptual one – that is, 'the mere recitation of a generic computer cannot transform a patent-ineligible abstract idea into a patent-eligible invention'.[10]

However, subsequent cases and revisions of practice guidelines within the US Patents and Trade Marks Office (USPTO) appear to bring that country's approach closer to that of the European Patent Office (EPO), which includes within the scope of patentability software innovations that produce a new 'technical effect' within the functioning of a computer system itself.[11] An instructive example from the United Kingdom applying the EPO approach is the case of *Symbian v Commissioner of Patents*, which concerned an application to patent an improved method of accessing data on a computer device. Although initially rejected, this decision was overturned on appeal. The Court of Appeal held:

> [N]ot only will a computer containing the instructions in question 'be a better computer' … it can also be said that the instructions 'solve a "technical" problem lying with the computer itself'. Indeed, the effect of the instant alleged invention is not merely within the computer programmed with the relevant instructions. The beneficial consequences of those instructions will feed into the cameras and other devices and products, which … include such computer systems.[12]

---

8    *Commissioner of Patents v Rokt Pty Ltd* (2020) 379 ALR 86, [109]. See, also, *Encompass Corporation Pty Ltd v InfoTrack Pty Ltd* (2019) 372 ALR 646.

9    IP Australia, *Patents for Computer Implemented Inventions (Software Patents)* (2020). Available: <https://www.ipaustralia.gov.au/ip-for-digital-business/idea/software-patents>.

10   *Alice Corporation Pty Ltd v CLS Bank International*, 573 US 208 (2014), 223.

11   Ben Klemens, 'Software Patents Poised to Make a Comeback under New Patent Office Rules', *Ars Technica*, 11 January 2019.

12   *Symbian v Commissioner of Patents* [2008] EWCA Civ 1066, [54], as cited by Ian Lloyd, *Information Technology Law* (Oxford University Press, 2017), 309.

Given the potential commercial value of technology patents, it is not surprising that expensive litigation takes place between the largest corporate players. For example, the mobile phone patents of companies Apple and Samsung were at the centre of the so-called patent wars that lasted from 2011 until a settlement was reached in 2018.[13] The dispute ranged not only over the patents held in relation to the technical programs underlying the operation of the competitors' products, but also over design features that were said to assist functionality. This illustrates that, in practice, various forms of intellectual property overlap.

The problem of multiple overlapping patent and other rights has sometimes been referred to as a 'patent thicket', defined as 'a dense web of overlapping intellectual property rights that a company must hack its way through in order to actually commercialize new technology'.[14]

This is seen as an impediment to the development of new or improved technology, due to legal and regulatory compliance costs for entrants into a market dominated by companies with large numbers of discrete patents over many aspects of a single product such as a mobile phone (eg operating system, screen, wi-fi transmission, antenna, sound system, etc). The risks of patent infringement claims pose significant barriers to new entrants.

> The patent thicket is especially thorny when combined with the risk of holdup, namely the danger that new products will inadvertently infringe on patents issued after these products were designed. The need to navigate the patent thicket and holdup is especially pronounced in industries such as telecommunications and computing in which formal standard setting is a core part of bringing new technologies to market. Cross licenses and patent pools are two natural and effective methods used by market participants to cut through the patent thicket, but each involves some transaction costs.[15]

The market solution to the patent thicket problem has been an array of licensing agreements that allow competitors to use the technology covered by each other's patents. However, this is somewhat limited by the fact that only those market players with sufficient patent portfolios to negotiate with others have bargaining power, while newer entrants may still struggle.[16]

Another obstacle to navigating the patent system is so-called patent trolls, who are not primarily engaged in the development of new technologies and products but make their profits from buying and selling others' patents and licences. The effect on the market is to impose additional, and arguably unproductive, transaction costs.

> Instead of investing capital to develop inventions, patent trolls wait for the industry to utilize a patented technology and then enforce their patents on the alleged infringers. And because patent trolls have no incentive to reach business solutions, target companies are left with two options: pay up or litigate.[17]

---

13  Jon Lee, 'Double Standards: An Empirical Study of Patent and Trademark Discipline' (2020) 61 *Boston College Law Review* 5.

14  Carl Shapiro, 'Navigating the Patent Thicket: Cross Licenses, Patent Pools, and Standard-Setting' (2000) 1 *Innovation Policy and the Economy* 119.

15  Ibid, 120.

16  Ralph Siebert and Georg von Graevenitz, 'Does Licensing Resolve Hold Up in the Patent Thicket?' (2008) *Discussion Papers in Business Administration* 1.

17  Jeremiah Chan and Matthew Fawcett, 'Footsteps of the Patent Troll' (2005) 10 *Intellectual Property Law Bulletin* 1.

While some reforms of patent law and enforcement actions against patent trolls using anti-competition and deceptive trade practices laws have occurred, the approach of granting limited monopolies for the advancement of inventive and creative industries will seemingly always be prone to forms of market manipulation and abuse by bad actors.[18] One response has been the emergence of 'open source' models, particularly in the development of computer software, whereby code is released into the public domain for refinement and adaptation by others without the rigorous enforcement of intellectual property rights, including both patents and copyright.[19]

# Copyright and entertainment industries

Copyright is the form of intellectual property that protects original literary, musical and dramatic works, as well as sound recordings and films. It does not require registration, unlike a patent, and arises as soon as the work is created in some material form (eg by being written down). This means that almost all of us are copyright owners, although few will ever apply for a patent. For example, a letter or blog post is protected under copyright law, despite the fact that there are few circumstances in which anyone would want to bring infringement proceedings against the maker of a copy.[20]

In the world of entertainment, by contrast, copyright is a valuable asset and infringement proceedings are commonplace. Every new film that is released in cinemas is the product of significant investment of creative effort and investment dollars, usually in the many millions, and the movie studios and others who hold the associated copyrights are prepared to defend their creations against unauthorised copying by instigation of civil or criminal infringement proceedings. The former normally involves demands that alleged infringers desist from making or distributing unauthorised copies, followed up by civil claims for damages; while the latter involves a complaint to police or other public authorities, followed by investigation, possible prosecution, and the imposition of fines or other criminal penalties.[21]

While copyright and its enforcement has been a feature of the legal landscape for hundreds of years, the advent of the internet and digital storage has resulted in rapid and radical change. Rather than a vertical supply chain for music and film, new technology enabled peer-to-peer (P2P) or horizontal distribution. This became most apparent in the late 1990s and early 2000s with file-sharing sites such as Napster.[22]

---

18  Grace Heinecke, 'Pay the Troll Toll: The Patent Troll Model Is Fundamentally at Odds with the Patent System's Goals of Innovation and Competition' (2015) 84 *Fordham Law Review* 1153.

19  Kevin Carillo and Chitu Okoli, 'The Open Source Movement: A Revolution in Software Development' (2008) 49(2) *Journal of Computer Information Systems* 1. An example is the Linux operating system. See, eg, Open Source, *What is Linux?* (2020). Available: <https://opensource.com/resources/linux>.

20  For information on copyright law generally, there are numerous general texts, such as Lionel Bently et al, *Intellectual Property Law* (5th ed, Oxford University Press, 2018). Such texts cover the subsistence and ownership of copyright in great detail, whereas the following discussion will focus mainly on infringement.

21  Gregor Urbas, 'Public Enforcement of Intellectual Property Rights', *Trends and Issues in Crime and Criminal Justice*, No 177 (Australian Institute of Criminology, 2000).

22  Raymond Shih Ray Ku, 'The Creative Destruction of Copyright: Napster and the New Economics of Digital Technology' (2002) 69 *University of Chicago Law Review* 263.

Despite a series of legal judgments holding the operators of such file-sharing services liable for contributing or inducing copyright infringement by their users, this had little discernible effect, particularly as new sites sprang up to replace the old, and usually with even more distributed storage and sharing mechanisms.[23] In particular, the advent of bit torrent enabled files to be stored in fragments distributed across networks of users, waiting to be assembled as complete copies at users' requests using advanced protocols. An example of this service was The Pirate Bay (TPB), founded by a group of Swedish developers, which was prosecuted in 2009.

> It was started in 2003 and has constantly been increasing in number of visitors … According to the site-ranking company Alexa, in May 2008, TPB entered the top 100 of the most visited sites globally and by November the same year had 20 million unique peers for the first time since the site was launched. In April 2011, it had climbed to number 86 and in May 2012, it had reached place 63 for the most visited sites in the world with more than 5 million registered users. On the 17 of April 2009, four men were sentenced to one-year prison terms and fined roughly euro 35,000,000 (SEK 30,000,000), for assisting in violations of copyright law through the Pirate Bay site. Both sides appealed, and the three that were re-tried in the autumn of 2010 were all found guilty yet again and sentenced to higher damages … but somewhat shorter prison sentences.[24]

Despite the guilty verdicts in this case and sentences of one year in prison and substantial fines, The Pirate Bay continues to operate and has spawned a number of political parties.[25] Further developments under Australian copyright law are discussed later in this chapter.

The *Convention on Cybercrime* deals with copyright and related rights in the context of criminal offences required to be adopted by signatory states.[26] Article 10 provides:

1. Each Party shall adopt such legislative and other measures as may be necessary to establish as criminal offences under its domestic law the infringement of copyright, as defined under the law of that Party, pursuant to the obligations it has undertaken under the Paris Act of 24 July 1971 revising the Bern Convention for the Protection of Literary and Artistic Works, the Agreement on Trade-Related Aspects of Intellectual Property Rights and the WIPO Copyright Treaty, with the exception of any moral rights conferred by such conventions, where such acts are committed wilfully, on a commercial scale and by means of a computer system.

2. Each Party shall adopt such legislative and other measures as may be necessary to establish as criminal offences under its domestic law the infringement of related rights, as defined under the law of that Party, pursuant to the obligations it has undertaken under the International Convention for the Protection of Performers, Producers of Phonograms and Broadcasting Organisations (Rome Convention), the Agreement on Trade-Related Aspects of Intellectual Property Rights and the WIPO Performances and Phonograms Treaty, with the exception of any moral rights conferred by such conventions, where such acts are committed wilfully, on a commercial scale and by means of a computer system.

---

23  Stefan Larsson, 'Metaphors, Law and Digital Phenomena: The Swedish Pirate Bay Court Case' (2013) 21 *International Journal of Law and Information Technology* 354, 358.
24  Ibid, 359.
25  For example, the Pirate Party in Iceland.
26  The Council of Europe's *Convention on Cybercrime* is discussed in detail in Chapter 7.

**3.** A Party may reserve the right not to impose criminal liability under paragraphs 1 and 2 of this article in limited circumstances, provided that other effective remedies are available and that such reservation does not derogate from the Party's international obligations set forth in the international instruments referred to in paragraphs 1 and 2 of this article.

The restriction to criminalisation of infringing acts that are committed 'wilfully [and] on a commercial scale' reflects the domestic law in many countries. This means that, while individual downloaders from known illegal file-sharing sites may be subject to civil penalties and sanctions such as cancellation of internet services, normally they will not be prosecuted. Rather, the criminal law is used to prosecute those who upload and/or distribute copyright material for profit. This includes some illegal file-sharing services, and on occasion, some individuals. Criminal penalties were increased under Australian copyright law in the mid-2000s to ensure that indictable as well as summary proceedings could be prosecuted, with maximum penalties of up to five years' imprisonment as well as substantial fines. Despite this, terms of imprisonment have rarely been imposed for copyright infringement in Australia. A rare exception was a video piracy case in which a shop owner was sentenced to 12 months' imprisonment for sales of pirated movies, with the sentencing judge finding that the repeated conduct was 'deliberate, flagrant, calculated offending motivated by the prospect of substantial profits'.[27]

In the United States, by contrast, copyright and trade mark infringement are prosecuted and sentenced with comparatively greater vigour. A specialised unit within the Department of Justice called the Computer Crimes and Intellectual Property Section (CCIPS) is prosecuting the Megaupload.com case. This website generated approximately US$200 million in advertising revenue associated with a massive online piracy enterprise and resulted in seven individuals and associated companies being charged by the US Department of Justice.

> The individuals each face a maximum penalty of 20 years in prison on the charge of conspiracy to commit racketeering, five years in prison on the charge of conspiracy to commit copyright infringement, 20 years in prison on the charge of conspiracy to commit money laundering and five years in prison on each of the substantive charges of criminal copyright infringement. The indictment alleges that the criminal enterprise is led by Kim Dotcom, aka Kim Schmitz and Kim Tim Jim Vestor, 37, a resident of both Hong Kong and New Zealand. Dotcom founded Megaupload Limited and is the director and sole shareholder of Vestor Limited, which has been used to hold his ownership interests in the Mega-affiliated sites ... The case is being prosecuted by the U.S. Attorney's Office for the Eastern District of Virginia and the Computer Crime & Intellectual Property Section in the Justice Department's Criminal Division. The Criminal Division's Office of International Affairs, Organized Crime and Gang Section, and Asset Forfeiture and Money Laundering Section also assisted with this case.[28]

27  *Ly v The Queen* (2014) 175 227 FCR 304, in which the defendant unsuccessfully appealed.
28  United States Department of Justice, 'Justice Department Charges Leaders of Megaupload with Widespread Online Copyright Infringement' (Media release, 19 January 2012). Available: <https://www.justice.gov/opa/pr/justice-department-charges-leaders-megaupload-widespread-online-copyright-infringement>.

In 2020, the process to extradite alleged leader Kim Dotcom was still being challenged in the New Zealand courts, with any prosecutions in the United States on hold in the meantime.[29] The US authorities had greater success in extraditing the alleged leader of an online copyright piracy group operating under the name 'DrinkOrDie' in the early 2000s. Resident in New South Wales, Hew Raymond Griffiths, after a lengthy but ultimately unsuccessful legal battle that led to the High Court of Australia, was extradited to the United States on charges of copyright infringement and conspiracy despite the fact that he had never been to that country prior to his removal by way of extradition. While there, he pleaded guilty and was sentenced to a lengthy prison term that was partly served before he returned to Australia.[30] The activities of the members of DrinkOrDie across various countries were outlined in 2002 by the Department of Justice after the sentencing of a member in the United States.

> DrinkOrDie was a well-organized, security-conscious, Internet software piracy group that specialized in acquiring new software, 'cracking' it (i.e., stripping or circumventing its copyright protections), and releasing the software over the Internet. DrinkOrDie consisted of approximately 65 group members from more than 12 countries, including the United Kingdom, Australia, Sweden, Norway, and Finland. Operation Buccaneer [was] a 14-month undercover investigation by the U.S. Customs Service that represents the largest international copyright piracy investigation to date by law enforcement. In addition to dismantling DrinkOrDie, Operation Buccaneer also netted members from a broad cross-section of leading online piracy groups. To date in the Eastern District of Virginia, 12 defendants have pled guilty, six have been sentenced. Six defendants have been formally charged in the United Kingdom as a result of Operation Buccaneer. More prosecutions are expected in the U.S. and abroad, including Australia, Finland, Sweden, and Norway.[31]

Most of the members of DrinkOrDie located in the United States pleaded guilty to charges, while others in the United Kingdom were convicted and sentenced to somewhat shorter terms. Apparently, only the Australian member was extradited rather than prosecuted at home.

While such enforcement actions can be regarded as heavy-handed protection of intellectual property rights of influential entertainment industries largely based in the United States, there are also legitimate consumer safety reasons for seeking to disrupt illegal downloading sites in that they are often used to distribute malware.[32]

---

29  Stephan Cassella, 'Hurdling the Sovereign Wall: How Governments Can Recover the Proceeds of Crimes that Cross National Boundaries' (2019) 22 *Journal of Money Laundering Control* 5.

30  See Gregor Urbas, 'Cross-National Investigation and Prosecution of Intellectual Property Crimes: The Example of Operation Buccaneer' (2007) 46 *Crime, Law and Social Change* 207. The investigation and prosecution aspects are further discussed in Chapter 10.

31  United States Department of Justice, 'Member of "DrinkOrDie" Warez Group Sentenced to 41 Months' (Media release, 2 July 2002). Available: <https://www.justice.gov/archive/criminal/cybercrime/press-releases/2002/Pattanay.htm>.

32  Jason Gull and Tim Flowers, 'Prosecuting Intellectual Property Crimes' (2016) 64(1) *United States Attorneys' Bulletin* 19, citing Digital Citizens Alliance, *Digital Bait: How Content Theft Sites and Malware are Exploited by Cybercriminals to Hack into Internet Users' Computers and Personal Data* (2015).

# Trade marks and business products

One of the most important intellectual property assets for any business is its trade mark(s), along with associated designators such as its business name, domain name and logo designs. While these require separate registration, they normally promote the business identity across various platforms. For example, XYZ Corporation may have registrations for 'XYZ' as a trade mark, or a series of trade marks incorporating the three letters; as a business name in its main or multiple places of trading; as the domain name 'XYZ.com'; and again as a stylised XYZ logo. Together, these assets protect business reputation and goodwill against imposters and free riders.[33]

A registered trade mark is infringed when it, or a mark that is deceptively similar to it, is applied to goods or otherwise used without the permission of the trade mark owner.[34] The growth of online commerce has increased trade mark infringement in two main ways. One is the expansion of the pre-existing trade in counterfeit goods into online marketplaces.

> The incidence of counterfeiting and trade mark infringement has surged with the widespread use of online marketplaces such as eBay, the Internet auction platform. As a result, such sites have faced a steady stream of lawsuits brought by prominent trade mark owners in United States and European courts in connection with the sale of counterfeit merchandise. Famous luxury brands, such as Tiffany, Louis Vuitton, L'Oréal, Hermès, and Rolex, have argued that eBay and other online market operators and service providers are liable for the sale of counterfeit products by their users. In these cases, the courts have had to address the critical issue of what level of knowledge is necessary to impose contributory liability on these intermediaries for sales by their users of infringing and counterfeit merchandise.[35]

The second way in which the growth of online commerce has increased infringement of trade marks and associated identifiers is by 'brandjacking'.[36] The deliberate use of another's brand may divert business that would otherwise be directed to the true owner, and may cause reputational harm.[37] Sometimes this occurs as part of a 'hacktivism' campaign directed

---

33 A 'free rider' in economic theory is one who takes a benefit from others' assets or efforts without paying – for example, a squatter in a building, or a train passenger who has not purchased a ticket. The excessive presence of free riders in a market will typically lead to a market failure and under-provision of goods and services; however, governments often intervene to provide public goods and services with the costs distributed across society through taxation or levies – for example, the provision of lighthouses may be financed in part by levies on shipping.

34 In Australia, the principal legislation is the *Trade Marks Act 1995* (Cth), with Part 12 governing infringement; see, eg, *Bing! Software Pty Ltd v Bing Technologies Pty Ltd (No 1)* (2008) 79 IPR 454; *E & J Gallo Winery v Lion Nathan Australia Pty Ltd* (2010) 241 CLR 144. For unregistered trade marks, deceptive use is dealt with under the common law action of 'passing off'.

35 Kurt M Saunders and Gerlinde Berger-Walliser, 'The Liability of Online Markets for Counterfeit Goods: A Comparative Analysis of Secondary Trademark Infringement in the United States and Europe' (2011) 32 *Northwestern Journal of International Law & Business* 37 (notes omitted). Note that the term 'counterfeit' is widely used to describe physical goods bearing infringing trade marks, otherwise known as 'knock-offs'. For a more recent update, see WIPO Advisory Committee on Enforcement, *Study on Approaches to Online Trademark Infringements* (2017).

36 Lisa P Ramsay, 'Brandjacking on Social Networks: Trademark Infringement by Impersonation of Markholders' (2010) 58 *Buffalo Law Review* 851.

37 See, eg, *Pokémon Company International, Inc v Redbubble Ltd* (2017) 351 ALR 676.

against a business, or it might be associated with 'phishing' activity that seeks to exploit consumer confusion for illegitimate gain: see Chapter 7 for further discussion.

Variations include website URLs that are deceptively similar to those of genuine websites, or hijacked hyperlinks, which lead visitors to spoof or fake websites where they can be defrauded. Simpler versions may exploit common misspellings of brand names, or the use of a different domain name (eg 'XYZ.net' instead of 'XYZ.com'). In each case, a form of deception is used. Thus, in addition to possible trade mark or other infringement proceedings brought by adversely affected businesses, consumer laws against misleading and deceptive conduct may also apply. Where fraud offences can be proved, criminal penalties may be imposed.

Another form of questionable behaviour involving websites and domain names is the use of so-called cybersquatting. This conduct is explained as follows by a European Union agency:

> Cybersquatting is the practice of registering as Internet domains identical or similar to a third party company name or trade mark, with bad faith intent to profit from the goodwill of a third party brand, or in the hope of reselling them at a profit. Cybersquatters exploit the first-come, first-served nature of the domain name registration system to register as domain names, third parties' trade marks or business names or names of famous people, as well as variations thereof. A common motive for cybersquatting is the intention to sell the domain name back to the trade mark owner, to profit from the goodwill of a third party brand, or to attract web traffic to unrelated commercial offers.[38]

While such conduct is not necessarily illegal, it is regarded as a 'bad faith' registration that can be cancelled by a domain name regulator such as the Internet Corporation for Assigned Names and Numbers (ICANN) in the United States, or the Australian registration authority (auDA). The latter provides a complaints and dispute resolution service for domain names.[39] Where cybersquatting is followed by extortion or fraudulent misuse of a domain name, these offences can, of course, be prosecuted using criminal laws.[40]

In Australia, criminal offences under copyright and trade marks legislation may apply to the fraudulent misuse of brand names, logos and domain names.[41] However, it is more usual for cybersquatting activities to be dealt with by way of civil action or complaints to regulators.

In addition to criminal and civil actions under trade marks legislation, the common law action of 'passing off' may be used, as well as consumer protection provisions relating to misleading or deceptive conduct.[42] Search engines such as Google have been the subject of investigations and enforcement action by regulators such as the Australian Competition and Consumer Commission (ACCC) over complaints of misleading search results (discussed also

---

38  European Union IP Helpdesk, *What is Cybersquatting?* (2020). Available: <www.iprhelpdesk.eu/node/3815>.

39  See, eg, Au Domain Administration Ltd. Available: <https://www.auda.org.au/about-auda/>.

40  John D Mercer, 'Cybersquatting: Blackmail on the Information Superhighway' (2000) 6 *Boston University Journal of Science and Technology Law* 290.

41  See *Copyright Act 1968* (Cth), Part V; and *Trade Marks Act 1995* (Cth), Part 14.

42  See *Trade Marks Act 1995* (Cth), s 230, which preserves passing off actions; and *Competition and Consumer Act 2010* (Cth), including the Australian Consumer Law (ACL) with provisions on misleading or deceptive conduct replacing former s 52 of the *Trade Practices Act 1974* (Cth).

in Chapter 5).[43] The state of this litigation has been summarised as follows, as regards the liability of Google:

> The question in *Google v ACCC* was whether Google had engaged in misleading and deceptive conduct contrary to s 52 of the *Trade Practices Act* 1974 (Cth) by displaying misleading and deceptive 'sponsored links'. At first instance, it was held that Google had not done so because it was simply a conduit which passed on the sponsored links without any adoption or approval of their contents. On appeal, the Full Court of the Federal Court of Australia held that Google had engaged in misleading and deceptive conduct by displaying sponsored links because the sponsored links were 'Google's response to a user's insertion of a search term into Google's search engine', which meant that Google did not merely pass on the contents of the sponsored links without adoption or approval …[44]

On appeal to the High Court, this decision was reversed and it was held that the primary judge was correct in finding that 'ordinary and reasonable users of the Google search engine would have understood that the sponsored links were advertisements' and that Google did not endorse them, but merely passed them on to its users.[45]

# Online enforcement of intellectual property rights

The enforcement of intellectual property rights in the online environment has posed considerable challenges, and resulted in innovative legal approaches. While there has been some litigation against downloaders of infringing content, the greater focus has been on the operators of file-sharing sites and the providers of internet services who support these sites. This includes telecommunications carriers or carriage service providers, internet service providers (ISPs) and content service providers (CSPs), as defined under the Australian *Telecommunications Act 1997* (Cth) and similar legislation in other jurisdictions.

By the end of the 20th century, it became increasingly clear that copyright and other intellectual property laws would have to be significantly clarified in their application to such intermediaries, given the amount of infringing content that was being downloaded through their services. In the United States, the *Digital Millennium Copyright Act* (DMCA) was passed in 1998, which included 'safe harbour' provisions for intermediaries against liability for third-party infringement. In Australia, similar provisions were added to the *Copyright Act 1968* (Cth) by the *Copyright Amendment (Digital Agenda) Act 2000* (Cth), including:[46]

---

43  *Google Inc v Australian Competition and Consumer Commission* (2013) 249 CLR 435, upholding an appeal by Google from the decision in *Australian Competition and Consumer Commission v Google Inc* (2012) 201 FCR 503.

44  *Trkulja v Google LLC* (2018) 263 CLR 149, [57]–[58] (summarising *Google Inc v Australian Competition and Consumer Commission*).

45  Ibid.

46  Section 36(1A) relating to copyright in artistic, musical and dramatic works; and an identical s 101(1A) for copyright in subject matter other than works, as well as s 39B, and a collection of provisions in Part V, Division 2AA, constitute the main 'safe harbour provisions' in the *Copyright Act 1968* (Cth).

## 36 Infringement by doing acts comprised in the copyright

**(1)**   Subject to this Act, the copyright in a literary, dramatic, musical or artistic work is infringed by a person who, not being the owner of the copyright, and without the licence of the owner of the copyright, does in Australia, or authorises the doing in Australia of, any act comprised in the copyright.

**(1A)**   In determining, for the purposes of subsection (1), whether or not a person has authorised the doing in Australia of any act comprised in the copyright in a work, without the licence of the owner of the copyright, the matters that must be taken into account include the following:

**(a)**   the extent (if any) of the person's power to prevent the doing of the act concerned;

**(b)**   the nature of any relationship existing between the person and the person who did the act concerned;

**(c)**   whether the person took any reasonable steps to prevent or avoid the doing of the act, including whether the person complied with any relevant industry codes of practice.

The following more recent section is specific to carriers and providers.

## 39B Communication by use of certain facilities

A person (including a carrier or carriage service provider) who provides facilities for making, or facilitating the making of, a communication is not taken to have authorised any infringement of copyright in a work merely because another person uses the facilities so provided to do something the right to do which is included in the copyright.

This form of provision excludes liability for so-called secondary infringement through express or implied authorisation of another's infringing activity. For example, an ISP would not be held liable for its customers' illegal downloads from a file-sharing site merely by providing ISP services; however, much turns on the modest word 'merely' in this context.

In two Australian cases in the mid-2000s, the position of ISPs in relation to infringing downloads was clarified. The first case was *Universal Music Australia Pty Ltd v Cooper*.

> The case involved Cooper's website that operated by providing hyperlinks to remote computers from which mp3 files were automatically downloaded upon users accessing the hyperlink. Cooper either placed these hyperlinks on the website himself or users could create their own hyperlink between a file and the website through the presence of a CGI-BIN gateway. Cooper arranged for his ISP to benefit from free advertising on his website in return for a waiver on domain name hosting fees. Cooper also collected additional revenue from vendors advertising on the site. All respondents were found liable for authorisation of the copyright infringements committed by the website's users and owners of the remote computers from which infringing copyright material was being downloaded.[47]

Notably, the ISPs were found liable on the basis of the special arrangement they had with the high-traffic website that Cooper was operating, with the judge observing that they 'were responsible for hosting the website and providing the necessary connection to the internet

---

47   *Universal Music Australia Pty Ltd v Cooper* (2005) 150 FCR 1, as summarised by Pam Foo, 'The Liability of Content Providers for Authorisation of Copyright Infringement in the Cases of *Cooper* and *Sharman*' (2006) 64 *Computers and Law* 13.

and therefore had the power to prevent the doing of the infringing acts. They could have taken the step of taking down the website. Instead, they took no steps to prevent the acts of infringement' and 'it could not be said that they were doing no more than "merely" hosting the website involved'.[48] Injunctive relief and costs were awarded against the respondents.[49]

The second case was *Universal Music Pty Ltd v Sharman*, handed down a few months later, with ramifications on an international scale.

> *Sharman* was decided on 5 September 2005 by Wilcox J after a prolonged battle between 30 record company applicants and 10 respondents consisting of Sharman, the operators of the Kazaa desktop program, and Altnet, who had co-operated with Sharman to supply legitimate music over the peer to peer file sharing program. Kazaa was a file sharing program that operated by users downloading and installing the software from the Kazaa website. Once installed, Kazaa searched for the files that were available to be shared between each user ... Sharman adapted the Kazaa program in order to comply with the two month deadline by restricting access to new users with Australian ISPs and issuing warnings to existing users. Sharman argued that the court order was ambiguous and that [it] applied only in the jurisdiction of Australia. There was no obligation to amend the program as it was accessed outside of Australia.[50]

This unclear resolution in the *Sharman* case highlighted the difficulties in enforcing copyright against intermediaries, particularly where these operate in an international environment with different restrictions and approaches operating in each jurisdiction. For example, the DMCA safe harbour provisions operating under US copyright law distinguish between four aspects of ISP operation, each having a different set of conditions on the shield against liability for third-party infringement:

(a)   transitory digital network communications;

(b)   system caching;

(c)   information residing on systems or networks at the direction of users; and

(d)   information location tools.[51]

An important aspect of the operation of safe harbours is whether there are any industry codes of conduct that apply, and what steps an intermediary such as an ISP has taken to warn its customers against infringing use of its services. In the case of *Roadshow Films Pty Ltd v iiNet Ltd*, the issue was whether the ISP (iiNet) was under an obligation to deal with individual customers, alleged by the Australian Federation Against Copyright Theft (AFACT) to have engaged in infringement through bit-torrent downloading of films, by way of terminating their internet access or otherwise warning them against continuing their activities. The High

48   *Universal Music Australia Pty Ltd v Cooper* (2005) 150 FCR 1, per Tamberlin J at [121], [126].

49   *Universal Music Australia Pty Ltd v Cooper* [2005] FCA 1878. An unsuccessful appeal followed a year later: *Cooper v Universal Music Australia Pty Ltd* (2006) 156 FLR 380.

50   *Universal Music Australia Pty Ltd v Sharman License Holdings Ltd* (2005) 222 FCR 465, as summarised by Pam Foo, 'The Liability of Content Providers for Authorisation of Copyright Infringement in the Cases of *Cooper* and *Sharman*' (2006) 64 *Computers and Law* 13.

51   See US Code Title 17 (Copyrights), §512: Limitations on liability relating to material online. These four aspects are adopted in the Australian *Copyright Act 1968* (Cth), in Part V, Division 2AA as introduced by the *US Free Trade Agreement Implementation Act 2004* (Cth). They relate only to civil liability.

Court dismissed an appeal from the Federal Court of Australia, which had found that there was no such obligation and consequently no infringement by authorisation, mainly because the ISP did not have the technical means of intervening in the use of bit-torrent.

> It is important to note that iiNet has no involvement with any part of the BitTorrent system and therefore has no power to control or alter any aspect of the BitTorrent system, including the BitTorrent client ... Whilst the relationship between iiNet and its customers involves the provision of technology, iiNet had no direct technical power at its disposal to prevent a customer from using the BitTorrent system to download the appellants' films on that customer's computer with the result that the appellants' films were made available online ...[52]

This result contrasts with the policy adopted in some countries, requiring ISPs to terminate customer access after several warnings about infringing use (eg the so-called Hadopi Law in France, and 'three-strikes' or 'graduated response' schemes in some other countries).[53] Controversial when implemented, these laws have been abandoned in France and some other countries.[54]

However, a somewhat different approach has been adopted in Australia, with a law allowing injunctions to be obtained against carriage service providers, requiring them to disable access to overseas-based websites that offer infringing content, being passed in 2015. This takes the form of an amendment to the *Copyright Act 1968* (Cth), adding new section 115A. There are a number of matters the court can consider in determining whether to grant an injunction.[55]

## 115A Injunctions relating to online locations outside Australia

*Matters to be taken into account*

(5) In determining whether to grant the injunction, the Court may take the following matters into account:

    **(a)**    the flagrancy of the infringement, or the flagrancy of the facilitation of the infringement, as referred to in paragraph (1)(b);

    **(b)**    whether the online location makes available or contains directories, indexes or categories of the means to infringe, or facilitate an infringement of, copyright;

    **(c)**    whether the owner or operator of the online location demonstrates a disregard for copyright generally;

---

52  *Roadshow Films Pty Ltd v iiNet Ltd* (2012) 248 CLR 42, per French CJ, Crennan and Kiefel JJ at [65]; Gummow and Hayne JJ agreed in a separate judgment. It was also noted that there was no industry code of conduct adhered to by all ISPs in relation to bit-torrent downloading, at [71]. The Federal Court proceedings included *Roadshow Films Pty Ltd v iiNet Ltd (No 3)* (2010) 263 ALR 215; and *Roadshow Films Pty Ltd v iiNet Ltd* (2011) 194 FCR 285.

53  Nicolas Suzor and Brian Fitzgerald, 'The Legitimacy of Graduated Response Schemes in Copyright Law' (2011) 34(1) *University of New South Wales Law Journal* 1; and Primavera De Filippi and Daniele Bourcier, "Three-Strikes' Response to Copyright Infringement: The Case of Hadopi'. In F Musiani et al (eds), *The Turn to Infrastructure in Internet Governance* (Palgrave-Macmillan, 2016).

54  'France Ends Three-Strikes Internet Piracy Ban Policy', *British Broadcasting Corporation News*, 10 July 2013.

55  Added by the *Copyright Amendment (Online Infringement) Act 2015* (Cth), later amended by the *Copyright Amendment (Online Infringement) Act 2018* (Cth).

**(d)** whether access to the online location has been disabled by orders from any court of another country or territory on the ground of or related to copyright infringement;

**(e)** whether disabling access to the online location is a proportionate response in the circumstances;

**(ea)** if the application under subsection (1) also sought for the injunction to apply against an online search engine provider – whether not providing search results that refer users to the online location is a proportionate response in the circumstances;

**(f)** the impact on any person, or class of persons, likely to be affected by the grant of the injunction;

**(g)** whether it is in the public interest to disable access to the online location;

**(ga)** if the application under subsection (1) also sought for the injunction to apply against an online search engine provider – whether it is in the public interest not to provide search results that refer users to the online location;

**(h)** whether the owner of the copyright complied with subsection (4);

**(i)** any other remedies available under this Act;

**(j)** any other matter prescribed by the regulations;

**(k)** any other relevant matter.

Shortly before the enactment of s 115A, the Federal Court had used its discretion under s 115 to order limited discovery of infringing customers of ISPs, in the *Dallas Buyers Club* case.[56] However, s 115A provided a more direct route to the blocking of so-called pirate websites. In the first major test case applying this provision, injunctions were granted to the applicants with the effect that carriage service providers were required to 'take reasonable steps to disable access' and redirect users to a 'landing page [that] had to state that access to the online location was disabled because the Federal Court had determined that it infringes, or facilitates the infringement of, copyright'.[57] While this development was welcomed by copyright owners, the overall effectiveness of such measures remained a matter of dispute.[58] Several other Federal Court decisions under s 115A also resulted in the grant of injunctions.[59] In a 2019 decision, injunctions were granted to prevent access to websites facilitating the 'ripping' of soundtracks embedded in YouTube videos.[60]

# Conclusion

The internet has presented a significant threat to the enforcement of intellectual property rights, particularly in regard to films, music and software. While this may increase access for those that could not otherwise afford to purchase them legitimately, it reduces revenue

56  *Dallas Buyers Club LLC v iiNet Ltd (No 4)* (2015) 327 ALR 702.
57  *Roadshow Films Pty Ltd v Telstra Corporation Ltd* (2016) 248 FCR 178.
58  For example, a VPN could be used to cloak the user's location and circumvent the IP address blocking; and website operators can shift to a different online location.
59  See, eg, *Universal Music Australia Pty Ltd v TPG Internet Pty Ltd* (2017) 348 ALR 493; *Roadshow Films Pty Ltd v Telstra Corporation Ltd* [2017] FCA 965; *Foxtel Management Pty Ltd v TPG Internet Pty Ltd* (2017) 349 ALR 154; and *Foxtel Management Pty Ltd v TPG Internet Pty Ltd* (2019) 148 IPR 432.
60  *Australasian Performing Right Association Ltd v Telstra Corporation Ltd* (2019) 369 ALR 529.

and the incentives and rewards available to artists and entrepreneurs to produce new digital creative content and other products. There has been an ongoing legal and technological struggle between content producers, such as film studios and software companies, ISPs and consumers.

As a wider range of businesses move online, the protection of business names and domain names will also continue to be a significant issue. It is clear that the issues discussed in relation to commercial transactions in Chapter 5 and cybercrime in Chapter 7 are closely related to several of those discussed in this chapter. The challenges associated with enforcing intellectual property rights in an online environment that are readily apparent in this discussion are also entwined with the global challenges associated with the investigation and prosecution of technology-related offences.

# 10

# INTERNATIONAL INVESTIGATION AND ENFORCEMENT

# Introduction

The growth of cybercrime, social media misuse and online intellectual property infringement discussed in the preceding three chapters presents new and significant challenges for regulating these aspects of technology law. Conducting investigations, determining jurisdictional scope and prosecuting offences all require a degree of adaptation, as compared to traditional areas of the law. The contrast between investigating a robbery from a bricks-and-mortar store on the one hand and the hacking of an e-commerce company's trade secrets is vast.

As will be discussed below, the problem of *attribution* for technologically based crimes is a significant difficulty, and investigators must adopt an arsenal of tracing techniques that differ from the physical identification of an offender in a more conventional crime such as an armed robbery. Once a probable offender has been identified, the question of *jurisdiction* must be considered. The traditional criterion of geographical connection between the criminal justice system of a country and the crime, either through its place of occurrence or the location, residence or nationality of the offender or victim, is complicated. The offender may be located in country A, the computing facilities used might include those located in country B, and victims may be located in country C. Which one, or more than one, can claim jurisdiction over the crime? Supposing that country A will not prosecute the alleged offender, can country B or C seek extradition?

Once within jurisdiction, a *prosecution* depends on making a credible case on the available evidence. This will involve dealing with electronic evidence and complex technologies, which have to be carefully explained to judges and juries tasked with reaching a verdict. Expert witnesses will invariably be involved, and the defence may either challenge their testimony and reports, or call their own expert witnesses. At times, courts are confronted with an array of conflicting expert views in highly technical areas of study. All of this can use up considerable resources within systems that have to deal with many other cases and demands on their funding and time. As a result, not all cases can be prosecuted. Finally, in the event that a conviction is obtained, *sentencing* must follow existing legislative constraints, but often with little precedent to follow in determining an appropriate punishment for technologically enabled crime.

# Investigation

The investigative approach involved in analysing a computer crime such as hacking involves tracing communications over the internet to their source and analysing the computer used in the crime.

> Investigators attempt to track communications to their source by collecting network logs. Computer networks normally are run by a system administrator, or 'sysadmin' for short, who is responsible for keeping the computer running and for troubleshooting difficulties. System administrators ordinarily set their computers to generate records known as logs that record how the network was used. For example, a server might be configured to record the incoming Internet Protocol (IP) addresses and times of every attempt to log in to an account on the server. (IP addresses are numerical addresses that are akin to Internet phone numbers. Every user connected to the Internet is assigned an IP address, and the address is used to send information to the user.) In the case

of an e-commerce site, it's a good bet that the network system administrator will have configured the network to generate access logs that recorded the time, IP address, and any other relevant information about each login into the network.[1]

Investigators must go step-by-step, tracing communications back to the offender and seizing their computer. Because there are no eyewitnesses, files on a suspect's computer are direct evidence connecting them to the crime.[2] Appropriate warrants must normally be obtained by police, both in relation to the tracking of communications through networks, and for the search and seizure of suspects' computers. The latter form of investigative intrusion is more closely related to the traditional search of premises and seizure of evidentiary material relevant to a suspected offence, for which police may obtain a warrant from a judicial authority. Legislative reform has extended and clarified the powers available under search warrants to analyse and otherwise deal with computers found at search premises. For example, the *Cybercrime Act 2001* (Cth) amended the *Crimes Act 1914* (Cth), under which the Australian Federal Police (AFP) may obtain search warrants, by adding the following provisions:

- Equipment may be brought by police to examine the contents of computers and devices found at the premises to determine whether they may be seized under the warrant: s 3K(1).

- Where it is more practicable or the owner consents, computers and devices may be removed to another location for examination: s 3K(2).

- Equipment found at warrant premises may be operated to determine whether it may be seized under the warrant: s 3K(4).

- Equipment found at warrant premises may be operated to access data (including data not held at the premises) if the data are suspected to constitute evidentiary material: s 3L(1) – noting that the words in parentheses allow *remote searching* within networks.

- Data accessed by operating electronic equipment at search premises may be copied to a storage device brought by police: s 3L(1A).

- Equipment providing access to evidentiary material may be seized or the material may be converted into documents to be seized, eg by printing from a computer: s 3L(2).

- Equipment may be locked away or placed under guard until expert assistance can be obtained to operate the equipment for search purposes: s 3L(4).

- Persons with knowledge of computers or computer systems may be required by order of a magistrate to provide assistance by way of access, copying of data or conversion of data into documentary form: s 3LA.[3]

The last of these provisions was somewhat contentious when first introduced, as it makes no reference to self-incrimination in situations where a person such as a computer network

---

1   Orin Kerr, *Computer Crime Law* (4th ed, *American Casebook Series*, West Academic Publishing, 2018), 5–6.

2   Ibid.

3   The *Crimes Legislation Amendment (Serious and Organised Crime) Act (No 2) 2010* (Cth) added s 3LAA, allowing equipment removed to another place to be operated.

manager is required to provide access to data protected by a password or encryption.[4] It is arguable that the traditional right against self-incrimination applies to what a suspect may say or do that might be self-incriminating, rather than to the compelled provision of a forensic sample (eg for DNA testing) or access to forensic material (eg the contents of a computer).[5] Alternatively, the common law privilege is presumably abrogated by s 3LA to the extent that it compels a suspect to give assistance to authorities.[6] In practice, a suspect may simply choose to comply with an order rather than resist.[7] The grant of such an order directed at a journalist whose home was searched for evidence of suspected national security information disclosures was recently considered by the High Court. However, in the high-profile case *Smethurst v Commissioner of Police*,[8] the court did not rule on the validity of the s 3LA order, as the main search warrant used by the AFP in that case was held by the court to be invalid in not properly stating the law or the alleged offence to which the search related.

The examination of a computer to determine whether it contains evidentiary material is a process typically undertaken by specialised technicians, who may be police officers or civilians contracted to perform forensic analysis for investigating agencies. The process of capturing the contents of a computer for analysis begins with 'forensic imaging'.

### The forensic image process

1. Proper acquisition of computer evidence requires the use of non-invasive advanced computer software specifically designed for the task. Such software recovers, searches, authenticates and documents relevant electronic evidence without compromising the integrity of the original evidence. PricewaterhouseCoopers currently use 'EnCase' software, which is the industry standard.

2. The cornerstone of the computer forensics is the 'forensic image' process. Quite simply this is the process of making an exact copy of all data, including all Operating System files, application files, user files (including deleted files, data fragments etc.) located on the 'target' hard drive. The image retains the identical data structure as it appeared on the original hard disk …

6. The image process also enables the computer evidence to be evaluated in the 'environment in which the evidence was created'. Operating System and Application Software files are preserved so that all steps that the user took to create the evidence can be duplicated by the computer forensics specialist and if necessary an independent examiner. This is vitally important in a case wherein sophisticated programs have been used, such as accounting software, electronic mail and Internet applications, or graphic design programs.

---

4    Nickolas James, 'Handing Over the Keys: Contingency, Power and Resistance in the Context of s 3LA of the Australian *Crimes Act* 1914' (2004) 23(1) *University of Queensland Law Journal* 7. Subsequent amendments have increased the maximum penalty for failure to comply with a s 3LA order to five years' imprisonment, or 10 years if the investigation relates to a terrorism or other serious offence: see, in relation to firearms trafficking, *DPP v Camaj* [2019] VCC 2200.

5    Discussed in Chapter 11 of Gregor Urbas, *Cybercrime: Legislation, Cases and Commentary*, 2nd edn (LexisNexis, 2020); see also, in relation to forensic procedures, Chapter 6 of this book.

6    *Luppino v Fisher (No 2)* [2019] FCA 1100, per White J at [33].

7    *R v Johnston* [2020] ACTSC 46, a child grooming case in which the offender had solicited nude pictures from a 10-year-old girl in the United States. He complied with a s 3LA order during the execution of a search warrant, providing access to his computer and mobile phones, and pleaded guilty to several offences.

8    (2020) 376 ALR 575.

7.  The adaptation of imaging to the investigation of computer data, together with the appropriate analysis software, now allows the forensic examiner access to data without fear of altering the original and with minimal disruption to the owner. A thorough search and complete identification of all evidence on a computer can take many hours per computer, depending on the volume, type and complexity of data stored, and the complexity of the search criteria. Without the forensic image process the analysis would be impractical and invasive.[9]

The creation of a forensic image of a computer to be analysed involves the least possible alteration to the computer's contents, so that the examination itself is not responsible for the alteration or deletion of any data. It also allows, in appropriate cases, computers and other equipment to be returned to their owners, reducing any need for compensation to be paid.[10] In other cases, however, legislation or court orders allow forfeiture of equipment.[11]

Where searching of electronic communications is required, other types of warrants are used. The ability of law enforcement, assisted by telecommunications providers, to use electronic means to listen in on telephone conversations has long been the subject of legal prohibition except with a warrant. Known as 'wiretapping' in the United States, the practice was held in a 1967 case to violate the Fourth Amendment to the US Constitution, unless a warrant was issued on probable cause.[12] The following year, Congress passed legislation to prohibit the unauthorised interception without consent of 'wire, oral, or electronic communications' by government agencies as well as private parties, with warrants available to government agencies to authorise such interceptions, as well as regulations governing the disclosure of material thereby obtained.[13] The legislation has been considerably expanded since, most notably by such statutes as the FISA and USA PATRIOT Acts.[14]

In Australia, the Commonwealth has mainly exercised its jurisdiction with respect to telecommunications through legislation such as the *Telecommunications (Interception and Access) Act 1979* (Cth), while the states and territories have enacted legislation dealing with listening or surveillance devices.[15] The conceptual difference between interception and surveillance is that the former involves a mechanism for intercepting an electronic communication between two points, while the latter involves covert listening or recording at the point of reception of the communication. However, the distinction has become increasingly blurred. For example, an application allowing a mobile phone conversation to be recorded by one party without the consent of the other may involve either interception or surveillance, and the Commonwealth has also enacted its own surveillance devices legislation that allows for three kinds of warrant to be issued:

---

9  *Grant v Marshall* [2003] FCA 1161, Annexure A. This Federal Court case involved civil litigation in which an order was made to allow searching of a party's computer by an accounting firm.

10  For example, s 3M of the *Crimes Act 1914* (Cth) provides for compensation for damage to equipment.

11  Part IE of the *Crimes Act 1914* (Cth) provides for the forfeiture of material and equipment involved in child abuse material offences (eg computers used in the production or distribution of child pornography).

12  *Katz v United States*, 389 US 347 (1967).

13  Title III of *The Omnibus Crime Control and Safe Streets Act of 1968* (Wiretap Act).

14  *Foreign Intelligence Surveillance Act* (FISA) of 1978; *Uniting and Strengthening America by Providing Appropriate Tools Required to Intercept and Obstruct Terrorism Act* (USA PATRIOT Act) of 2001.

15  For example, the *Listening Devices Act 1992* (ACT) and *Surveillance Devices Act 2007* (NSW). Both statutes contain an additional exemption from liability if one party records a conversation without the consent of the other where the recording is considered 'on reasonable grounds, to be necessary for the protection of that principal party's lawful interests': see *DW v The Queen* (2014) 239 A Crim R 192.

- surveillance device warrant
- retrieval warrant
- computer access warrant.[16]

These warrants complement telecommunications interception and stored communications warrants available to law enforcement and national security agencies under the *Telecommunications (Interception and Access) Act 1979* (Cth).[17] As discussed in Chapters 2 and 7, recent amendments require internet service providers (ISPs) and other telecommunications operators to retain metadata relating to communications for a period of two years. This is defined for telephone calls as phone numbers and duration (not content) and for electronic communications, email addresses and transmission times (again, not content).[18]

An interesting example of the use of a surveillance device warrant in investigating suspected criminal activity occurred in the following Victorian case.

> The warrant in question authorised the use of surveillance devices of various kinds in respect of the conversations and activities of the second applicant ('Mann'). In reliance on the warrant, police covertly uploaded computer software onto Mann's mobile telephone. They then used the software to activate the microphone on the telephone, so as to permit conversations taking place in the vicinity of the phone to be transmitted to police in a remote location and recorded … What is unusual about this case is that the device was the property not of the investigators but of a person who was the subject of the investigation, and it was in that person's possession. Ordinarily, of course, the use of property belonging to another without that person's permission would constitute an actionable tort (trespass to goods and/or conversion). Use of property is an exercise of a right of ownership.[19]

This kind of covert investigative technique is one of several that law enforcement agencies can deploy in criminal investigations. Another, described in Chapter 8, is the use of assumed identities online, such as where a fictional 'child' identity is used by police to investigate suspected child grooming.[20] This kind of deceptive investigation method or 'sting operation' may require additional law enforcement authorisations.[21] Obtaining such authorisations protects investigators from civil and criminal liability, as long as their actions stay within legislatively approved boundaries. For example, in investigating child exploitation activities online, it may be necessary for police to adopt the identity of an actual or potential offender,

---

16  *Surveillance Devices Act 2004* (Cth).

17  The use of telecommunications interception warrants is illustrated by *Nguyen v The Queen* (2018) 274 A Crim R 534. The use of stored communications warrants is illustrated by *R v Hardstaff* [2016] QSC 299 and *Tuioti and Minister for Home Affairs (Migration)* [2019] AATA 4423.

18  Australian Government, Department of Home Affairs, 'Lawful Access to Telecommunications: Data Retention'. Available: <https://www.homeaffairs.gov.au/about-us/our-portfolios/national-security/lawful-access-telecommunications/data-retention>.

19  *Watkins v DPP (Vic)* (2015) 304 FLR 105 per Maxwell P at [1]–[9].

20  For example, the case of *R v Stubbs* (2009) 228 FLR 221, discussed in Chapter 8; see also *R v Priest* (2011) 209 A Crim R 254, which involved a joint Australian–US covert operation that targeted a defendant who was engaged in grooming underage boys.

21  See *Crimes Act 1914* (Cth), Part IAB (Controlled operations) and Part IAC (Assumed identities).

or a victim, including engaging in obscene exchanges or sharing prohibited images with those under investigation.[22]

In some jurisdictions such as the United States, the legal doctrine of 'entrapment' can threaten to make covertly obtained evidence inadmissible in court. This applies to any operation in which a suspect may have been coerced or pressured into committing a crime that he or she was not already predisposed to commit, as well as the involuntary making of any admissions. Along with the 'fruit of the poisoned tree' doctrine, which applies to exclude evidence obtained in breach of lawful requirements, such doctrines serve to limit the power of investigators to use covert methods without due regard to suspects' rights.

In Australia, as well as other common law jurisdictions such as the United Kingdom, the admissibility of illegally or improperly obtained evidence is a matter of judicial discretion. For example, s 138(1) of the *Evidence Act 1995* (Cth) provides that such evidence 'is not to be admitted unless the desirability of admitting the evidence outweighs the undesirability of admitting evidence that has been obtained in the way in which the evidence was obtained'. A list of factors that must be considered in assessing this balance is found in s 138(3), as follows:

**(a)** the probative value of the evidence; and

**(b)** the importance of the evidence in the proceeding; and

**(c)** the nature of the relevant offence, cause of action or defence and the nature of the subject-matter of the proceeding; and

**(d)** the gravity of the impropriety or contravention; and

**(e)** whether the impropriety or contravention was deliberate or reckless; and

**(f)** whether the impropriety or contravention was contrary to or inconsistent with a right of a person recognised by the International Covenant on Civil and Political Rights; and

**(g)** whether any other proceeding (whether or not in a court) has been or is likely to be taken in relation to the impropriety or contravention; and

**(h)** the difficulty (if any) of obtaining the evidence without impropriety or contravention of an Australian law.

In *R v Stubbs*, where a New Zealand police officer posed as a 12-year-old girl online and engaged in multiple chats with the Australian defendant, a defence application to have the chat transcripts excluded under s 138 of the Evidence Act did not succeed. The Chief Justice of the ACT Supreme Court, Higgins CJ, ruled that the officer had done nothing illegal or even improper in his use of the fictitious identity to interact with the suspected child groomer, and even if there were any impropriety demonstrated, the evidence would still have been admitted on the discretionary balance, taking into account the listed factors.[23]

In Australia, and in some other countries, the prevalent attitude of the courts has thus been that covert investigations of online child exploitation using a degree of deception fall within

---

22  Controlled operations authorisations have been used to compromise child exploitation websites and to administer them for months at a time in order to gather evidence: Paul Bleakley, 'Watching the Watchers: Taskforce Argos and the Evidentiary Issues Involved with Infiltrating Dark Web Child Exploitation Networks' (2018) 92(3) *The Police Journal: Theory, Practice and Principles* 221.

23  *R v Stubbs* (2009) 228 FLR 221, [69]–[72]. A similar outcome was reached in *R v Priest* (2011) 209 A Crim R 254, where Penfold J rejected a defence claim of police impropriety.

the bounds of acceptable policing.[24] An interesting extension of this proposition is the use of automated programs to detect child sex offenders, such as the 'Sweetie 2.0' chatbot. Developed by the Dutch non-government organisation Terre des Hommes to study webcam child sex tourism (WCST), the deployment of the first version of the Sweetie avatar occurred in 2013.[25] The success of this technique led to a second research effort in 2016 by Terre des Hommes to ascertain what legal impediments might exist in public law enforcement agencies, as opposed to private researchers, in using a chatbot avatar such as Sweetie 2.0 in detecting WCST. The substantive and procedural criminal law of almost 20 countries, including Australian laws, was analysed, with the following research questions to be addressed.[26]

1. How is webcam sex with minors criminalised in selected jurisdictions?
2. To what extent do existing crime descriptions within substantive criminal law apply to virtual victims (ie chatbots like Sweetie 2.0)?
3. To what extent does the criminal procedure law framework allow for the (proactive) investigation of webcam sex offences using Sweetie 2.0, taking into account that: (a) Sweetie 2.0 is an AI that interacts with suspects without direct human control or intervention; (b) A 'fake identity' is used for the AI.
4. Are there specific limitations in criminal procedure when it comes to entrapment, and what are the consequences of this for using Sweetie 2.0?
5. Which forensic requirements apply to the collection of evidence using Sweetie 2.0?

The Australian legal framework around covert online investigations was found to be adequate to allow the adoption of Sweetie 2.0 by law enforcement, though legislative clarification to address the application of assumed identities and controlled operations laws was desirable.[27] By contrast, the criminal laws of many other jurisdictions within the comparative study were found not to extend to the use of such techniques by law enforcement, the major obstacles being that in many cases only offences committed against real children would be criminal, so that at best the doctrine of attempt would have to be relied on for a prosecution; and laws relating to entrapment would have to be carefully navigated by any such covert operations.[28] This kind of international comparative approach to dealing with technology-related crimes, which are particularly – but not exclusively – a product of the misuse of telecommunications such as social media and the internet, brings into focus the issues of jurisdiction and international cooperation.

---

24  Gregor Urbas, 'Protecting Children from Online Predators: The Use of Covert Investigation Techniques by Law Enforcement' (2010) 26(4) *Journal of Contemporary Criminal Justice* 410.
25  Terre des Hommes (2013), *Webcam Child Sex Tourism: Becoming Sweetie: A Novel Approach to Stopping the Global Rise of Webcam Child Sex Tourism.* Available: <https://www.terredeshommes.org/wp-content/uploads/2013/11/Webcam-child-sex-tourism-terre-des-hommes-NL-nov-2013.pdf>.
26  Ibid.
27  Gregor Urbas, 'Substantive and Procedural Legislation in Australia to Combat Webcam-Related Child Sexual Abuse' (Chapter 4, pp 135 ff). In Simone van der Hof et al (eds), *Sweetie 2.0: Using Artificial Intelligence to Fight Webcam Child Sex Tourism* (TMC Asser Press, Information Technology and Law Series, vol 31, 2019).
28  See, eg, Alisdair Gillespie, 'Substantive and Procedural Legislation in England and Wales to Combat Webcam-Related Child Sexual Abuse' (Chapter 7, pp 291 ff) and Jonathan Unikowski, 'Substantive and Procedural Legislation in the United States of America to Combat Webcam-Related Child Sexual Abuse' (Chapter 12, pp 491 ff). In Simone van der Hof et al (eds), *Sweetie 2.0: Using Artificial Intelligence to Fight Webcam Child Sex Tourism* (TMC Asser Press, Information Technology and Law Series, vol 31, 2019).

# Jurisdiction and international cooperation

It has been said that 'all crime is local', though cybercrime poses immediate challenges to this adage.[29] The tension is largely due to the geographically based legal assertion of jurisdiction, as opposed to the much less geographically confined nature of the offending.

> [T]he laws of virtually all modern democracies posit 'territoriality' as the basis for acquiring criminal jurisdiction, yet the criminal conduct in cybercrimes may originate from a number of geographical locations, and its impact may have been global. Who then has jurisdiction to prosecute? Related issues include situations where elements of an offence take place in more than one jurisdiction and access from one jurisdiction to digital evidence in another jurisdiction has the potential to raise concerns about privacy, security and national sovereignty.[30]

The Council of Europe's *Convention on Cybercrime*, discussed in Chapter 7, in relation to its coverage of substantive offences, also contains numerous articles relating to procedural matters, including jurisdiction.

## Article 22: Jurisdiction

1   Each Party shall adopt such legislative and other measures as may be necessary to establish jurisdiction over any offence established in accordance with Articles 2 through 11 of this Convention, when the offence is committed:

   a   in its territory; or

   b   on board a ship flying the flag of that Party; or

   c   on board an aircraft registered under the laws of that Party; or

   d   by one of its nationals, if the offence is punishable under criminal law where it was committed or if the offence is committed outside the territorial jurisdiction of any State.

2   Each Party may reserve the right not to apply or to apply only in specific cases or conditions the jurisdiction rules laid down in paragraphs 1.b through 1.d of this article or any part thereof.

3   Each Party shall adopt such measures as may be necessary to establish jurisdiction over the offences referred to in Article 24, paragraph 1, of this Convention, in cases where an alleged offender is present in its territory and it does not extradite him or her to another Party, solely on the basis of his or her nationality, after a request for extradition.

4   This Convention does not exclude any criminal jurisdiction exercised by a Party in accordance with its domestic law.

5   When more than one Party claims jurisdiction over an alleged offence established in accordance with this Convention, the Parties involved shall, where appropriate, consult with a view to determining the most appropriate jurisdiction for prosecution.[31]

---

29  Simon Bronitt and Miriam Gani, 'Shifting Boundaries of Cybercrime: From Computer Hacking to Cyber-Terrorism' (2003) 27(6) *Criminal Law Journal* 303.

30  Kim Soukieh, 'Cybercrime – The Shifting Doctrine of Jurisdiction' (2011) 10 *Canberra Law Review* 221, 222–3, notes omitted.

31  Council of Europe, *Convention on Cybercrime*, Treaty No 185, opened for signature in Budapest on 23 November 2001 (hence, often referred to as the 'Budapest Convention').

Thus, the two most important traditional bases for asserting jurisdiction, being territoriality and citizenship, are reflected in the *Convention on Cybercrime*. However, there is some uncertainty about precisely when a cybercrime is committed in the 'territory' of a state.

> The interpretation of particularly the location of the act will create problems in cybercrime, where the origins and destinations of the crime are usually in different locations, and where the means, computer networks and IP packets, usually cross numerous territories.[32]

Examples of cross-border cybercrime abound, ranging from remote hacking through to online stalking across national boundaries, but a particularly interesting case is the following, reported by the US Federal Bureau of Investigation (FBI) in mid-2003.

> Two Romanian citizens accused of hacking into the National Science Foundation's Amundsen-Scott South Pole Station science research facility were arrested in a joint FBI/ Romanian police operation last month.
>
> On May 3, 2003, an anonymous email was simultaneously received by the Foundation's U.S. Antarctic Program network operations center and by technical staff at the South Pole. 'I've hacked into the server of your South Pole Research Station,' it read. 'Pay me off, or I will sell the station's data to another country.' The email contained data found only on South Pole computer systems, demonstrating that it was not a hoax. The threat hinted that the South Pole network had been widely penetrated, potentially with harmful software that would cause harm if triggered by the hacker.
>
> NSF and its contractor, Raytheon Polar Services Company, immediately isolated the entire station's computer network to prevent future moves by the hacker. For part of each day the station is naturally isolated from the Internet because of limited satellite coverage, and by the time satellite access returned the next day the NSF team had locked down the station while beginning to restore essential services such as email and telemedicine and to isolate the known hacked computers from the local network.
>
> … While the network was being secured and service restored to the personnel isolated at the bottom of the world, the NSF contacted the FBI, and the agencies worked together to find those behind the scheme. The Washington Field Office helped the NSF preserve evidence and use cyber-investigative techniques to track the path of the extortionist's emails. The FBI Information Technology Division and the Cyber Division collaborated to determine that the hackers were accessing their emails from a cyber café in Romania. A call to the FBI Legal Attaché in Bucharest revealed that the Romania suspects were the target of other investigations out of the Mobile and Los Angeles Field Offices. The investigation was so far along in Mobile that the agents working with the Romania police had already made controlled payments to the suspects in an effort to flush them out further.
>
> In executing a search warrant of the suspects' residence, the Romanian authorities seized documents, a credit card used in the extortion scheme, and a computer that contained the very email account that was used to make the demands of NSF. The Romanian police had all they needed and arrested two individuals and charged them with the crimes.[33]

---

32  Susan Brenner and Bert-Jaap Koops, 'Approaches to Cybercrime Jurisdiction' (2004) 4(1) *Journal of High Technology Law* 3, 44; see also Susan Brenner and Bert-Jaap Koops (eds), *Cybercrime and Jurisdiction: A Global Survey* (TMC Asser Press, Information Technology and Law Series, vol 11, 2006).

33  Federal Bureau of Investigation, 'The Case of the Hacked South Pole' (Media release, 18 July 2003). Available: <https://archives.fbi.gov/archives/news/stories/2003/july/backsp_071803>.

Hackers located in one country and committing crimes against a target located in or owned by another are not immune to investigation, or even prosecution, by the latter's justice system.

Australian criminal law provides for extraterritorial criminal jurisdiction in various ways. For example, the law of New South Wales extends to conduct that satisfies all the elements of a crime disregarding geographical considerations, as long as there is some 'geographical nexus' between that state and the offence by way of its commission wholly or partly in the state, or where the offence is committed wholly outside the state but has an effect within the state.[34] An example might be where a NSW resident is the victim of an online scam originating and operated from a foreign country; examples of such scams are discussed in Chapter 7.

At the Commonwealth level, there is considerable flexibility in the jurisdictional reach associated with each offence created by statute. The Commonwealth Criminal Code provides for either 'standard geographical jurisdiction' to apply, or one of four gradations of 'extended geographical jurisdiction' labelled category A to category D. Category A is as follows:

## 15.1 Extended geographical jurisdiction–category A

(1) If a law of the Commonwealth provides that this section applies to a particular offence, a person does not commit the offence unless:

(a) the conduct constituting the alleged offence occurs:

(i) wholly or partly in Australia; or

(ii) wholly or partly on board an Australian aircraft or an Australian ship; or

(b) the conduct constituting the alleged offence occurs wholly outside Australia and a result of the conduct occurs:

(i) wholly or partly in Australia; or

(ii) wholly or partly on board an Australian aircraft or an Australian ship; or

(c) the conduct constituting the alleged offence occurs wholly outside Australia and:

(i) at the time of the alleged offence, the person is an Australian citizen; or

(ii) at the time of the alleged offence, the person is a body corporate incorporated by or under a law of the Commonwealth or of a State or Territory; or

(d) all of the following conditions are satisfied:

(i) the alleged offence is an ancillary offence;

(ii) the conduct constituting the alleged offence occurs wholly outside Australia;

(iii) the conduct constituting the primary offence to which the ancillary offence relates, or a result of that conduct, occurs, or is intended by the person to occur, wholly or partly in Australia or wholly or partly on board an Australian aircraft or an Australian ship.[35]

34  See *Crimes Act 1900* (NSW), Part 1A – Geographical Jurisdiction, particularly s 10C.

35  *Criminal Code Act 1995* (Cth), s 15.1. This category of extended geographical jurisdiction applies to telecommunications offences in Part 10.6, per s 475.2; and to cybercrime offences in Part 10.7, per s 476.3. Categories C and D differ in minor ways, while category D requires no geographical nexus at all and applies to a small range of offences such as war crimes offences in Part 5.1 and terrorism offences in Part 5.3.

Given that cybercrime 'knows no borders' in its potential reach, there are often multiple jurisdictions involved in investigating any particular incident or pattern of offending.[36] Even before the formal legal machinery related to prosecution comes to be applied, there is ample scope for international cooperation at an informal, investigatory level. It is not uncommon for police in one country to 'tip off' their counterparts in another about suspected criminal activity by the second country's nationals or appearing to target victims in that country. As an example, the child grooming investigation discussed in the *R v Stubbs* case was originally conducted by an officer in New Zealand posing as a 12-year-old girl, who indicated that 'she' would be travelling to Canberra, Australia and it was then that the defendant, located in Canberra, arranged to meet her at a bus station. He was met there not by any girl, but by AFP officers who had been alerted by the Auckland officer.[37] Similarly, in the case of *R v Priest*, the defendant came to the attention of German authorities in relation to downloading of child exploitation material, who then alerted the AFP. His child grooming activities were then detected by an American detective posing as a 14-year-old boy, who contacted the AFP and coordinated with an AFP officer posing as a 12-year-old Canberra boy with whom the defendant was put in touch, again culminating in an arranged meeting at which an arrest was made. The judge rejected defence protestations in the latter case that this coordinated sting operation was like shooting 'one fish in a barrel', noting:

> The problem for Mr Priest is that the criminal law and the criminal justice system are not a game with rules designed to ensure a challenge for all participants and an enjoyable spectacle for observers. Certainly the criminal justice system involves more rules based on fairness than any game or sport I can think of, but those rules are aimed at protecting 'the integrity of the administration of criminal justice' ... at ensuring that police officers and other officials do not abuse their powers, and at ensuring that innocent people are not wrongly convicted ...
>
> [The police] cannot be criticised for failing to give, to a person who commits an offence voluntarily and without inducement, a sporting chance of avoiding prosecution or conviction.[38]

Efficient information-sharing between police in different countries is assisted by the work of international networks combatting child exploitation, such as the Virtual Global Taskforce, with members including the European Union, Canada, the United States, the United Kingdom, Australia and New Zealand, as well as some members from Asia, the Middle East and Latin America.[39] Cooperative efforts have been successful in detecting and dismantling several global child exploitation networks.[40] Recognising that such informal contacts between investigating agencies in different countries do occur, the *Convention*

---

36  Lauren Moraski, 'Cybercrime Knows No Borders' (2011) 8(2) *Infosecurity* 20; see also Susan Brenner, 'Cybercrime Investigation and Prosecution: The Role of Penal and Procedural Law' (2001) *Murdoch University Electronic Journal of Law* 8.

37  See *R v Stubbs* (2009) 228 FLR 221, per Higgins CJ at [9]–[20]. The application to exclude the evidence as illegally or improperly obtained under s 138 of the *Evidence Act 1995* (Cth) was unsuccessful. The facts of this case are set out in greater detail in Chapter 8.

38  *R v Priest* (2011) 209 A Crim R 254, per Penfold J at [8]–[24], [65]. The application to exclude the evidence as illegally or improperly obtained under s 138 of the *Evidence Act 1995* (Cth) was unsuccessful.

39  Virtual Global Taskforce, 'Member Countries'. Available: <http://virtualglobaltaskforce.com/member-countries/>.

40  Virtual Global Taskforce, 'Operations'. Available: <http://virtualglobaltaskforce.com/operations/>.

*on Cybercrime* seeks to facilitate both informal and formal international cooperation in investigations and prosecutions in the form of '24/7' contact.

## Article 35: 24/7 network

1   Each Party shall designate a point of contact available on a twenty-four hour, seven-day-a-week basis, in order to ensure the provision of immediate assistance for the purpose of investigations or proceedings concerning criminal offences related to computer systems and data, or for the collection of evidence in electronic form of a criminal offence. Such assistance shall include facilitating, or, if permitted by its domestic law and practice, directly carrying out the following measures:

   a   the provision of technical advice;

   b   the preservation of data pursuant to Articles 29 and 30;

   c   the collection of evidence, the provision of legal information, and locating of suspects.

2   a   A Party's point of contact shall have the capacity to carry out communications with the point of contact of another Party on an expedited basis.

   b   If the point of contact designated by a Party is not part of that Party's authority or authorities responsible for international mutual assistance or extradition, the point of contact shall ensure that it is able to co-ordinate with such authority or authorities on an expedited basis.

3   Each Party shall ensure that trained and equipped personnel are available, in order to facilitate the operation of the network.[41]

This contact mechanism is supplemented by provisions allowing one party to request another to ensure expedited preservation of stored computer data (art 29), expedited disclosure of preserved traffic data (art 30), and trans-border access to stored computer data with consent or where publicly available (art 32). In addition, there are numerous articles relating to the provision of mutual assistance, and extradition. In particular, the *Convention on Cybercrime* can serve as a basis for processing extradition requests between member states even where there is no bilateral extradition agreement in place between them (art 24).

Extradition and mutual legal assistance agreements are more formal mechanisms, but their operation tends to involve considerable periods of time, making them unsuitable to rapidly evolving investigations. However, once a suspect is identified and amenable to justice processes, the territorial boundaries that otherwise impede cross-national law enforcement operations can be overcome. An example is the case involving the DrinkOrDie online copyright piracy group that was discussed in Chapter 9. This group contained approximately 65 members from more than a dozen countries, including the United Kingdom, Australia, Sweden, Norway, and Finland. Most were able to be prosecuted in their home countries, but an alleged co-leader, Hew Raymond Griffiths, was extradited from Australia to the United States, a country where he had never set foot until being sent there. The international enforcement effort leading up to this was called 'Operation Buccaneer'.[42]

The extradition request sent by the United States to Australia, alleging copyright infringement and conspiracy, was initially considered by a magistrate who declined to issue

---

41  Council of Europe, *Convention on Cybercrime*, art 35.

42  United States Department of Justice, 'Extradited Software Piracy Ringleader Sentenced to 51 Months in Prison' (Media release, 22 June 2007); see also Gregor Urbas, 'Cross-National Investigation and Prosecution of Intellectual Property Crimes: The Example of Operation Buccaneer' (2007) 46(4–5) *Crime, Law and Social Change* 207.

an extradition order as he was not satisfied that the 'double criminality' test required for extradition applied in the circumstances, reasoning that the process usually involved sending an alleged offender back to his home country, which was very different from sending an Australian resident who allegedly committed crimes against US interests to that country for prosecution. However, the Federal Court took a different view both as to the operation of 'double criminality' requirements and to where the offending had occurred:

> In my respectful opinion, the Magistrate approached the matter with a number of fundamental misconceptions.
>
> First, internet fraud, though relatively new, involves nothing more than an application of the legal principles applicable to communication by post and telegraph. As Gleeson CJ observed in *Lipohar*, these developments commenced over 100 years ago. True it is that the Internet has a wider reach and wider field of applications but the problem of widely disseminated communication is, as Gleeson CJ, McHugh, Gummow and Hayne JJ pointed out in *Dow Jones & Co Inc v Gutnick* (2002) 210 CLR 575 at 605 ('*Gutnick*'), much older than the Internet and the World Wide Web. As their Honours said in *Gutnick* at 605, the law has had to grapple with cases of this kind ever since newspapers and magazines, and later radio and television came to be made available to large numbers of people over wide geographic areas. To this may be added telephones, mobile phones and fax machines.
>
> Second, the fact that Mr Griffiths is not, as the Magistrate described him, a 'fugitive' fleeing from the United States is irrelevant. This was not a bar to extradition in *Schoenmakers v Director of Public Prosecutions* (1991) 108 FLR 457, where the person whose extradition was requested by the United States, returned to Australia from Holland where his illegal activities took place. In any event, 'fugitive' is merely a term which describes the person whose extradition is requested. There is no requirement that the person be fleeing the jurisdiction of the requesting state. A well known example of this is to be found in *Regina v Bow Street Metropolitan Stipendiary Magistrate; Ex parte Pinochet Ugarte* [2000] 1 AC 61 in which Spain sought the extradition of General Pinochet from England to Spain on charges of the murder of Spanish citizens in Chile.
>
> Third, it is wrong to characterise the acts of Mr Griffiths as acts physically committed in New South Wales. It is made plain in *Doot* and *Lipohar* that conspiracy is a continuing offence. Even if the conspiracy was formed outside the jurisdiction, the agreement is performed in it when a co-conspirator, acting as agent of the others, carries out an overt act inside the jurisdiction.
>
> Fourth, it is not correct to say that conspiracy to breach copyright in the jurisdiction of the requesting state is an unusual kind of extradition offence. *Regina v Bow Street Metropolitan Stipendiary Magistrate; Ex parte Government of USA* [1999] UKHL 31; [2000] 2 AC 216 is an example of such an extradition offence. There, the United States Government sought the extradition from England of a person charged with conspiracy to secure unauthorised access to the American Express computer system with intent to commit fraud.[43]

Where mutual legal assistance and extradition agreements exist, they can thus be used to assist in bringing suspected offenders to justice across international borders. Another method, understandably not widely reported, is to use a sting operation to entice suspects within jurisdictional reach.

---

43 *United States of America v Griffiths* [2004] FCA 879, per Jacobson J at [116]–[122], with the Full Federal Court dismissing an appeal against this decision in *Griffiths v United States of America* (2005) 143 FCR 182. Special leave to appeal to the High Court of Australia was refused in 2005.

# Prosecution decision-making

Prosecution services are among the key gatekeepers of the criminal justice system.[44] Not every case will go to a contested trial, either because prosecutors and defence representatives are able to agree on a suitable plea deal, or because the case is assessed as not suitable to proceed. The two main grounds on which prosecutors may decide not to take a case further are lack of sufficient admissible evidence to support a conviction, and public interest considerations. In Australia, such decision-making is governed by published policies such as the following.

> The initial consideration in the exercise of the discretion to prosecute or not prosecute is whether the evidence is sufficient to justify the institution or continuation of a prosecution. A prosecution should not be instituted or continued unless there is admissible, substantial and reliable evidence that a criminal offence known to the law has been committed by the alleged offender.
>
> When deciding whether the evidence is sufficient to justify the institution or continuation of a prosecution the existence of a bare prima facie case is not sufficient to justify the prosecution. Once it is established that there is a prima facie case it is then necessary to give consideration to the prospects of conviction. A prosecution should not proceed if there is no reasonable prospect of a conviction being secured. In indictable matters this test presupposes that the jury will act in an impartial manner in accordance with its instructions. This test will not be satisfied if it is considered to be clearly more likely than not that an acquittal will result.
>
> ... Having satisfied himself or herself that the evidence is sufficient to justify the institution or continuation of a prosecution, the prosecutor must then consider whether, in the light of the provable facts and the whole of the surrounding circumstances, the public interest requires a prosecution to be pursued. It is not the rule that all offences brought to the attention of the authorities must be prosecuted.
>
> The factors which can properly be taken into account in deciding whether the public interest requires a prosecution will vary from case to case. While many public interest factors militate against a decision to proceed with a prosecution, there are public interest factors which operate in favour of proceeding with a prosecution (for example, the seriousness of the offence, the need for deterrence). In this regard, generally speaking the more serious the offence the less likely it will be that the public interest will not require that a prosecution be pursued.[45]

Factors relevant to the evaluation of the public interest in prosecution are then set out.

> (a) the seriousness or, conversely, the relative triviality of the alleged offence or that it is of a 'technical' nature only;
> (b) mitigating or aggravating circumstances impacting on the appropriateness or otherwise of the prosecution;
> (c) the youth, age, intelligence, physical health, mental health or special vulnerability of the alleged offender, a witness or victim;
> (d) the alleged offender's antecedents and background;
> (e) the passage of time since the alleged offence when taken into account with the circumstances of the alleged offence and when the offence was discovered;

---

44  Russell Smith, Peter Grabosky and Gregor Urbas, *Cyber Criminals on Trial* (Cambridge University Press, 2004), Chapter 3.

45  Commonwealth Director of Public Prosecutions (CDPP), *Prosecution Policy of the Commonwealth*. Available: <https://www.cdpp.gov.au/sites/default/files/Prosecution-Policy-of-the-Commonwealth_0.pdf>.

(f)  the degree of culpability of the alleged offender in connection with the offence;

(g)  the effect on community harmony and public confidence in the administration of justice;

(h)  the obsolescence or obscurity of the law;

(i)  whether the prosecution would be perceived as counter-productive, for example, by bringing the law into disrepute;

(j)  the availability and efficacy of any alternatives to prosecution;

(k)  the prevalence of the alleged offence and the need for deterrence, both personal and general;

(l)  whether the consequences of any resulting conviction would be unduly harsh and oppressive;

(m) whether the alleged offence is of considerable public concern;

(n)  any entitlement of the Commonwealth or other person or body to criminal compensation, reparation or forfeiture if prosecution action is taken;

(o)  the attitude of the victim of the alleged offence to a prosecution;

(p)  the actual or potential harm occasioned to an individual;

(q)  the likely length and expense of a trial;

(r)  whether the alleged offender is willing to co-operate in the investigation or prosecution of others, or the extent to which the alleged offender has done so;

(s)  the likely outcome in the event of a finding of guilt having regard to the sentencing options available to the Court;

(t)  whether the alleged offence is triable only on indictment;

(u)  the necessity to maintain public confidence in the rule of law and the administration of justice through the institutions of democratic governance including the Parliament and the Courts;

(v)  the need to give effect to regulatory or punitive imperatives;

(w) the efficacy, as an alternative to prosecution, of any disciplinary proceedings that have been found proven against the alleged offender to the extent that they encompass the alleged offence; and

(x)  the adequacy in achieving any regulatory or punitive imperatives, of relevant civil penalty proceedings, either pending or completed, and whether these proceedings may result, or have resulted, in the imposition of a financial penalty.[46]

In many cybercrime prosecutions, the defendant is relatively youthful and without a significant prior criminal history.[47] The case of the 15-year-old schoolboy in Montreal who, under the guise of 'Mafiaboy', launched a sophisticated denial-of-service attack that brought down the websites of major corporate entities and was sentenced to a period in youth detention on more than 50 charges was discussed in Chapter 7. In such cases, both the weight of a public prosecution and the imposition of an appropriate sentence are balanced against an offender's youth, recognising that no punishment will likely reflect the degree of damage and loss caused by the conduct under consideration.

In other cases, however, a more significant outcome may be sought by prosecutors and imposed by sentencing courts. For example, in a recent Australian case, the sentencing magistrate remarked:

> Cybercrime and crimes of the type committed by this offender are serious because they attack and undermine the confidence of citizens in financial institutions. As a result

---

46  Ibid, para 2.7.
47  See, for example, *Soyke v The Queen* [2016] NSWCCA 112.

offences such as these call for the imposition of sentences that pay significant regard to the need for both general and specific deterrence. The cost to financial institutions in seeking to prevent this type of conduct means that there is a resultant cost to the community who rely on the safety and security of the funds that they faithfully and diligently deposit into banks. Members of the community who deposit their funds in this way have a legitimate expectation that they will be kept safe. Conduct that undermines that expectation is to be treated with the utmost seriousness.[48]

A decision for both prosecutors and defence lawyers in any contested proceedings is the calling of expert witnesses.[49] Where complex technology is involved, it is advisable to have such experts available to explain the workings of the technology to judges and jurors. For example, a technical expert might be called to explain what effect a worn vehicle component might have had in causing a collision in which the vehicle was extensively damaged. In some cases, an expert conducts preliminary investigations and compiles a written report for the court. For example, a computer expert might have been asked to make and analyse a forensic image of a computer located during a search, looking for search terms suggesting that the data contained in the computer was of evidentiary relevance.[50]

Expert witnesses are required by applicable codes of conduct to be impartial witnesses, primarily there to assist the court to understand the evidence and not partial to either side. For example, the Federal Court of Australia's *Expert Witness Code of Conduct* provides: 'An expert witness is not an advocate for a party and has a paramount duty, overriding any duty to the party to the proceedings or other person retaining the expert witness, to assist the Court impartially on matters relevant to the area of expertise of the witness.'[51]

An important requirement is for experts to state explicitly any information or assumptions on which their specialised opinions are based.[52] This allows courts to evaluate whether that information or those assumptions are supported by other evidence, which will affect the weight to be given to the expert opinion. In court testimony, it is permissible for an expert to be given a hypothetical scenario and to be asked to comment on it. Experts may also give their evidence with the aid of charts, graphs and similar material.[53]

A final topic for consideration is the role and experience of victims. Although victims are not parties in such proceedings as criminal trials and sentencing, they play an important role in giving evidence relevant to the prosecution, and in informing sentencing decisions. Where they have been victims of technology-enabled crimes such as online stalking, harassment or sexual exploitation, their perspective is invaluable in making clear the negative and often harmful consequences of the offending behaviour involved.

---

48  *R v Zhong* [2018] NSWLC 1, [10]. The defendant had entered pleas of guilty to computer and financial advantage offences, and was sentenced to a total term of three years' imprisonment. A similar sentence was imposed in the Western Australian case of *Larkin v The Queen* [2012] WASCA 238.

49  An expert is a 'person who has specialised knowledge based on the person's training, study or experience': *Federal Court Rules 2011* (Cth), Schedule 1; reflecting the wording of the specialised knowledge exception to the opinion rule in s 79(1) of the *Evidence Act 1995* (Cth).

50  See, eg, *Sabel v The Queen* (2014) 242 A Crim R 49; and *R v Tahiraj* [2014] QCA 353.

51  Federal Court of Australia, *Harmonised Expert Witness Code of Conduct*, Practice Note GPN-EXP, October 2016. Available: <https://www.fedcourt.gov.au/law-and-practice/practice-documents/practice-notes/gpn-expt#AnnexureA>.

52  Ibid, Appendix A. This reflects decisions such as that of Heydon JA in *Makita (Australia) Pty Ltd v Sprowles* (2001) 52 NSWLR 705.

53  *Evidence Act 1995* (Cth), s 29(4).

Victim impact statements may be tendered by the prosecution at a sentencing hearing. Their requirements vary across jurisdictions, but in general are meant to 'describe the impact of the offence on the victim, including details of the harm suffered by the victim as a result of the offence'. Such a statement may be in writing, or read out to the court by the victim, a relative or a person approved by the court, including a prosecutor.[54] Online victimisation is both similar to, but in important ways different from, physical criminal victimisation.

> Along with the unusual speed, intensity and extent with which crimes are committed online, interactions in cyber space foment highly criminogenic factors, such as: greater anonymity; greater impulsiveness, thoughtlessness and naivety in decision-making by the victim, who is frequently prisoner to impulsive consumerism; a lost sense of privacy, leading to a tendency to indiscriminately provide personal data to strangers; greater exhibitionism of feelings and corporeity, a source of greater imprudence that acts as an attractive force (for sexual harassers or swindlers); and a multiplication of the degrading effects, victimisation being suffered on a global stage.[55]

It is known that severe psychological harm can be caused by online victimisation, including driving victims to take their own lives, such as the Lori Drew and Amanda Todd cases discussed in Chapter 8. The latter case, in particular, reinforces the jurisdictional issues discussed above, as its resolution awaits the extradition of a Dutch offender to answer to charges in relation to his Canadian victim.[56]

# Conclusion

The investigation of technology-enabled offences poses challenges, ranging from the application of search and seizure laws to the question of jurisdiction where geographical boundaries have been crossed. Domestic and international laws have adapted to new and complex circumstances, making the adoption of harmonised approaches such as the Council of Europe's *Convention on Cybercrime* important in the global response to online offending.

Where appropriate legal mechanisms such as mutual legal assistance and extradition are available, they help to bring alleged offenders within jurisdictional reach, wherever they may be located. The case involving the extradition of an Australian co-leader of the global piracy group DrinkOrDie to the United States exemplifies how this can work in practice. Informal means of international police cooperation are also helpful, such as the contact mechanism enabled through the *Convention on Cybercrime*.

Further, the ability of law enforcement officers to exploit online anonymity has proved invaluable in relation to some types of investigations. Although regulatory reforms to allow such possibilities may still be required, there is a discernible trend in creative adaptation on the part of law enforcement authorities to the challenges of transnational online and other technology-enabled crime.

---

54  *Crimes Act 1914* (Cth), s 16AAA. This provision was introduced in 2013, making victim impact statements available in proceedings for Commonwealth offences. An example of statements being made in an online child exploitation case is *Martin v The Queen* [2019] NSWCCA 197.
55  Jose Agustina, 'Understanding Cyber Victimization: Digital Architectures and the Disinhibition Effect' (2015) 9(1) *International Journal of Cyber Criminology* 35.
56  David Lester et al, 'Suicide and the Internet: The Case of Amanda Todd' (2013) 15(2–3) *International Journal of Emergency Mental Health and Human Resilience* 179.

# 11

## FUTURE DIRECTIONS IN TECHNOLOGY LAW

# Introduction

We began with the observation that technology law, as defined by this text, is now an important field in its own right. This importance will continue to grow as the progress of technology and its application in society continues to create gaps in the legal framework that require regulation. No-one can predict exactly what new technologies are coming, what their implications will be, or what laws will be needed, but by studying theoretical approaches to ethics and regulation and the legal problems that have arisen to date, and how these have been responded to, we are better prepared to deal with future challenges. The COVID-19 pandemic of 2020 provides a stark reminder that unanticipated events can change the societal landscape in a matter of weeks and provide compelling reasons for technologies to be quickly applied in new ways. This concluding chapter will consider the future directions of technology law by reflecting on technology and society, noting the areas of law and regulation that have been covered, and reflecting on themes that have arisen.

During the last century, bold predictions were being made about the state of technological advancement by the end of the millennium and its impact on human existence. The following excerpt from a 1954 book, *The Technological Society*, provides an example of what people thought would be occurring in the year 2000.

> [V]oyages to the moon will be commonplace; so will inhabited artificial satellites. All food will be completely synthetic. The world's population will have increased fourfold but will have been stabilized. Sea water and ordinary rocks will yield all the necessary metals. Disease, as well as famine, will have been eliminated; and there will be universal hygienic inspection and control. The problems of energy production will have been completely resolved. Serious scientists, it must be repeated, are the source of these predictions, which hitherto were found only in philosophic utopias.
>
> ...
>
> Knowledge will be accumulated in 'electronic banks' and transmitted directly to the human nervous system by means of coded electronic messages. There will no longer be any need of reading or learning mountains of useless information; everything will be received and registered according to the needs of the moment. There will be no need of attention or effort. What is needed will pass directly from the machine to the brain without going through consciousness. In the domain of genetics, natural reproduction will be forbidden. A stable population will be necessary, and it will consist of the highest human types. Artificial insemination will be employed.[1]

Society's relationship with technology, itself a product of social organisation and endeavour, oscillates between joy at the technical advances that improve lives or avert dangers, to dread at the apparent and inexorable 'rise of the machines'. Today's developments in artificial intelligence, and particularly deep learning, mark a significant shift in this development. We embrace rapid and ubiquitous telecommunications networks, but baulk at aspects of hyper-surveillance that these networks facilitate.[2] Medical applications of modern genetics

1 Jacques Ellul, *The Technological Society* (1954; Vintage Books, 1964), 432.
2 Karen S Glover, 'Citizenship, Hyper-Surveillance, and Double-Consciousness: Racial Profiling as Panoptic Governance'. In M Deflem and JT Ulmer (eds), *Surveillance and Governance: Crime Control and Beyond* (*Sociology of Crime, Law and Deviance, Vol 10*; Emerald Group Publishing, 2008).

are welcomed, but some view the use of genetically modified food sources or of vaccination programs with trepidation.[3] Robotics and automation increase productive capacity, but many fear the displacement of human labour and mass unemployment.[4] And while many in developed countries, and increasingly even in the developing world, are constantly attached to a mobile phone, there is ongoing concern about the threats of cyberbullying and exposure to harmful images and information.[5]

Many of the real or imagined harmful effects of technology have resulted in regulatory responses through legislation, litigation and industry-level codes of conduct. These range from the punitive approach of criminal sanctions for misbehaviour through to rewards for compliance with agreed standards.[6] The chapters of this book have highlighted, among others, laws relating to:

- national security and data storage (Chapter 1)
- cyberspace and genetics (Chapter 2)
- privacy rights and sensitive data (Chapter 3)
- genomics, reproduction and cloning (Chapter 4)
- digital currencies, online markets and robotics (Chapter 5)
- DNA identification and other biometrics (Chapter 6)
- computer intrusion, damage and warfare (Chapter 7)
- online harassment and sexual exploitation (Chapter 8)
- technology patenting, and online copyright infringement (Chapter 9)
- international law enforcement cooperation (Chapter 10).

Without reprising all of these discussions, it is evident that some common themes have emerged.

# Access, control and risk

Technologies such as the internet have improved *access* to information and radically transformed social, business and government activities. For almost every physical interaction, there is a possible online alternative, be it shopping, banking, voting or dating. Coupled with the vast coverage of telecommunications networks, at least outside remote areas, and the proliferation of smartphones with affordable internet plans, the access that most people have to electronic data and transactions is almost instant and ubiquitous. This is radically transforming how businesses are set up, operated and used by customers.[7] An example is

---

3   Robert B Lull and Dietram A Scheufele, 'Understanding and Overcoming Fear of the Unnatural in Discussion of GMOs'. In Kathleen Hall Jamieson et al (eds), *The Oxford Handbook of the Science of Science Communication* (Oxford University Press, 2017); Gordon Leslie Ada and David Isaacs, *Vaccination: The Facts, the Fears, the Future* (Allen & Unwin, 2000).

4   Martin Ford, *The Rise of the Robots: Technology and the Threat of Mass Unemployment* (Oneworld, 2015).

5   Pamela Whitby, *Is Your Child Safe Online? A Parent's Guide to the Internet, Facebook, Mobile Phones and Other New Media* (Crimson Publishing, 2011).

6   Ian Ayres and John Braithwaite, *Responsive Regulation: Transcending the Deregulation Debate* (Oxford University Press, 1995); and John Braithwaite, 'Fasken Lecture: The Essence of Responsive Regulation' (2011) 44 *University of British Columbia Law Review* 475.

7   As discussed in Chapter 5.

the emergence of fully online banking services, also known as 'neobanks', which go beyond the extension of existing banking to online options.

> The best solution for all in the market could be to work together – where the smaller neo banks do what they do best and offer a fast and efficient payment platform and the bigger bank provides the expertise with greater capital backing. The big banks are always going to be one step behind the neo-banks, so working together could be the ideal solution. The very nature of a neo-bank as opposed to a 'big bank' will be more appealing to many tech driven entrepreneurs creating practical barriers to big banks.[8]

Clearly, this purely online business model offers customers great convenience, and factors such as opening hours, car parking and queuing for service become obsolete. On the other hand, physical security concerns are now replaced by online security questions: Is the app used for online transactions secure? Is the website on the screen genuine or a fake site? Can the wireless connection between device and network, especially a public network such as a mobile hotspot, be trusted? Can anyone hack into that connection and gain illegitimate access to personal and financial data that is stored on the device or passing through the network?[9]

Questions of security and privacy relate to issues of *control*. It can be difficult to determine whether the system being used for a given interaction is solely in the hands of the parties to the interaction, or also within the control of a range of intermediaries. The fewer links in the chain, the more control is usually retained by those connected to the chain. To return to the banking example, in the old world of 'bricks-and-mortar' institutions, the security of deposits and transactions was largely ensured by the bank itself, its security staff (which might include private contractors), and physical features such as strong doors, locks and safes. A relatively small number of staff and service providers worked together to ensure the safety of customers and their funds in a controlled way. The online equivalent is arguably equally secure, at least that is the promise made by banks offering online services, but the range of technology developers and providers involved in creating and maintaining online facilities is very different, and probably unknown at many points within the system. Does the bank really know every technological contributor to the systems it has bought or hired from commercial technology companies? And if the bank doesn't know, how could the consumer know?

The issue of control can be further illustrated in relation to control of health information. Patients may provide private information about symptoms and conditions to their physicians, as well as biological specimens such as blood and urine for pathology testing, on the basis that this information will only be used for providing helpful medical advice and treatment. The serious threat of COVID-19 necessitated governments taking action to limit the spread of the disease, including making full use of any available technologies. Emergency public health powers allowed actions to be taken that would be unimaginable under normal circumstances.[10] These measures – including travel bans, closing businesses and quarantine – also

---

8   Olly Jackson, 'MREL Rules Could Derail Progress of Challenger Banks', *International Financial Law Review*, 3 September 2018.

9   As discussed in Chapters 7 and 8.

10  On 18 March 2020, the Australian government declared a human biosecurity emergency under provisions of the *Biosecurity Act 2015* (Cth).

involved law enforcement agency use of surveillance technologies. These include closed-circuit television cameras, metadata access, automated numberplate recognition, financial transaction and GPS tracking.[11] The use of smartphone metadata and applications that employ Bluetooth technology to communicate with phones in their vicinity, rather than track users' locations, was widespread. In Norway, where the government application did employ GPS tracking, its operation was suspended due to privacy concerns.[12]

The rapid rise of genomics and the ever-expanding amount of information that can be derived from biological specimens, noted in Chapter 4, has ongoing implications for the control of this type of material. As discussed in previous chapters, privacy laws around health information mean that there are strict exceptions to the requirements that such information may only be collected and used in accordance with the purposes for which consent has been given by the patient.[13] However, this does not always prevent information from being obtained and used more widely than may have been intended. As discussed in Chapter 6, genetic information disclosed in ancestry searches provided by private companies may be obtained by law enforcement agencies, and in some cases has been obtained and contributed to a conviction.

One controversial response to the issue of genetic information in health databases being exploited by law enforcement in ways that the public may find questionable is the creation of vastly more comprehensive forensic databases. Large forensic databases of fingerprints, DNA profiles and photographs able to be used for facial recognition now exist in many countries, including Australia, Canada, the United States and United Kingdom, and within the European Union.[14] Some authors have argued that, in view of the utility of large forensic databases, the future will bring the creation of universal databases so that entire populations can be checked against crime scene samples.[15]

In the United Kingdom, an offence of DNA 'theft' has been created under the *Human Tissue Act 2004*, making it unlawful to have human tissue with the intention of its DNA being analysed, without the consent of the person from whom the tissue came.[16] In Australia, a similar proposal was advanced by the Australian Law Reform Commission, but this has yet to be enacted into legislation and protection remains based on general privacy laws.[17]

As with other sensitive personal and financial information, questions remain. How secure are the databases on which our genetic and health information are kept secure against intrusion, either by external hackers or inquisitive governments and their agencies? Is data

---

11  Kelly Servick, 'COVID-19 Contact Tracing Apps are Coming to a Phone Near You. How Will We Know Whether They Work?', *Science*, 21 May 2020.

12  Ibid.

13  Mainly in Chapters 3 and 4; law enforcement uses of genetic information, such as DNA identification and other biometric matching, are discussed in Chapter 6.

14  See, eg, Helena Machado and Rafaela Granja, 'DNA Databases and Big Data'. In Helena Machado and Rafaela Granja, *Forensic Genetics in the Governance of Crime* (Palgrave, 2020).

15  Marcus Smith, 'Universal Forensic DNA Databases: Balancing the Costs and Benefits' (2018) 43(2) *Alternative Law Journal* 131.

16  *Human Tissue Act 2004* (UK), s 45(1)(a)(ii) and Schedule 4, cl 5(1)(d), with an exception for law enforcement.

17  Australian Law Reform Commission, *Essentially Yours: The Protection of Human Genetic Information in Australia* (ALRC R96, 2003), Chapter 12. The Model Criminal Law Officers' Committee issued a discussion paper in 2008 that similarly suggested an offence of non-consensual genetic testing, but no legislation has eventuated.

security the same, irrespective of whether the database is managed by a public agency or a private company? Can laws sufficiently protect us, when it seems that technological measures can be breached?

More generally, with technology-associated misuse, such as the failure to secure databases, or allowing the information contained in such databases to be shared for purposes not initially consented to, the question of allocation of *risk* becomes important. Should the risk and its consequences be borne by the individuals who hand over their data, the business or government agency entrusted with it, or a third party who acquires and uses the data unlawfully or improperly? The answer will depend on the situation, and allocation of risk at all stages may be required.

An illustrative discussion in this context is the increasingly powerful role of social media in our lives and the level of provider responsibility that this entails. In the past, internet and other telecommunications providers have been able to rely on various safe harbours, first in relation to defamation law and intellectual property infringement, and later in relation to various categories of prohibited content such as child exploitation material. Intermediary and service provider responsibility for such content was discussed in Chapters 7 and 8.

Social media platforms such as Facebook, YouTube, Instagram and TikTok have grown rapidly in terms of their influence on everyday life. As would be expected, they have instituted various mechanisms for review of content that violates policies on community standards or domestic laws. Facebook's internal guidelines for review of content state:

> We aim to prevent potential offline harm that may be related to content on Facebook. While we understand that people commonly express disdain or disagreement by threatening or calling for violence in non-serious ways, we remove language that incites or facilitates serious violence. We remove content, disable accounts and work with law enforcement when we believe that there is a genuine risk of physical harm or direct threats to public safety. We also try to consider the language and context in order to distinguish casual statements from content that constitutes a credible threat to public or personal safety. In determining whether a threat is credible, we may also consider additional information such as a person's public visibility and the risks to their physical safety.[18]

The timeliness in which these policies can be implemented will be an ongoing concern. This context was brought into sharp focus by the 2019 mass shootings in Christchurch, New Zealand, which were live-streamed by the shooter on Facebook, as discussed in Chapter 8. Australian legislation threatens large fines for social media platforms that fail to expeditiously remove abhorrent material. However, the costs of identifying and removing objectionable content are not negligible, or limited to financial costs. Facebook and YouTube moderators are likely to be at risk of post-traumatic stress disorder as a result of doing their jobs. While artificial intelligence can do some of this work, there will always be a need for human involvement. As social networks continue to develop and play a central role in people's lives, new strategies, including more widespread government regulation of system architecture, will be needed in order to regulate them effectively.

---

18  Facebook, 'Community Standards' (2020). Available: <https://www.facebook.com/communitystandards/objectionable_content>.

# Conclusion

The future of technology law will be shaped by the interaction between our societies and the technologies they produce. As discussed, this interaction is not uniformly positive, and many of the discussions throughout the text have described the negative consequences that can result. To some extent, these risks can be managed, either through system architecture or legal regulation, or a combination of both. While the impending introduction of driverless vehicles promises to reduce the risk of human error, the risk of mechanical and computer dysfunction may be impossible to eliminate. More generally, we confront choices in retaining or relinquishing levels of access and control, including in relation to our own personal, health and financial data. To a large extent, technology law will reflect the choices that our society makes in regulating the impact of technology on human existence and experience.

Law and regulatory responses to technological advancement need to balance competing objectives and be cognisant of ongoing development. Formulating responses to technologies that are continually developing will remain an issue. The time to consult, research, analyse, take advice and formulate laws can take years, by which time the technology may have progressed and been adapted so as to render that law obsolete. The challenge for government is to harness the benefits of this technology for society and limit the costs in a globalised world, where there are financial incentives for these technologies to be implemented quickly.

The law has an important role to play in establishing regulation that balances the complex relationship between technology, individuals and society. It must take account of its potential to improve the way humans communicate, obtain information and access services while limiting the potential impact on individual rights in liberal democracies.

# INDEX

Printed in the United States
by Baker & Taylor Publisher Services